Congress in Context

CONGRESS
in
CONTEXT

JOHN HASKELL

WESTVIEW
PRESS
A MEMBER OF THE PERSEUS BOOKS GROUP

Library of Congress Cataloging-in-Publication Data
Haskell, John, 1959–
  Congress in context / John Haskell.
    p. cm.
  Includes bibliographical references and index.
  ISBN 978-0-8133-4412-6 (alk. paper)
  1. United States. Congress. 2. Legislative power—United States. 3. Represen-
tative government and representation—United States. I. Title.
  JK1021.H38 2010
  328.73—dc22
                                        2009038747
10 9 8 7 6 5

CONTENTS

LIST OF ILLUSTRATIONS

EXHIBITS

TABLES

FIGURES

PREFACE

The unifying concept of this book is that Congress's central function in our separated system is to be, borrowing from James L. Sundquist, the "board of directors" of the federal government, empowered by the Constitution to authorize, fund, and supervise the activities of the government—that is, the executive branch agencies. Drawing on my varied experiences as a college professor, a congressional staffer, and an instructor for federal agency personnel, this textbook seeks to help people make sense of Congress in the context of its role in our separated system of government. The aim of *Congress in Context* is to convey my experiences working in government and with government officials, informed by the relevant political science literature, in a format that is lively and conveys a real-world sense of the first branch.

The journey that led to writing this book was a long one. I first taught a university-level course covering Congress—called "Congress and the Presidency"—as a graduate student in the fall of 1986. The sections on the two branches were clearly differentiated in the syllabus. Overall, the course was presented as a series of topics—the Congress in *The Federalist Papers*, congressional elections, leadership and committees in Congress, then the president in the Constitution, presidential personality, presidential elections, and so forth. As a grad student, I was too wrapped up in other more pressing matters to impose much organizational coherence on the course. To be honest, it never occurred to me to do that. The syllabus was handed down, as it were, and I did as I was told.

When I moved on to full-time teaching and a tenure-track job, my portfolio included separate courses on Congress and the presidency. I continued to teach Congress more or less as a set of differentiated topics, albeit with an introduction emphasizing that members have two roles, legislative and representative. Generally speaking, students seemed to enjoy the course, but I still did not impose the kind of structure or coherence that the material deserved.

One year I had the good fortune to work on Capitol Hill through the American Political Science Association Congressional Fellowship Program. From day one of my assignment I was disturbed to find out how ignorant I had been about what members of Congress and their staff were up to on a day-to-day basis. I knew almost immediately that I had been stressing the wrong things in my Congress course, or at least had not been conveying to students what really mattered about the institution. At first I could not put my finger on exactly what I had missed. Eventually my thinking began to crystallize: What members were doing was primarily aimed at changing government programs and agency policies and practices to the benefit of their constituents in particular, and sometimes to the benefit of broader groups across the country. I was in dozens of meetings involving a wide range of members and staff. Although a lot of these meetings were primarily "political," even those usually touched at least a little bit—and often much more than that—on what the members could do in law or by other means to change federal programs to the people's benefit.

This realization changed the way I taught Congress when I returned to the classroom. I covered the same main topics—elections, committees, party leadership, and so forth—but changed the focus to looking at congressional policymaking in the context of the institution's role in the federal government. I began to stress that Congress *matters* . . . to the extent that what it does in law and through other methods alters or creates government programs that invariably have tangible effects on people's lives. Understanding how a bill becomes a law has intrinsic importance only insofar as a law may change, for example, Interior Department policies that affect the management of federal lands or the populations of endangered species, or as a law may involve funding one type of research instead of another at the National Institutes of Health (NIH).

In 2000 I had the good fortune to land a job at the Government Affairs Institute (GAI) at Georgetown University. GAI has a unique mission among nonprofit educational institutions: We endeavor to explain how Congress works to executive branch officials. The notion is that the government functions better when the people who work in the two branches understand each other. Executive branch officials are in constant communication with members of Congress, and especially congressional staff, but most of them have trouble mastering the specialized lingo, understanding the complex authorization and appropriations processes, and grasping members' perspective on the world. This is where GAI comes in.

Teaching federal agency personnel about Congress brings into clear relief the most salient function of Congress: directing, through legislation and oversight, the work of the agencies and departments of government. It is tremendously important for executive branch officials, students at the undergraduate and graduate levels, and interested citizens to understand the legislative process and what drives members' decision-making on Capitol Hill. After all, government programs as created by Congress and administered by executive branch officials have a profound effect on all of our lives. The federal government now constitutes well over 20 percent of the American economy, and it is not about to get any smaller or less significant. It is Congress that provides the statutory basis for the work of the agencies. Understanding congressional policymaking tells us a great deal about the kind of government we have now and will have in the future.

Gaining this understanding is what drives *Congress in Context* and its unique focus on exploring Congress as a board of directors. In addition to introducing this concept, the first three chapters of the book introduce the student of Congress to the institution, its constitutional underpinnings, the basic organizational units of the House and Senate, the importance of the bicameral structure, the impact of the representative role on the policymaking process, and the role and influence of campaigns and elections on everything the members do.

The book then turns to how Congress carries out its legislative duties. Chapters 4, 5, and 6 cover the authorizing power, the funding power, and the conduct of oversight (the supervisory power), respectively. The aim is to give the reader a full understanding of the legislative process, Congress's role in establishing government agencies, how Congress directs the agencies through its funding power, and how the institution looks into the performance and conduct of agencies and programs and attempts to influence agency policy through oversight.

Chapter 7 covers the important exception: war powers, an area in which Congress has for the most part failed in recent decades to exert its influence effectively and in fact has been weak and subordinate to the executive branch. The chapter examines the reasons for this recent lack of congressional effectiveness in the exercise of its war powers, as well as the public policy consequences of presidential dominance.

In the last chapter, we assess the congressional board of directors in the twenty-first century. Ultimately, Chapter 8 addresses the question of whether the unwieldy institution of Congress is up to the great challenges of the years to come.

ACKNOWLEDGMENTS

Among the many people to whom I owe a debt of gratitude, two deserve to be singled out for extra kudos. They are Ken Gold, the director of the Government Affairs Institute, and Marian Currinder, senior fellow at GAI. Without their assistance, Chapters 3 and 7 probably could not have been completed and, at the very least, would be of much inferior quality.

Valerie Heitshusen, formerly a GAI faculty member and now with the Congressional Research Service, went through early drafts of Chapter 4 with a fine-toothed comb and otherwise helped me with the informal nuances of congressional procedure. In particular, her up-to-the-minute knowledge enabled me to capture some of the recent trends in how leaders in both chambers deal with complex legislation.

Arthur Burris of the House Budget Committee staff and a couple of anonymous Appropriations Committee staffers have helped me with examples and details of the budget process. Former Appropriations Committee staffer Charlie Flickner has been invaluable as well, providing insights into some of the uses of report language and general provisions in appropriations law. Jonathan Etherton, formerly of the Senate Armed Services Committee staff, has over the years shared vital insights into the role of hearings and the construction of authorization bills. Robert Dove, former Senate parliamentarian, has been a great resource on the ways of the "upper chamber." Mark Harkins, former chief of staff for Representative Brad Miller; Brenna Findley, chief of staff for Representative Steve King; and Jean-Louise Beard, chief of staff for Representative David Price, have been very helpful in giving me a better sense of the workings of the personal office. I am very much indebted to Jonathan Degner, a campaign consultant who has been involved with several congressional campaigns and has run independent expenditure efforts, for sharing his knowledge of congressional politics on the ground. Jeffrey Birnbaum of the *Washington Times* has been helpful by conveying a sophisticated sense of the "real story" of the role of interest groups and lobbyists in the policymaking process on Capitol Hill.

Nitt Chuenprateep and Travis Forden designed the artwork and provided help on other high-tech matters that was desperately needed. Sarah Wohl, Amy Meyers, Daniel Fischer, and Chris Walker provided research assistance.

The entire staff of the Government Affairs Institute—Worth Hester, Howard Stevens, Jim Hershman, Susan Sullivan Lagon, LaJuan Alexander, Meg Tice, and Katina Slavkova (Ken Gold and Marian Currinder too!)—was incredibly patient and forgiving toward the cranky writer in their midst over the last couple of years.

The staff at Westview Press—editors Steve Catalano and Toby Wahl, as well as development editor Brooke Kush and Kelsey Mitchell—has been helpful and incredibly responsive at every step. Toby in particular was full of insightful suggestions that kept me on the beam. Also, I appreciate the dozens of ideas for improvement from anonymous reviewers.

This book would not have been possible without the help of every single person listed here as well as many others. But, unfortunately, I have to absolve them all of responsibility for any errors in its contents.

CHAPTER ONE

CONGRESS AS THE
BOARD OF DIRECTORS

The U.S. Congress is by far the least popular branch of the federal government. It is also probably the least understood. Even some high-ranking officials in the executive branch do not understand the basic dynamics of the institution and how it exercises its power. Amazingly, experienced professional staff members in the Congress itself get confused from time to time about the intricacies of the legislative process. It is the aim of this book to demystify the institution—to give the reader a practical yet sophisticated overview of Congress and the legislative process.

Congress in Context takes a different approach than most textbooks. Usually Congress is treated in isolation from the rest of the government. But the Framers of the Constitution explicitly intended for the branches of government to be interdependent. The aim here is to introduce readers to Congress's critical role within this interdependent system. Specifically this book focuses on Congress in the context of its relationship with the executive branch.

FIVE EXAMPLES OF THE FEDERAL GOVERNMENT IN ACTION

The initial focus of this chapter is counterintuitive. It is to look *away* from the Congress itself and examine a few examples of the results of the policymaking process in Washington. These examples represent the federal government in action.

Some of what the government does appears on the front pages of the nation's newspapers every day—the president pursues a new strategy in the Iraq War, major changes are made in the tax code, a prescription drug program for senior citizens is implemented by Medicare, and so on. Although most government activities are far more mundane than these front-page headlines, make no mistake about it: The federal government is literally everywhere, involved in our lives and communities in innumerable ways, big and small. The scope of the government is almost impossible to fathom. It is a $3.5 trillion enterprise that accounted for fully 25 percent of the entire U.S. economy in 2009—easily the largest single entity on the planet.

The following examples are not likely to make headlines, but they do typify the federal government's ongoing involvement in the lives of its citizens.

Example 1: Keeping Tabs on the Fish We Eat

At the National Oceanographic and Atmospheric Administration's National Marine Fisheries Service (NOAA Fisheries), an agency of the U.S. Commerce Department, scientists make determinations as to whether fish such as the Pacific salmon are "endangered" or "threatened."

These fish have a complex life cycle spanning periods spent in both freshwater and saltwater. They begin life inland and eventually find their way to the ocean. After maturing, they reverse course, heading back upriver to where they were born in order to reproduce and ultimately die.

Overfishing and loss of habitat have brought most salmon stocks in the Northwest United States to a fraction of their historic levels. Recent improvements in ocean conditions have helped the population, but the salmon remains on a kind of "watch list." NOAA Fisheries is required by federal law—the Endangered Species Act—to monitor the populations and conditions of the salmon habitat.

In addition, NOAA Fisheries is responsible for maintaining sustainable populations of all the fish popular at restaurants and grocery stores, including tuna, swordfish, and halibut. The Sustainable Fisheries Act (1996) charged NOAA with balancing the sustainability of fish populations with the economic concerns of communities on the coasts and the interests of recreational anglers.

In May 2008, NOAA Fisheries adopted a change in halibut quotas for chartered fishing vessels in southeast Alaska. Anglers can now keep only one halibut per day instead of the previous limit of two. Citing the influx of new chartered boats in the region, the agency aims to reduce harvest levels and ensure a healthy halibut population.[1]

Example 2: Combating Drugs and Gangs

In 1988, at the height of the drug wars in New York City and around the country, twenty-two-year-old police officer Edward Byrne was guarding the house of a family who had defied drug dealers and agreed to testify against them in court. Four young gang members, on the instructions of a jailed drug kingpin, ambushed Officer Byrne and shot him dead with no warning. This heinous crime was the catalyst for the creation of the Byrne Formula Grant Program, established by an act of Congress in 1988, to be administered by the Bureau of Justice Assistance (BJA) in the U.S. Justice Department.

BJA is authorized to award grants to states for use by state and local government entities to provide personnel and training for more widespread apprehension, adjudication, and rehabilitation of drug law offenders. Grants may also be used to provide assistance to victims. In recent years, the Congress has appropriated nearly $200 million for the program annually.[2]

Example 3: Joint Military Training Goes High-Tech

Most significant war-fighting operations conducted by the U.S. military involve at least some level of jointness—that is, coordination and communication among the branches of the armed services: the Army, Navy, Air Force, and Marines. Yet, historically, most military training has been branch-specific—handled by one branch for that branch.

In the last twenty-five years, the U.S. Defense Department has enhanced its efforts to provide joint training. To that end, a major initiative, the Joint National Training Capability (JNTC), was established in 2003, to be managed by the United States Joint Forces Command. JNTC is intended to update certain types of joint training for the high-tech twenty-first-century environment of modern warfare. A fully interactive global communications network is scheduled for permanent installation by 2010. The aim is to provide "live, virtual, and constructive" training that covers all of the joint war-fighting capabilities: training for people in live environments (live), training for people in partially simulated environments (virtual), and training for entirely simulated environments (constructive).[3]

Ideally, with the updated training program, military personnel will better understand the purposes and objectives of joint operations from both a strategic perspective and an actual, on-the-ground, tactical perspective. Military experts maintain that improved jointness training is especially important in countering terrorist threats. In this area, special operations involving highly trained personnel capable of conducting delicate and intricate joint incursions are essential. JNTC is expected to be crucial to the training and eventual success of special operations forces.

Example 4: Controlling Animals

The Animal and Plant Health Inspection Service (APHIS), a division of the U.S. Department of Agriculture, has a wide-ranging mission. It is best known for its efforts in maintaining the safety of the food supply, but it is also charged with the responsibility of protecting people, airplanes, and local economies from damage caused by wild animals.

For example, animal biologists at Wildlife Services (WS), an agency within APHIS, work with local authorities to control bird populations along airport runways to prevent the rare but hazardous situation of larger birds being sucked into an airplane's engines, damaging the craft, and potentially bringing the plane down. This was a low-profile activity before the double bird strike that brought down US Airways Flight 1549, which landed in the Hudson River shortly after taking off from LaGuardia Airport on January 15, 2009. Miraculously, no one died in the incident. Not so lucky were the twenty-four passengers on board an Air Force plane on a routine mission in Alaska in 1995. Normally, Wildlife Services works to disperse heavy concentrations of geese and other large birds, but sometimes the agency has had to eliminate birds that pose a hazard.

In Mississippi, Wildlife Services is very busy. The aquaculture industry suffers about $5 million in losses annually from fish-eating birds such as cormorants and pelicans, but the losses would be much worse if it were not for the nonlethal harassment methods employed by the agency. Wildlife Services conducts regular aerial surveys of cormorant populations and provides data on heavy concentrations to aquaculture producers in the affected areas so that they can plan appropriate harassment activities. In extreme situations, the agency helps producers obtain a "depredation permit" from the U.S. Interior Department's Fish and Wildlife Service—in other words, a federally sanctioned license to kill some birds.[4]

Beavers have kept Wildlife Services busy in Mississippi as well. Beavers were once considered a net economic gain, but reduced demand for beaver products has led to an increase in population. Although there are some benefits to beaver infestation, including increased wetlands, there have been many detrimental effects, including damage to roads, bridges, farm products, and other property. The Beaver Control Assistance Program was established in 1990 to address this situation. This program authorizes the relocation or killing of problem beavers and the destruction of beaver dams.[5]

Example 5: Providing Recreational Opportunities in the Heartland

The U.S. Army Corps of Engineers' main mission includes flood control, environmental protection, and emergency preparedness, but Congress often instructs the agency to build particular projects with other functions in mind. For example, in 1986 Congress appropriated funds to the Rock Island District of the Corps to develop the Greenbelt Program, which constructs recreational facilities in central Iowa. The Des Moines Riverwalk , a 1.2-mile path around the Des Moines River that may cost upward of $50 million to complete, is being funded as part of this program.

The Riverwalk will act as a link to other recreational facilities—some built by the Corps—in the area. The plan does not end there: The Corps will create other projects that improve the appearance and accessibility of Des Moines. Residents and tourists can look forward to an outdoor ice skating rink, a sprawling "long-look" garden, and an open plaza.

Despite its focus on enhancing the leisure options of Iowans, the project does connect its recreational purposes to the flood protection mission. Since the Riverwalk will be built alongside the preexisting Des Moines Flood Protection Project, new construction will incorporate improvements to the levees and floodwalls that protect the city from emergency water situations, such as the devastating flood of 1993.[6]

As one might conclude from just these few examples, the federal government takes on a wide range of discrete, relatively little-known projects. For our purposes, it is important to look a little more closely at exactly who is doing the work described in these examples.

In the first example, it is NOAA Fisheries in the Commerce Department. The second involves an office of the Justice Department, the Bureau of Justice Assistance. In the third case, the United States Joint Forces Command in the Defense Department is doing the work. The fourth example shows us Wildlife Services, an agency of the Agriculture Department, at work, and in the fifth example, the Des Moines Riverwalk, it is the Army Corps of Engineers.

What all of these government agencies and departments have in common is that they are in the executive branch of government. The legislative branch, the U.S. Congress, manages no federal programs and is not out there getting its hands dirty dealing with fish and beavers. It is the vast executive branch that does the work of government. In a sense, Congress does not *do* anything at all.

And the fact is that, perennial cynicism about a "do-nothing Congress" notwith-standing, in our federal system the legislative branch was not *meant* to do anything.

CONGRESS AS THE BOARD OF DIRECTORS

Laying Down the Law

If Congress is not meant to do the work of government, then what exactly is its role? As the political scientist James L. Sundquist put it, Congress operates as the "board of directors" of the federal government.[7]

A board of directors can take many different forms, depending on the type of en-tity it governs in the business or nonprofit world. In a college or university, for exam-ple, the board of directors holds ultimate power and is largely not answerable to anyone.

Congress's board-of-directors function more closely resembles that of a corpora-tion. A corporation that issues stock is owned, in effect, by its shareholders, who se-lect the members of the board. In fulfilling its function—typically establishing the policies of the corporation and approving the corporation's budget—the board is answerable to those shareholders. Generally the board gives wide latitude to those who are responsible for the day-to-day management of the corporation.

Congress's situation is very similar. The members are chosen by the voting public and are held accountable by regular and frequent elections. Congress sets forth in law the policies that guide the government, just as the corporate board sets forth company policy, and Congress is in charge of determining the budget for the government. Given the immense size and complexity of the government, Congress usually must give a great deal of discretion to the president and the lower-level executive branch agency officials in running day-to-day operations.

There is one major difference between Congress and its corporate counterparts: Except in extraordinary circumstances, Congress does not get to choose the presi-dent, while the corporate board gets to choose the chief executive officer (CEO), who is fully answerable to it. An institutional rivalry between the legislative and ex-ecutive branches was intentionally built into the federal government.

Still, Congress has tremendous leverage in the separated system of government. To put it succinctly, as the board of directors, it has three powers as set forth or im-plied in the Constitution:

1. Congress *authorizes* in law the activities of the government—which is to say, the executive branch.

2. Congress passes laws to *fund* what the executive branch does.
3. Congress, when it sees fit, *supervises* the executive branch (a function usually referred to as *oversight*).

Congress was not designed to manage fisheries or build a levee; it was designed to decide, based on its collective wisdom, whether the government will manage a particular fishery or build a particular levee, to allocate money for these activities, and to check up on the executive branch agencies it has made responsible. In almost every case, Congress creates in law the agencies it assigns to perform government functions.

This authority comes from Article I, Section 1, of the Constitution, which explicitly gives Congress the lawmaking power: "All legislative powers herein granted shall be vested in a Congress of the United States, which shall consist of a Senate and a House." (Most of these legislative powers are specified in Section 8 of Article I.) Notably the legislative power includes the power to appropriate money—also explicitly granted in Section 9 of Article I: "No money shall be drawn from the Treasury, but in consequence of appropriations made by law." In sum, Congress has the power to set up agencies and government programs, determine the policies carried out by those agencies, and establish the budgets for their operations.

The courts have always considered the supervisory or oversight function of the Congress a legitimate extension of Congress's legislative power, for two reasons. First, Congress needs to be able to make sure the laws it passes are being faithfully executed. After all, what good would there be in having the power to authorize and fund the activities of the government if the executive branch agencies could ignore the law and carry out programs as they saw fit or spend money in ways that might be prohibited? Just as a corporation is answerable to its board of directors, Congress must have the authority to demand documents or otherwise investigate the executive branch to make sure the agencies are doing its bidding.

Second, Congress needs to be able to conduct oversight in order to inform its decision-making, in both the authorization process and the appropriations (funding) process. If a government program is not working, members of Congress need to be able to find out why so that they can consider making changes in the law to improve it. They may also choose either to fund the program at a higher level the next year, so that it can perform better, or reduce and maybe even cut off its funding stream. Information is crucial to Congress's ability to legislate, and oversight is the main way in which Congress gathers the data it needs.

In all five of our examples of "government in action," executive branch agencies are carrying out responsibilities assigned to them in law. As noted in the first case, NOAA Fisheries is required to carry out certain functions—assessing the status of particular fish populations and balancing various legitimate interests (recreational, economic, and so on) in the sustainability of fisheries—pursuant to the Endangered Species Act, in the first instance, and the Sustainable Fisheries Act, in the second. Similarly, BJA is authorized to implement the Byrne grants program as part of the Anti–Drug Abuse Act, and the Beaver Control Assistance Program authorizes Wildlife Services to deal with burgeoning beaver populations. The Defense Department was prodded by Congress to move in the direction of improved joint forces integration by the Goldwater-Nichols Act in 1986, as well as by subsequent authorizing legislation. The Army Corps of Engineers is periodically authorized in law to undertake projects in the Water Resources Development Act.

Holding the Purse Strings

It is important to note that in nearly all of these specific cases, Congress went a step further than what is described in the last paragraph. Although Congress often delegates a great deal of authority to executive branch agency officials, it is not always satisfied with simply providing broad guidelines and mission statements and leaving the details to the experts in the bureaucracy. Sometimes the members of Congress get into the specifics by detailing exactly where and how some of the money appropriated for government functions should be spent.

For example, in explanatory language accompanying a recent appropriations law—language that is not statutory, thus technically nonbinding—Congress told NOAA Fisheries how to break down its $90 million allotment for salmon recovery state by state. Furthermore, as can be seen in Exhibit 1.1, members of Congress inserted sections urging the agency to spend the funds provided for salmon recovery in specific places for specific purposes: $100,000 for the United Fishermen of Alaska's subsistence program, $3.368 million for the Fairbanks hatchery facilities, $1 million for conservation mass marking at the Columbia River Hatcheries, and so on.[8]

In 2008, Congress did an interesting thing regarding BJA's Byrne grants. It gave the agency $191,704,000 for competitive grant awards. The idea of competitive grant programs is to have experts in executive branch agencies evaluate proposals that come in from around the country and allocate money according to a set of objective criteria. In this case, state and local governmental entities must make the case that they have a useful idea to address drug and gang problems in their communities.

But in explanatory language accompanying the appropriations law (again, not statutory, thus not technically binding to the agency), Congress gave BJA a ten-page,

EXHIBIT 1.1
CONGRESS GIVES SPECIFIC DIRECTION TO NOAA IN
LANGUAGE ACCOMPANYING APPROPRIATIONS BILL

Pacific Coastal Salmon Recovery

The conference agreement provides $90,000,000 for Pacific Coastal Salmon Recovery, instead of $80,000,000 as proposed by the House and $99,000,000 as proposed by the Senate. Language is included extending authorization for this program in fiscal year 2005 and authorizing participation by the State of Idaho.

Funds provided under this heading shall be allocated as follows: $24,000,000 for Alaska; $13,000,000 for California; $2,500,000 for Columbia River Tribes; $4,500,000 for Idaho; $13,000,000 for Oregon; $8,000,000 for Pacific Coast Tribes; and $25,000,000 for Washington.

With respect to the amounts for Alaska, the conferences agree to the following allocation: $3,500,000 is for the Arctic Yukon-Kuskokwim Sustainable Salmon initiative; $1,000,000 is for the Cook Inlet Fishing Community Assistance Program; $500,000 is for the Yukon River Drainage Association; $3,368,000 is for Fairbanks hatchery facilities; $250,000 is for an initiative to redefine optimum goals for sockeye, chinook, and coho stocks; $2,500,000 is for the NSRAA Hatchery; $500,000 is for Coffman Cove king salmon; $250,000 is for the State of Alaska to participate in discussions regarding the Columbia River hydro-system and for fisheries revitalization; $100,000 is for the United Fishermen of Alaska's subsistence program; $3,500,000 is to restore salmon fisheries in Anchorage at Ship Creek, Chester Creek, and Campbell Creek, including habitat restoration and facilities; $500,000 is for Alaska Village Initiatives to enhance salmon stocks; $800,000 is for Bristol Bay Science and Research Institute; $1,100,000 is for the Alaska Fisheries Development Foundation; $150,000 is for the State of Alaska for fishing rationalization research; $1,500,000 is for the State of Alaska for fisheries monitoring; $1,500,000 is for the Alaska SeaLife Center to restore salmon runs in Resurrection Bay; $500,000 is for the southeast Revitalization Association for its fleet stabilization program; $1,000,000 is for the Kenai River; and $200,000 is to restore the Craig watershed.

Of the amounts provided to the State of Washington, $3,500,000 is for the Washington State Department of Natural Resources and other State and Federal agencies for purposes of implementing the State of Washington's Forest and Fish report, and $3,000,000 is for the purchase of mass marking equipment used at Federal hatcheries in Washington State to promote selective fisheries and protect threatened and endangered species.

Of the amounts provided to the State of Oregon, $1,000,000 is for conservation mass marking at the Columbia River Hatcheries.

The conferees agree that NOAA shall report to the Committees by March 31, 2005, on final performance measures for this program, including an assessment of cumulative program effects on Pacific salmon stocks, and the identification of recovery needs of specific salmon populations as a resource for determining future funding allocations.

Source: Explanatory "report language" attached to the fiscal year 2005 appropriations bill for the U.S. Commerce Department.

In this passage from nonstatutory report language, Congress strongly encourages NOAA Fisheries to spend its funds for salmon recovery in specific ways, including the ways spelled out in the three passages highlighted in the text. Agencies almost always follow the guidance given in report language, even though they are not legally obligated to do so, because Congress's "power of the purse" gives it tremendous leverage.

single-spaced list of suggested grant recipients. Congress put it this way: "[The agency] is expected to review the following proposals, provide grants if warranted, and report to the Committees on Appropriations regarding its intentions." The total of the hundreds of grants suggested was exactly the amount of money appropriated: $191,704,000.[9] If the agency chose to fund this congressional wish list, it would in effect have no money remaining for an open competitive awards process. It is important to note that the agency did in fact comply with all of Congress's suggestions, even though those suggestions were not legally binding. In later chapters, we consider why it is that agencies are loathe to ignore such nonstatutory "suggestions" made by the board of directors.

Members of Congress also like to make sure that animal control money for Wildlife Services goes where they want it to go. The strong suggestion from Congress in 2006 was to direct "$539,000 for the management of beavers in Mississippi."[10]

The lesson is that agencies, in doing the work of government in pursuit of their missions, ultimately are answerable not just to the head of the executive branch, the president of the United States, but also to the board of directors on Capitol Hill. Congress may, if it chooses, give both general and specific instructions to those who do the work of government. If such instructions are signed into law by the president, the agencies are required to comply. When Congress, or some subset of members of Congress, conveys its wishes in less formal, nonstatutory ways, agencies can be put in a very difficult spot: Sometimes the instructions from the president and the congressional overseers are in conflict, and sometimes the instructions do not jibe precisely with the agency's mission as established in law.

Circumstances such as these lead to some of the most interesting clashes in our separated system of government. The constitutional design calls for the Congress, with its particular perspective and way of doing business, to direct the executive branch, which is made up of dozens of agencies, with as many different corporate cultures. Unsurprisingly, as often as not, the two branches do not see eye to eye on the details of the work of government. The Framers, however, intentionally built this tension into our system of government: They believed that the way to protect the people's liberties was to ensure that the branches do not have the same perspective.

CONGRESS IN A SEPARATED SYSTEM

As mentioned at the beginning of this chapter, Congress is often studied in isolation from the rest of the government. In this book, the aim is to understand Congress in context—specifically in the context of its role as the board of directors in a separated system of government.

Although it is common to hear our institutions of government described as "separated powers," this is not a complete or precise characterization. In fact, as the Framers made abundantly clear, ours is a system of *separate institutions sharing powers.*[11]

The genius of the checks and balances in the American political system is that each branch of government has been granted in the Constitution checks on the other branches. In fact, the idea was *not* to give branches truly separate powers. If one branch of government had truly separate, unchecked powers, the ambitious people in that branch of government (and the Framers firmly believed that people in politics *are* ambitious!) would be tempted to run wild with that power, which was just the situation the Framers were trying to avoid. Their number-one priority was to prevent the central government from unnecessarily infringing upon the people's liberties. Pitting the branches against one another was thought to be the best way to accomplish this goal.

In particular, the Framers were concerned about controlling the political branches, the executive and legislative. The judicial branch was thought to be the "least dangerous branch," since its pronouncements, to have any effect, would require the acquiescence of the political branches to fund them (the Congress) and enforce them (the president).[12] In the parlance of the time, the judicial branch would have neither the "purse" nor the "sword," so it would be in no position to run away with its authority.

Whether the judicial branch has actually been constrained over the long course of American history is a matter of considerable debate. Many people feel that the lack of sufficient effective institutional checks on the Supreme Court and the lower federal courts led in the latter half of the twentieth century to a runaway judiciary that has done more than just adjudicate the disputes brought to its attention. Even so, it remains the case that the judiciary usually does not participate in the day-to-day functioning of the government but most often serves as the referee; the main players are the political branches, legislative and executive.

The Framers focused on balancing the checks the two political branches had on one another. As a result, those two branches are inextricably linked to each other by the Constitution. To get a sophisticated sense of what each branch does in the government, one must see it in the context of the other branch. *What Congress does is not meaningful unless seen in the context of its interactions with the executive branch.*

In other words, what Congress does has tangible importance in our lives only insofar as its decisions are translated into the actions taken by officials in the executive branch agencies—whether they are tracking infectious disease, subsidizing public housing, prosecuting people accused of violating federal statutes, or patrolling the borders.

Congress and the Execution of the Law

The relationship between the two political branches is not as simple as it might at first seem. Their interaction is not just a matter of one branch, the Congress, creating laws, and the other branch, the executive, implementing them.

Although members of Congress have to vote on every imaginable issue, including highly technical ones, it is impossible for them to be expert on everything. Members of Congress are generalists who have some knowledge of a lot of things but in-depth knowledge of very few. Because the laws written by the generalists in Congress are frequently—and often intentionally—broad, vague, or even ambiguous, there are almost always differing opinions on how to interpret and implement these laws. Furthermore, no law can anticipate all future circumstances; all laws require constant reinterpretation.

Congress recognizes these facts of life and often leaves a great deal of decision-making authority to the discretion of experts in the executive branch agencies. In exercising their discretion, executive branch officials may not necessarily make decisions that correspond with the views of at least some current members of Congress. (This is especially common in times of divided government, when the president and congressional majorities have ideological differences.) Confrontations between the branches, and even occasionally major headline news, may result.

The branches are, in effect, in a continuous feedback loop. The implementation of Congress's imprecise statutes by the executive branch often attracts the attention of congressional overseers, who then may use various methods of persuasion and coercion (hearings, informal communications, and other types of oversight) designed to get the agencies to reconsider their decisions. Sometimes Congress reacts by introducing and passing new legislation with the hope of making its intentions clearer.

Much of this interaction revolves around funding. Because agencies' funding levels are reconsidered annually, members of Congress have a regular opportunity to poke around in executive branch business to make sure money is being spent wisely and according to their wishes.

The Executive Branch and the Legislative Process

Not only, then, is Congress sometimes an active player in the execution of the law, but importantly, the executive branch is a player in the legislative process. At the top of the executive branch, the president has the veto power, which puts him in the thick of any legislative activity in which he takes an interest. Congress historically has found it extremely difficult to make law by mustering the two-thirds majority required by the Constitution to override a veto, and thus it is almost always necessary for it to take the president's views into consideration.

In addition, the Constitution allows the president to recommend legislation to the Congress (Article II, Section 3). Over time the White House has institutionalized its participation in the legislative process through the Office of Management and Budget (OMB), an agency in the Executive Office of the President that officially conveys the president's views on pending legislation.

Furthermore, the agencies, where much of the expertise in government resides, often are the source of legislative proposals to fix government programs or address particular needs. In other words, while it is technically true that only members of the legislative branch may introduce legislation, in fact Congress often finds itself considering bills suggested and written by the White House or executive branch agencies instead of writing the bills itself.

In summary, in our system of government, Congress is not just concerned with legislation but is fully entitled to play a role in the execution of the law by checking up on how the agencies carry out its wishes; similarly, the executive branch is not limited to the implementation of the law but is fully entitled to play a role in the writing and even the interpretation of the law.

This relationship results in a constant struggle between the two inextricably linked political branches—just as the Framers intended. In our conception of Congress as the board of directors of the federal government, we recall that it lacks one key power enjoyed by a corporate board: It does not get to choose the chief executive officer. And of course, this was entirely intentional. Striving for businesslike efficiency was not the point of the constitutional arrangement; ensuring the liberties of the people was. The branches would share powers but have separate bases of support; it was understood that this arrangement would often lead to disagreement and a less-than-efficient lawmaking process.

Unlike legislatures in most countries, which play a decidedly subordinate role to the chief executive, the U.S. Congress has retained its fundamental powers throughout American history. Congress remains powerful in many of the key ways in which a corporate board of directors is powerful; in particular, it establishes policy and determines the level of funding for government activities. It is not always a hands-on board; the government is way too big for Congress to delve into all the specifics.

But no one can understand our system of government without grasping Congress's undeniably crucial role.

Congress is a complex institution arranged unlike almost any other organization, and this often makes its ways subject to misinterpretation. Its internal workings are confusing, and it has its own vocabulary and rhythms. It is the aim of this book to interpret the institution of Congress, giving the reader a better understanding of the role of the legislative branch in our system of government.

THE PLAN OF THE BOOK

In this book about Congress in the context of its relationship with the executive branch, the first objective is to establish a basic working knowledge of the institution, and that is the aim of Chapters 2 and 3. The student of legislative branch policymaking needs to understand the constitutional underpinnings of Congress's power, the nature of the institution, and the roles and motivations of the members.

Congress's essential characteristics are shaped by the Constitution of the United States. A twofold understanding of the institution is derived from that document. First is the idea that Congress is both a lawmaking body and a representative institution, accountable and responsive to the public. Second is the fact that the Congress comprises two chambers, the House of Representatives and the Senate. The student of Congress needs to understand what it means for members of Congress to serve as both legislators and representatives, as well as how the two very distinct chambers operate.

Chapter 2 covers these fundamental aspects of Congress's nature. Congress's legislative and representative roles often prove extraordinarily difficult for members to reconcile. The tension between these roles may lead them at times in directions that they would not necessarily go if they only had one or the other responsibility. The chapter focuses in particular on the pressures that members face in their capacity as representatives. Members are on the frontlines, hearing from all manner of groups and individual constituents with an interest in the work of Congress. The reader will get a sense of the pressures to which members are subject and the motivations that drive their behavior; these pressures and motivations have a profound effect on their legislative work as the board of directors of the federal government.

Congress's bicameral composition, the topic of the second half of Chapter 2, is the source of much confusion. Few people—and not even all those who work on Capitol Hill—are fully aware of the ways in which the bicameral makeup of the institution drives the legislative process. The fact is that the Congress comprises two uneasily coexisting chambers that are truly separate and distinct, yet that must work together in order for the institution to perform its board-of-directors function. Chapter 2 includes an introduction to the dynamics of the relationship between the House and Senate and covers the organizational makeup of the two chambers, focusing on the party leadership and committees.

Chapter 3 develops the representative role of Congress further, looking at the electoral pressures faced by members of Congress. This chapter describes congressional elections, the recruitment of candidates, the importance of fund-raising, electoral strategies, and the meaning of congressional election results. The thematic focus of the chapter is on the impact of the unrelenting pressure to campaign for reelection. Members face what amounts to a continuous campaign, especially in the House. In recent years, there simply have not been enough hours in the day for many members to give full attention to their legislative role. The work of the board of directors has been profoundly affected as a result—a theme we return to in Chapter 8.

In Chapters 4 through 6, we move to the main thrust of the book: explaining how Congress directs the work of government through the exercise of its authorizing, funding, and oversight powers—Congress's three board-of-directors functions. Chapter 4 discusses the institution's authorizing responsibility. Congress is responsible for producing the legislation that authorizes the work of government carried out by the executive branch agencies. In drafting the bills that set policy for federal agencies, congressional committees do most of the heavy lifting in carrying out the authorizing responsibility. We look at the different ways in which Congress exercises power over federal agencies and programs, even to the extent of producing legislation that reshapes and reorganizes government departments and agencies. A case study of the 2004 restructuring of the federal government's foreign intelligence function illustrates the lengths to which Congress can go in asserting its powers.

Chapter 4 also covers the essentials of the legislative process in the House and Senate. That process is always evolving and frequently deviates from the "how a bill becomes a law" chart familiar to most people. We look at how the process really operates in today's Congress, focusing on the increasingly active role played by party leadership in the last fifteen years. The chapter ends with a discussion of evolving trends in Congress's handling of its authorizing responsibility, especially the consequences of its inability to complete much of its work in this area in a timely manner.

Once a federal program has been established, Congress has to decide whether to fund it. Congress's funding role, the so-called power of the purse, is generally regarded as its most important function; after all, no agency can carry out a government program without money. This is the subject of Chapter 5. The funding process, controlled by Congress's Appropriations Committees, attracts more attention year in and year out than any other congressional activity. In fact, some of Congress's authorizing and oversight functions frequently ride piggyback on the appropriations process. As one prominent congressional staffer said: "Most years everything in Congress revolves around the appropriations process; all else is just window dressing."[13]

In this chapter, we look at the federal budget writ large, examining its vast scope and the major categories of spending. That analysis is followed by an examination of the congressional budget process, starting with the submission of the president's budget request in early February and following it through the passage of the concurrent budget resolution and the appropriations bills. The chapter ends by highlighting some of the most controversial issues surrounding the budget, including debates about deficit spending and the national debt, earmarking, and the common failure of the Congress to complete appropriations bills on time.

Once federal programs are put in place, Congress has a responsibility to look into how they are operating. Chapter 6 looks at Congress's supervisory or oversight function. Almost every committee in Congress has oversight responsibility over several federal agencies and dozens or even hundreds of programs. Congressional committees keep tabs on the work of government they have authorized or funded in order to inform the legislative process. Congress's activities in this area take many forms. Committees may conduct full-fledged investigations of federal agencies or hold hearings to question federal officials. Individual members may simply make phone calls or write letters inquiring about particular programs. Congress is supported in these efforts by the Government Accountability Office (GAO), its investigative support agency. Sometimes oversight can be the principal activity of the Congress. In effect, the board of directors may substitute oversight activities for actual legislation in its efforts to influence federal agencies. At the end of the chapter, we discuss the political motivations that drive Congress's oversight activities.

Chapter 7 takes a brief detour to look at one area of public policy in which Congress has been unmistakably eclipsed by its executive branch rival: war powers. Congress's role in the area of war powers is important, but perennially controversial. Unlike in domestic policy, in important ways Congress's power is limited in the national security arena, although that may not at all have been the intent of the Constitution's Framers, who seemed explicitly to give Congress the power to commit troops to battle in almost all circumstances. We look at why Congress's war powers role has diminished quite suddenly and dramatically since the end of World War II. The chapter concludes with a case study of the government's decision to go to war in Afghanistan in 2001 and Iraq in 2003, as well as Congress's unsuccessful efforts to alter the conduct of the latter war in 2007–2008.

The concluding chapter, "The Board of Directors in the Twenty-First Century," gives us an opportunity to take a step back to review what we have learned about Congress in its role of directing the work of the federal government, as well as to assess the quality of that work. To a significant degree, the Congress of the twenty-first century is a product of the constitutional design. It is and always will be slow-moving, parochial, and unfocused. But not everything about the institution is determined. Congress has changed in fundamental ways in response to the larger political and social environment. The party system, for example, did not exist in anything like its current form in the early days, and it has evolved in ways that affect the performance of the board of directors every bit as profoundly as the unalterable characteristics written into the Constitution. The pressures of the constant campaign and the ubiquitous influence of interest groups have changed the policymaking environment on Capitol Hill as well.

In many ways, when all is said and done, the fact is that the institution is falling down on the job. It is not keeping up with its authorizing responsibilities, it regularly fails to act in a timely fashion on crucial legislation to fund the functioning of the government, and it spends less time than in the past on conducting oversight of federal programs. We take a therapeutic approach to the institution and these evident failings: The first step is to identify the problems. This is a tremendously important inquiry—after all, Congress will be in the middle of the great challenges of the twenty-first century. Laws will be required to get the nation's fiscal house in order, fix the health care system, and deal with global climate change, among other things. Whether the board of directors is up to the task will say a great deal about the nation's future.

QUESTIONS FOR DISCUSSION

1. A corporate board of directors answers to the company's shareholders, while the members of Congress, as the board of directors of the federal government, answer to the voters. Are there similarities in the kinds of demands that shareholders and voters make of their respective boards? What are some key differences?

2. In its capacity as a board of directors, how active should the Congress be in providing specific direction to the agencies of government? Are there any general rules or principles it should follow in determining when to get involved in the execution or implementation of the law?

SUGGESTIONS FOR FURTHER READING

Madison, James. *The Federalist Papers*. Nos. 47, 48, 49, and 51.

NOTES

1. U.S. Commerce Department, National Oceanographic and Atmospheric Adminis-tration, Northwest Regional Office, "ESA Salmon Listings," available at: http://www.nwr.noaa.gov/ESA-Salmon-Listings/ (accessed November 28, 2006).

2. U.S. Department of Justice, Bureau of Justice Assistance, "Edward Byrne Memorial State and Local Law Enforcement Assistance," available at: http://www.ojp.usdoj.gov/BJA/grant/byrne.html (accessed November 7, 2006).

3. United States Joint Forces Command, "Joint National Training Capability (JNTC) Frequently Asked Questions," available at: http://www.jfcom.mil/about/faq_jntc.htm.

4. U.S. Department of Agriculture, Animal and Plant Health Inspection Service, Mis-sissippi Wildlife Services, "State Report," available at: http://www.aphis.usda.gov/ws/state reports/mississippi.html.

5. Ibid.

6. See "Principal Riverwalk," available at: http://www.absolutedsm.com/index.php?option=com_content&view=article&id=729%3Aprincipal-riverwalk&catid=61%3Adown town-central&Itemid=172; and U.S. Army Corps of Engineers, Rock Island District, "About the Greenbelt Program," available at: http://www2.mvr.usace.army.mil/Greenbelt/.

7. James L. Sundquist, *The Decline and Resurgence of Congress* (Washington, DC: Brook-ings Institution Press, 1981), pp. 38–39. Sundquist gives credit to W. F. Willoughby for first developing the board-of-directors analogy in the 1930s.

8. See "Conference Report for the Omnibus Appropriations Act for Fiscal Year 2005: Joint Statement of Managers (Pacific Coastal Salmon Recovery)."

9. See "Consolidated Appropriations Act for Fiscal Year 2008: Edward Byrne Discre-tionary Grants."

10. See "Agriculture and Related Agencies Appropriation Act for Fiscal Year 2006: Joint Statement of Managers (Wildlife Services)."

11. See especially Charles O. Jones, *The Presidency in a Separated System* (Washington, DC: Brookings Institution Press, 2005); and Richard Neustadt, *Presidential Power and the Modern Presidents* (New York: Free Press, 1991).

12. Alexander Hamilton, *The Federalist Papers*, No. 78.

13. Mark Harkins, then chief of staff to Representative Brad Miller (D-NC), interview with the author, April 16, 2006.

CHAPTER TWO

THE NATURE OF CONGRESS

There is a common expression that people are "products of their environment." Even though there is obviously some truth to that claim, no one doubts that many of an individual's most important traits are heavily influenced by genetics as well. In a similar vein, the U.S. Congress has certain characteristics and exhibits behaviors that have been shaped by the American political version of the genome: the seven articles, as amended, of the U.S. Constitution. Article I of the Constitution establishes the powers and responsibilities of the legislative branch and, together with Article II, sets forth its relationship with the executive branch.

The Constitution gives Congress two distinct responsibilities: lawmaking and representation. Congress's essential nature is to a significant degree determined by the tension between these two roles. Lawmaking entails serving as the board of directors of the U.S. government—authorizing, funding, and supervising its activities. The second responsibility is essentially political: Each member of Congress represents and is accountable to a discrete group of people who make up the member's constituency.

The Constitution established a bicameral legislature, with a House of Representatives and a Senate, to carry out these roles. The two chambers have different constituencies, profoundly dissimilar rules, some different responsibilities, unequal stature, and, in sum, divergent perspectives on the political world. Congress's two-headed quality makes it an institution that is particularly hard—bordering on impossible at times—to coordinate.

The first part of this chapter describes Congress's legislative and representative roles and looks at the potential for conflict between them. The discussion begins with the seeming contradiction between the popularity of individual members of Congress and the low regard the public usually has for the institution as a whole. Even though members of Congress are often criticized for being "out of touch," in fact nothing could be further from the truth. Their popularity derives from their responsiveness to constituents as they address citizens' public policy concerns and help them navigate the confusing government bureaucracy.

Members are also accused of being "beholden to special interests." It is true that interest groups are major players in the legislative process, but for the most part not exactly in the way most people think. Members' relationships with interest groups and lobbyists are more often than not tied directly to matters of concern to their districts and states, especially jobs and the provision of services.

It is no mystery, then, why members of Congress are popular. They are good at the representative role—tending to the needs of the people back home. The representative role is priority number one for most members most of the time. What this means is that, in understanding the nature of Congress, one can never lose sight of the importance of members' district and state concerns as they make national policy and pass laws in their capacity as the board of directors.

The section ends by explaining why members' individual popularity does not necessarily translate into goodwill toward the institution as a whole. Congress has, to put it mildly, a public relations problem unique to its structure and tied to the behavior of some members in their efforts at self-promotion.

The second part of the chapter covers the structure of the House and Senate, as well as the chambers' major similarities and differences. The two bodies are organized along roughly parallel lines, with party leadership and committees designed to plan and conduct legislative business. We look at how leaders are selected, the committee structure, and the ways in which members attempt to secure positions of influence. Ultimately these organizational units are meant to help the institution and its members balance their representative and legislative responsibilities.

THE NATURE OF CONGRESS, PART I:
TWO DISTINCT RESPONSIBILITIES

The Legislative Role

As mentioned in Chapter 1, Congress is explicitly given the lawmaking function at the beginning of the Constitution, in Article I. Subsequent sections of that article flesh out this role, and Section 8 spells out Congress's constitutional powers in setting policy for the government:

- "To lay and collect taxes, duties, imposts and excises
- To pay the debts [of the nation]
- [To] provide for the common defense and general welfare
- To borrow money on the credit of the United States
- To regulate commerce [with foreign nations, among the states, and with the Indian tribes]
- To establish a uniform rule of naturalization
- To establish uniform laws on the subject of bankruptcies
- To coin money and regulate [its] value
- [To] fix the standard of weights and measures
- To provide for the punishments [for] counterfeiting
- To establish post offices
- To promote the progress of science and the useful arts by securing for limited times to authors and inventors the exclusive right to their respective writings and discoveries
- To constitute tribunals inferior to the Supreme Court
- To define and punish piracies and felonies committed on the high seas
- To punish offenses against the law of nations
- To declare war
- To grant marque and reprisal and make rules concerning captures on land and water
- To raise and support armies [and a navy] and make rules [for governing the armed forces]
- To provide for calling forth the militia to execute the laws of the union
- To suppress insurrections and repeal invasions
- To provide for organizing, arming, and disciplining the militia and for governing such part of them as may be employed in the service of the United States
- To exercise exclusive legislation over [the District of Columbia]
- To exercise . . . authority over [forts, depots, navy yards, and so on]
- To make all laws which shall be necessary and proper for carrying into execution the foregoing powers and all other powers vested by this Constitution of the United States"

Section 9 of Article I establishes Congress's "power of the purse," the power that most regularly provides the leverage needed to direct the work of government.

Section 10 establishes Congress's authority over the states in crucial policy areas, including tariffs and military affairs.

Furthermore, some of the most important amendments to the Constitution—including the one that permitted a federal income tax in 1913 (Amendment XVI) and those that were meant to ensure equal rights and voting rights for all Americans (Amendments XIII, XIV, XV, XIX, XXIV, and XXVI)—further expanded the legislative reach of the Congress, in some cases very dramatically. For example, Amendment XIX giving women the vote (ratified in 1919) says: "The right of citizens of the United States to vote shall not be denied or abridged by the United States or by any State on account of sex. *Congress shall have power to enforce this article by appropriate legislation*" (emphasis added). In effect, Congress's authority was explicitly expanded to do what it deems legislatively necessary to protect women's suffrage. The Fifteenth Amendment (1870) has an almost identical provision giving Congress the power to act if the right to vote is denied based on "race, color, or previous condition of servitude."

The purpose of the Constitution was to establish a federal government strong enough to keep together a nation of far-flung states. The constitutional Framers recognized that the first national governing document, the Articles of Confederation (1777–1788), was unable to do this. That document set up a confederation in which the states retained many important powers independent of the central government. The central government lacked critical enumerated powers, such as laying and collecting taxes, and there was no chief executive separate from the legislative body. (The president was merely the presiding officer for the legislative body.)

The Framers' notion was that the legislative body needed to have clearly delineated powers that could not be nullified by the states. In the *supremacy clause*, Article VI of the Constitution explicitly states that federal laws take precedence over state laws. Most of the Framers also felt that a separate chief executive was needed to enforce the laws of the land.

Essentially the U.S. Congress was given the responsibility to establish federal policy in law. As a practical matter, Congress was the board of directors, charged with creating programs to address the nation's needs and the departments and agencies of government to carry them out. As if this job was not big enough, the Framers gave Congress another job every bit as important.

The Representative Role

The Framers of the U.S. Constitution set up a *republic*. In a republic, sovereignty is vested in the voting citizenry instead of in a monarch. But since it is impractical (and many thought unwise) for the voting citizenry literally to govern itself, the republican form of government gives power to the citizens' elected representatives. The elected representatives must face regular and frequent elections to retain their positions of authority.

To make the American republic operational, the original Constitution set up a popularly elected House of Representatives. All of its members would be up for reelection every even-numbered year. The Constitution stipulates that no bill may become law without passing both the House and Senate in identical form, making it impossible for the government to impose anything on its citizens without the concurrence of their directly elected representatives. The provision in Article I that contains this stipulation is called the *presentment clause*:

> Every bill which shall have passed the House of Representatives and the Senate, shall, before it become a law, be presented to the President of the United States. If he approve he shall sign it, but if not he shall return it, with his objections to that House in which it shall have originated.

Originally, members of the Senate, who were given six-year terms, were not directly elected. The Constitution stated that they would be chosen by the state legislatures. This was changed in 1913 with Amendment XVII, which requires the direct election of senators in the states. Since that time, all members of Congress have been directly elected. However, unlike with the House, only one-third of the Senate seats are contested in each election cycle.

There is one exception to the rule that every sitting member must be directly elected: When a senator dies or retires in the middle of his or her term, most states give the governor the power to appoint a temporary successor until the next election cycle. On the other hand, when vacancies occur in the House, the seat may not be filled by appointment even temporarily; a special election must be held to fill the spot.

What was established in the Constitution was a system of *accountability*, which is the core principle of a republic. Citizens—who are the sovereign in a republic—control the politicians they put in power by exercising the voting franchise. It is true that politicians may do what they want while in office, but if they intend to keep their jobs, they are unlikely to stray too far from voters' wishes.

It is impossible to overemphasize the importance of accountability in a representative democracy. In such a system, it is extremely difficult for those who do not have the voting franchise to get the attention of the elected officials who wield power.

This is best illustrated by the situation of African Americans even after slavery was abolished. In much of the old Confederacy and the border states, African Americans were denied the vote for almost one hundred years following the end of the Civil War in 1865, even though the Fifteenth Amendment, ratified in 1870, was meant to ensure that the franchise could not be taken away based on race. When forceful and authoritative legislation in 1965 finally secured access to the voting booth for African Americans in these states, even the most dismissive of southern segregationist members of Congress became attentive within just a few years to the concerns of their newly enfranchised constituents. The example of Senator Strom Thurmond of South Carolina, described in Box 2.1, illustrates this point well.

The American republic was arranged so that the elected representatives would be accountable to particular constituencies: to districts in the House and to states in the Senate. The House districts were to be apportioned to the states based on population, with the total number determined in federal legislation. (This number was set at 435 in 1911 and has not been changed since.[1]) Each state would get two senators.

This constitutional arrangement creates the *representative role* for members of Congress. Thus, all members of the institution must serve two functions—one primarily involving policymaking for the government and the other being primarily political. A member's job is a complicated one: Setting federal policy *and* looking after the interests of one's constituents is a lot of work. Moreover, the two roles are not necessarily always compatible. Understanding the tension between being a lawmaker and being a representative is the key to grasping the essential nature of the institution, and ultimately to gaining a sophisticated sense of the Congress in its role as the board of directors for the federal government.

Reconciling the Two Roles: The Public's Mixed Feelings

One useful way to get at the interplay between the two roles of members of Congress is to look at how the public regards Congress.

Survey your friends, your work associates, your classmates, or almost any other group, and you will probably discover that there is general dissatisfaction with the performance of the Congress. Scientific public opinion surveys regularly test this very issue, asking a random and representative sample of the public whether they approve of the performance of Congress. The results have varied a fair amount, depending on the circumstances. But as can be seen in Figure 2.1, a review of polling conducted by the Gallup organization over the past thirty years indicates a generally low level of approval of the institution. The ratings tend most of the time to range from about 20 to 50 percent. In 2006 they tended toward the low side: Often the

BOX 2.1
SENATOR THURMOND CHANGES HIS TUNE

Strom Thurmond was first elected to the Senate from South Carolina in 1954 after having served as the state's governor and as the 1948 presidential candidate of the "Dixiecrats." Officially the States' Rights Party, the Dixiecrats were a breakaway group of southern Democrats who were disenchanted with a move by some prominent party leaders at the 1948 convention to embrace a civil rights platform. Thurmond took five southern states in the general election that year, capturing the vote of traditional Democrats who opposed any infringement on the states' right to maintain the racial status quo of legal segregation.

Thurmond achieved notoriety as a senator for his leadership in 1956 in promoting the "Southern Manifesto," a document signed by most southern members of Congress to protest the Supreme Court's *Brown v. Board of Education* desegregation decision of 1954. In 1957 he filibustered for over twenty-four hours—a record for the Senate—in opposition to the 1957 civil rights bill. In short, Thurmond was a steadfast opponent of integrating schools and other public facilities and institutions in the South. He even went so far as to leave the Democratic Party and become a Republican in 1965 when it became evident that the party was intent on moving more aggressively on the civil rights front.

That same year the Voting Rights Act was signed into law, ending forever the disenfranchisement of the African American community in his home state and across the South. Thurmond's hard line started to change. His office began to provide constituent services for African Americans, as it had always done for the white population in the state. He was one of the first southern senators to hire a black staff member, and many observers were stunned when he voted for the reauthorization of the Voting Rights Act some years later as well as for the controversial establishment of a federal holiday commemorating Martin Luther King's birthday.

While Thurmond never was able to secure consistently widespread support from South Carolina's African Americans in his reelection efforts, his constituent service operation in the state certainly contributed to a productive working relationship with the black community. And he did improve his percentage of the vote among African Americans as the years went by, usually besting the performance of other Republican southern senators.

Source: Michael Barone and Richard E. Cohen, *The Almanac of American Politics 2002* (Washington, DC: National Journal, 2001), pp. 1367–1368.

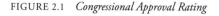

FIGURE 2.1   *Congressional Approval Rating*

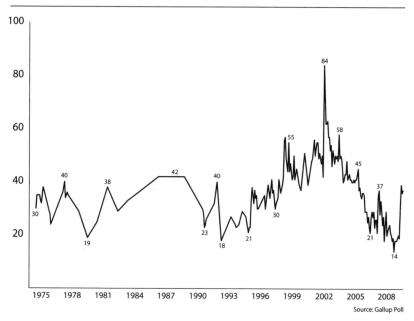

approval rating was somewhere around 25 percent. There was a brief upswing in early 2007, followed by a sharp drop in the late summer and fall. In 2008 the approval numbers went even lower. On the positive side, the months after the September 11, 2001, attacks yielded not only great popularity for President George W. Bush, whose approval ratings reached a high of 90 percent, but stratospheric (by historical standards) ratings for Congress of about 60 percent. Those ratings represented, as the saying goes, the exception that proved the rule.[2]

Interestingly, there is always a curious and sizable discrepancy between the paltry ratings the institution usually receives and the relatively favorable ratings given individual members. As can be seen in Figure 2.2, when polling organizations asked people whether their own member was doing a good job and deserved reelection, typically well over half gave the thumbs-up and the favorable ratio was better than two-to-one. Even in 2006, a year when Congress was held in especially low repute owing to lobbyist scandals and other factors, the majority of the public thought their representative deserved to be returned to Congress.

Even more telling are the reelection rates enjoyed by members. In the House in recent years, well over 90 percent of members seeking reelection succeed in their quest. It is not uncommon for that number to reach 98 percent or even higher. Even

FIGURE 2.2   *People May Disapprove of Congress, but They Approve of Their Representative*

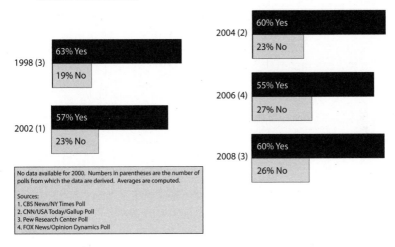

Generic poll question: "Would you tell me whether the U.S. Representative in your District deserves to be re-elected?"

1998 (3)
63% Yes
19% No

2002 (1)
57% Yes
23% No

2004 (2)
60% Yes
23% No

2006 (4)
55% Yes
27% No

2008 (3)
60% Yes
26% No

No data available for 2000. Numbers in parentheses are the number of polls from which the data are derived. Averages are computed.

Sources:
1. CBS News/NY Times Poll
2. CNN/USA Today/Gallup Poll
3. Pew Research Center Poll
4. FOX News/Opinion Dynamics Poll

in 1994, the year of the "Republican Revolution," when more than fifty Democratic seats were lost in a wave of dissatisfaction with the performance of the party that had held the chamber for forty years (and most of the previous sixty-four years), 90 percent of incumbents were returned to office. (See Figure 3.4 for a graphic presentation of reelection rates in the House.) In 2006, another year when public disgust with the Congress led to a change in party power, 95 percent of those who sought reelection to the House of Representatives won. The same was true in 2008. In the Senate, usually over 80 percent of incumbents win reelection. (In 2006 the figure was exactly 80 percent, which was sufficient to swing six seats to the Democrats and give them the majority in the chamber.) The bottom line: Individual members are much more popular than the institution in which they serve.

What Explains the Seeming Contradiction?

What is going on here? How can there be such a discrepancy between the public's views of the institution and its views of the members of that institution?

Let's start with the favorable ratings of the members. How do they garner these good reviews? First and foremost, members of Congress take their representative role very seriously. Constituent service is the first priority for many if not most of them.

FIGURE 2.3   *Typical House Member's Office Structure*

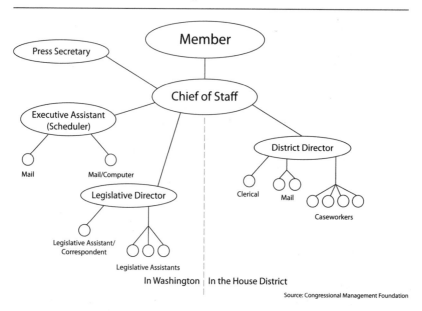

Source: Congressional Management Foundation

In Figure 2.3,[3] one can see the most common staffing arrangements for members of the House. A description of each aide's duties is included in endnote 3. Most members have multiple offices in their districts or states, staffed by people whose exclusive duty is attending to constituents' problems with one or another government agency.

In this capacity, congressional offices are performing a function that can be traced back to classical antiquity—the *ombudsman* role, or serving as an intermediary between the citizen and the government. Members have staff dedicated, for instance, to helping seniors cope with the new Medicare prescription drug plan, sorting out travelers' passport snafus at the State Department, and handling constituents' problems with Immigration and Customs Enforcement or even with the Internal Revenue Service.

In fact, some members' staffs are legendary for their ability to untangle bureaucratic knots. Former New York senator Alfonse D'Amato, who served from 1981 to 1999, was affectionately nicknamed "Senator Pothole" because of his willingness to look into seemingly the smallest problems that New Yorkers had with government services. And the crack staff of five-term North Carolina senator Jesse Helms had a reputation as the "go-to guys" for constituents trying to get information from federal or even state and local agencies. Although it may be impossible to quantify precisely the effect that good ombudsmanship has on the popularity of a member of Congress, certainly it is safe to conclude that the overall effect is positive.[4]

Even in their Washington offices, members commit considerable staff time to dealing with constituents' concerns about issues they are following or pending legislation. In many offices, responding to constituent questions takes up more resources than any other single activity. Members receive thousands of e-mails, faxes, and letters every month, not to mention the dozens of phone calls that come in every day, and most offices attempt to answer all of these promptly. In fact, many members' public positions on emerging issues of the day are formulated in response to constituent concerns expressed in writing. An informal poll conducted by the author of chiefs of staff for members of the House indicated that somewhere between 55 and 75 percent of staff hours in the Washington office are spent directly addressing constituent concerns. Members firmly believe that their ability to stay in office hinges on their responsiveness to constituents' concerns. They are probably right.

Another factor that explains the ability of members to cultivate good feelings is more organic. Members, with a few notable exceptions, are from the district or state they represent. They may have grown up there, and it may be their ancestral home; often they have relatives and friends in influential positions back home. As a result, they have an instinctive feel for the people and for their views, ambitions, and political leanings. Of course, many members, especially in the Senate, have diverse constituencies, or demographic shifts have changed their constituencies over time. These members must expend more time and effort to foster the trust and identification that is so crucial to effective representation and reelection.

Members who do not originally hale from the district or state of their constituency, such as former New York senator Hillary Clinton, try extra hard to get to know the people they are representing. Clinton's reelection margin in 2006 far exceeded the margin in her initial 2000 race for the seat, probably as a result of her persistence in getting to know the state and addressing the needs of her constituents. Box 2.2 describes her efforts to identify with and develop familiarity with the needs and concerns of her New York constituents.

Are Members of Congress Out of Touch?

It would be amusing to members, if it were not so frustrating, that they are frequently accused of being "out of touch" with the people. Nothing could be further from the truth. In fact, scholars and journalists who study Congress are nearly unanimous in criticizing members for being *too* responsive, unwilling to take risks that

BOX 2.2
SENATOR CLINTON BUILDS TRUST
IN HER NEW HOME STATE

Congressional scholar Richard Fenno has long maintained that developing trust and fostering a relationship with constituents is first and foremost in the minds of members of Congress.* After all, in order to be able to address policy matters of interest, members must first stay in office, and voters are much more inclined to support a politician with whom they can identify.

This relationship-building is tougher—but not impossible—when, in the rare case, the candidate is not from the district or state they seek to represent. First Lady Hillary Clinton was, of course, well known to New Yorkers when she ran for the Senate in 2000. But she had never lived in the state. She was raised in Illinois, and her adult life had primarily been spent in Arkansas and then Washington, D.C. But there was an open seat in New York being vacated by the retirement of longtime senator Patrick Moynihan. Clinton was encouraged to run by the fact that New York had experience in electing nonresidents to high office: President John F. Kennedy's brother, Robert F. Kennedy, had only briefly lived in New York as a child, but was elected senator in 1964.

Clinton was able to discourage potential primary opponents within the Democratic Party with her fund-raising prowess and key local endorsements. But Republicans saw the opportunity to pick up a Senate seat in a Democratic state by tagging her as a "carpetbagger." After New York City mayor Rudolph Giuliani, the party's hottest prospect, decided not to run, the party settled on Rick Lazio as its candidate. He was a Long Island congressman with a reputation as a responsible, moderate legislator and effective campaigner.

Clinton expected to do well in New York City and figured that her biggest hurdle would be relating to voters in upstate New York, where the Republican Party was stronger. At the very least, she needed to tamp down Lazio's margins in those areas in order to win the state. For the better part of a year before election day, she focused on meeting voters in small towns upstate and visited every county, most of them repeatedly. Her "listening tour" bore fruit. With the tour and effective debate performances, she was able to limit Lazio's margins in Republican strongholds and win the election going away, 55 to 43 percent.

Clinton's efforts to connect with New Yorkers did not lag after she was sworn into office in January 2001. She sought to solidify and even expand on her support and to dispel once and for all the carpetbagger charge. Within a year and a half of taking office, she had made more than 130 trips upstate alone. Ultimately, her efforts and prodigious fund-raising scared away most potential challengers to her reelection effort in 2006. She faced a weak general election opponent and won 67 to 31 percent.

* Richard Fenno, *Home Style: House Members in Their Districts* (Boston: Little, Brown and Co., 1978); see also William T. Bianco's *Trust: Representatives and Constituents* (Ann Arbor: University of Michigan Press, 1994).

threaten to put some distance between them and their constituents on controversial issues of the day.[5] Former members, such as former Indiana congressman Tim Roemer, are sharply critical of today's members for their unwillingness to take controversial stands for fear of stirring up opposition back home. Roemer suggests that "members need to recognize that there are issues worth losing your seat for."[6]

Most members spend more time at home interacting with constituents than in Washington. Even members from as far away as California, or even Hawaii and Alaska, hop on a plane almost every weekend to get back for meetings, events, and perhaps a little time with their families—and these "weekends" are sometimes longer than the workweeks, lasting from Thursday afternoon until midday the following Tuesday. In 2009, as Congress attempted to process President Barack Obama's ambitious agenda, members spent a bit more time in Washington most weeks—often almost four full days.

In addition to weekends, members jealously guard the more extended recesses from legislative business—during federal holidays most of them take a week away from Washington and some as long as a month—in order to go to town meetings, hold local office hours, give speeches at graduations, and spend time with their families. In 2007, Congresswoman Debbie Wasserman-Schultz (D-FL) made it clear that she wanted to guard her district time in order to continue to take an active role in raising her kids back in Florida. Most members do not move their families to Washington when they win a congressional seat.[7]

Members have incredible demands on their time, since the public expects responsiveness from their representatives and senators. To stay in office, members try to deliver.

It is a simple fact that many senators and representatives regard it as their responsibility to reflect the preferences of their constituents, not to vote based on their own independent views on the issues of the day. They go to great lengths to gauge what is of salience to the people back home and keep tabs on voters' thinking through polling, frequent meetings, and contacts with key community leaders. At the very least, members know that they must be able to provide a satisfactory explanation for any position they take that does not correspond neatly with the views of a majority of their constituents or those of a key group within the district or state.

The result of all these efforts is a happy one for most. In the House, most members have established so much credibility back in the district that they enjoy comfortable reelection margins. Even in a relatively competitive year like 2006, only 15 percent of the House races were decided by less than ten percentage points. And effective representation may pay another dividend: Some members can weather

BOX 2.3
SCANDALS DO NOT NECESSARILY MEAN
THE END OF A CAREER

Representative Ken Calvert (R-CA) has been in Congress since 1992, rising to a coveted slot on the House Appropriations Committee, despite facing an embarrassing scandal in his first term. In April 1994, the *Riverside Press-Enterprise* reported that Calvert had been stopped by police late the previous year while he was in a car with a prostitute. The newspaper printed some of the details of the report, and the congressman soon admitted that in fact he had engaged in "inappropriate" activities, but he maintained that he had not known the woman was a prostitute. Calvert was later quoted as saying he was "depressed about his recent divorce and his father's suicide and had wanted companionship."[*] Just six months after the congressman's tryst came to light, he was reelected by a 55 to 38 percent margin.

In 1983, Representative Gerry Studds (D-MA) was the subject of an investigation that was looking into sexual relationships that members of Congress were allegedly having with congressional pages. It was determined that, in 1973, Studds had in fact had relations with a seventeen-year-old male page. The congressman acknowledged the affair, but he refused to apologize, stating that "the affair was a mutually voluntary, private relationship between adults." Despite receiving official censure from his colleagues, Studds was reelected six more times before retiring from Congress in 1996.[†]

In 2005, Representative William Jefferson (D-LA) found himself under investigation by the Justice Department for bribery and other crimes. As his reelection campaign geared up in early 2006, it was revealed publicly that FBI agents had found $90,000 in cash (allegedly out of $100,000 that had been delivered by an informant as part of a bribery scheme) in his freezer in various plastic containers. The Justice Department further stated that investigators had collected evidence linking Jefferson to at least seven other cases in which he "sought things of value in return for his performance of official acts." Jefferson went on to win reelection that year in Louisiana's Second District with 57 percent of the vote. He was indicted in June 2007 for racketeering, bribery, obstruction of justice, wire fraud, and money laundering. Jefferson's problems did eventually take their toll—he was narrowly defeated in the 2008 election cycle.[‡] In August 2009, he was convicted of eleven out of sixteen corruption charges and may face twenty or more years in prison.

---

[*] Philip D. Duncan and Christine C. Lawrence, *Politics in America 1998* (Washington, DC: CQ Press, 1997), p. 211.

[†] Peter Perl, "Rep. Gerry Studds: Democrat from Massachusetts Has Been Elected Six Times," *Washington Post*, July 15, 1983, p. A10; and Jonathan Alter and Margaret G. Warner, "Sex and Pages on Capitol Hill," *Newsweek*, July 25, 1983, p. 16.

[‡] "Congressman William Jefferson's Corruption Charges Lead to Political Uproar on Capitol Hill," Foxnews.com, June 6, 2007, available at: http://www.foxnews.com/story/0,2933,278080,00.html; and Peter Whoriskey, "Jefferson Win Poses Dilemma for Party," *Washington Post*, December 11, 2006, p. A3.

embarrassing scandals—a Justice Department corruption investigation, an arrest for drunk driving, sexual peccadilloes—on election day and serve another term. Box 2.3 describes some interesting cases of members surviving such scandals.

Interest Groups and the Representative Role

Another common complaint about politicians in Washington is that they are in the pocket of the special interests that employ high-paid lawyer-lobbyists. Instead of looking out for the little guy, members of Congress are suspected of siding with interest groups, particularly those who "pay to play"—that is, those who contribute to their reelection campaigns. In effect, the complaint is that members, in directing the work of the federal government, are beholden to those with access and power and consider their needs ahead of the interests of the general public.

Interest group lobbyists are, in fact, hugely important in the day-to-day activities of Congress. There are over 30,000 registered lobbyists in Washington, and far more than 100,000 people working in some capacity in the lobbying industry.[8] Every imaginable interest is represented, including corporations, unions, charitable organizations, issue and cause groups, trade associations, county and state governments, and universities.

Interest group activity has mushroomed in the last forty years in Washington. Lobbyists working for various corporate concerns by trying to secure government contracts, tax breaks, or favorable regulatory rulings have been fixtures in Washington for decades, but historically the scope of interest group activity was fairly circumscribed. From the 1930s into the early 1960s, the major battles often came down to a relatively few corporate interests pitted against the AFL-CIO, by far the biggest union player. The federal government certainly mattered in American life in the first half of the twentieth century, but it tended to stay out of the affairs of the states in areas such as health, housing, education, and social issues.

The 1960s changed all that. Massive new government programs were put in place during the Great Society of President Lyndon Johnson and into the early years of Richard Nixon's presidency that involved heavy federal involvement in health care, education at all levels, housing, welfare, race relations, women's issues, consumer protection, the environment, the arts, science, and a host of other areas. Rather suddenly, nothing in American life remained untouched by federal policies in some significant way.

Many of the new government programs of that era affected corporate America, and in the eyes of some sectors of the corporate world, often not in a good way. Businesses geared up in unprecedented ways to try to mitigate some of the effects of what they regarded as burdensome new government regulations and tax burdens. They established Washington offices (or hired lobbyists from Washington law firms) to lobby members of Congress to change laws or at least take their concerns into consideration. Issue-oriented groups interested in the environment, consumer issues, women's rights, the rights of welfare recipients, women's reproductive issues, and many other issues sprouted up and became a Washington presence. Universities and state and local governments also wanted a piece of the action.

The journalist Jonathan Rauch describes a kind of *hyperpluralism* that developed at that time.[9] The term *pluralism* describes a political system in which no one particular group dominates the decision-making processes. Instead, numerous groups—economic, cultural, and ethnic—share power in shifting coalitions, depending on the issue. One group may hold the upper hand for a time in collaboration with some other group or groups, but their interests never coincide perfectly for long, so other combinations of groups coalesce to challenge existing coalitions for influence.[10]

In a country as diverse as the United States, thousands of identifiable groups and interests vie to protect or advance their position in society. Not all of them have traditionally found it necessary to expend the time and effort to lobby decision-makers in Washington, but as Washington's reach extended into every imaginable sphere of American life in the 1960s and 1970s, it became apparent that, to avoid getting the short end of the stick in federal policy, interest groups need to have a presence in Washington.

Hyperpluralism developed in the 1970s as all economic sectors, cultural groups, issue-oriented groups, universities, and so on, recognized that, to remain competitive and protect their interests in Washington, they had to make concerted efforts to influence the board of directors and agency officials in the executive branch. Corporations realized that if they did not have a presence, their competitors would win the day in the competitive marketplace with tax breaks and favorable regulatory rulings. State university systems saw that they would lose out on federal grants if they were not in Washington making their case. Governors who lacked a Washington office would lose highway funding. And people opposed to legal abortion, fearing the increasing influence of women's groups, rapidly organized to agitate for more restrictions.

Total numbers are hard to measure accurately. Health analysts estimate that the number of health-related groups has increased more than twentyfold since the 1970s. The number of citizen groups has gone up roughly tenfold in that period. Five or six times as many corporations base their operations in Washington as was the case forty years ago. All in all, the number of organized interests active in Washington has probably at least quintupled since the 1960s.[11]

Gaining Influence

As members of Congress decide what government programs to fund, what regulations to impose on business, and what the tax code will look like, lobbyists for organized interests pursue a range of strategies to try to influence the board of directors on Capitol Hill.

First and foremost, lobbyists try to be helpful to congressional staff and members. "Being helpful" can take many forms. Members and staff need good information from a wide range of sources to make considered decisions on public policy. The lobbyist who goes to great lengths to be the "go-to" person on a particular issue, providing reliable and verifiable information to Congress, is the lobbyist who has the ear of the decision-makers, which of course is the key to getting his or her views heard. Lobbyists who are unreliable or who provide bad information do not get in the door to make their case. Access is the essential ingredient to influence in Washington. By being useful and well-connected, good lobbyists become integral parts of the legislative process, helping congressional staff with crafting legislation, anticipating roadblocks to success, and building coalitions in support of mutually held objectives.

It should be noted that interest groups are very good at luring some of the best talent away from Capitol Hill. Experienced congressional staffers frequently move to the private sector to help law firms, companies, trade associations, and other groups influence members of Congress. There is a simple reason for this: The private sector can pay better than the federal government, which imposes strict pay caps on all federal employees. As a result, these former insiders are able to be quite useful to congressional staff and members, who often know less about the legislative process and lawmaking than they do. Of course, former members of Congress can make valuable lobbyists for the same reasons—who better to influence current members than a former colleague? Trent Lott, a former Republican Senate leader from Mississippi, upon his retirement in 2007 joined with his former Senate colleague John Breaux (D-LA) to form one of the most formidable lobbying teams in Washington. Billy Tauzin, a onetime Louisiana congressman who could write his own ticket after chairing the Energy and Commerce Committee in the House, signed on to head the Pharmaceutical Research and Manufacturers of America, one of the most powerful lobbies in Washington.

One way in which organized interests gain access is by setting up a political action committee (PAC), which is the legal mechanism by which an organization may make campaign contributions. Fund-raising events are a great place to make contacts with members. But campaign contributions rarely (and almost never explicitly) take the form of a quid pro quo arrangement whereby the member agrees to do something legislatively in exchange for a contribution. (Moreover, quid pro quo arrangements are illegal.) Instead, campaign contributions go to members of Congress who already support the interest group's position—the interest group, in effect, is helping an ally stay in office—as well as to those who may be undecided and thus open to persuasion. The *Washington Post* depicted the relationship this way:

> W. J. "Billy" Tauzin, a former Republican House member from Louisiana who runs the Pharmaceutical Research and Manufacturers of America (PhRMA), said campaign contributions from his industry simply reflect participation in American democracy.
>
> "We do what most people do in political systems: We support people with whom we agree and with whom we believe in," Tauzin said, adding, "We also support other people who don't always agree with us but are honest and fair and open-minded."[12]

But the fact is that the vast majority of organized groups do not have a PAC and thus make no campaign contributions at all. Interestingly, these groups do not necessarily feel at a great disadvantage in their efforts to influence Congress. So how do they gain access and influence the board of directors without "paying to play"?

Interest Groups and the Constituent Connection

The key to gaining access and influencing the board of directors is this: Show members of Congress the impact of a particular piece of legislation on the people who "hired" them—the voters back home.

Lobbyists from the National Association of Counties (NACo) report that they do not need a PAC to get access. Federal regulatory decisions on land use frequently vex county officials, especially in the western states. And counties across the country are interested in federal legislation in a wide range of areas, from Medicaid to transportation spending to educational requirements. NACo lobbyists bring county officials and sometimes ordinary citizens to Washington to meet their representatives and senators. The members of Congress, knowing full well that they are meeting leaders in the communities they serve, are almost always attentive to their concerns on pending legislation. Box 2.4 describes this sort of relationship and exactly how a group can be persuasive without the benefit of campaign contributions.

When the Parkinson's Action Network advocates for stem cell research money, it brings afflicted constituents to Capitol Hill to meet their representatives to press the case. If Congress is considering decreasing the number of F-22 Raptors (a fighter aircraft) that it funds for the Air Force, the manufacturer not only makes sure that

BOX 2.4
NACO STOPS ACTION ON KEY ELECTIONS BILL

In 2007 the National Association of Counties (NACo) lobbied Congress to prevent the passage of the "paper trail" elections bill that would have required every county to provide physical backup documentation for every vote cast. The association's press secretary described its strategy this way*:

> [We] used effective media relations in concert with . . . one lobbyist . . . and NACo members [around the country] to help defeat the "paper trail" bill. This bill (H.R. 811) had more than 200 House co-sponsors, an early editorial endorsement from *The New York Times* and pressure from the new Speaker of the House to get [it] to the floor for fast approval. It never got there in large part because of counties' opposition to the legislation which was frequently reported in national and Capitol Hill news media at critical times in the legislative process. We felt the bill—while well-intentioned—was a huge unfunded mandate on counties. It was ill-advised . . . and would have created mass confusion for the 2008 presidential election.
>
> It all started when [a NACo lobbyist] issued an Action Alert to her [association members] which generated hundreds of letters of protest to Congress. I used those letters with the media to show fatal flaws in the bill. I pitched a story to *The Hill* [an influential Washington publication] about how county election officials and NACo were effectively stalling the bill at the committee level. They assigned a reporter and ran a story, which led to other stories in *USA Today* and *The Washington Post*. Stories reported how a member of Congress had a stack of our letters in his hand during a markup in the House Administration Committee and said basically, "What are we doing?" The bill eventually died without even getting to the floor despite four editorials in *The New York Times*.

* James E. Phillips, Media Relations Manager, National Association of Counties, e-mail correspondence with the author, September 11, 2008.

members and their staffs know how many jobs will be lost in their districts, but probably brings in a local worker or two to put a human face on the issue. In fact, the principal manufacturer, Lockheed Martin, makes a point of producing parts for the F-22 in as many states and congressional districts as possible in order to bolster the constituent connection to members of Congress.

The point is that the most common and most effective strategy for interest groups is to *show the district and state effects of policy to the representatives and senators.* Most members see policy first and foremost in terms of the impact on their constituency. Interest groups do not for the most part rely on abstract arguments; they rely on tangible effects. If jobs in the district, educational opportunities, or health care access are at stake, the advocate has to make the local impact clear. That gets the member's attention.

Interest group activity in Washington is more comprehensive and thoroughgoing than most people realize. Not only are groups lobbying members and their staffs directly, providing advice on bill language, testifying at hearings, and contributing to campaigns, but they go to great pains to promote their causes to policymakers indirectly. Most effective groups collaborate with other groups with common interests, just as in the pluralist model. They gin up grassroots support for their positions by encouraging their membership to contact members of Congress by e-mail, phone, and regular mail. Many groups have sophisticated public relations operations that they use to create a better climate for their issues by developing relations with key people in the major media and even going so far as to create major advertising campaigns.[13]

Interest groups can be thought of as "organized public opinion," in the words of Jeffrey Birnbaum of the *Washington Times*, one of journalism's foremost authorities on lobbying.[14] Most Americans—some estimates approach 80 or 90 percent—are represented in Washington by one or more interest groups. Although it is true that not all interest groups are created equal—the well-heeled ones, on balance, are more effective at influencing the board of directors—it is also true that nearly every group can make a legitimate claim that it is acting on behalf of an identifiable group of citizens. Interest groups are not some alien force—interest groups are us. They represent us according to our views on social issues, they represent us in our occupations, they represent our communities and local governments, they represent corporations that provide us with jobs, they represent the universities that educate our children, and the list goes on.

The point is not to deny that there are some bad effects of the undeniable influence of interest groups. Members in recent years have been caught taking bribes from lobbyists for legislative actions, most notably Congressman Duke Cunningham of California (see Box 2.5), and enjoying lavish vacations at corporate expense. But these are the exceptions. The overwhelming majority of lobbyists operate within the rules and can be effective without resorting to questionable activities.

The central point is that, for the most part, interest groups are influential in Washington to the extent that they bring home to the members the impact of what

BOX 2.5
CONGRESSMAN CUNNINGHAM CAUGHT TAKING BRIBES

Representative Duke Cunningham (R-CA), a member of the influential Appropriations Committee, had a precipitous fall from grace in 2005 after a widely publicized lobbyist scandal.

For years Cunningham had arranged to direct federal funds—a process frequently called *earmarking*—for government contractors in the defense and intelligence industries. In and of itself, this is neither illegal nor at all unusual. Most members try to earmark funds to address particular needs, in both the private and public sectors, to enhance services or create jobs in their districts or states. Cunningham, however, had an ulterior motive.

The congressman insisted on a cut for each earmark he put into federal legislation, on a sliding scale depending on the size of contract. In fact, he wrote down specific sums for clients on his congressional letterhead stationery. All told, Cunningham was discovered to have received about $2.4 million in bribes and numerous extravagant gifts, as well as the use of a yacht while in Washington, all courtesy of corporate lobbyists. He pleaded guilty to conspiracy to commit bribery, tax evasion, and other charges. He is currently in federal prison serving out an eight-year, four-month term and was required to forfeit his multimillion-dollar home and $1.8 million in cash and other items.

Sources: Debbi Baker, "Foggo Pleads Guilty to Fraud," *San Diego Union-Tribune*, September 29, 2008, available at: http://www.signonsandiego.com/news/politics/cunningham/20080929-1220-bn29foggo.html; and Gig Conaughton, "Congressman, War Hero, Found Guilty of Bribes," *North County (San Diego) Times*, November 29, 2005, available at: http://nctimes.com/articles/2005/11/29/news/top_stories/112805193248.txt.

they are planning to put into law. Members are indeed beholden to interest groups— *when those groups express effectively the needs and concerns of their constituents.*[15] Otherwise, chances are good that the lobbyists will not gain the access they need to argue their case. It is an essential part of the representative role to listen to constituents— members' popularity and reelection efforts depend on it. And constituents' voices are often most effectively heard when organized according to shared values and concerns by interest groups.

Two Roles, One Field of Vision

Everything about a member of Congress's job involves some combination of the two essential roles—representative of the people back home and legislator crafting public policy for the nation. Although we can analytically distinguish between these two functions, in fact nothing a member does involves only one or the other.

Representatives and senators are constantly campaigning, especially those in the House, whose seats are contested every two years. As a result, their schedules are full of events back in their district or state staged for maximum political benefit. A Democrat might schedule a speech at the local union hall to energize labor support, encouraging active members to go door-to-door in his next campaign. A Republican might do the same thing at an exurban mega-church to motivate her base. Members advertise open town hall meetings or try to attract local media to speeches—all with the aim of attracting positive publicity and ultimately active support and votes in the next election.

But none of these campaign activities occurs in a vacuum. The union gathering will be attended by people who want to ask the member what he is doing about making health care more portable. The most politically attuned church members will wonder whether their representative is using her membership on the Ways and Means Committee to alleviate the marriage penalty in the tax code. Speeches and town halls also have to include question time—a golden opportunity for community activists to get face time and question the member on the Middle East, or housing subsidies, or his or her latest vote on a controversial bankruptcy bill. Even though members are primarily trying to promote their reelection prospects by appearing at public events, they always know that they have to be able to address the legislative side of their work. They cannot neatly detach one role from the other.

"Right-Eye Dominance"

One consequence of serving two very different roles in one job is that at times the two roles may come into conflict. This is one of the occupational hazards of being a member of Congress.

Much of the time—perhaps most of the time—a member's sense of what is good public policy in the national interest is congruent with the views of his or her constituents. After all, members are elected at least in part based on their views on the major issues of the day, and the people tend to send the candidate to Washington who better reflects their positions. In addition, on matters of little concern to their constituents, representatives can exercise their judgment with little or no fear of retribution on election day.

BOX 2.6
DANGER LURKS FOR THE INATTENTIVE MEMBER

The fact that most members are easily reelected—usually by a wide margin—often leads to the following prescription from critics: Since the member has such a safe seat, and hence does not have to worry about reelection, perhaps he or she could focus less on the narrow needs of the district or state and instead render independent judgment on issues and, even more importantly, spend more time addressing the big and controversial issues of the day, such as promoting energy independence, ensuring the solvency of Social Security, or addressing spiraling medical costs.

This advice misses the basic point: Members are safe *because* they address the concerns of their constituents and the interests important to their districts or states. Their careers are dependent on a district- or state-centered view of things. In fact, in each election cycle there are always a few members who lose touch with their constituencies and get punished at the polls. They become poster children for the remaining members, reminding them of first priorities.

In 2004 it was Democratic senator Tom Daschle of South Dakota, whose ascension to the top Senate leadership position in his party and presidential ambitions led him in a direction counter to the views of too many constituents in his conservative state. He became the first Senate leader (he was minority leader at the time) to lose his seat in half a century. In 1994 the same thing happened to Speaker of the House Tom Foley of eastern Washington State, whose prominent national position with the Democratic Party was perceived as too liberal by his rural, conservative-leaning district.

Congressman Earl Hilliard (D-AL), who rarely had any substantial competition for his seat, was suddenly swept out of office in 2002 after it seemed to voters that he was spending a little too much time focusing on foreign affairs, at the expense of his home district.* Similarly, Republican Congressman Curt Weldon's forays into controversial intelligence and national security matters, as well as a potential corruption investigation, seemed to cost him back home in his eastern Pennsylvania district. He lost in 2006 after serving ten consecutive terms. The message from these examples is heard loud and clear in both chambers: Nobody is truly safe—forget the people back home at your peril.

Having said all that, most members feel that they can stray every so often, exercising their own judgment and voting against the apparent views of the majority of their district or state, or even a key faction or interest group in that constituency. But in *every case* they also recognize that they had better have a good explanation for their actions. Perhaps the most crucial part of crafting a position on an issue is explaining why you have taken that view. Voters want to know the reasoning and need to know that the member has thought the issue through. Even if they disagree, voters are more likely to give their representative a pass on a controversial issue if they understand why he or she took a particular position and feel certain that the representative listened to them and was open to all viewpoints when formulating that position.

* Mary Orndorff, "Hilliard, Davis Take New Money to Airwaves," *Birmingham News*, June 18, 2002, p. 2B; and Michael Barone and Richard E. Cohen, *The Almanac of American Politics* (Washington, DC: National Journal, 2008).

Inevitably, however, conflicts emerge. How do members resolve strong differences of opinion on the merits of policy between themselves and key groups in their constituencies? How do members resolve conflicts between their own oft-stated principles or ideological predispositions and legislation that would adversely affect their state or district?

The best way to get at members' thinking is to understand how they see the world.

Members understand, probably instinctively in most cases, that although they have two seemingly distinct roles, these roles are usually impossible to disentangle. As noted, nearly everything in their job involves *both* policy and political considerations.

To develop a useful metaphor, members may have one field of vision, but that field includes the perspective of their right eye, which sees the issues of the day in terms of the impact on constituents (the representative role), and the left eye, which sees issues in terms of the public policy merits (the legislative role). Most of the time there is no conflict in the field of vision. But when there is, the member's dominant eye takes over. Most members are "right-eye-dominant" most of the time, and some emphasize the representative role all of the time. Their careers depend on their ability to see district or state needs and preferences clearly. Box 2.6 describes some high-profile instances of members who lost their focus.

People are often critical of representatives and senators for their "right-eye dominance"—that is, for their focus on their representative role. But many members, maybe most of them, are strongly inclined to view their responsibilities in terms of being a delegate rather than a trustee in the traditional formulation. This difference has been debated in political theory since representative democracy was invented: Should representatives in a republic exercise their own judgment (the trustee model), or is their responsibility to reflect the views of their constituents as best they can discern those views (the delegate model)?[16]

It is not the intention here to resolve the delegate-versus-trustee debate, but rather to explain the reality of representation in the Congress. Although there are exceptions that illustrate the rule, the fact is that members tend to put their constituents first. The first two of the following examples are typical. The next two examples show members who charted their own, potentially perilous, course.

Senator Kennedy the Environmentalist—Senator Edward Kennedy's (D-MA) tenure in the Senate was almost exactly coterminous with the environmental movement in this country, and that was not entirely a coincidence. Kennedy was first elected in

1962 when he won the seat once held by his then-president brother. At about this time, Rachel Carson (whose trailblazing book *Silent Spring* was published in 1962), Ralph Nader, and others were raising public awareness of the damage being done to the environment by various pollutants. As Kennedy became more influential in the Senate, he was an important congressional ally for the movement. In recent years, the major national, nonpartisan arm of the environmental movement, the League of Conservation Voters, rated Kennedy's voting record as high as 100 percent.

But Kennedy adamantly opposed an $800 million renewable energy project proposed for the federal waters off of Nantucket Sound. The project, called Cape Wind, would create the first offshore energy project in the United States, and the largest of its kind in the world. If completed, it would provide a substantial amount of the power needed for Cape Cod and the nearby islands.[17] Cape Wind has been enthusiastically embraced by major left-leaning interest groups, including the Sierra Club, the Union of Concerned Scientists, and U.S. Public Interest Research Group.

In a May 2006 press release, Kennedy called for a "federal policy to be put in place before a project of this magnitude is given approval." He also expressed concern that the project might "[wreak] havoc" on "Massachusetts' fishing and tourism industries, the Coast Guard, navigation and national security."[18] Ultimately the senator opposed comprehensive energy legislation on the Senate floor owing to special waivers he claimed were included for Cape Wind.

Senator Bond Says No to Science—Senator Christopher "Kit" Bond (R-MO) has always been determined to fund water projects that provide jobs for the people of Missouri. In recent years, Bond has advocated spending the rather substantial sum of $1.7 billion to improve the Mississippi waterway connecting farmers in the Midwest with New Orleans and the open sea. Navigating this route requires passing through a series of locks; Bond has pushed for longer locks to reduce congestion (and thus lower shipping rates). Bond's office has estimated that the project would generate 48 million work-hours for carpenters.[19]

The problem, as good government advocates see it, is that numerous studies going back to the early 1990s have shown that the improvements are not even close to worth what they would cost. Furthermore, much less expensive innovations would suffice to reduce congestion.

The Army Corps of Engineers, which commissioned the original study and would be responsible for construction, sponsored other studies that proved more favorable to the idea. Unfortunately these studies were criticized by the National Academy of Sciences for poor methodology. The original conclusion held: The lock expansion would cost far more than it would be worth, and it would make more sense to do much cheaper innovations, or even to do nothing at all. The senator did not budge; jobs, to be paid for by the nation's taxpayers, were at stake.[20]

––––––––––

We do not mean to pick on these two senators, both of whom have distinguished records and a long history of working productively on issues of national importance with members of the opposing party. Kennedy and Bond are in many ways model members of Congress. Rather, we mean to stress what is normal, expected, and even often necessary in most instances. Members must stick up for the people they represent or they will not stay in Washington to make the contributions their experience makes possible in health care, defense, foreign policy, and other matters. There is a common saying in Washington that "you can't save the world if you don't save your seat." The renowned political scientist David Mayhew put it this way in his seminal work, *Congress: The Electoral Connection*: Whatever a member's goals are in terms of solving the pressing problems of society, his immediate goal always must be to win reelection.[21]

Members by the dozen advocate tax reform and simplification, yet aggressively push for add-ons to tax legislation to provide tax breaks for groups or particular industries in their districts. Self-professed free-traders often turn around and support protections for industries that provide employment in their states. Scores of members voted for stringent spending limits in the Balanced Budget Act of 1997 and then turned around in 1998 to vote for a budget-busting transportation bill in order to have roads and bridges built or repaired in their districts or states. Good government and ideological consistency are important, but not necessarily top priorities. One could charge members with hypocrisy—and it would be hard to quarrel with that interpretation—but there are other ways to look at this kind of behavior.

First of all, members do a faithful job of reflecting the views and preferences of their constituents. Most Americans want a simpler tax code, but they also want businesses in their hometowns to thrive in a competitive global environment—a goal that is enhanced by targeted tax breaks. Similarly, people want the cheaper goods and services that free trade brings, but they also want people in their community to keep their jobs; a stiff tariff can achieve the latter goal. And everyone thinks that the government should balance the books, but few seem able to identify major programs that should be cut to make this possible; certainly no members will vote for cuts in transportation funding when their constituents complain about traffic, potholes, and decaying bridges. And everyone knows that raising taxes is almost always a political nonstarter. The fact is that the public has conflicting and contradictory desires that put cross-pressures on members of Congress.

Furthermore, doing what needs to be done to simplify the tax code, make Medicare solvent, or balance the budget is incredibly difficult. The political reality is that achieving these goals requires an extraordinary ability to cooperate and work with people with very different backgrounds and views. There is no place in life where it is easy to work with people whose priorities you do not share and whose outlook is opposed to your own. Congress is no different. There is a tremendously wide range of viewpoints and backgrounds among the membership. So if members cannot save the world in the near term, at least they can serve their people and save their seats.

Having said all of that, there are times when members go against the strongly held views of their constituents. Some members do it on a regular basis. Sometimes it costs them their seat, and sometimes they survive in spite of it.

Congressman Shays Prevails in Spite of His Support for the Iraq War—Not all members take the path of least resistance, bowing to constituent pressures on the major issues of the day. Republican Christopher Shays of Connecticut represented the largely well-heeled, socially liberal suburbs of New York City. The district usually went for the Democratic candidate for president but continued to send Shays to Washington— and had done so since 1987, when he first won office in a special election.

Nevertheless, election day had not been easy for him in the first decade of the new century. In 2004, with President Bush running behind Democratic challenger John Kerry in the district, a worthy challenger came within four percentage points of ousting Shays in Connecticut's Fourth District. The 2006 election looked even tougher: Shays was running against the same challenger, who would be even better-funded this time around.

In addition, Connecticut looked to be even more fertile ground for Democrats than usual. The incumbent Democratic senator, Joe Lieberman, had lost a late summer primary to a political novice because of his support for the president's policies in Iraq. The state's other two Republican House members, Rob Simmons and Nancy Johnson, seemed imperiled as well, if only because of the "R" that would appear next to their names on the ballot. Shays had been a more vocal and far more high-profile supporter of the war than they were. Key observers thought that Shays was in serious trouble and the most likely to be a Connecticut Republican casualty on election day.[22]

As it turned out, Simmons and Johnson were both defeated and Shays survived, confounding the experts. Shays only barely trimmed his sails regarding Bush's policies in Iraq, and he lambasted the popular liberal Senator Edward Kennedy when he came to the state to campaign for Shays's opponent. Doing an about-face on Iraq would have been the easy way out. Shays prevailed—barely—even though he stuck to his guns.

By the 2008 election cycle, the Iraq War was no longer the big issue it had been— some progress seemed to have been made with the surge strategy employed in 2007. Ironically, it was then that the Democrats finally succeeded in defeating Shays, in large measure owing to the wave of support for Democratic presidential candidate Barack Obama at the top of the ticket.

The Firebrand Survives, Time and Again—Iowa senator Tom Harkin, an uncompromising advocate for labor, civil rights, environmentalism, feminism, and similar causes, has been a leader of the liberal wing of the Democratic Party in the Congress since the 1970s. In 1992 Harkin became a national figure when he waged a spirited campaign for the Democratic presidential nomination, which was ultimately won by Bill Clinton. Harkin proved to be far too much of an unreconstructed New Deal liberal for the national Democratic primary electorate that year.

Harkin has been in the Senate since 1984, representing a decidedly middle-of-the-road state—in fact, a state that seesaws between supporting Democratic and Republican presidential candidates. During this period, Iowa has almost always had a Republican-controlled House delegation, and Harkin's Senate colleague from the state is the moderately conservative Republican Charles Grassley.

Harkin has not taken the path of least resistance. And he has had to fight hard to keep his seat. Prominent House members have challenged him every time, always attracting national support and plenty of funds. Harkin has managed—though just barely one time—to beat every one of them. By comparison, Grassley, whose views seem to fit more neatly with the Iowa electorate, has not received a serious challenge for his seat in decades.

———————

Harkin (like Shays when he served) does not ignore his constituents. He knows that, to have a chance at reelection, members have to address the needs of their constituents through targeted federal spending, good ombudsman work, and overall responsiveness. But neither does he trim his sails much on major national issues in order to ensure an easy path to reelection. He wins in spite of his positioning on some issues, not because of it.

This is a risky strategy, as Senator Rick Santorum (R-PA) learned the hard way in 2006. Much like Harkin, Santorum was often out of step with his state on major national issues. Far more conservative than the broader Pennsylvania electorate, which has trended Democratic in recent presidential elections, Santorum managed to win squeakers through hard work and spirited campaigning to secure two terms in the Senate, but in a year that was particularly unpropitious for Republicans, he could not withstand the tide, losing by an overwhelming eighteen-point margin.

The lesson is clear: A "right-eye-dominant" perspective is the easy way to go for members of Congress, and most take that approach. The other strategy takes a lot more skill and carries greater risks. Members have to be able to explain to the satisfaction of their constituency any controversial positions they take. Even then, incongruent views may be costly.

Conclusion: The Primacy of the Representative Role

To understand Congress as it carries out its duties as the board of directors of the federal government, it cannot be stressed too much how important it is to appreciate the motivations of the members. Their elected position makes them accountable to the people in their districts or states. Nearly every decision point that members face in the legislative process starts with a calculation of whether and how a given policy affects the people back home.

Probably the simplest useful way to think of the Congress is to view it as an institution comprising 535 people scrapping furiously for the interests of the people they represent. Much of this battling is done in full view of the public on C-SPAN, over the Internet, and through various news outlets during floor speeches, press conferences, and committee hearings. Furthermore, members fight hard to enhance their party's chances of retaining or regaining the majority in their chamber, because majority status enhances members' ability to pursue the interests of their constituents and any policy or ideological goals of their own. Majority status has its privileges: Only the majority members may chair committees and subcommittees, and the majority leadership controls the schedule on the floor of the two chambers.

Often members' most effective tactic to boost their party's electoral prospects is to tear down the other party, making theirs look better by comparison. Voters are cynical enough to find the argument that the other party is dastardly more persuasive than the contention that the member's own party will solve the major problems of the day. Negative campaigning is, in short, more convincing.

This reality does not make a pretty picture. No wonder the public dislikes the Congress: 535 aggressive, district- and state-focused people fighting over public policy, with an overlay of partisan bickering, is not a good starting point for developing good public relations. In fact, Congress is *overly* engaged in public relations—all the members and committees have press people who promote individual members, but almost never do they promote the institution. In reality, self-promotion in the Congress is often linked to the denigration of the institution, as in "Congressman Doe is fighting for the people against the evil forces in the Capitol that are in cahoots with corrupt lobbyists and special interests."

Compare that to the White House, which strictly controls the flow of information and has a sophisticated press relations shop dedicated to making the president, the presidency, and indeed the government look good. And don't forget the Supreme Court, which allows very little press access and shrouds its decision-making process in almost total secrecy, which gives it a certain mystique that cannot be matched by the other branches.

The irony of the public's negative view of Congress is that *we, the people, want Congress to do many of the very things that make it look bad.* We want our members to fight for our interests. During reelection campaigns, members stress what they bring home to the district or the state because they know that these benefits and services are often exactly what makes them look good to us. Democratic senator Robert Byrd is a legend in West Virginia because he tends to the state's interests so effectively; Republican representative Bud Shuster was similarly revered in central Pennsylvania for delivering highway improvements in rural areas; Maryland congressman Steny Hoyer is credited for his tireless work on behalf of the federal workers and military families who populate his district; and the list goes on. Some voters may have high-minded expectations that their representatives should address major issues such as war, global warming, and the solvency of Medicare. But members know that they risk getting punished at the polls if they forget the particular needs of their district or state.

Strip away all the accoutrements of Washington and the intricacies of the legislative process, and we can see that this is the fundamental nature of Congress: a rough-and-tumble partisan arena, composed of 535 representatives drawn from a tremendously diverse country looking out for the people back home. *The representative role affects nearly everything members of Congress do in the legislative arena as they authorize, fund, and supervise the work of the federal government.*

THE NATURE OF CONGRESS, PART II: HOUSE AND SENATE

The Constitution set up a bicameral legislature to carry out the critical function of directing the work of the government. The decision to go with this arrangement was a tremendously important one; it affected virtually every aspect of the institution. In this section, we look in detail at the two chambers. The first part gives an overview of the constitutional debate and the key differences between the House and Senate. We then look at how the two chambers organize themselves for business by giving agenda-setting power to party leadership and assigning legislative and oversight responsibilities to committees.

The Great Compromise

The composition of the board of directors was a matter of great contention at the Constitutional Convention. Virginians put forward a plan that, among other things, proposed a single-chamber national legislature with representation based on population. Less populated states opposed the plan. Led by the New Jersey delegation, they proposed establishing a legislature that would be similar to the one set up in the Articles of Confederation, with each state receiving equal representation regardless of population.

Ultimately, Connecticut's Roger Sherman and Oliver Ellsworth put forward what came to be called "the Great Compromise." It proposed a bicameral arrangement with one chamber's representation based on population and the other having equal representation for every state. Although there were many details that remained to be resolved, it was this plan that was adopted.

Such a plan was defended by some at the time on the grounds that it would be much more difficult for unwise legislation to pass two such differently constituted chambers. With their very different perspectives, the members of the two chambers would have difficulty coming together on particular legislative solutions. The idea was that bad bills would be filtered out in the process. An inefficient legislative body was actually thought to be a virtue, because it would provide more time for careful consideration and identification of the public interest. It was feared that streamlined processes in a unicameral legislature would be more likely to result in laws that harmed the people.

Distinct Qualifications and Responsibilities

The two chambers were set up to give the Congress a wider range of representative characteristics than would have been possible had there been only one chamber. Not only were the members of the chambers to be answerable to different constituencies, but they were given different time perspectives as well. The six-year term was thought to give senators the ability to take the long view. House members, it was thought, would be more likely to consider the immediate impact of legislation given the fact that they had to vie for reelection every two years. (In fact, a lot of people at the Constitutional Convention thought a two-year term was too long; fearing that members would not be tied closely enough to their constituents, they advocated annual reelection for representatives.)

In addition, as noted earlier, senators were not originally to be selected directly by the people. State legislatures selected them, making them more removed from the public than House members. While the Constitutional Convention recognized that it was necessary to make Congress directly accountable to the people, the prevailing view was that it would be better not to have the public, which might be prone to rash and ill-considered collective judgments, directly elect the entire Congress. A directly elected House was deemed sufficient to achieve a truly accountable lawmaking body.

The Senate was also given a higher age requirement: Senators must be thirty years old, while House members may be as young as twenty-five. Presumably with age comes wisdom. Again, the Senate was expected to be less impulsive and more statesmanlike in its decision-making in order to check a more reactive House.

To reinforce this point, the Senate was made "more equal"—it was given some weighty responsibilities that the House does not have. For a treaty to become the law of the land, the Constitution stipulates that it must gain the Senate's approval. (Two-thirds of the Senate is required to ratify a treaty.) The House was given no such role, and as a result the Senate became a much bigger player in the realm of foreign affairs. The Senate's approval is also needed for the president's high-ranking executive branch appointments—now numbering nearly 1,000. Again, the House has no role in this process. And nominations to the federal judiciary, all the way up to the Supreme Court, also require Senate approval, with the House having no say.

On the flip side, the House was given the exclusive responsibility to originate revenue bills. The seeming advantage, however, is really not all that significant: The Senate must also pass tax bills for them to become law, and senators are not constrained by the Constitution from amending House-passed revenue measures in any way they see fit.

There is another important way in which the Constitution insulates the Senate as a body from immediate political pressures. The electoral cycle puts every seat of the House up for grabs every two years. The chamber as a whole is expected to be attuned and responsive to the political climate in the nation. In the Senate, on the other hand, only one-third of the seats are contested every two years. At any given time, then, most senators do not have to be immediately concerned about the upcoming election. The thinking at the Constitutional Convention was that the Senate would take the long view on legislation, balancing the House's tendency to address the people's immediate concerns.

The Key Difference Between the House and Senate? It's a Matter of Perspective
Many House members represent constituencies that are homogeneous in terms of some combination of partisanship, ideology, economic status, race, or other factors. Most senators, representing entire states, have much more diverse constituencies in all or most of these respects. (Only seven states are so sparsely populated that they have only one House member. California is the most populated state; it has fifty-three representatives in the House.) When we remember that members of Congress are "right-eye-dominant"—they look at the political world first in terms of their constituents' interests—we see that the relative homogeneity or heterogeneity of the constituencies leads to very different tendencies and approaches in the two chambers.

Many House members come to Washington with a strongly partisan or ideological take on their legislative work and the issues of the day because their districts are either overwhelmingly Democratic or Republican. And there are many who focus their work primarily on a particular sector of the economy if most of their constituents' livelihoods are dependent on it. On the other hand, most senators have to balance the needs of a wider range of economic interests with the views of more people across the political spectrum and the perspectives of people of more races and backgrounds.

For example, senators from North Carolina have to consider the views of different kinds of farmers (the state is one of the leaders in both tobacco and pork production); balance the needs of the banking industry in Charlotte with the high-tech and pharmaceutical industries in the Research Triangle as well as the furniture industry in the Greensboro area; advocate for a wide range of tourism and recreational interests from the mountains to the coast; and listen to the constituent needs of a diverse population that includes a growing number of Hispanics, American Indians, and a large African American population, as well as the majority who are white. The thirteen House members from the state do not individually have to take into account anywhere near as many interests and viewpoints.

Essentially the chambers have different styles and political contexts because of their different constituencies. As a rule, the House is a more partisan body that tends to focus on parochial, narrow concerns. The Senate, on the other hand, tends to be less bitterly partisan and is somewhat more apt to approach issues with a big-picture perspective. One can overstate these differences—for example, it is not uncommon for the Senate to have partisan struggles, and senators certainly look out for the particular economic interests of their states. But the two chambers do have distinct tendencies.

The Prestige Gap

In large part because of the Senate's enhanced legislative responsibilities, it is generally considered more prestigious than the House. There are additional reasons for the Senate's exalted position.

Senators tend to be more widely known, if only because of the fact that, in today's Congress, a senator is one of 100 and a House member is one of 435. Senators also are more likely to receive far more coverage in the media, both nationally and back at home. They often comment on major international issues (remember, they are the ones who handle treaties) and are frequently mentioned as presidential or vice presidential prospects. House members rarely make credible runs for the White House. In the last fifty years, seventeen senators have appeared on major party presidential tickets, while only two sitting House members have been selected.

Back home, senators benefit in most states from being one of only two in their chamber, while House members sometimes get lost in the shuffle among many other representatives. In addition, senators represent the whole state, while all but seven House members do not. Senate rules also give senators, as individuals, much greater power and leverage in the legislative process than House members have.

All of these factors contribute to the tendency of the Senate to attract interest from prospective candidates who have already accomplished a great deal politically or in the private sector. Governors or former governors often run for the Senate, but much less often the House. Famous athletes, such as Bill Bradley, a starter on two NBA championship teams, have made a run for the Senate as their first foray into electoral politics. John Glenn, the famous astronaut, also aimed first for the Senate. His initial effort was not successful, but he eventually served with distinction as a senator from Ohio. Wealthy entrepreneurs and military heroes also often go for the more prestigious chamber rather than face toiling in a junior position in the House. As one might expect, House members usually regard a run for the Senate as a potential upgrade.

The House of Representatives

The two chambers have parallel organizational units: party leadership and the committees. The party leadership in each chamber is responsible for organizing the chamber's legislative business, although the way that happens is quite different in the two bodies. The committees are specialized units that handle the essential legislative business for the board of directors. This section describes these organizational units and looks at how they are meant to help the institution reconcile the tension between its legislative and representative responsibilities.

Majority Party Leadership

The presiding officer of the House of Representatives is the *speaker*, or the *speaker of the House*. The speaker is the only official position in the House listed in the Constitution, although the Constitution does say that the House membership has the power to choose other officers. The Constitution puts the speaker second in line for the presidency after the vice president.

The speaker is chosen from among the majority party in the House. This is not a constitutional requirement; in fact, the Constitution does not contemplate the existence of organized political parties. In practice, however, the two parties each choose a candidate for speaker, with a roll call vote of the whole House membership determining the winner. This roll call is a formality, since the majority party candidate is always the winner.

The speaker, in a real sense, runs the House of Representatives. We will see in subsequent chapters how he or she does this, but the essential point is that the speaker determines the agenda of the chamber. In addition, the speaker appoints people to administrative positions to take care of the day-to-day operations of the House.

The speaker needs help in managing the legislative business of the House, so the majority party chooses other top leadership positions. The top leadership for the majority Democrats at the beginning of the 111th Congress included:

Speaker of the House—Nancy Pelosi (D-CA)
Majority leader—Steny Hoyer (D-MD)
Majority whip—James Clyburn (D-SC)
Caucus chair—John Larson (D-CT)

All of these top leadership positions, as well as some lower-level positions, were determined by a secret ballot vote in a caucus of House Democrats. Members running for these positions must secure a majority of 50 percent plus one to win the slot. If no candidate for a position receives the necessary majority, the last-place finisher is eliminated and a new balloting is held. Races for top leadership posts attract a lot of attention and can be rather suspenseful, as depicted in Box 2.7.

BOX 2.7
COUNTING VOTES IN LEADERSHIP RACES

Races for leadership in the parties can be very controversial, and close contests are not unusual.

In 2003 the Democrats held a vote for a vacancy in the caucus chair position, and Robert Menendez of New Jersey and Rosa DeLauro of Connecticut vied for the coveted slot. Both claimed that they had sufficient support to win, but when the votes were counted, it was Menendez who was declared the winner, 104–103.* One of the votes for Menendez, however, was cast by Mike Feeley of Colorado, *who never served in the House of Representatives.*

In November 2002, Feeley had run for Colorado's Seventh District seat against Republican Bob Beauprez. The vote count was extremely close—Beauprez was ahead by only about one hundred votes, and there were many more contested ballots than the margin of seeming victory for the Republican. Recounts and court challenges dragged on into the new year. Democrats were confident enough that Feeley would prevail that they permitted him to participate in the caucus vote. Ultimately, Beauprez would get the nod and represent the Seventh District, but the damage to DeLauro's cause was done by that time.

Current-speaker Nancy Pelosi first won a major leadership position in 2001 when she was elected over Steny Hoyer to be minority whip for the Democrats. The campaign for votes was intense. Before the caucus was held, Pelosi claimed 120 commitments—12 more than the 108 needed for victory that year. Hoyer claimed 110 commitments. Someone had to be wrong. In the end, Pelosi won, 118–95, proving that she could count votes better than Hoyer.†

Since it was a secret ballot vote, no one really knows for sure who indicated support for *both* candidates, but clearly some people did. Hoyer may have misinterpreted ambiguous comments as indications of support. Perhaps some members made it clear to both candidates that they were open to supporting them but ultimately got what they wanted—a choice committee assignment perhaps—from Pelosi. Or maybe Hoyer exaggerated his support, intentionally or unintentionally. It is unlikely that we will ever know for sure.

* Mildred Amer, "CRS Report to Congress: Majority Party Leadership Election Contests in the House of Representatives, 94th to 109th Congresses," Congressional Research Service, May 4, 2006.

† Mark Sandalow, "Pelosi Breaks House Glass Ceiling," *San Francisco Chronicle*, October 11, 2001, available at: http://www.sfgate.com/cgi-bin/article.cgi?file=/chronicle/archive/2001/10/11/MN47587.DTL.

The top majority party leaders have the following duties:

Speaker of the House—Oversees the operations of the whole House and signs off on the agenda for floor consideration. The speaker also selects his or her party's members and the chairs for select committees, such as the Select Committee on Intelligence. In addition, the speaker names the chair and all of his or her party's members on the Rules Committee.

Majority leader—Assigned by the speaker to develop the majority party's agenda for the floor of the House. The majority leader communicates that agenda to the whole House on the floor. Normally the majority leader is charged with resolving differences among committee chairs on pending legislation.

Majority whip—Assigned by the speaker to canvass the opinions of the membership of the majority party on bills scheduled to come to the floor. As the official vote-counter, the majority whip apprises the majority leader and the speaker when the party is likely to have the votes to move forward on its agenda.

Caucus chair—Responsible for running the meetings of the majority party caucus. In addition, the caucus chair manages the public relations strategy for the majority party, keeping members informed about how the leadership would like for them to describe the issues of the day when speaking to the media and the public.

All the top leaders hire aides, called *leadership staff*, to help them with their duties. In addition, the leaders select deputies among the rank-and-file members in the party; in particular, the whip assigns trusted colleagues to keep tabs on the thinking of other party members in their states or regions.

The leadership in the House also runs *party committees*, comprising both senior and more junior members of the party, to handle various important matters of party business. Democrats in the 111th Congress have the following party committees:

Democratic Policy Committee—Helps the party leadership by doing research and polling on major policy issues. This committee may also propose potential legislative solutions.

Democratic Steering Committee—Charged with assigning Democrats to committees and recommending committee chairs, this committee comprises a regionally representative sample of party members, with leadership getting a weighted vote.

Democratic Congressional Campaign Committee—Recruits candidates for potentially winnable races, coordinates campaign activities, and raises money.

Minority Party Leadership

The minority party has decidedly less influence in the House of Representatives. It serves essentially as the "loyal opposition," typically opposing the majority's agenda but without the ability to pursue an agenda of its own.

The minority party, like the majority, elects members to leadership positions by secret ballot. The Republican minority in the 111th Congress calls its meeting of all members a *conference* instead of a *caucus*. The top Republicans elected for the 111th Congress were:

> *Minority leader*—John Boehner (R-OH)
> *Minority whip*—Eric Cantor (R-VA)
> *Conference chair*—Mike Pence (R-IN)

The duties of the minority party leadership are as follows:

Minority leader—Runs the minority party's operations in the House of Representatives and assigns members of his or her party to select committees and to the Rules Committee; also names the ranking members of these committees. The minority leader usually takes on the responsibility of making the case to the American people for his or her party and against the majority agenda on the House floor and in other places.

Minority whip—Assigned by the minority leader to canvass the opinions of minority party members on pending legislation that is under consideration by the majority. As the chief vote-counter for his or her party, the whip tries to keep the party in line in opposition to key majority party agenda items.

Conference chair—Given the task by the minority of running the meetings of all Republicans. In addition, the conference chair is in charge of managing the party's public relations strategy with an eye toward undermining the majority party's legislative agenda and promoting minority party alternatives.

As with the majority, the minority leadership has staff to help them with their duties, and they similarly deputize rank-and-file members for assistance.

Republican Party committees in the 111th Congress mirror their Democratic counterparts. They, too, have a Policy Committee and a Steering Committee, with similar responsibilities. The Republicans' House campaign committee is called the National Republican Congressional Committee, or the NRCC.

Committees in the House

The House of Representatives is not a continuous body. This means that the House, in effect, goes out of business at the end of a two-year Congress and must be "reconstituted" at the beginning of a new Congress. The chamber adjourns sometime late in the even-numbered election year (often in December after the election) and before the entire elected or reelected membership is sworn in for the new Congress on January 3. After the swearing-in, the House passes a resolution that organizes the chamber and establishes its rules for the upcoming two-year Congress. This document is prepared by the majority party leadership and ordinarily passes over whatever objections the minority may have.

One of the most important things this resolution does is establish the legislative committees, these committees' policy jurisdictions, and the number of members and the ratio of majority to minority members on each. For the most part, the committees, their jurisdictions, and even the ratio of members remain nearly the same from one Congress to the next. But when a new party takes power in the House, the changes are dramatic.

The House currently has twenty-two committees, as listed here; most of them are authorizing committees charged with considering legislation that authorizes and sets policy for the programs and agencies of the federal government. Some of the most prominent include the Energy and Commerce Committee, the Ways and Means Committee, and the Armed Services Committee. The House has one committee whose sole responsibility is to write bills to fund the functions of the government—the Appropriations Committee. All the authorizing committees as well as the Appropriations Committee conduct oversight over the executive branch agencies and programs in their jurisdiction. The Committee on Oversight and Government Reform is notable in that it has oversight jurisdiction over the entire government. The Rules Committee does not explicitly have any of the board-of-directors functions, but it is powerful nonetheless because it writes the rules that govern the consideration of legislation on the House floor.

Committees in the House of Representatives
(authorizing committees appear in italics)

- *Agriculture*
- Appropriations (principal duty is funding)
- *Armed Services*

- *Budget*
- *Education and Labor*
- *Energy and Commerce*
- *Financial Services*
- *Foreign Affairs*
- *Homeland Security*
- House Administration (handles House administrative tasks)
- *Intelligence*
- *Judiciary*
- *Natural Resources*
- Oversight and Government Reform (principal duty is oversight)
- Rules (draws up rules for the consideration of legislation on the House floor)
- *Science and Technology*
- Select Committee on Energy Independence and Global Warming (has no legislative authority)
- *Small Business*
- Standards of Official Conduct (handles ethics issues)
- *Transportation and Infrastructure*
- *Veterans' Affairs*
- *Ways and Means*

When the Democrats took over the Congress in 2007 after having been in the minority for twelve years, they renamed a couple of committees without substantially changing those panels' jurisdictions. The Government Reform and Oversight Committee was renamed Oversight and Government Reform to highlight the party's intention to put the Republican Bush administration under scrutiny. The Education and the Workforce Committee was renamed Education and Labor, which served to emphasize the importance of organized labor, a key Democratic constituency. Some minor jurisdictional adjustments were made to various committees. In addition, the Democrats created the Select Committee on Energy Independence and Global Warming to focus attention on the key emerging environmental issues of interest to many Democratic members.

Most committees have several subcommittees that reflect further specialization of the committees' work. The House Armed Services Committee, for example, authorizes all activities of the Defense Department and the Army, Navy, Air Force, and Marines. This vast jurisdiction is divided up among seven subcommittees.

House Armed Services Committee Subcommittees

- Air and Land Forces
- Military Personnel
- Oversight and Investigations (of the Defense Department)
- Readiness
- Seapower and Expeditionary Forces
- Strategic Forces
- Terrorism, Unconventional Threats, and Capabilities

The Senate Armed Services Committee, with essentially the same jurisdiction, works in a similar way with the following six specialized subcommittees. The major difference is that the Senate has no subcommittee dedicated explicitly to oversight and investigations.

Senate Armed Services Committee Subcommittees

- Airland
- Emerging Threats and Capabilities
- Personnel
- Readiness and Management Support
- SeaPower
- Strategic Forces

The House Ways and Means Committee, which handles taxes, major entitlement programs, and trade, is another tremendously important committee. The Senate Finance Committee has a similar jurisdiction. The two also divide up their work similarly, although Senate Finance seems a little more imaginative in the naming of its subcommittees. The Senate Finance Committee also has jurisdiction over energy policy that the House committee does not have.

House Ways and Means Committee Subcommittees

- Health
- Income Security and Family Support
- Oversight
- Select Revenue Measures
- Social Security
- Trade

Senate Finance Committee Subcommittees

- Energy, Natural Resources, and Infrastructure
- Health Care
- International Trade, Customs, and Global Competitiveness
- Social Security, Pensions, and Family Policy
- Taxation, IRS Oversight, and Long-Term Growth

As noted earlier, a new majority party adjusts the ratio of party members on each committee and determines the number of members serving on each. In 2007 the Democrats put a majority of their party's members on each committee, a change from the Republican majorities of the previous twelve years.

The understanding is that the ratios on the committees should mirror the ratio of the overall chamber. The 2008 elections gave the Democrats a 257–178 edge in the House—a 59-to-41 ratio. In January 2009, Democrats established ratios on most committees closely approximating that overall ratio, although they did give themselves an added advantage on a few key committees, including Ways and Means (26–15, or 63 percent of the slots) and Appropriations (36–23, or 61 percent). As usual, the minority complained but really had no recourse, since the majority party gets its way on organizational matters and most other things in the House. The majority does feel constrained in giving itself lopsided committee majorities by the fact that they will someday, maybe sooner rather than later, be in the minority and would like to be treated fairly in that eventuality. The largest committee in the House is Transportation and Infrastructure, with seventy-four members. New members clamor to get on it in order to deliver highway funding and other infrastructural assistance to their districts.

The one committee that always has an overwhelming majority party advantage is the Rules Committee, which for almost four decades has had a 9–4 edge for the majority party regardless of the chamber ratio. The majority party, Republican or Democrat, has found it essential to have a clear working majority on this committee because it has the all-important duty of structuring debate and the amendment process on legislation on the House floor. The committee's membership is hand-picked by leadership.

Committee Assignments—Getting good committee assignments is crucial for members of the House. Committees are where the serious legislative work of establishing and funding government programs, as well as writing tax law, is accomplished. To be a player in the Congress, members must be on one or more committees that give them influence over government policy. The party's Steering Committees make the

BOX 2.8
REPRESENTATIVE TRAFICANT IS DENIED
COMMITTEE ASSIGNMENTS

Members of Congress have to come to their party's steering committee to receive committee assignments. Even nominally independent members of Congress may receive assignments, even though independents are not guaranteed committee slots by House or Senate rules. They can show their allegiance, albeit unofficial, to a party by voting for that party's candidate for speaker of the House and supporting that party's position on the organizing resolution in the House or Senate. Vermont's Bernie Sanders, an independent, has done just that in support of the Democratic Party. As a result, he received committee assignments from House Democrats while serving in that chamber and also, since his election to the Senate in 2006, from Senate Democrats.

Democratic Representative James Traficant of Ohio found himself in a highly unusual predicament in January 2001 after voting for Republican Dennis Hastert in the roll call vote for speaker. (Traficant had been siding with Republicans more and more often on issues for several years, but had always run for reelection in northeast Ohio as a Democrat.) Democrats proceeded to strip him of his committee assignments after the Hastert vote. He turned to the Republicans, who indicated no interest in giving him any assignments either.

The reason? Traficant was under federal investigation at the time for misuse of the funds he had been allotted to run his congressional office, and Republicans did not want to be associated with him. He was the first member of Congress in more than one hundred years not to serve on at least one committee. (In 2008 two Republicans, John Doolittle of California and Rick Renzi of Arizona, were stripped of committee assignments by their leadership after they came under federal investigation for potential wrongdoing. Neither ran for reelection.) The next year Traficant was convicted on ten felony counts, including bribery, racketeering, and tax evasion, and sent to prison. His House colleagues, Democrat and Republican alike, voted to expel him from the chamber.

Source: Alison Mitchell, "House Votes, with Lone Dissent from Condit, to Expel Traficant from Ranks," *New York Times*, July 25, 2002, available at: http://query.nytimes.com/gst/fullpage.html?res=9F01E5D91038F936A15754C0A9649C8B63.

assignments. It is only in extremely rare cases, as can be seen in Box 2.8, that members are denied committee slots.

Members of the House may get multiple committee assignments. Some have as many as four. But members who serve on Energy and Commerce, Appropriations, Rules, Ways and Means, or Financial Services are, by both parties' rules, limited to one assignment. These committees are referred to as *exclusive* committees. However, exceptions are made and many waivers are granted by the Steering Committees, especially on the Democratic side.[23] This enables members not only to serve on an exclusive committee but also to serve on a committee that addresses the particular needs of their constituents. Democrat Earl Pomeroy of North Dakota enjoys membership on both the Ways and Means and Agriculture Committees, a perk that his leadership hopes will solidify his electoral position in a strongly Republican state.

Most members stick with the committee assignments they have when a new Congress convenes, although some may lobby for exclusive committee slots that open up owing to retirement or electoral defeat. New members always lobby for assignments that enable them to serve their constituents' interests, but they also look for assignments that are intellectually interesting to them or where their professional expertise may be particularly useful. Exclusive committee assignments give representatives a considerable amount of leverage with their colleagues, but freshman members rarely land one of them.

In very rare cases, members may be stripped of committee assignments by leadership because of acts of egregious disloyalty to the party. The Traficant example described in Box 2.8 is noteworthy for being exceptional—he was under indictment and went to jail. Speaker Newt Gingrich provoked intense internal dissent among House Republicans in the 1990s when he moved to strip a junior congressman of a coveted slot on the Appropriations Committee after that member had been disloyal. The speaker was forced to back down. His successor, Dennis Hastert, had better luck in the 2000s, twice going so far as to strip members of committee chairmanships.

Committee Chairs—The position of committee chair in the House is a very important one. Committee chairs set the agenda of their committees and are in charge of legislation in their areas of jurisdiction. Every chair is a member of the majority party. Chairs get to hire the committee's majority party expert, or *professional staff*—anywhere from twenty-five to seventy-five people, depending on the committee's importance and jurisdiction—and direct their work. The *ranking member*, or top person from the minority party (who would be chair if his or her party were in control), gets the resources to hire about half as many professional staff. The majority needs the additional staff because it is responsible for setting up hearings, establishing an agenda, and moving legislation through the committee and to the House floor.

In decades past, the selection of a committee chair was automatic: The senior member in terms of service on the committee from the majority party would get the gavel. But in the 1970s, Democrats reformed the process by putting in place a mechanism by which the larger membership of the party—the party caucus—could make the determination in a secret ballot vote.[24] Although Democrats usually kept to the seniority principle, there was competition for a chair position several times when an aggressive junior member of a committee would be willing to take on an elder. A few times those challenges were successful. The current chair of the Appropriations Committee, David Obey of Wisconsin, was first installed in that position after challenging the more senior Neal Smith of Iowa in 1994. Deemed more able by his colleagues, Obey bested Smith in the caucus vote.

After taking over the House in 1995, Republicans took far less heed of seniority in making chair selections. Speaker Newt Gingrich employed very different criteria and essentially handpicked the chairs. To him, what mattered were loyalty, an ability to raise large sums of money for the Republican Party, and a sophisticated understanding (as well as an ability to convey that understanding in public) of the major issues confronting the committee.

Gingrich's successor, Dennis Hastert from Illinois, who took over the speakership in 1999, installed a different process, although he seemed to use essentially the same criteria for selection as Gingrich did. Prospective committee chairs presented their case before the Republican Steering Committee, which voted to recommend its favorite to the Republican conference. The conference ratified the Steering Committee's recommendation every time. (In one instance, Hastert's weighted vote carried the day in the Steering Committee, giving Bill Thomas of California the helm at Ways and Means.)

This method of selecting committee chairs gave the leadership considerable control over the agenda of the chamber. Gingrich put able people in control of writing legislation—able people whom he selected for their loyalty and fund-raising prowess. In addition, the party imposed six-year term limits on committee chairs. As it turned out, after members had served their term, some wanted to chair another committee. It helped their cause to have demonstrated their loyalty and competence during the previous six years.

When the Democrats took over in 2007, they initially kept the six-year term limit on committee chairs, but in 2009, at the beginning of the 111th Congress, the term limit was removed. All the Democratic committee chairs for the 110th Congress were the senior members on those committees. Speaker Pelosi made no effort to supplant anyone with a loyalist. In the 111th Congress, however, the most senior Democrat (in fact, the longest-serving member in congressional history), John Dingell of Michigan, was challenged for his slot on the Energy and Commerce Committee by Henry Waxman of California. Waxman defeated Dingell in a vote of the caucus, becoming the only chair not to be senior in time of service on his committee.

Subcommittee chairs for the 111th Congress were determined on the basis of seniority, subject to the approval of the party caucus. All subcommittee chairs, like committee chairs, are members of the majority party. No member may chair more than one. There are 104 subcommittees in the House in the 111th Congress. Subcommittee chairs on Energy and Commerce, Ways and Means, Appropriations, and Financial Services also must be approved by the Steering Committee. When the Republicans were in charge, Gingrich and Hastert paid special attention to the subcommittee chairs on Appropriations, who were typically more rigorously vetted than the chairs of other committees.

Members' Offices

As noted earlier, members of the House may hire staff to assist them with constituent services and legislative work in Washington and in their district offices. Members all represent approximately the same number of constituents—about 700,000—and they get the same budget for setting up offices and hiring assistants. The budget is about $1.4 million in total. There is some small variation to account for differences in travel expenses back to the district. To work in both their Washington and district offices, House members may hire as many as twenty-two staff members, but only eighteen may be full-time. Most members have between one and five district offices, depending on the geographical size of the district.

The Senate

Majority Party Leadership

The presiding officer of the Senate, as stipulated in the Constitution, is the vice president of the United States.[25] Rarely, however, does the vice president actually preside—in modern times he has usually taken on that duty only when it looks as though a vote in the Senate may end up tied and the president has an interest in the outcome. In that eventuality, the vice president may cast a vote. Both vice presidents Dick Cheney and Al Gore appeared in the Senate to break ties on crucial budget and tax bills. Otherwise, they stayed away from official duties.

The Constitution requires that the Senate select a *president pro tempore*, although that has become a largely ceremonial position held by the senior member of the majority party, who has no more interest than the vice president in the tedious work of presiding over endless debates and votes.

The person who really runs the Senate is the majority leader. By custom, the majority leader of the Senate has the right to be recognized first on the floor, which gives him the power to set the agenda in the chamber. The majority party has two top leadership positions, and in the 111th Congress they are held by:

Majority leader—Harry Reid (D-NV)
Assistant majority leader—Richard Durbin (D-IL)

As in the House, these positions are determined by secret ballot in a caucus of Democratic senators.

The majority party leaders have the following duties:

Majority leader—Determines the agenda on the floor of the Senate, usually in close consultation with the minority leader. The majority leader selects his party's members for select committees, including the Select Committee on Intelligence.

Assistant majority leader—Assists the majority leader in developing the agenda of the Senate. The assistant leader helps to negotiate agreements among committee chairs on complex legislation and is in charge of canvassing the party's membership on upcoming votes.

As in the House, the majority party leaders hire staff to help them with their duties. Also as in the House, the majority party of the Senate has *party committees* to handle important party business. Senate Democrats have the following committees in the 111th Congress:

Democratic Policy Committee—Conducts research and polling on the major issues of the day. Also assists the majority leader in scheduling the floor agenda.

Democratic Steering and Outreach Committee—Assigns new Democratic senators to committees and makes any assignment adjustments in a new Congress.

Democratic Senatorial Campaign Committee—Helps recruit candidates for upcoming Senate races, coordinate campaign activities, and raise money.

Democratic Technology and Communications Committee—Assists the leadership in internal communications among members of the party and coordinates external messaging.

Minority Party Leadership

Every member of the Senate, including those in the minority party, has a great deal of power owing to standing rules, precedents, and customs. This fact enables the minority party to be a player in the establishment of the legislative agenda. (In the House, the minority is in a much weaker position.)

The minority party leadership is elected in a caucus of party members, just as the majority party leadership is. The top Senate Republicans in the 111th Congress are:

> *Minority leader*—Mitch McConnell (R-KY)
> *Assistant minority leader*—Jon Kyl (R-AZ)

With the assistance of the staff they are also allowed to employ, the minority leadership carries out the following duties:

Minority leader—Regularly negotiates with the majority leader over proposed legislative agenda items, representing the interests of his or her caucus. The minority leader's other responsibilities include naming members of his or her party to select committees, including the Select Committee on Intelligence.

Assistant minority leader—Assists the minority leader in dealings with the majority party in matters related to the agenda. The assistant leader's other responsibilities include canvassing his or her party's members on pending legislation.

Republicans have a party committee structure similar to the Democrats' structure. The Republicans handle committee assignments through the Committee on Committees, but they do not have a Technology and Communications Committee, as the Democrats do.

Committees in the Senate

Technically the Senate is a continuous body, unlike the House, since two-thirds of its membership remains in place every election cycle. As such, the Senate does not have to be reconstituted every two years, as the House does. If there is a switch in party control, the new majority brings forward a resolution amending the existing rules of the Senate. But even if the party control remains the same in the Senate after the election, senators are often interested in changing the makeup of the committees—especially if the majority has added or lost a significant number of seats. This happened after the 2008 elections, when Democrats added eight seats to their majority.

The Senate, then, may either leave alone or adjust the committee structure, jurisdictions, and ratios for each new two-year Congress. The Senate has twenty committees in the 111th Congress, as listed here. In many respects, the committee structure of the Senate resembles the House's structure, but few committees match up exactly. (There is no official liaison between the two chambers to enforce corresponding committee and subcommittee arrangements.) Only the Appropriations Committees in the two chambers have exactly matching jurisdictions and subcommittees.

> *Committees in the Senate* (authorizing committees are italicized)
> - *Agriculture, Nutrition, and Forestry*
> - Appropriations (handles funding)
> - *Armed Services*
> - *Banking, Housing, and Urban Affairs*
> - *Budget*
> - *Commerce, Science, and Transportation*
> - *Energy and Natural Resources*
> - *Environment and Public Works*
> - *Finance*
> - *Foreign Relations*
> - *Health, Education, Labor, and Pensions*
> - *Homeland Security and Governmental Affairs*
> - *Indian Affairs*
> - *Intelligence*
> - *Judiciary*
> - Rules and Administration (handles internal rules and administrative tasks)
> - Select Committee on Aging (has no legislative jurisdiction)
> - Select Committee on Ethics (handles ethics issues)
> - *Small Business and Entrepreneurship*
> - *Veterans' Affairs*

There is one particularly notable difference between the two chambers that speaks to the profound variance in their operating environments: The Senate has no equivalent to the House Committee on Rules, which has tremendous power in structuring how legislation is handled on the House floor. In fact, no committee structures floor debate in the Senate; instead, formal and more often informal agreements are reached between the majority and minority leaders to move legislation along. (The Senate does have a panel called the Committee on Rules and Administration, but its main task is to handle administrative matters as well as internal Senate rules.)

As in the House, most Senate committees are so-called authorizing committees—that is, they deal with legislation to authorize government agencies and programs. The Senate, too, has one committee that controls funding, the Appropriations Committee. The Senate committee that focuses mostly on oversight of government programs and agencies is called the Committee on Homeland Security and Governmental Affairs. Unlike its House counterpart (Oversight and Government Reform), it has authorizing jurisdiction over much of the Department of Homeland Security.

Also as with the House, most Senate committees have specialized subcommittees to carry out the committees' work. As a general rule, House subcommittees play a larger role in the legislative process than do Senate subcommittees. House members are typically on fewer committees and subcommittees than senators and are better able to turn their attention to narrower areas of policy. In a chamber with only one hundred members, most senators are stretched very thin (many have multiple positions of authority in the chamber) and are unable to focus effectively at the level of subcommittee specialization.

The ratios between the parties on Senate committees always reflect very closely the ratio of the overall chamber. The prerogatives that all members have in Senate rules enable the minority to block attempts by the majority party to stack committees in their favor. (In the House, the majority can impose almost any ratio it wants, although, as we saw, the majority party is somewhat motivated to keep the numbers more or less in line with the party breakdown in the overall chamber.) As a result, at the beginning of the 111th Congress, with Democrats holding a chamberwide 58–41 edge[26] (including the two independents, Bernie Sanders and Joe Lieberman, who both side with the Democrats on organizational matters), most committees had a three-seat margin for the majority. The ratio was 11–8 on the Judiciary Committee, 13–10 on Finance, and so on. Democrats did get agreement on holding a four-seat edge on Appropriations (17–13).

Committee Assignments—Getting good committee assignments is crucial in the Senate, just as it is in the House. Senators develop expertise in their committee work, which usually results in considerable deference in their areas of specialty. Of course, senators try to get on committees that serve their constituents' needs and their own personal interests, as House members do, but senators are more likely to try to get on the Armed Services Committee or the Foreign Relations Committee in order to enhance their plausibility as a presidential candidate in the future.

All senators serve on multiple committees, usually three or four. There simply are not enough of them to make it feasible to establish exclusive committees, as the House does. But not all committees are created equal. The Senate has a long list of what it calls "A" committees:

Senate A Committees

- Agriculture, Nutrition, and Forestry
- Appropriations
- Armed Services
- Banking, Housing, and Urban Affairs
- Commerce, Science, and Transportation
- Energy and Natural Resources
- Environment and Public Works
- Finance
- Foreign Relations
- Health, Education, Labor, and Pensions
- Homeland Security and Governmental Affairs
- Intelligence
- Judiciary

Among these A committees, Appropriations, Armed Services, Finance, and Foreign Relations have exalted status and are referred to as "super A" committees. Democrats add one more committee to their super A list—the Commerce, Science, and Transportation Committee.

Returning members usually stick with the assignments they already have in order to accrue seniority, which is necessary to achieve chair or ranking member status. New members must lobby their party committee (the Committee on Committees for Republicans and the Steering and Outreach Committee for Democrats) for preferred assignments. Senate rules dictate that all members get one super A slot.[27] Members also are entitled to another of the A committee slots, as well as at least one other assignment.[28] Assignments are doled out differently by the two parties.

The Republican Committee on Committees sticks mainly to a seniority formula in determining committee slots. The Democrats' Steering and Outreach Committee also relies on seniority, but it considers several other factors, including the length of time since a particular state has been represented on a committee, the expertise of the new members, and their expected level of loyalty to the party.[29]

Committee Chairs—As with the House, the rank of committee chair comes with many privileges. The chair determines the agenda of the committee and gets to hire the bulk of the professional staff who work for the committee. As with the House, the minority ranking member can also hire staff. Senate resources are usually more evenly divided between the parties than in the House. (In recent Congresses, while the resource ratio on House committees has been about two-to-one in favor of the majority, in the Senate the majority has gotten 55 to 60 percent of the funding. In the 111th Congress, Democrats enjoy about 60 percent of the funding.)

As with the House, the majority party in the Senate gets all the committee and subcommittee chair positions. Both parties in the Senate still adhere to the seniority tradition in determining committee chairs and ranking members, and it is not uncommon for a particular senator to be senior in service on more than one committee. In these cases, the senator may chair only one committee. The late senator Edward Kennedy, for example, was the senior Democrat on both the Armed Services Committee and the Health, Education, Labor, and Pensions Committee at the beginning of the 111th Congress. He chose to chair the latter, which he did briefly in 2009 before ill health forced him to step down. Subcommittee chairs are also determined by seniority accrued on the subcommittee. There are seventy-two subcommittees in the Senate in the 111th Congress. Every Democrat chairs at least one.

The seniority tradition in the Senate has come under fire in recent years, especially in the Republican Party. In 1995 Republican Mark Hatfield of Oregon was named chair of the Appropriations Committee when his party took power, but his liberal views and a controversial vote against a balanced budget amendment to the Constitution almost led to his undoing. His more conservative colleagues lobbied internally to strip him of his position, but Hatfield managed to hold on to it.[30] In 2005 Arlen Specter of Pennsylvania, in line to take over the Judiciary Committee, came under heavy scrutiny from conservative Republicans for his pro-choice stance on abortion. After Specter promised not to get in the way of President Bush's nominees to the federal judiciary, his opponents laid off.[31] Later, in 2009, Specter switched parties, in part because of heavy Republican criticism of his vote for President Obama's stimulus package (he was one of only three Republicans in the Congress to do so), and in part as a way to improve his chances of keeping his seat in the 2010 elections.

The fact that the seniority system remains in place in the chamber gives committee chairs a measure of freedom from the dictates of the majority party leadership that their House counterparts do not always have. Another difference between the chambers is that Senate Democrats, on taking power in 2007, did not put in place the six-year term limit on chairs that Republicans had enforced when they were in the majority. As noted earlier, the House Democrats abolished the term limit in 2009.

Members' Offices

Senators represent varied constituencies. Unlike the House, where the districts are all nearly the same size in terms of population, states range from Wyoming's approximately 500,000 residents to California's 36 million.

California senators do not quite get to hire seventy-two times as many staff members as Wyoming's senators do—which would reflect proportionally the populations of the two states—but they do get more resources than the senators from the sparsely populated states. The big-state senators usually hire sixty to eighty staffers to cover the Washington and state offices, while the smaller-state senators have the resources to hire thirty to forty-five employees, depending on the state. Even with the larger allotment, California's senators are still not able to provide the kind of personalized service to their constituents that senators from sparsely populated states like Wyoming can deliver.

House and Senate Organization and the Pressures of the Legislative and Representative Roles

A useful way to think about the major organizational components of the two chambers is that they are meant to aid the institution and its members in balancing their legislative and representative responsibilities.

Committees, the workhorses of the institution, have the responsibility to study, formulate, and refine legislation in all areas of federal policy. In addition, these panels conduct oversight to keep track of how the executive branch agencies are implementing the laws passed by Congress and spending the money it provides. In short, congressional committees and subcommittees are the place where the serious work on national security, agriculture, taxes, and so forth, goes on. As has been noted, the authorizing and appropriations committees all have delineated policy domains and jurisdiction over specific federal agencies and departments. If one had to point to one place in Congress where the board-of-directors role is carried out, it would be in the committees.

But committees are hardly immune from the political pressures inherent in the representative role. Members of the House serve on anywhere from one to four committees. Senators usually serve on three or four committees. As we saw, these assignments are not made randomly. Members lobby within their parties to secure desired committee assignments. In fact, for newly elected members, this becomes a preoccupation. To demonstrate back home that they are relevant players in Washington, it is crucial for new members to get on good committees. Naturally, members try to get on the panels most relevant to their constituencies—perhaps the Armed Services Committee for the representative who has naval bases in his or her district, or the Agriculture Committee if farming is important. Many reelected members make concerted efforts to land a desired slot on the most prestigious committees (super A committees in the Senate and exclusive committees in the House) when openings occur.

The upshot is that members, as they work on policy in committee, are carefully attuned to the political ramifications back home of the decisions they make and the bills they craft in their role as the board of directors. The job of legislator cannot be separated from the job of representative.

As the other main organizational unit in the two chambers, the party leadership decides what legislation to bring to the floor. The two parties embody distinct, if overlapping, philosophies of governance. The party that happens to be in the majority is in the advantageous position of being able to pursue its national policy goals in legislation, but to pursue that agenda successfully, party leaders must carefully consider their rank-and-file members' representative responsibilities. After all, they need to corral a sufficient number of votes actually to pass bills.

In other words, crafting as well as scheduling and passing legislation must be done with an eye toward the views and interests of members' constituencies. Congress cannot make law based solely on some abstract concept like "good public policy" or "the public interest"; nor can its members simply pursue their own ideological or philosophical agendas. Political considerations must be part of every calculation.

In the 111th Congress, the majority leadership of the Democrats is struggling with exactly this sort of dilemma. The party, long a friend of the environmental movement, has made addressing the looming global warming crisis a top priority. But the leadership of the party is having trouble moving legislation that would address the problem. Although the party's membership is largely supportive of dramatic efforts to increase fuel efficiency in the vehicle fleet and reduce industrial carbon emissions, the sizable number of Democrats who represent coal regions and automobile manufacturers are standing in the way. They complain that they cannot support that particular approach to the problem because too many jobs are at stake. Ultimately, on matters of crucial importance to a district, leadership efforts to enforce party loyalty and cohesion can be frustrated, with constituent interests taking precedence.

CONCLUSION

The Framers gave two jobs to the Congress they created: lawmaking and representing. In this book, we focus on the lawmaking side—Congress as the board of directors of the federal government. But the student of Congress must understand the ramifications of the representative role that looms so large for every member. Members' representative responsibilities profoundly affect the institution's performance in directing the work of government. In fact, it is no exaggeration to say that the political perspective of the representative role bleeds—and bleeds profusely—into the realm of policymaking, whether in authorizing, appropriations, or oversight.

The Constitution divided the board of directors into two very differently constituted chambers with different time perspectives and very different types of constituencies to represent. It is a branch of government that does not have a central organizing body. The two chambers of Congress are quite literally *uncoordinated*— they do not have a central nervous system. And without a central nervous system, it is an institution that regularly has a great deal of difficulty coming together to make big decisions on directing the work of the government.

Still, the Constitution requires the House and Senate to work together to produce legislation. This is a tricky business and no easy task, nor was it meant to be. Many of the Framers were far more concerned about preventing a proliferation of bad legislation than creating an efficient and smoothly functioning legislative process. They seem to have succeeded.

QUESTIONS FOR DISCUSSION

1. Does Congress deserve its generally bad reputation? Or, given its structure, does it perform about as well as can be expected?

2. Interest groups are undeniably influential in the Congress. In what ways, if any, should their activities in trying to influence the board of directors be regulated?

3. Members of Congress take their representative role very seriously and go back to their districts or states as often as possible to be in closer touch with voters. Would it be wise to require members to spend more time in Washington so that they could focus more on their legislative role?

SUGGESTIONS FOR FURTHER READING

Birnbaum, Jeffrey. 2008. "Mickey Goes to Washington." *Washington Post*, February 17, p. W10.

Hibbing, John R., and Elizabeth Theiss-Morse. 2002. *Stealth Democracy: Americans' Beliefs About How Government Should Work*. Cambridge: Cambridge University Press.

Madison, James. *The Federalist Papers*. No. 10.

Pearson, Kathryn, and Eric Schickler. 2009. "The Transition to Democratic Leadership in a Polarized House." In *Congress Reconsidered*, 9th ed., edited by Lawrence C. Dodd and Bruce I. Oppenheimer, pp. 165–188. Washington, DC: CQ Press.

Rauch, Jonathan. 1994. *Demosclerosis*. New York: Three Rivers Press.

NOTES

1. At this writing, the 111th Congress is considering legislation that would add two seats to the House: one for the District of Columbia and one for Utah. Some critics of this proposal maintain that the Constitution permits only states, not the District of Columbia, to have voting representation in the House.

2. One of the best studies of public opinion and the Congress is John R. Hibbing and Elizabeth Theiss-Morse, *Congress as Public Enemy* (Cambridge: Cambridge University Press, 1996).

3. The basic office structure depicted in the diagram is used, with some alterations, by most House members. Senators typically use a similar structure, but they will have more staff overall – anywhere from about 35-80 total staff depending on the state. (Senators representing states with larger populations get a larger operating budget than those representing sparsely populated states.) Senators employ more legislative assistants (LAs) and caseworkers, and they will have more people handling relations with the media. House members are restricted to 18 full-time staff and 4 part-time staff. The Senate does not have similar restrictions.

The district office is largely concerned with addressing specific problems constituents have with federal programs and agencies. Caseworkers focus on that sort of work under the direction of a district director or the chief of staff if he or she is in the district. Everyone – in the district and in Washington – is answerable to the chief of staff and ultimately the member of Congress.

In the Washington office, the legislative director (LD) oversees the office's legislative work. The LAs and the LD do a number of things. Each has a portfolio of issues to follow. They track any legislation in their portfolio that the member is interested in – remember members of Congress have to vote on every matter that comes before the body. LAs and LDs support the member in his or her committee assignments. They write speeches and talking points for the House or Senate floor and appearances back home. They draft or perfect existing letters that respond to constituent inquiries. Senate offices will always have legislative correspondents (LCs) to write first drafts. Some House offices also do. The central focus of the Washington office almost always is on legislation that has an effect on the district or state the member represents.

The press secretary (sometimes called the communications director) is in charge of handling media inquiries and polishing speeches and talking points. Most press secretaries are very aggressive in trying to place stories in the press back home and securing coverage by the local television news stations, all in the interest of burnishing the reputation of the member back home.

The executive assistant or scheduler has to deal with the hundreds and hundreds of requests that come into every office for face time with the member. Members are in constant demand to give speeches and meet with groups from back home or even individual constituents. A member's schedule will be loaded with short, usually 15 or 30 minute, meetings.

4. See George Serra, "What's in It for Me?" *American Politics Research* 22, no. 4 (1994): 403–420; and Albert Cover and George Serra, "The Electoral Impact of Casework," *Electoral Studies* 14, no. 2 (June 1995): 171–177.

5. Even a former congressman, Lee Hamilton (D-Ind.), suggests that members are too responsive; see his book *How Congress Works* (Bloomington: Indiana University Press, 2004), pp. 54–55.

6. Tim Roemer, interview with the author, May 11, 2007.

7. Up until about thirty years ago, members did tend to move to the capital. In those days, however, members' spouses did not usually have a career that they might wish to continue back home. Furthermore, the advent of jet travel had already made regular trips back and forth each weekend more feasible than it had been in the past.

8. Dr. James A. Thurber, Distinguished Professor and Director, Center for Congressional and Presidential Studies, American University, "Lobbying Reform: The Importance of Enforcement and Transparency," testimony before the U.S. Senate Committee on Rules and Administration, February 8, 2006.

9. Jonathan Rauch, *Demosclerosis* (New York: Three Rivers Press, 1994).

10. In *Disjointed Pluralism: Institutional Innovation and the Development of the U.S. Congress* (Princeton, NJ: Princeton University Press, 2001), Eric Schickler describes how the idea of pluralism has played out through the development of the institution.

11. See Rauch, *Demosclerosis*, ch. 3, esp. p. 39; and Anthony Nownes, *Pressure and Power* (Boston: Houghton Mifflin, 2001), ch. 2.

12. Dan Eggen, "Health Sector Has Donated Millions to Lawmakers," *Washington Post*, March 8, 2009, p. A9.

13. A particularly interesting description of a concerted public relations campaign designed to affect federal public policymaking can be found in Jeffrey Birnbaum, "Mickey Goes to Washington," *Washington Post*, February 17, 2008, p. W10.

14. Jeffrey Birnbaum, interview with the author, October 21, 2006.

15. Richard Hall, *Participation in Congress* (New Haven, CT: Yale University Press, 1996), provides a nuanced treatment of how members make decisions in allocating their scarce time and efforts in the legislative process.

16. See *The Portable Edmund Burke* (New York: Penguin, 1999).

17. Elizabeth Mehren, "Cape Cod Wind Farm Project May Be Headed for Pasture," *Los Angeles Times*, May 5, 2006; and Rick Klein, "Kennedy Faces Fight on Cape Wind," *Boston Globe*, April 27, 2006.

18. Office of Senator Edward Kennedy, "Floor Statement on the Cape Wind Project" (press release), May 9, 2006.

19. Sebastian Mallaby, "Kit's Caboodle," *Washington Post*, June 7, 2004, p. A23.

20. Michael Grunwald, "Army Corps Delays Study over Flawed Forecasts," *Washington Post*, October 5, 2000, p. A33.

21. David Mayhew, *Congress: The Electoral Connection* (New Haven, CT: Yale University Press, 1974).

22. Amy Walter, then of the *Cook Political Report*, interview with the author, September 7, 2006.

23. Democrats give waivers to the majority of members who serve on exclusive committees. In fact, at this writing, only one Democrat on the Financial Services Committee has that as his only assignment—the chair, Barney Frank of Massachusetts.

24. See David Rohde, *Parties and Leaders in the Post-Reform House* (Chicago: University of Chicago Press, 1991).

25. The Chief Justice of the Supreme Court presides in the case of an impeachment trial, as stipulated in the Constitution.

26. The Minnesota Senate election was still contested at the beginning of the 111th Congress. Eventually, in the summer of 2009, after Democrat Al Franken was declared the winner and Arlen Specter switched parties from Republican to Democrat, the Democrats had a 60–40 edge.

27. The so-called Johnson Rule, named after Lyndon Johnson when he was the majority leader in the 1950s, established the precedent that all members would get one prestigious committee slot. Before that time, senior members were more inclined to hoard these assignments, at the expense of newer members.

28. Judy Schneider, "CRS Report for Congress: Senate Committees: Categories and Rules for Committee Assignments," Congressional Research Service, January 18, 2005.

29. Judy Schneider, "CRS Report for Congress: Committee Assignment Process in the U.S. Senate: Democratic and Republican Party Procedures," Congressional Research Service, November 3, 2006.

30. Joshua Wolf Shenk, "An Endangered Species: Senator John Chafee Is Fighting an Uphill Battle to Moderate the Republican 'Revolution,'" *Washington Monthly*, December 1995.

31. "Abortion-Support Threatens Arlen Specter's Political Future," November 9, 2004, available at: http://www.lifesitenews.com/ldn/2004/nov/04110904.html (November 9, 2004); and Andrea Stone, "Specter Pushes for Judiciary Chair," *USA Today*, November 8, 2004.

CHAPTER THREE

CONGRESSIONAL ELECTIONS

In a political system based on the idea that public officials are to be regularly and frequently held accountable for their actions by the voters, the next election cycle always casts a long shadow. As a consequence, members of Congress are constantly concerned about the potential electoral consequences of their legislative actions, both setting government policy in the authorizing process and making decisions about funding in appropriations bills. Furthermore, members frequently try to use their supervisory or oversight power to their electoral advantage by shining a light on government programs that they believe are not delivering for their constituents or to take credit for those that are.

The time-consuming nature of the modern congressional campaign—including especially the incredible fund-raising burden faced by members—has its own independent effect on the work of the board of directors. The bottom line is that one cannot understand how Congress does its work in directing the agencies of the federal government without understanding the electoral context.

The chapter starts with three vivid examples of what the political scientist David Mayhew calls the *electoral connection* to the legislative work of members of Congress. Representatives and senators of both parties and across the political spectrum pursue specific legislative goals in order to impress upon their constituents the relevance of the work they do.

The next section looks at the fundamentals of the electoral context from the perspective of a potential candidate for the House or Senate. We look at the eligibility requirements for the job, what sorts of people choose to run, what motivates candidates, and the candidate recruitment efforts undertaken by the two parties.

The subsequent section looks at the geographical context of congressional elections. We cover the process of apportioning House seats among the states, as well as the rules governing the drawing of district lines. Of particular importance is the politics surrounding the drawing of these lines, which invariably involves partisan battles at the state level and sometimes brings up considerations of race and ethnicity.

The context of a congressional election campaign is typically conditioned by the existence of an incumbent seeking reelection. The discussion of geographical context is followed by a look at the tremendously important incumbency advantage enjoyed by sitting members of the House and Senate. As noted in the last chapter, members almost always win reelection, usually by a large margin. Why are they so hard to beat, and what do they do to exploit their advantage?

We go on to examine the most crucial aspect of the incumbency advantage: campaign finance. Money is the key building block to all aspects of a congressional campaign, including hiring staff, producing advertisements, and raising yet more money. We look at the pressures on all candidates to raise sufficient funds, either to squelch potential opposition or just to be competitive. Individual donors, political action committees (PACs), and the parties are the big players in campaign finance.

Then we turn to campaign themes and issues. Primary elections and general elections present distinct challenges for congressional candidates. Different issues may need to be addressed at each of these stages, requiring different strategies and themes—and always money. To a large degree, candidates rise or fall based on their campaigning abilities, fund-raising, and strategy. But sometimes external events and national conditions can overwhelm even the best-laid plans.

Ultimately we address the stakes in congressional elections. Every two years every House seat and about one-third of the Senate seats are up for grabs. Congressional elections are tremendously consequential, not just because the immediate career interests of the members are on the line, but also because elections may portend shifts in national priorities. The party that captures a majority of seats gets to set the agenda for the next two years in that chamber, deciding the issues to focus on, the government programs that deserve more money, the new initiatives that should be considered, and so forth. What are the key factors that determine success for a political party? What do parties do to enhance their chances?

We conclude by looking at the impact of campaigns and campaigning on the legislative and oversight work of members of Congress. In the twenty-first century, running for Congress can be nearly a full-time job in itself, cutting into the time needed to direct the work of government. The "continuous campaign" has tremendous consequences for Congress as an institution as it struggles to fulfill both its legislative and representative responsibilities.

THE ELECTORAL CONNECTION

Example 1: Senator Stevens and America's Forty-Ninth State

Alaskan Ted Stevens's work in the federal government began when his home state was still a territory. As an employee of the Interior Department in the 1950s in the administration of President Dwight Eisenhower, he was instrumental in Alaska's gaining statehood in 1959.

Less than a decade later, in 1968, Stevens was first elected to the U.S. Senate. He represented the state for more than forty years. Stevens was a master legislative craftsman and immediately began work on matters affecting his home state. In fact, his accomplishments were staggering for a junior member. Within little more than a decade, he had played a major role in passing the Alaska Native Claims Settlement Act; authorizing the Trans-Alaska Pipeline; bringing about a major broadening of wildlife refuges, national parks, national monuments, and preserves; and sponsoring the Magnuson-Stevens Act, which established federal policy on the management and conservation of the nation's fisheries (Alaska's being the largest).

In subsequent years, Stevens worked on amendments to these acts—notably the Sustainable Fisheries Act, which amended Magnuson-Stevens—and other areas of particular concern to Alaskans. In particular, as a leader and onetime chair of the Appropriations Committee, Stevens was able to direct a disproportionate amount of federal spending to his sparsely populated state.

Example 2: Representative Murtha Looks After Johnstown, Pennsylvania

As chairman of the House Appropriations Committee's Defense Subcommittee, Representative John Murtha (D-PA) secured forty-eight earmarks amounting to $150.5 million in the 2008 military spending bill. Murtha's biggest earmark directed $23 million to the National Drug Intelligence Center, which is located in his congressional district and employs three hundred workers.

The power that Murtha exercises over military spending, combined with his commitment to creating jobs for the people he represents, has prompted some defense contractors to relocate to his district. And for some of these contractors, the move has proven quite profitable. For example, Concurrent Technologies Corporation, a defense research firm that employs eight hundred people in Murtha's hometown of

Johnstown, has received hundreds of millions of dollars over the past decade, thanks to Murtha's efforts. In addition to directing money to his defense industry constituents, Murtha has targeted federal funds for new roads, water projects, an airport, medical facilities, and federal offices in his district.

Taxpayers for Common Sense, a nonpartisan watchdog organization, estimates that Murtha has directed more than $2 billion to his district since he joined the House Appropriations Committee. At a 2007 campaign fund-raiser, Representative Murtha claimed that bringing federal dollars to his district "is the whole goddamn reason I went to Washington."[1]

Example 3: Mississippi's Bennie Thompson and the Aftermath of Hurricane Katrina

When Mississippi Democrat Bennie Thompson assumed chairmanship of the House Homeland Security Committee in January 2007, he removed from the committee's hearing room walls photographs of the Pentagon and World Trade Center after the terrorist attacks of September 11, 2001, and replaced them with photographs of the destruction caused by Hurricanes Katrina and Rita. "The chairman last year was from New York. I'm from Mississippi, a state that was hit hard by Katrina. It's the chairman's prerogative to put whatever he or she wants [on the hearing room walls]," Thompson said when asked why the September 11 photos were replaced.[2]

Hurricane Katrina significantly damaged Thompson's district, and many of his constituents suffer from homelessness, joblessness, and ill health. Since taking the committee's helm, Thompson has stepped up oversight of the disaster response efforts of the Federal Emergency Management Agency (FEMA). He has used his chairmanship to investigate the health effects of formaldehyde in FEMA-provided trailers, the post-Katrina housing crisis on the Gulf Coast, and FEMA's preparedness, response, and recovery missions. When he campaigns for reelection, Thompson regularly highlights his chairmanship of the committee that oversees federal disaster response as well as his ongoing oversight efforts. The congressman never misses a chance to claim his full share of the credit for the improvement in the agency's preparation for natural disasters.

———————

It would be naive to think that electoral pressures do *not* influence the way members of Congress do their jobs in directing the work of government. After all, the republic was set up so that elected officials would be accountable to the public. Representatives and senators sponsor legislation that resonates with their constituents, secure federal funds for programs and projects that are important back home, and oversee the implementation of federal laws and programs that affect their district or state.

Senator Stevens achieved almost iconic status in Alaska for his prodigious legislative achievements over four decades, even managing almost to win reelection in 2008, at the age of eighty-four, less than two weeks after being convicted on seven felony counts in federal court. (Stevens's conviction was overturned in April 2009— which was, of course, too late to save his seat in the Senate.) Representative Murtha's overriding focus on creating jobs in his district through earmarks in appropriations bills has made him a tough candidate to beat. The unemployment rate in Murtha's hometown of Johnstown dropped from 24 percent in 1983 to around 5 percent in 2007, owing in part to his efforts. Voters know that replacing Murtha with an inexperienced freshman member could be economically devastating for the district.[3] Representative Thompson's oversight of FEMA's disaster response efforts is extremely important to his constituents, many of whom lost family members, homes, or jobs to Hurricane Katrina. On the campaign trail, Thompson frequently reminds voters that he chairs the committee that oversees FEMA. By doing so, he is reminding them of his relevance to their lives.

People get into politics for a lot of reasons—to address specific issues and problems, for instance, or to advance policy goals. But as these examples illustrate, members must focus on first principles—the needs of the people in their districts and states— to win reelection and give themselves the opportunity to pursue loftier ambitions.

RUNNING FOR CONGRESS

Eligibility

The laws governing who is eligible to run for Congress are established in the Constitution. Article I, Section 2, states that House members must be at least twenty-five years of age, U.S. citizens for at least seven years, and inhabitants of the states from which they are elected (though not necessarily the districts they hope to represent). Article I, Section 3, requires that senators be at least thirty years of age, U.S. citizens for at least nine years, and inhabitants of the states from which they are elected. Neither the states nor Congress can alter or expand upon these qualifications.

Interestingly, in the early 1990s there was a major movement, spearheaded at the grassroots level by thousands of activists across the country, to change a key aspect of congressional representation by imposing term limits on service in Congress.

TABLE 3.1   *The Demographic Makeup of the 111th Congress*

	HOUSE	SENATE
Women	73 (17%)	17
African Americans	42 (9%)	0
Hispanics	25 (6%)	3
Asian Americans	7 (2%)	2
Roman Catholic	132 (30%)	24
Jewish	32 (7%)	13
Protestant	250 (57%)	52
Military experience	92 (21%)	25
Professional background		
Public service/politics	182 (42%)	32
Business	175 (40%)	26
Law	152 (35%)	54
Average age	56	63
	(23 under 40)	(none under 40)

Source: *Congressional Quarterly.*

Term limits advocates proposed limiting congressional tenure to as little as six years in the House, although most supported a twelve-year limit for both chambers. In a few cases, these activists succeeded in changing state laws or constitutions to put their plans in place. But in a 1995 case challenging state-imposed term limits on members of Congress, the Supreme Court established that qualifications for holding congressional office could be changed only by a federal-level constitutional amendment.[4]

In practice, voters have tended to hold congressional candidates to a higher standard than do the basic constitutional requirements. Voters, for example, seem to prefer the experience that typically comes with age. Table 3.1 provides a broad demographic profile of the 111th Congress. As can be seen, at the beginning of the 111th Congress, House members averaged fifty-six years of age, and senators averaged sixty-three years of age. There were only twenty-three House members under the age of forty. No senators under the age of forty serve in the 111th Congress.

And while the Constitution does not require congressional candidates to reside in the districts or states they represent for a set period of time before running, voters have demonstrated a strong preference for candidates with long-standing connections to the places they wish to represent. Voters tend to shun so-called carpetbagger candidates because they lack ties to the district or state—notwithstanding a few notable exceptions, such as Hillary Clinton's successful election and reelection efforts in New York (discussed in Chapter 2).

Deciding to Run

Individuals seek elective office for personal and political reasons. Ambition, a desire to help others, an interest in public policy, and pressure from party officials rank high on the list of motivating factors for those who decide to run for Congress. Whatever their reasons for running, the candidates themselves play a pivotal role in electoral politics. Make no mistake about it—running for federal office requires tremendous initiative and drive. The candidate must generate voter interest, be a tireless fund-raiser, and know how to handle a range of media.

Before examining how parties select and recruit candidates, it is useful to consider more carefully the personal factors that motivate politicians. The political scientist Joseph Schlesinger argues that candidates are driven to a significant degree by their own ambitions. There are discernible patterns of office-holding, according to Schlesinger, and these patterns give direction to candidates' ambitions.

Some elective positions—namely those that typically serve as stepping-stones to higher office—are more likely than others to attract candidates with what Schlesinger calls "progressive ambition." For example, serving on the city council is often a stepping-stone to serving in the state legislature. And serving in the state legislature is often a stepping-stone to serving in Congress. This kind of progression allows an individual to build contacts and credentials over time with key groups and the party organization.

Schlesinger suggests that by studying the political behavior of politicians who serve in these "stepping-stone" offices, we can make certain inferences about what they want to be next.[5] More than 50 percent of the sixty-six new members (fifty-six representatives and ten senators) who were elected to Congress in 2006 had served in their state legislature prior to running for Congress.

But naked ambition is not the only thing that matters, despite the prevailing stereotype of the career politician as someone purely seeking self-aggrandizement. Running for public office often appeals to individuals who see elective office as a way to help others. Members of Congress can assist constituents in obtaining their Social Security, disability, Medicaid, and veterans' benefits, expedite their passport applications, and respond to immigration and citizenship queries. Members from areas afflicted by floods or hurricanes can be instrumental in delivering federal assistance to relieve the suffering. Many members of Congress describe working with constituents as the most rewarding aspect of their jobs.

Former congressman Martin Frost, who represented Texas's Twenty-fourth District from 1979 to 2005, says that "many of my colleagues either pursued or contemplated pursuing a career as a clergyman in their faith."[6] For many politicians, it is that urge to help people—just as a minister, priest, or rabbi does—that drives them into politics. Many politicians even use the same language commonly used with regard to clergy—they see politics as their "calling." Former congressman Tim Roemer of Indiana cites the drive to "serve the community," instilled in him by the Catholic Church, as the source of his motivation to run for elective office.[7]

In contemporary politics, congressional candidates are also frequently driven by a desire to shape the larger direction of public policy and the role of government in society. Many of the House Democrats elected in 1974—a year when many Democrats won office in the aftermath of President Nixon's Watergate scandal—were liberal activists who were highly critical of what they perceived as the chamber's conservative policy bias. Many of these members had not previously held elective office and ran for Congress to shake things up and accomplish their policy goals. In many respects, they did just that.

The House speaker at the time, Tip O'Neill of Massachusetts, said that senior House members referred to these new members as "outsiders" because "they had not come up through the state and local political systems." They had never "rung doorbells, or driven people to the polls, or stayed late stuffing envelopes at campaign headquarters." O'Neill was struck by how many of the newcomers had decided to run because of Vietnam, civil rights, or environmental and consumer issues. Many had been inspired by the civil rights movement in the 1950s and 1960s and by the presidential campaign of Robert Kennedy in 1968.[8]

Similarly, the seventy-three Republicans who were newly elected to the House in 1994—a landslide year for the party—were also interested in shaking things up and pursuing their big-picture policy goals. Many of them had been recruited for that very purpose by Republican leaders, especially then–minority whip Newt Gingrich of Georgia. They ran for office in the service of conservative goals, such as deregulating the economy, cutting tax rates, and reducing the size of government. Indeed, most had signed onto the "Contract with America," a policy platform on which Republicans campaigned in 1994.

The journalist Alan Ehrenhalt, in one of the most trenchant studies of political ambition in the United States, observes that there has to be a strong motivation for people to go through what they have to do to get elected to office, whether at the state legislative level or the federal level for the House or Senate. In the U.S. system, so much depends on initiative to get a campaign going. In short, a candidate has to be a self-starter. Most of them have to put their careers on hold, spend a tremendous amount of time away from their families, and suffer the indignity of begging for campaign funds—all for a job that does not come with a lucrative paycheck.

What Ehrenhalt finds is that people are motivated by the desire to make a difference—not just in the lives of people by serving as ombudsman but also by addressing bigger issues, such as the environment, taxes, government regulation, or health care. He notes that successful people in American politics in the late twentieth century were good public speakers, often worked as teachers, lawyers, or salespeople, and were driven to get involved by the big issues of the day, just as O'Neill had noticed in the 1970s and Gingrich capitalized on in the 1990s.[9]

The Work of the Party Committees

The Democratic Senatorial Campaign Committee (DSCC) recruits Democratic candidates for the Senate, and the Democratic Congressional Campaign Committee (DCCC) recruits Democratic House candidates. The Republican counterparts are the National Republican Senatorial Committee (NRSC) and the National Republican Congressional Committee (NRCC). These organizations dedicate their resources to locating qualified candidates, encouraging them to run, and often giving them a boost during the campaign. Most recruiting takes place during the electoral off-season (odd-numbered years). Recruiting scouts fan out all over the country, focusing on districts and states where party officials believe their candidates can be competitive, either against an incumbent of the other party or in an open-seat race to replace a retiring member.

The committee scouts interview local party officials, business and community leaders, and political activists, among others, in order to find talented candidates. What exactly makes a good candidate? The short answer usually is: experience in politics. A person who has won an election is more than likely to have the media savvy and fund-raising skills that are needed in a run for Congress. In short, those with political experience know what they are getting into and what it takes to succeed. Former athletes, business leaders, celebrities, and hometown heroes may also fit the bill without necessarily having held elective office. They may bring instant name recognition or built-in fund-raising networks to the table—both invaluable assets.

The issues of the day can also influence the kinds of candidates the party committees want to recruit. During the 2006 and 2008 election cycles, both parties focused on recruiting Iraq War veterans to run for Congress. They were better able to speak with authority on a key issue in voters' minds than some other potential candidates.

Locating strong candidates is one thing, but convincing them to run is quite another. After the campaign committee scouts have screened and interviewed their preferred candidates, they turn to their higher-profile colleagues for help in making the pitch. Prospective candidates can expect phone calls and meetings with national party officials, key fund-raisers, sitting U.S. representatives and senators, governors, and sometimes even the president or vice president.

The goal is to flatter prospective candidates, convince them that they can win, and assure them that they will have support at every stage of the campaign. Party operatives can also address any questions or concerns a prospect may have about the costs and benefits of running for office and what to expect during the campaign.

It is not easy at all to persuade someone to run. The main reason, as noted earlier, is that running for office is a grueling business that takes a person away from family and career, and the job is tenuous, requires yet more hard work (much of it unrewarding and often downright demeaning), and does not offer a fantastic salary. The recruiters strike out as often as not. Factors like the national political environment and the competitiveness of the seat come into play as well. A strong economy and a popular president can motivate potential candidates who share the president's party label, while the opposite conditions tend to shift the incentives to the out-party's prospects.[10] Naturally, if a district or state is overwhelmingly Democratic- or Republican-leaning, it is considerably more difficult for the nondominant party to recruit candidates.

Put simply, candidates are rarely interested in running for office when they stand little chance of winning. When the president of the College of Charleston, Alex Sanders, a Democrat who had served on the South Carolina Supreme Court, challenged Republican representative Lindsey Graham in 2002 for one of South Carolina's U.S. Senate seats, he knew he faced long odds. Republicans dominate South Carolina politics, and Graham was the early favorite. Although just a House member, Graham had developed a statewide—indeed, nationwide—reputation for his leadership in the effort to impeach President Clinton. On the campaign trail, Sanders would frequently joke that he was the DSCC's eighth choice and became the nominee because the committee's top seven choices knew better than to waste their time running as a Democrat in South Carolina. Sanders's concerns were borne out—he lost to Graham by ten percentage points.

Sometimes the party's preferred candidate faces competition in the primary election. Traditionally, parties have not taken sides during primaries in order to avoid dissension within the ranks. More recently, however, the national organizations have gotten involved. Democratic and Republican operatives have occasionally gone to great lengths to discourage opposition to their favored prospect. This can take the form of actively discouraging local political and business leaders from contributing money to another candidate or even, in the extreme case, challenging the validity of signatures on petitions that would gain a spot on the ballot for the nonfavored candidate.

Republican Party officials tried desperately to persuade Representative Katherine Harris (R-FL) *not* to challenge a sitting senator, Bill Nelson (D-FL), in 2006. Party operatives viewed Harris, who gained prominence as Florida's secretary of state during the 2000 presidential election recount, as a weak candidate. After Harris refused to drop out of the Senate race, Republican leaders began a very public search to find a stronger candidate. Florida governor Jeb Bush was tapped to recruit Florida state house speaker Allan Bense, but Bense was not interested. Senator Elizabeth Dole (R-NC), chair of the NRSC that year, then flew by private plane to New York in an unsuccessful attempt to recruit conservative commentator and former Florida representative Joe Scarborough to run.[11] Ultimately the Republicans were unable to recruit a stronger candidate, Harris got the nomination, and Nelson was easily reelected to his Senate seat.

That same year the party did everything it could to discourage a conservative primary challenge to sitting liberal Rhode Island Republican senator Lincoln Chafee. Chafee, in their view, was the only sort of Republican capable of winning a statewide race in Rhode Island. Activists on the right had other ideas, however, and supported the candidacy of Cranston mayor Stephen Laffey. Although Laffey's challenge was unsuccessful, Chafee's resources were depleted as he headed into the general election, and he was defeated convincingly by Democrat Sheldon Whitehouse.[12]

How active the party organization should be at the primary stage remains a matter of debate. The voter turnout rate for congressional primary elections typically hovers around 20 percent, and those who vote in congressional primaries tend to be highly motivated partisans.[13] While the party organization tends to favor candidates who they think have a more realistic shot at winning the general election, even if it means compromising on the issues, party activists want candidates who share their political ideologies. Box 3.1 details the controversial efforts of the DCCC in 2006—what turned out to be a big year for the Democrats.

Protecting the Freshman Members

The work of the party committees is not over after a successful campaign. In fact, the campaign committees never rest. Immediately after the election, they work to

---

BOX 3.1
FINDING THE RIGHT FIT: RAHM EMANUEL AND
THE DEMOCRATIC TAKEOVER OF THE HOUSE

To win seats in Congress, party leaders believe they need to find an ideological fit for the district or state in question. In the Chafee-Laffey Republican primary in Rhode Island, the Republican campaign committee was focused on helping the kind of Republican it felt had a chance to win in New England, a region of the country less hospitable to strongly conservative candidacies. On the flip side, Democratic leaders look for candidates to compete in southern or western states who are not so liberal as to be uncompetitive. In recent years, the congressional campaign committees have become increasingly aggressive and sophisticated in targeting competitive seats and recruiting candidates who fit the constituencies.

In 2006 then–DCCC chair Rahm Emanuel of Illinois had a plan for his party to win a majority in the House of Representatives for the first time in twelve years. His methods were controversial. One of the defining issues that year was the Iraq War, which was very unpopular, particularly among activists in the Democratic base. But Emanuel marshaled the resources of the party behind several moderate to conservative Democrats who were not necessarily critical of the war. He also put the power of the party behind military veterans, whose critiques of the war he felt would have more credibility with voters.

Emanuel was especially sensitive to the need to recruit candidates, whatever their views on the war, who opposed gay marriage and abortion and supported gun rights. Socially liberal candidates, he calculated, stood no chance in a general election in parts of the Midwest, the Rocky Mountain states, and most of the South. The liberal base of the party argued vehemently that Emanuel and the DCCC were in violation of party rules that forbade the party from endorsing candidates in the primaries. But Emanuel did not back off. He thought his way was the only path to capturing a majority of the House.

And his efforts paid off for the party. Democrats won twenty-one seats in 2006 in districts that had gone for President Bush in 2004—in more than half of these districts Bush had won by more than ten percentage points. Among them were five districts in the South and border states, three in the rural Midwest, and two in the Rocky Mountains.

Source: "The View from the DCCC," post by Tom Bevan on Real Clear Politics, November 10, 2006, available at: http://www.realclearpolitics.com/blog/2006/.

persuade the congressional party leadership to give newly elected members from marginal districts plum committee assignments and help with finding someone to run their congressional office. Many new members have few Washington connections. And running a House or Senate office is nothing like running a state legislative office—or almost anything else for that matter! The newly elected officials need to be able to hit the ground running because their constituents are going to be in touch from day one. Coping with the thousands of requests, e-mails, and letters that come in every week is no easy task.

Republican leaders, when they were in control of Congress in the 1990s and the first decade of this century, did everything they could to help their freshman members bring home tangible legislative achievements to aid in their reelection efforts. Newt Gingrich, the Republican speaker from 1995 to 1998, gave some new members exclusive committee assignments, and nearly all were rewarded with earmarked federal funding in their districts. Party leaders knew that their majority depended on the success of the freshmen.

When Democrats took over in 2007, their leadership took the unusual step of giving freshmen members subcommittee chairs—especially those who had been elected from districts that had historically gone Republican. In this way the freshmen could influence legislation and demonstrate their effectiveness to their constituents right away. The party also has been generous with committee assignments. Bobby Bright, elected in 2008 from a strongly Republican Alabama district, was rewarded with two significant assignments—the Armed Services and Agriculture Committees—that address the needs of his district. Normally, freshmen feel fortunate when they can land one key committee assignment.

These tactics are important because members are most vulnerable the first time they run for reelection. The opposing party is watching every move of the freshmen for missteps. New members not only must deliver the goods to their district but need to spend time building up a war chest of campaign funds for the next cycle. If they stumble in either of these areas, look out! The elections expert Charles Mahtesian of *Politico* says that the parties' campaign committees are like lions tracking a herd of antelope. They look intently for the weaker members of the herd—usually from among the freshmen—to pick off.[14] They target the vulnerable ones and put the party machinery behind carefully selected challengers. In this way the parties can add to their numbers in the next Congress and either solidify their majority or, if they are in the minority, make progress toward regaining control of the House or Senate.

THE GEOGRAPHICAL CONTEXT OF
CONGRESSIONAL ELECTIONS

House Apportionment

In Article 1, Section 2, the Constitution mandates that a census of the population be taken every ten years for the purpose of determining the allocation of House seats. Following the first census in 1790, the number of House seats was set at 105, with each House member representing a constituency of approximately 33,000. As the population grew and new states were added, House membership increased. After the 1910 census, House members agreed to cap the number of seats at 435. In 2009 the Congress considered legislation to add two seats—one for Utah and one for the District of Columbia. This was highly controversial, since the Constitution seems to limit voting membership in the House to the states. (The District of Columbia, Puerto Rico, Guam, the Virgin Islands, the Northern Mariana Islands, and American Samoa each send a nonvoting member to the House.) In general, attempts to increase membership beyond the states have been met with strong resistance. Some members have argued that a larger body would probably hinder legislative productivity, and no doubt there is also concern that a larger membership would only further dilute the power of individual members.

Today congressional districts average about 700,000 people. Every ten years, the U.S. Commerce Department's Bureau of the Census collects population data, and that information is used to reapportion the House's 435 seats among the fifty states. As the nation's population shifts, states may lose or gain House seats. The "method of equal proportions" is used to calculate how many seats each state is awarded once each state's population is determined.[15]

This system for allocating House seats was the result of a decade's worth of congressional debate and is designed to make the proportional differences between districts as small as possible.[16] The Constitution entitles each state to at least one representative, but districts are not always equal because of population disparities between the states. For example, Wyoming's entire population is about 500,000, so its single district is the least populous. Montana has a population of approximately 1 million, making its single district the most populous. It does not quite qualify for a second seat.

The politics of determining state population has in recent decades been a matter of considerable controversy. Members of Congress, as well as state and local officials, want the Census Bureau's population count to be as accurate as possible because the numbers are used not only for reapportionment but also for allocating federal aid for many government programs. However, counting the population is a massive, logistically challenging task. The homeless, people who rent, and the poor are typically undercounted because they are often difficult to locate. Critics of the Census Bureau's methodology argue that statistical adjustments should be made to correct for undercounting. The Supreme Court, however, has rejected using statistical projections to adjust the census figures and instead requires what amounts to a head count of the population.[17]

House Districting

Every ten years, after the census is taken and House seats are reapportioned, it is the individual state's job to reconfigure congressional districts. In 1964 the Supreme Court applied the "one-person-one-vote" principle to congressional districts and held that district populations must be roughly equal within the states.[18] Prior to 1964, district populations had varied enormously in size. For some states, these variances resulted when the state's population shifted internally (for example, people moved from the state's rural areas to the state's urban centers) but congressional district lines remained static. More often, however, the failure to adjust district lines in response to population shifts was quite intentional. Entrenched political interests associated with rural areas were intent on maintaining their power at the expense of urban centers.

The Court determined that unless all congressional districts have about the same number of people in them, one person's vote in one district may be worth more (or less) than one person's vote in another district. *Malapportionment*, as the justices called it, violates the constitutional principle requiring that representation in the House be apportioned according to population.

Although the Court's actions have nearly equalized each citizen's voting influence in the House, they have in some ways reinforced the political disconnect between citizens and their representatives. Rather than draw district lines in ways that encompass natural political communities, district mapmakers may cut across city and county lines to ensure that the district conforms to the "one-person-one-vote" principle. Some congressional districts thus become strange geographical conglomerations whose constituents have little in common, and members representing these districts can have a hard time communicating a coherent campaign message as they attempt to reach different constituencies within the district. Sometimes the sheer size of a district makes campaigning and constituent service extremely taxing. One chief of staff reports that she drives as much as 1,200 miles in a long weekend attending events with or on behalf of her boss, the congressman.[19]

The Politics of Redistricting

The redistricting process is handled in most states by the state legislature in the regular legislative process, and it normally requires the sign-off of the governor. But six states have turned the job over to nonpartisan boards or commissions. Even in those states, the elected politicians have to ratify the decision.

The party that controls the state legislature after the census is conducted initiates the redistricting for the U.S. House seats. The new district lines usually hold for ten years until after the next census is taken, although a high-profile exception occurred in Texas in 2003–2004.[20] The events surrounding the mid-decade redistricting in that state are described in Box 3.2. It matters a great deal which party controls the state legislature and the governor's office in the year after the census, because they are the ones who determine the district lines. As a result, every ten years, toward the end of a decade, both parties invest large sums of money in state legislative races and gubernatorial campaigns with the hope of controlling the redistricting process.

When states lose a seat or more in the reapportionment process after the census, incumbent members of the House get very jittery. Invariably the new districts have to pit two incumbents against one another. For this reason, the number of members retiring from Congress tends to spike at the beginning of each decade.

Partisan Gerrymandering

The practice of drawing district lines in ways that benefit certain individuals or groups is known as *gerrymandering*. The term originated in 1812, when the Massachusetts state legislature created a district that was shaped like a salamander. Elbridge Gerry was governor of Massachusetts at the time, so the salamander-shaped district (of which he approved) soon became known as a "gerrymander." Today the term "gerrymander" is used to describe the practice of drawing districts to benefit incumbents, political parties, or racial and ethnic minorities.

When the party in control of the state legislature wants to create districts that maximize the chances of its candidates winning, it can either *pack* the opposing party's supporters into as few districts as possible or *crack* the opposing party's supporters into a number of small clusters dispersed into more districts.

Packing minimizes the number of seats the minority party can win, while cracking disperses that party's supporters throughout the state. By packing the opposing party's supporters into a few districts, the controlling party ensures that its candidates will win by large, comfortable margins in most of the districts. Maryland's districts, as depicted in Figure 3.1, are a classic example of packing. Democrats drew the lines to concentrate Republicans in Districts 1 and 6, giving their incumbents in Districts

BOX 3.2
TEXAS REDISTRICTS MID-DECADE

A recent exception to the redistrict-every-ten-years rule serves to illustrate the political stakes. Texas has been a strongly Republican state in recent decades, at least in terms of national politics. Nonetheless, the state typically sent a majority of Democrats to Washington in its House delegation, in part because Democrats were able to cling to a Democratic majority in at least one of the houses of the state's legislature. (The 1990 House districting had been established by a Democratic governor together with a Democratic legislature.)

In 2001, after the census, the Republican governor, Rick Perry, and the Democratic legislature were unable to come to a redistricting agreement. Ultimately, a federal court redrew the lines, maintaining the districts much as they had been in the 1990s. On that basis, Democrats won seventeen seats to the Republicans' fifteen in the 2002 elections.

But those elections brought Republican majority control to both houses of the state legislature, and Governor Perry secured a full term as well. (Perry had been the lieutenant governor under George W. Bush and took the top job in 2000 after Bush was elected president.) Spearheaded by then–U.S. House majority leader Tom DeLay, Republicans attempted to redraw the lines in mid-decade for the 2004 election cycle.

This was not done without controversy. Democrats in the State Senate went to great lengths—at one point they holed up in another state to avoid capture by authorities—to deny Republicans a quorum and the ability to act in that chamber. DeLay was accused of various abuses in the matter, including illegal campaign contributions and intimidation of federal officials. In the end, Republicans gained a quorum and prevailed, although court challenges to the redistricting plan dragged on into 2006. The results were good for the majority. The Texas delegation to the House was 21–11 Republican after the 2004 election, a gain of six seats for the party.*

Why don't states engage in mid-decade redistricting more often? After all, if the party control of the state legislature and the governor's office changes, why not engineer more seats for your party in Congress? The reason is that redistricting is a very labor-intensive and controversial task. Most legislatures meet for limited periods of time in a given year—many states consider legislative seats only part-time positions and pay accordingly. There is always plenty of other pressing business on education, health care, transportation, and other issues. There simply is not the will or the time to revisit the House district lines. State legislatures normally act only when they have to—which is after the census.

* Charles Lane and Dan Balz, "Justices Affirm GOP Map for Texas," *Washington Post*, June 29, 2006, p. A1; and "Republicans Take Four of Five Targeted Democratic Seats," *USA Today*, November 2, 2004.

FIGURE 3.1   *Maryland "Packs" Republican-Leaning Voters into Districts 1 and 6*

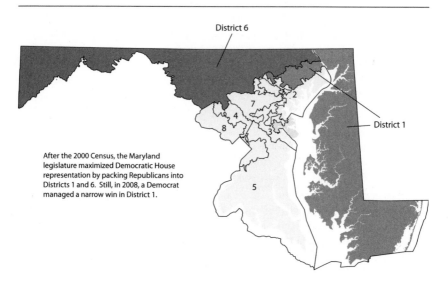

District 6

District 1

After the 2000 Census, the Maryland
legislature maximized Democratic House
representation by packing Republicans into
Districts 1 and 6. Still, in 2008, a Democrat
managed a narrow win in District 1.

FIGURE 3.2   *Illinois' 17th District: A Classic Gerrymander*

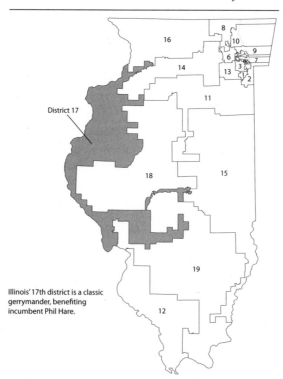

District 17

Illinois' 17th district is a classic
gerrymander, benefiting
incumbent Phil Hare.

2 through 5 and 7 clear sailing and making the Eighth District tougher to hold for the incumbent Republican.[21] (Republican Connie Morella had represented that district for sixteen years, but the newly formed district had enough additional Democrats to deny her reelection in 2002.) In 2008 the Democrats managed to win one of the districts that had been drawn to concentrate Republican-leaning voters.

The idea of cracking is to introduce competition into more districts, which can make winning elections more challenging for the controlling party's candidates. But if the majority party's candidates win under a cracking scheme, the party can often claim control of a greater number of the state's House seats.[22]

In 1986 the Supreme Court ruled that partisan gerrymandering could theoretically be egregious enough to violate the *equal protection clause* in the Fourteenth Amendment.[23] As of this writing, the Court has not identified any gerrymandering arrangements that violate this principle. The Court even upheld the 2003 Texas redistricting scheme (see Box 3.2) that was engineered by former U.S. representative Tom DeLay. The Court found that although the Republican-controlled Texas state legislature had acted "with the sole purpose of achieving a Republican majority," it had not, they said, gone *too* far. The question of how much partisanship is too much remains unresolved.[24]

Sweetheart Gerrymandering

Sweetheart gerrymandering can be seen as a type of partisan gerrymandering, but its main motivation is the protection of incumbent members of the House regardless of party. Like partisan gerrymanders, sweetheart gerrymanders may take unusual forms. Figure 3.2 depicts the Illinois Seventeenth District, which is considered one of the most oddly shaped configurations for ensuring an incumbent's reelection. (Democrat Phil Hare is the beneficiary.) Rather than attempting to expand the number of seats they hold, parties that choose the sweetheart option take the path of least resistance and focus on protecting the seats they control. Furthermore, leaders in a state legislature may recognize that it is valuable to protect incumbents, regardless of party, if those incumbents have accrued considerable seniority and are adept at delivering federal funds and projects to the state.

Sweetheart gerrymandering is quite common when divided government reigns at the state level. Many of the 2000 redistricting efforts across the country were aimed at protecting incumbents, and election results in 2002 and 2004 confirmed the success of this strategy. In the 2004 elections, for example, only thirteen House seats switched parties, and only seven incumbents lost in the general election. More than 85 percent of all House incumbents won with majorities greater than 60 percent—a whopping twenty points or more! In California, not one of the 153 seats in the California state legislature or in its 53-seat U.S. House delegation changed hands. Most were uncompetitive.

California's Republican governor Arnold Schwarzenegger responded to this outcome by proposing that the responsibility for district mapmaking be turned over to a panel of retired judges in the state. Criticizing the system for its lack of accountability and competition, he asked, "What kind of democracy is this? The current system is rigged to benefit the interests of those in office and not those who put them there."[25] Schwarzenegger's proposal was placed on the ballot in a November 2005 special election but failed to win the support of voters.

Racial Gerrymandering

Redistricting in ways that deliberately dilute the vote of minority groups is forbidden by the Voting Rights Act of 1965 and its subsequent amendments. Beginning in 1980, the Supreme Court began to narrow the act's definition of what constitutes racially discriminatory intent in the drawing of district lines. In *Mobile v. Bolden* (1980), the Court held that the fact that an African American (or a person from another racial minority group) had never been elected under the particular system in question did not prove discriminatory intent. Congress responded by amending the Voting Rights Act to outlaw any practice that has the effect of discriminating, regardless of intent.

As a result, in 1986 the Court pivoted away from its *Mobile* decision and issued a ruling that required lawmakers to demonstrate that they had done all they could to maximize minority voting strength. In *Thornburg v. Gingles*, the Court determined that six of North Carolina's state legislative districts unlawfully diluted the voting strength of African Americans. Because few blacks had been elected from these districts, the Court reasoned that the system violated the law. The decision was widely interpreted to mean that mapmakers must design districts that include a majority of minorities wherever residence patterns make this even remotely possible.[26]

The 1990 census was followed by the creation of a number of "majority-minority" districts—districts in which the majority of the population was either black or Hispanic. As a result, in the 1992 elections African Americans gained thirteen additional House seats and Latinos gained seven. But these newly created districts quickly came under scrutiny. North Carolina's Twelfth District, which patched together a number of heavily African American communities along Interstate 85 through the middle of the state, is perhaps the best-known. It is shown as it was configured at the time in Figure 3.3.

FIGURE 3.3   *North Carolina's 12th District*

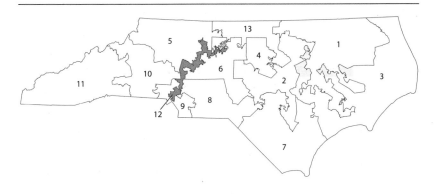

North Carolina's 12th District was originally drawn to improve the chances of an African American getting elected to the House. While the original configuration was struck down as unconstitutional, the district remains oddly shaped, snaking up Interstate 85 in the Piedmont.

The district was challenged in 1993 by five white North Carolinians who argued that it violated their right to equal protection under the law by diluting the strength of their votes. In *Shaw v. Reno*, the Supreme Court ruled that districts drawn for the purpose of enhancing minority representation might violate the constitutional rights of white voters. Three years later, in *Miller v. Johnson* (1995), the Court held that using race as the "predominant factor" in drawing districts is presumed to be unconstitutional unless there is evidence of a compelling government interest.

As one might expect, there was considerable confusion as to exactly what this meant. Throughout the 1990s, federal district courts responded to these decisions by ordering a number of states to redraw districts that were deemed unconstitutional racial gerrymanders. In 1999, just before the 2000 census, the Supreme Court heard another North Carolina case, *Hunt v. Cromartie*, and ruled that mapmakers could use race as a factor in drawing district lines if the primary motive was to achieve greater partisan balance rather than to ensure the election of a black or Hispanic representative.[27] The Court provided some clarification in *Bartlett v. Strickland* (2009), saying that legislatures did not have to go to great lengths to enhance the chances of a district electing a minority candidate if the minority population was below 50 percent.

Ironically, as a number of scholars have noted, while minorities elected in these districts have always been Democrats, the overall effect of packing African Americans or Hispanics may have been to increase the number of seats held by Republicans in the affected states. There is considerable disagreement, however, over the extent to which this is the case.[28]

Senate "Districts"

The question of reapportionment does not arise in the U.S. Senate because senators represent states with fixed boundaries. As we have seen, as part of the Great Compromise, the Framers decided that seats in the House would be awarded by population and Senate seats would be awarded in accordance with the principle of equal representation. Thus, every state—regardless of its population size—has two seats in the Senate.

The principle of "one-person-one-vote" simply does not apply in Senate representation. As the political scientist Gary Jacobson has noted: "The nine largest states are home to 51 percent of the population but elect only 18 percent of the Senate; the smallest twenty-six states control 52 percent of the Senate, but hold only 18 percent of the population."[29] In effect, the votes of those who reside in populous states count for less than the votes of those who live in less populous states. A senator from California represents about seventy-two times more people than a senator from Wyoming.

––––––

While the parties put a great deal of effort into recruiting candidates who fit particular districts, at the same time they try to create districts that maximize their chances of winning seats. Partisan gerrymandering in particular helps the parties craft districts that are safe for their incumbents or that better fit their candidates.

In House districting, parties are pulled in two directions: On the one hand, the incumbent members of the House usually push the state legislatures hard for sweetheart arrangements that will make reelection easier for them; on the other hand, party leaders sometimes push "cracking" strategies to put more seats in play, with the hope of electing more members of their party to the House—even though those strategies may make life a little more difficult for some incumbents. It is interesting to note that Majority Leader DeLay's aggressive mid-decade redistricting plan was a classic and successful effort at cracking. (Republicans picked up six Texas seats in 2004.) He even put his own seat in jeopardy in order to put more conservative voters in neighboring districts to make them more Republican-friendly. After his retirement in 2006, his district was held for one term by a Democrat.

THE INCUMBENCY ADVANTAGE

Upon taking office, members of the House and senators immediately begin to accrue the considerable advantages of incumbency that contribute to high reelection rates. Not the least of those advantages is their effective participation as members of the board of directors. As we have already seen, members pass legislation and conduct oversight in ways that benefit their districts or states—funneling funds to specific needs and keeping agencies that deliver services to their constituents on their toes. It is only natural that incumbents highlight their accomplishments in Washington when they run for reelection.

The Congress scholar David Mayhew claims that, "if a group of planners sat down and tried to design a pair of national assemblies with the goal of serving members' reelection needs year in and year out, they would be hard pressed to improve on what exists."[30] Indeed, members of Congress have significant advantages over those who challenge them for their seats. Generally speaking, these advantages can be broken down into two categories: institutional and political.[31]

Institutional Advantages

As we saw in Chapter 2, members strive to get on committees that address the needs and interests of their constituents. The committees are where most of the detailed legislative work and oversight of government programs is done; effective members are able to get provisions into legislation that help back home. The key is to be able to plausibly take credit, for instance, for a tax break that enables more people to afford community college, or for funding to refurbish a levee that yields hundreds of jobs, or for a research grant for a new lab at the local university.

A typical tactic might be for a member to introduce a specific, limited bill to rebuild the levee system on a river in his district, and then, through his membership on the Transportation and Infrastructure Committee, making sure his idea is included in a much larger public works bill. The small bill itself probably would never go anywhere, but the larger bill has so many other similar projects that it will have broad support in the chamber. In this way, the member can point to a discrete bill with his name on it and, most importantly, deliver the goods.

All is not lost, however, if the member does not happen to serve on the committee that deals with the area of policy affecting his district or state. A member who serves on the Agriculture Committee is in a position to bargain with a member who serves on Armed Services. Members build alliances with their colleagues—there are always members on Armed Services who have farming interests in their districts, just as there are always members on Agriculture who have naval installations or Air Force bases back home. Once members show that they are effective legislators, they can become part of the deal-making that can be used to their district's advantage. The bottom line in Washington is that committee work—the more powerful the committee the better—is a member's key to being able to show constituents that he or she is effective.

Incumbents also benefit from an array of institutional resources. House members serving in the 111th Congress received an annual members' representational allowance (MRA) of approximately $1.4 million. Senators receive substantially more than House members; as noted in the last chapter, their allocations vary in relation to the population of the state they represent. The MRA is used to cover all of the office's non-campaign-related operating expenses, including staff and member salaries; equipment such as computers, fax machines, printers, and Blackberries; the rent on district office space; and member and staff travel to the district. While MRA funds cannot be used for campaign-related expenses, members obviously benefit electorally from having staff who respond to constituent requests and work on policy issues that matter to the district or state.

They also benefit from having the technical resources necessary to stay in constant touch with constituents. Both chambers have facilities where members can tape radio and television messages free of charge, and members have access to WATS lines, which allow unlimited long-distance calling, and also maintain websites. Many members now provide an array of web-based services for their constituents.

Members also benefit from the franking privilege, which allows them to send mailings to their constituents using their signatures (the "frank") instead of stamps. The frank is intended to provide members with a way to communicate legislative information to their constituents, but it also aids members in their reelection efforts. The essential point is that members do everything they can to connect their legislative work in Washington to the people back home. Most members use the frank to blanket their districts with newsletters or to send targeted information to specific groups, such as senior citizens, persons living in particular communities or neighborhoods, or constituents who have shown an interest in environmental issues.

Critics of the frank argue that it gives members a free way to advertise their work and to reach out to constituents, and there is undoubtedly some truth to the charge. Members maintain that they have a duty to apprise the people who sent them to Washington of their legislative and oversight activities. But the law does forbid them from directly soliciting political support with these mailings, and they cannot send mass mailings in the ninety days preceding an election.

The political scientist Morris Fiorina has argued that incumbents gain an advantage not only by advertising themselves but by creating needs among their constituents, then catering to those needs. When Congress increased the size and scope of the federal government in the decades following World War II, it also created demand from citizens who wanted to take advantage of various federal programs. Members responded to this demand by expanding staff and increasing their capacity to communicate and work with constituents.[32] Today most—if not all—members believe that good constituency service is the key to getting reelected.

Political Advantages

Political party organizations provide a number of services that help their incumbent candidates get reelected. As previously discussed, most states give the job of congressional redistricting to the party that controls the state legislature. And it is common for parties to draw sweetheart gerrymanders to protect their incumbent candidates, sometimes regardless of party.

When parties have to subtract districts (based on census results), the job of drawing safe-incumbent districts becomes more challenging. Running in a district that has been substantially redrawn can present challenges for incumbent members. Nonetheless, incumbents almost always benefit from higher name recognition, a record of constituency service, and the adroit use of the board-of-directors powers to deliver projects to their districts and states. When two incumbents are pitted against one another after reapportionment and redistricting, the competition is almost always extremely intense—and of course someone has to lose.

Incumbent candidates are usually the ones who benefit from the various campaign services available to them through the congressional campaign committees. Although all incumbents are entitled to baseline services from their party's congressional committees (policy talking points and campaign advertising templates, for example), at-risk incumbents are also provided with fund-raising, advertising, and campaign staff assistance. At a minimum, congressional parties want to hold all of the seats they control in the chamber; providing campaign support for at-risk incumbents naturally is central to this goal.

Constituent voting behavior also tends to favor incumbent candidates. Voters are often criticized for their inattentiveness to the issues of the day and their inability sometimes to identify the major party candidates running for federal office. Data show that a sizable number of voters, especially in House races, recognize the name of only one candidate on the ballot—the incumbent. Presumably they are thus more likely to vote for the incumbent.[33] But there is logic to keeping a House member or senator in office. Experienced incumbents, regardless of party or their position on hot-button issues, are more likely to be able to deliver tangible benefits in the form of federal dollars for their constituencies than a newcomer would be. A voter may be viewed as fully rational in supporting an incumbent, even when the voter is not

FIGURE 3.4   *U.S. House Reelection Rates, 1964–2008*

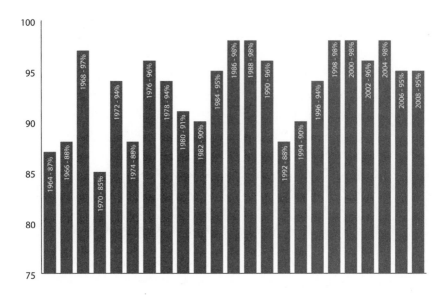

of the same party or disagrees with the incumbent on some issues. An argument can be made that often even a scandal-plagued member would serve his or her district better than a newcomer.

The Incumbency Advantage: The Bottom Line

Perhaps incumbents' most important advantage is the ability to discourage challengers from running. The bottom line is that incumbents are tremendously difficult to defeat. The average House incumbent reelection rate has been around 93 percent over the past six decades, and in recent years it has been even higher. The average reelection rate for incumbent senators has been about 80 percent in that time period—and again, it typically has been even higher in recent times.

Even in 2006, when majority control of the House switched from Republican to Democratic, 95 percent of all House incumbents won reelection. Figure 3.4 shows the reelection rates of members of Congress.

These statistics confirm that challenging an incumbent is a daunting task that most potential challengers choose not to attempt. Almost all incumbents begin their general election campaigns with higher name recognition, more political experience, more money, and a better campaign organization than their challengers. They also benefit from the mere fact that constituents and political elites expect them to win.[34]

These expectations influence media coverage of the campaign, donor contribution decisions (most donors want to give money to a winner), the likelihood of attracting campaign volunteers, and ultimately voter support.

FINANCING THE CAMPAIGN

One of the most important—if not *the* most important—advantages that incumbents have over their non-incumbent challengers is campaign money. As elected officials in charge of directing the work of government, incumbents are positioned to help not only their constituents but also any interests that have policy concerns in their committees' jurisdictions. Their ability to attract campaign contributions is based in large measure on the influence they have in the legislative process and in their dealings with federal agencies.

For example, constituents are more likely to contribute to an incumbent who helped them secure Social Security benefits for their parents than to an unfamiliar challenger who has done nothing for them. Likewise, a trade association that worked closely with an incumbent to secure a policy that benefits association members is more likely to contribute to the incumbent than to his or her challenger. Giving money to a challenger is a speculative venture; the incumbent is more of a sure thing.

Put simply, incumbents are often rewarded financially through campaign contributions for the work they do in Congress. By constantly emphasizing their board-of-directors responsibilities, incumbents remind contributors (and potential contributors) of the power they exercise over the authorization, appropriations, and oversight processes. People often view campaign fund-raising as little more than candidates begging for money from interest groups and citizens. But there is another side to it: Incumbents are not shy about reminding potential contributors of the power they wield, implicitly suggesting that access to them is not a given and that continued financial support for their campaigns would be appreciated.

The Fund-Raising Burden

Non-incumbent candidates face an upward battle when it comes to raising campaign money. As suggested earlier, in many ways they represent the unknown, and most investors prefer security and predictability. The high rate at which incumbents are re-elected also convinces many contributors that money given to a non-incumbent is money wasted.

In the 2008 elections, House incumbents raised an average of $1.2 million, while their challengers raised an average of $325,000. Senate incumbents raised an average of $8.8 million in 2008, while their challengers averaged $1.5 million.[35] But these numbers are deceptive. In an era when challengers going after more vulnerable incumbents are able to raise $1 million or more, House incumbents may have to raise two or three times the average in order to deter strong potential opposition. And the sky's the limit in potentially competitive Senate races.

BOX 3.3
WHAT DOES A CONGRESSIONAL CAMPAIGN LOOK LIKE?

Challenging an incumbent, with all the institutional and political advantages they have, is no easy task for an aspiring politician. What some people do not realize is that setting up a political campaign is a lot like setting up a small business. Probably the biggest obstacle comes in the form of a very problematic catch-22: It is difficult for challengers to convince people to give them money for what is likely to be a doomed effort to take down an incumbent, while it takes a great deal of start-up money for a campaign to establish its credibility.

There is no one-size-fits-all campaign organization for either House or Senate races because there is no one-size-fits-all district or state. Even though House districts all have about 700,000 people in them, they vary dramatically—from districts that cover all or nearly all of an entire rural state (the Third District of Nebraska covers most of the territory of the state and consists entirely of small towns) to suburban districts to compact districts in densely populated cities. What works for a campaign in Nebraska or Iowa is not going to work in Orlando, Florida, or northern New Jersey.

A competitive House race (there may be only fifty or fewer of these in a typical election cycle) may require a couple of hundred thousand dollars to start up. A campaign also typically needs anywhere from four to eight paid staff—occasionally House campaigns hire as many as ten staff members. The *campaign manager* is the number-one person; the other two essential jobs are *finance director* and *field director*. The finance director heads the fund-raising effort and typically takes on the duty of treasurer and ensures that the campaign abides by federal guidelines in disclosing its contributions. The field director organizes the work in the district to contact voters, distribute campaign information, organize volunteers, and the like.

Additional paid staff in a rural or small-town district are likely to include deputy field directors and perhaps a press secretary. (Usually one of the top three paid staff doubles as press secretary.) In rural areas, where people tend to expect personal contact and there is often no major media market, fieldwork is crucial.

In a typical House campaign, the candidate relies heavily on unpaid informal advisers—a kind of "kitchen cabinet." These advisers are old hands who are knowledgeable about the district and—especially important—have good fund-raising networks. Most campaigns depend on local campaign contributions, but particular personal attributes may enable some candidates to tap into broader

Running for office requires that candidates campaign for both money and votes. As can be seen in Box 3.3, campaigns are complex and expensive undertakings; without money, candidates cannot pay for campaign staff, advertising, polling, consultants, direct mail, transportation, and various other campaign expenses. Independently wealthy candidates may choose to foot the bill for their own campaigns, but most candidates

national sources of campaign cash. For example, a trial lawyer, a realtor, or a doctor may be able to make appeals through trade associations. A strong environmentalist may tap into national groups promoting those issues.

In addition, volunteers are crucial to almost every House campaign. Usually candidates rely on volunteer help for scheduling, driving, managing the office, and canvassing. Candidates must be able to inspire the sort of commitment required to get people to work for a cause for no pay.

Even with all these staff members and functions in place, there is still a lot to be done in a campaign, and much of it will need to be contracted out. Web page work, as well as advertising and polling, are often done by outside firms. Campaigning in an urban or suburban district often requires a great deal of money for advertising because television time is more expensive. Depending on the experience of the campaign manager and others in the campaign, the task of obtaining and analyzing voter lists is sometimes handled by a consultant.

For Senate races, paid staff will range from ten all the way up to fifty people for the most populous states. The Senate campaign staff is an expanded version of the House campaign, with more paid people in the field, more paid people working on finance, and usually a paid communications director or press secretary. (The media normally pay much more attention to Senate races.) The need for outside expertise in the form of strategic and media consultants is also usually greater in a Senate race.

For House races, it may be necessary to begin gearing up shortly after the last election. Some campaigns start twenty months before election day, and others closer to a year before. The difference may come down to whether a candidate anticipates a primary election to determine his or her party's nominee. If so, an early start is crucial. Even if the candidate is home free until the general election, it may be necessary to begin building the campaign early if name recognition is a problem in major parts of the district, as it usually is in a House race.

For Senate races, the fund-raising efforts almost always must begin much earlier. Building a statewide organization is a painstaking task. Successful Senate challengers often begin organizing three or more years before the election.

Source: Jonathan Degner, Democratic Party operative, interview with the author, September 25, 2008.

do not have that luxury.[36] (Campaign operatives report that independently wealthy candidates are often less successful than people think, usually because they prove unable to generate support among party activists who provide the crucial volunteer services that are necessary for a winning campaign.) Instead, they must spend countless hours on the phone, dialing for dollars. Representative David Price (D-NC) confesses that the cost of running for office the first time drove him and his wife to "shed our inhibitions and contact our Christmas card lists from years past, our professional colleagues at home and across the country, and far-flung family members." Price adds that he and his wife then did something they had said they would never do—they took out a $45,000 second mortgage on their home.[37]

Reforming Campaign Financing: The New Rules

In 1974 Congress overhauled federal campaign finance laws in response to public outrage over recent scandals and the lack of strict reporting requirements and meaningful enforcement of the existing law. The Federal Elections Campaign Act (FECA) placed limits on campaign contributions and expenditures by individuals and groups, made political action committees legal, and created the Federal Elections Commission (FEC) to enforce the law.

About two months after the FECA was enacted, its constitutionality was challenged in court. In *Buckley v. Valeo* (1976), the Supreme Court upheld the act's limits on contributions, but found its restrictions on total campaign expenditures unconstitutional. Limits on contributions were justified, according to the Court, because such limits prevented the appearance (and potentially the reality) of corruption. But limits on campaign expenditures, according to the Court, violated candidates' right to free speech guaranteed in the First Amendment. In effect, the Court said that by limiting how much money candidates could spend on their campaigns, the act also limited candidates' ability to express themselves. Congress responded to the Court's decision in 1976 by amending the portions of the act deemed unconstitutional.

Congress continued to tinker with federal campaign finance laws but did not pass another major reform package for almost three decades. The Bipartisan Campaign Reform Act (BCRA) of 2002, sometimes called "McCain-Feingold" owing to the leadership of Senators John McCain (R-AZ) and Russ Feingold (D-WI) in passing the bill, was Congress's most recent attempt to regulate the money spent on federal elections. The act's central goals were to ban national parties and congressional campaign committees from raising and spending so-called soft money and to prevent outside groups from running issue ads before election day that mention candidates by name.[38]

TABLE 3.2   *Contribution Limits for Federal Offices, 2007–2008*

	TO CANDIDATE (OR CANDIDATE COMMITTEE)	TO NATIONAL PARTY	TO STATE/ LOCAL PARTY	TO OTHER POLITICAL COMMITTEE	SPECIAL LIMITS
Individual may give:	$2,300	$28,500	$10,000 (combined)	$5,000	$108,200
National party may give:	$5,000	No limit	No limit	$5,000	$39,900 to Senate candidates
State/local/ district party may give:	$5,000 (combined)	No limit	No limit	$5,000 (combined)	No limit
PAC may give:	$5,000	$15,000	$5,000 (combined)	$5,000	No limit

Source: *Federal Election Commission.*

Soft money contributions—sometimes called nonfederal contributions—had not been subject to FECA restrictions. People could give any amount to the parties, and many wealthy people had given tens or hundreds of thousands of dollars—a few even gave millions. These contributions were meant to be used only for so-called party-building activities (getting out the vote for the whole ticket, registration drives, infrastructure, and so on) rather than for the purpose of supporting particular candidates. But the practice of soliciting soft money donations became controversial after the 1996 election when both parties exploited a gray area in the law in a big way. They used soft money funds to pay for advertising that seemed clearly to benefit specific candidates rather than for promoting the party ticket more broadly. Compounding the problem, President Clinton was found to have been particularly aggressive in courting soft money donors with deep pockets, having invited some to stay the night in the White House's Lincoln Bedroom. The practice appeared unseemly. BCRA ended the solicitation by the parties of big-money donors; the parties would instead have to rely on regulated contributions in much smaller amounts.

BCRA also doubled and indexed to inflation contribution limits for individuals (the limits had not been adjusted for inflation since the 1970s) and placed new limits on individual contributions to national, state, and local party committees. Table 3.2 lists the federal contribution limits for the 2007–2008 election cycle.

Candidates for federal office must fully disclose to the FEC the sources of their campaign contributions. The national party committees and federally registered PACs also must report to the FEC the sources of their contributions. The FEC makes this information available to the public through its website.

Political Action Committees

Federal law prevents corporations, federal contractors, and labor unions from contributing money directly from their treasuries to candidates. These groups can, however, encourage their employees, stockholders, or members to support particular candidates. They can also engage in independent spending and recommend the election or defeat of particular candidates, as long as they do not coordinate their efforts with candidate campaigns.

More commonly, these groups participate in the electoral process by forming political action committees. A PAC is best understood as the electoral arm of a corporation, labor union, interest group, or some other organized entity.[39] Although federal law prohibits these groups from giving directly from their treasuries to candidates, it allows them to establish separate, segregated accounts from which campaign contributions and other political expenditures can be made. PACs can solicit contributions from individuals affiliated with the sponsoring organization, then make contributions to political candidates. For example, a corporation cannot give directly to political candidates, but its PAC may do so. The important thing is that PACs rely on *voluntary* contributions from the organization's membership, employees, or supporters. It is against federal law to compel employees to give to the PAC.

Beginning in 1974, PACs were required to register with the FEC and report their receipts and contributions. Corporate PACs totaled 89 in 1974, labor PACs totaled 201, and trade association, membership, and health care industry PACs totaled 318. As of 2008, the FEC counted 1,578 corporate PACs, 272 labor PACs, and 928 trade association, membership, and health care PACs; overall, there were 4,292 PACs registered with the FEC in 2008. PACs contribute to candidates for a variety of reasons, including partisanship, ideology, incumbent voting records, and influence in the House or Senate. The candidates to whom PACs contribute vary in accordance with a given PAC's political and policy goals.

PAC contributions, contrary to popular belief, are not primarily intended to sway members' votes on the floor or influence their legislative work, although it is certainly helpful to give to an open-minded member of Congress, since a contribution may give an organization the opportunity to make its case. More commonly, such contributions are made to help keep like-minded legislators in office (or to help a like-minded challenger get elected).

Members know that adding a provision to a bill that benefits a contributor and has no connection to their constituency can generate very bad publicity and may in some circumstances even violate the law. Congressman Don Young of Alaska did just that with a provision in a 2006 transportation bill that aided the interests of a Florida-based campaign contributor. (The so-called Coconut Road earmark was actually added to the bill *after it passed the House and Senate* and before it appeared on President Bush's desk. Young acknowledged this irregular process, contending that the earmarked addition was a correction.[40]) This incident was front-page news, put Young's seat in jeopardy, and led to a congressional ethics investigation.

Political action committees can give up to $5,000 per candidate, per election. For this reason, their contributions are especially attractive to House incumbents, who have to run for office every two years. During the 2006 election cycle, House members collected just over 40 percent of their total contributions from PACs; Senate Republicans collected 24.2 percent from PACs, and their Democratic counterparts took in 14 percent of their total contributions from PACs, according to the Center for Responsive Politics. FEC data show that total PAC contributions to congressional candidates topped $348 million in the 2006 election cycle. Political action committees can also bundle contributions from supporters, then present them all together to candidates. (Individuals may do this as well.[41]) This strategy can help PACs show their clout and gain influence with the candidates they favor.

Leadership PACs, which are established by politicians (independent of their campaign committees), are a form of the traditional political action committee. Like other PACs, leadership PACs can contribute up to $5,000 per candidate, per election. Funds can be used to pay for travel, political consultants, overhead, meals, and other activities that can benefit the member's political fortunes.

Members use their leadership PACs to give money to their colleagues, to candidates, and to their party committees. By "spreading the wealth," members can build support for their parties as well as their own ambitions. Those interested in pursuing leadership positions, committee chairmanships, or higher office can gain support by giving generously. Senators and representatives who are contemplating a run for the presidency often use their leadership PAC money to travel in key presidential primary states on behalf of local candidates. Leadership PACs were relatively rare throughout the 1970s and 1980s. But by the mid-1990s, the number of registered leadership PACs began to expand as more rank-and-file members sought to increase their power and influence in the chamber. There were 54 registered leadership PACs in 1994, 86 in 1996, and 285 in 2006.⁴² Leadership PACs contributed $42 million to federal candidates during the 2006 election cycle—$25 million more than just six years earlier, according to the Center for Responsive Politics.

Party Committees

We have seen how the four congressional campaign committees—the Democratic Congressional Campaign Committee, the Democratic Senatorial Campaign Committee, the National Republican Congressional Committee, and the National Republican Senatorial Committee—are involved in recruiting candidates for federal office. They, together with the national party bodies (the Democratic National Committee [DNC] and the Republican National Committee [RNC]), also assist congressional candidates in crucial ways during campaigns.

First, they *give money directly to candidates*. The two Democratic congressional campaign committees raised a total of $255 million for the 2008 election cycle, and their Republican counterparts raised $182 million.⁴³ The national and congressional party committees can give House candidates $5,000 per candidate, per election. The law allows the national and senatorial party committees to give Senate candidates a combined total of $17,500 per election cycle.

Increasingly, the congressional campaign committees have called on their own to give for the good of the whole. Both parties now require incumbents who are not in competitive races to pay dues to the committees—those filling a more prestigious committee chair (or even in some cases a subcommittee chair) or holding a ranking member position may be assessed in the hundreds of thousands of dollars. For example, an Appropriations Committee subcommittee chair in the House is expected to give at least $250,000 to the DCCC for efforts in electing and reelecting more vulnerable Democrats. An exclusive committee chair is assessed $500,000.

Although this dues system is meant to encourage "team spirit," it also provides party leaders with a way to gauge member support for the party. Safe incumbents who do not "pay in" are much less likely to be rewarded with key committee assignments or positions of power. These contributions are of the highest priority to the leadership of both parties and are considered a crucial component of a strategy to either maintain or gain power in the House or Senate.

Second, party committees can *make coordinated expenditures to pay for the campaign-related services, such as advertising, consultants, and polling*, requested by the candidate. When expenditures are coordinated, the candidate has a say in how the money is spent. For example, a candidate can request that the party committee purchase television airtime or pay for a series of polls. These expenditures, which can only be made during the general election, are capped at $33,780 for House candidates.[44] Party committees can coordinate with Senate candidates to spend two cents (adjusted for inflation) for every person of voting age in the state.

Third, the party committees may also make uncoordinated *independent expenditures* on behalf of candidates. The committees can pay for campaign ads and direct mail, sponsor get-out-the-vote efforts, and underwrite phone banks. As long as they do not coordinate with the candidate—and that means no connection whatsoever between the party apparatus and the candidate's campaign—the parties can spend an unlimited amount in independent expenditures.

It is not uncommon for the party committees to spend $1 million or more on a competitive House race or many millions on a Senate campaign. In 2008 the Democratic congressional campaign committees spent over $100 million on independent expenditures, and in twenty-seven House races they spent over $1 million. The Republicans spent about $40 million in similar efforts.[45] Usually these expenditures come late in the race, and often they consist of various forms of negative advertising (leaflets, television, radio, and so on). This is advantageous for the candidate for whom the effort is made, as he or she can plausibly deny any direct connection to the attacks made on the opposing party's candidate.

Often the independent efforts of the parties come in the form of massive infusions of money in the last two or three weeks of the campaign. The parties wait to see which of their challengers are gaining traction and which of their incumbents are losing ground. And then they pull the trigger. These crucial late-in-the-day decisions often determine winners or losers in tight races. Observers credit late independent expenditures with saving Representative Dave Reichert's (R-WA) seat in 2008, as well as with putting Democrat Frank Kratovil over the top in his upset win in Maryland's First District that year.[46] Sometimes the party committees have been known to pull the plug when a candidate appears to be losing ground. The Democrats initially invested heavily in the 2006 Senate race of Representative Harold Ford (D-TN), but as soon as he appeared to lose ground in his race against Republican Bob Corker, the committees decided to redirect their money to other more competitive races.

Sometimes the party committees invest in campaigns against candidate wishes. When Senator Russ Feingold (D-WI) ran for reelection in 1998, the DSCC spent vast amounts of money in independent expenditures on his race. Feingold, who built his reputation in the U.S. Senate on the issue of campaign finance reform—especially the importance of limiting money in politics—and other "good government" issues, strongly objected to the party's efforts on his behalf. He does not accept money from

TABLE 3.3   *Sources of Campaign Contributions to House and Senate Candidates, 2000–2006*

| | AVERAGE CONTRIBUTIONS | CONTRIBUTIONS FROM: | | | | |
		INDIVIDUALS	PARTIES	PACS	CANDIDATES	UNKNOWN
House						
2000	$661,472	53%	1%	35%	7%	4%
2002	699,736	50	1	37	9	3
2004	766,752	57	0.6	36	4	3
2006	953,044	54	1	35	5	5
Senate						
2000	5,305,051	55	0.2	14	25	6
2002	4,013,845	68	0.9	20	8	3
2004	5,418,860	76	0.6	17	4	2
2006	7,943,700	68	0.3	13	13	5

Source: *Gary C. Jacobson,* The Politics of Congressional Elections, *7th ed. (New York: Pearson Longman, 2009), p. 66 (drawn from FEC data).*

special interests, but the DSCC does; therefore, he did not want the committee's money being spent on his behalf. The committee was more concerned with holding his seat for the Democrats and chose to ignore his protests. Feingold went on to narrowly win reelection.

Putting It All Together

Candidates have a number of sources they can turn to for campaign money, including individuals, political action committees, and party committees. It comes as a surprise to some people that most contributions to federal candidates come from individuals. As shown in Table 3.3, House Democrats and Republicans collected just over 50 percent of their total contributions from individuals in the 2006 election cycle. Senators amassed more than two-thirds of their total contributions from individuals.

Under current law, individuals can contribute up to $2,300 per candidate, per election. Candidates who run in both primary and general elections thus can collect up to $4,600 from individual contributors. The majority of individual contributors, however, do not "max out" their contributions to candidates but instead give in smaller amounts. Candidate campaign committees keep track of which contributors have maxed out and which have not; those who can legally give more are typically contacted by the campaign (often repeatedly!) and encouraged to give again.

Running a competitive campaign requires that candidates constantly be on the lookout for new sources of money and campaign assistance. With the brief two-year election cycle they face, many House members stay in an almost constant campaign mode. But senators, too, expend a great deal of time and effort on fund-raising throughout their terms. Raising anywhere from $5 million to $20 million or more in small denominations, as most need to do, is no easy task. Most members view fund-raising as a "necessary evil"—something they loathe but must do.

As the cost of running a viable campaign continues to climb, members devote more and more time to fund-raising. More than anything else, the pressures of fund-raising cut into the time that members can devote to their legislative and oversight work. We return to this critical issue in the chapter's conclusion.

CAMPAIGN THEMES AND ISSUES

Many different factors influence the kind of campaign run by candidates for the House or Senate. When people decide to throw their hat into the ring, they presumably have a good sense of *why* they are running for office. Perhaps the candidate believes that the incumbent is doing a poor job, or that important issues are being ignored. Perhaps the candidate is driven by a sense of public duty or by personal ambition. Whatever the reasons, most candidates enter a campaign with a game plan for winning. The best-laid plans, however, can be shattered by unforeseen events. Scandal, a terrorist attack, skyrocketing gas prices, or local events can force candidates to adjust their message in midcampaign. Indeed, a campaign that encounters no unexpected bumps and bruises along the way is rare.

Primary and General Elections

Primary campaigns tend to be quite different from general election campaigns. During the primaries, candidates of the same party are pitted against each other. Whoever wins the primary goes on to run in the general election against the opposing party's candidate.[47]

Election specialists have traditionally depicted the dynamics that shape elections in terms of a bell curve.[48] The middle of the curve represents the median voter—most voters, the theory goes, reside here—and the outer edges of the curve represent partisan, ideologically driven voters. This sort of configuration of the electorate is depicted in Figure 3.5. Voter turnout for primaries is typically low, and the people who do participate tend to be the party's "true believers" or "the base"—highly motivated partisans who have strong policy preferences. To win the primary, candidates must

FIGURE 3.5   *Median Voter Hypothesis*

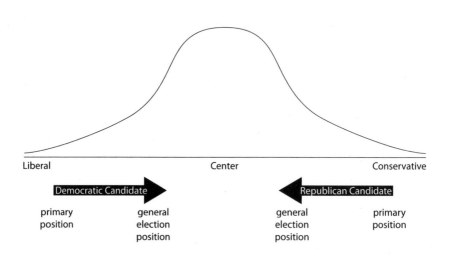

appeal to these voters. Conventional wisdom says that Democrats have to prove they are liberal enough, and Republicans have to prove they are conservative enough. As a result, primary candidates tend to campaign out on the edges of the bell curve. They frame their messages to appeal to primary voters, emphasizing their partisan credentials.

The bell curve model presumes that candidates will moderate their messages in the general election to appeal to the largest proportion of voters—those who reside in the middle. Turnout rates are much higher in the general election, and a broader spectrum of voters participates. Candidates sometimes reframe their primary campaign messages accordingly, to attract moderate support. During the general campaign, the theory goes, candidates typically meet with more diverse groups of voters, expand the range of issues they discuss, and continually travel the district or state.

But to the extent that a House seat is safe for a particular party, appealing to the center of the political spectrum may not be necessary. Districts may have been gerrymandered to achieve one-party dominance. Or a district may be dominated by one party without gerrymandering, perhaps because it includes a contiguous group of counties or a city with generally like-minded voters. For example, Nebraska's

FIGURE 3.6   *District with Democratic Skew*

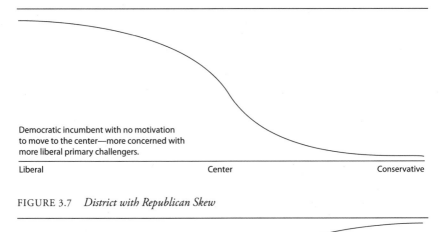

Democratic incumbent with no motivation
to move to the center—more concerned with
more liberal primary challengers.

Liberal   Center   Conservative

FIGURE 3.7   *District with Republican Skew*

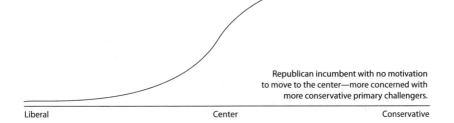

Republican incumbent with no motivation
to move to the center—more concerned with
more conservative primary challengers.

Liberal   Center   Conservative

Third District consists of most of the state's land mass and the lion's share of its counties. Nebraska 3 is strongly Republican. Most of California's Eighth District is the city of San Francisco; its voters are overwhelmingly liberal and Democratic. The distribution of voters in these sorts of districts might look something like Figures 3.6 and 3.7.

Incumbents who hold seats from such districts tend to worry more about primaries than general elections. With a district heavily skewed to favor one party, that party's candidate almost always wins the general election. Surviving the primary, then, is often the key to reelection.

Although House incumbents do not want to offend moderate voters, if the primary is the only potential stumbling block in the path toward reelection, the incumbent only needs to play to the base. Democrats from overwhelmingly liberal districts discourage opposition in the primary by taking liberal issue positions down the line, just as Republicans from conservative districts are consistently and strongly conservative to achieve the same end.

In 2008 only two House incumbents lost in primary elections, and in both cases moderation turned out to be a disadvantage. Wayne Gilchrest, a moderate Republican who represented Maryland's First District—a district drawn to favor the GOP—lost to a candidate who challenged him from the right. And Albert Wynn, a moderate Democrat who represented Maryland's strongly Democratic Fourth District, lost to a candidate who challenged him from the left. Because these incumbents were moderates, emphasizing their accomplishments in Congress seemed only to highlight their moderate records to activist primary voters attuned to ideological distinctions.

Because senators represent entire states, they usually must appeal to a broader spectrum of voters than their House counterparts in districts dominated by one party. States tend to have something more closely resembling the bell curve distribution of voters in Figure 3.5. As a result, senators have to look both ways—to their flank to avoid a primary challenge as well as to the center for the general election in order to defeat any serious opposition that may have materialized in the opposing party.

Senators who assume that they will face a well-funded opponent in the general election often try to build a record of moderation in the first few years of their term; if a primary opponent gains traction, however, the incumbent senator must take more ideological stands as the primary approaches. Finding the right balance is tricky and takes a great deal of political and rhetorical skill.

In early 2009, moderate Republican senator Arlen Specter of Pennsylvania was trying to do exactly that. The right wing of his party seemed poised to support a serious primary challenge from former congressman Patrick Toomey. Specter began to tack to the right, but after a poll came out showing him far behind Toomey in a Republican primary, he decided that his record of moderate and even liberal positions had made it impossible for him to get the support he would need. He switched parties in April that year, reasoning that his only path to reelection would be to run as a Democrat.

Six-term Democratic senator Max Baucus of Montana has walked this tightrope very effectively in recent years. Montana is a Republican state, but in recent election cycles Baucus has managed to stave off serious primary and general election opposition by developing a record of independence on major issues of salience to his state. He has won his last two terms, in 2002 and 2008, against weak Republican general election candidates after little or no primary opposition.

The Emerging National Factor in Congressional Elections

Congressional candidates must make strategic decisions about the issues or themes they will emphasize in their campaigns. These decisions are driven to a great extent by the political environment and, as noted, are also subject to change over the course of a campaign. Incumbents naturally focus on their accomplishments in office and run on themes that emphasize their experience, popularity, and constituency service. The evidence shows that incumbents are on safe ground to the extent that the campaign stays focused on these themes.

Keeping the focus on district and state concerns, however, is not as easy as it used to be. Although it is important to stress that incumbency is still a crucial advantage for all the reasons already covered and state and local issues often still predominate, national issues, party differences, and the president's popularity are now much more likely to creep into the equation.

In 1994 congressional Republicans undertook a novel approach to winning the House by, in effect, nationalizing their campaign message. Democrats had controlled the chamber since 1954, and many Republicans viewed themselves as a permanent minority. Minority whip Newt Gingrich convinced his colleagues that they would never win majority control if they continued to run localized, "every man for himself" campaigns. Gingrich argued that if voters understood what the Republican Party stood for nationally, they would vote Republicans into the majority. Perhaps more importantly, he spent several years contrasting the Republicans with Democrats. The Republicans were the "party of reform," while the Democrats were depicted as scandal-plagued, corrupt, "inside the beltway" operatives who were out of touch with the real concerns of the people. Gingrich had led the campaign to force Speaker Jim Wright's resignation based on ethics charges in 1989. And he hammered mercilessly on Democrats for their overall arrogance in running the House— including their attempt to raise congressional salaries by more than 50 percent in the dead of night and their move to permit check-kiting through the House bank. He even criticized the free ice deliveries that every Capitol Hill office got every day at taxpayer expense.

On the positive side, he created the "Contract with America." The Contract was a ten-point platform that served as the campaign centerpiece for many Republican congressional candidates in 1994. It clearly stated the party's common principles and legislative goals—ending corruption, doing away with wasteful spending, cutting taxes, and so on. Republicans pledged to enact the items outlined in the Contract if they were elected to the majority. Although the themes were national, Republican leaders encouraged their candidates to emphasize those that were most relevant to their constituents. Ultimately the combination of hitting Democrats where they were weak while also pointing to a policy agenda in the Contract proved successful, and Republicans won majority control for the first time in forty years.

One of the Republicans' greatest triumphs that year exemplifies this approach. Longtime Democratic congressman Neal Smith of central Iowa found himself in a tough general election race for the first time in many years. Smith, a highly influential subcommittee chair on the Appropriations Committee, had brought back millions of dollars to the district for everything from recreational facilities to university research centers. Although scandal-free, he could be depicted as the consummate Washington insider simply because he had served for so long. Out of the woodwork came a self-funded Republican challenger, plastic surgeon Greg Ganske. He drove around the central Iowa district in a 1958 automobile symbolizing the year Smith was first elected. His ads attached Smith to what Ganske depicted as the corrupt pork barrel activities of the Appropriations Committee and claimed that, as a newcomer to politics, he would be the kind of congressman needed to clean up the nation's capital and save taxpayer money. Smith didn't know what hit him, and Ganske won an upset victory.

Democrats took notes and waited for their opportunity, which finally arrived in 2006. The party had been in the minority since the 1994 Republican takeover and, until 2006, had lacked an overarching national message on which to run. But in 2006 a number of bribery scandals involving Republican members of Congress and an increasingly unpopular war gave them the national themes they needed. The Democratic Party committees encouraged their candidates to focus their campaign messages on Republican corruption (and to stress their support for ethics reform) and the unpopular Iraq War. Democratic candidates also repeatedly tied Republican candidates to President Bush, whose approval ratings hovered around the 30 percent mark. The message worked: Democrats picked up more than enough seats to take over the House and just enough to take the Senate.

But ultimately the fallback position for an incumbent is to stress what he or she has done by way of constituent service and delivery of federal funds. Heading into the 2008 elections, Republican leaders advised their candidates to run localized campaigns. Tom Davis, former NRCC chair and at that time a Republican congressman from northern Virginia, circulated a twenty-page memo to his House colleagues stating that "the political atmosphere facing House Republicans this November is the worst since Watergate and is far more toxic than the fall of 2006 when we lost 30 seats and our majority, and came within a couple of percentage points of losing another 15 seats."[49] Because the Republican brand name was "in the dirt," Davis suggested that candidates would be better off focusing their campaign messages on local issues and constituent services. By emphasizing national themes, Republican candidates risked reminding voters of their affiliation with an unpopular Republican president, the Iraq War, and a faltering economy. Davis's strategy may have saved some seats; however, Democrats still gained an additional twenty-one seats in the election. They also picked up seven Senate seats on election day.

Incumbents hold significant advantages over their challengers, but it has always been the case that they are vulnerable if they lose touch with their constituencies. A generation ago, the prevailing view was that incumbents should stress, almost to the exclusion of everything else, their individual qualities and their ability to deliver for the district. In the twenty-first century, the situation is somewhat different. The examples cited here suggest that parties and their candidates now need to be cognizant of the larger political environment in which they are working and campaigning, especially in marginal districts. If national conditions are bad for a party, major investments need to be made to shore up its incumbents and other candidates in close races; conversely, parties need to put themselves in a position to take advantage of good national conditions by recruiting strong challengers and raising lots of money. In today's environment, losing sight of national factors—the economy, the president's popularity, and so forth—can have catastrophic consequences for parties and candidates on election day.

THE STAKES IN CONGRESSIONAL ELECTIONS

Every two years, congressional elections involve 435 House races and 33 to 35 Senate races. (One-third of the Senate is up every cycle, but there is usually an election or two to fill out the remainder of the term of senators who died or resigned from office.) The outcome of each race is determined to a significant degree, as we have seen, by the quality of the individuals running as well as by local or state issues. But the cumulative effect of these races is national: Because the overall results determine which party controls each of the chambers, *the majority party's leadership gains the opportunity to shape the congressional agenda and drive national policy for the next two years.* In other words, the views and policies of the board of directors is at stake on election day, potentially affecting which government programs will be enhanced or created and which agencies will suffer cuts in funding.

BOX 3.4
COMPETITIVENESS IN HOUSE AND SENATE RACES

Senate races are on average much more expensive to run than House races, for obvious reasons—in a statewide race there are more media markets, more constituents to reach, more territory to cover, and so forth. At first glance, one might assume, then, that Senate incumbents are safer than House incumbents. After all, raising $10 million or so to put up a serious challenge to a sitting member would seem to be almost impossible to do.

But in fact the opposite is true: A much higher percentage of Senate races are competitive than House races (typically 30 percent versus 10 percent), and senators are more vulnerable to defeat. Why is this so?

There are a number of factors. First, consider some key differences between the typical House district and a Senate "district." In a populous state, it is next to impossible for a senator to be able to deliver the level of service that an energetic House member and his or her staff can in a relatively compact, 700,000-person district. As a result, senators seem more remote and inaccessible to constituents. In addition, the Senate constituency itself is likely to be much more diverse in terms of partisanship, racial composition, economic status, ideology, and every other way than the typical House constituency. It is harder for a senator to connect with constituents and keep most of them reasonably happy with his or her stances on the issues of the day. All of this means that a greater proportion of voters are open to supporting a challenger.

Second, Senate races attract a lot more media attention than House races, giving challengers the potential for more free publicity than House challengers can get. And because Senate seats are also more prestigious than House seats, Senate seats frequently attract the interest of ambitious politicians who have already made a name for themselves, such as former governors, celebrities, or professional athletes. These types of people have no problem with name recognition, can often raise lots of money, and may even have a network of supporters in place.

Source: Gary C. Jacobson, *The Politics of Congressional Elections*, 7th ed. (New York: Longman, 2009), pp. 101–103.

The Landscape

As noted earlier, not all congressional races are close. In fact, the overwhelming majority of House seats are won easily by incumbents—in 2006 only 15 percent of House races were decided by fewer than ten percentage points, *and this was an unusually competitive electoral cycle.* (The definition of a *marginal district* is usually one in which the race is within that ten-point differential.) Many incumbents have no opponent, and many others have only token, underfinanced, and unknown challengers. In the Senate, of the thirty-three to thirty-five seats typically up for grabs, usually over two-thirds are judged to be uncompetitive in most cycles. In 2008, twelve of thirty-five races proved to be competitive. Box 3.4 explains why Senate races tend to be more competitive.

Majority control of the two chambers—power in the Congress—usually comes down to twenty-five to fifty tight House races and five to twelve competitive Senate races. The two parties' committees focus tremendous attention each cycle on these campaigns because the stakes are so high. They pay particular attention to competitive *open-seat* races. Open seats have no incumbent. If the district demographics do not skew strongly toward one party or the other in an open-seat district, no candidate has a built-in advantage.

National Trends

Observers have noted a fairly regular trend in the results of House elections. In a presidential election year, the party of a newly elected or reelected president almost always picks up seats. In the midterm election, when the presidency is not contested, the president's party almost always loses seats.

Table 3.4 shows the results of House races since 1950. Although the party swings are not always dramatic—and in fact President Clinton's Democrats *picked up* seats in 1998, as did President Bush's Republicans in 2002—the trend is clearly in favor of the president's party in a presidential election year and against his party in the off-year.

Political scientists believe that the winning presidential candidate helps his party pick up seats, although the level of that assistance from a strong presidential candidate may be exaggerated in journalistic circles. A good turnout for a presidential candidate may add 3 to 5 percent to the vote for a House or Senate candidate of his party.[50] These additional votes, of course, can be crucial at the margin.

In midterm elections, the president's popularity is often mentioned as a factor in his party's fortunes. Another key factor is the performance of the economy. A strong

TABLE 3.4   *House Election Swings, 1950 to the Present*

ELECTION YEAR	NET GAIN OR LOSS FOR PRESIDENT'S PARTY*	PRESIDENTIAL RACE RESULT
1950	−28	(Midterm for Democratic President Truman)
1952	+22	Eisenhower (R) 55–44% over Stevenson (D)
1954	−18	
1956	−1	Eisenhower 58–42% over Stevenson
1958	−48	
1960	−20	Kennedy (D) elected, 50–50% v. Nixon (R)
1962	−4	
1964	+37	Johnson (D) 61–38% over Goldwater (R)
1966	−48	
1968	+4	Nixon 44–43% over Humphrey (D)
1970	−12	
1972	+15	Nixon 61–38% over McGovern (D)
1974	−48	(Watergate and Nixon resignation)
1976	+1	Carter (D) 50–48% over Ford (R)
1978	−15	
1980	+33	Reagan (R) 51–42% over Carter
1982	−26	
1984	+17	Reagan 59–41% over Mondale (D)
1986	−5	
1988	−1	Bush I (R) 53–46% over Dukakis (D)
1990	−8	
1992	−9	Clinton (D) 43–37% over Bush I
1994	−54	(GOP "Contract with America")
1996	+3	Clinton 49–41% over Dole (R)
1998	+5	
2000	0	Bush II (R) elected (50–50% v. Gore [D])
2002	+6	
2004	+3	Bush II 51–48% over Kerry (D)
2006	−31	
2008	+21	Obama (D) 53–46% over McCain (R)

* *In a presidential election year, the figure represents the net gain or loss in House seats of the president-elect's party.*

Source: *Adapted from Norman J. Ornstein, Thomas E. Mann, and Michael J. Malbin,* Vital Statistics on Congress 2008 *(Washington, DC: Brookings Institution Press, 2009).*

economy helps the incumbent president's party, at least at the margin. But the fact is that presidents are not always unpopular in the middle of their terms, nor is the economy always performing poorly. So why does their party tend almost always to lose seats?

One key factor that tends to work against the president's party is often overlooked in midterm elections. The president's very success in the previous election may have brought into office candidates of his party who won in spite of themselves, who may have won districts that would normally go for the other party. In other words, the president's party has more vulnerable incumbents in a midterm election, while the other party has had its vulnerable members weeded out. (Political scientists say that a party in this predicament has greater "exposure.") The party out of the White House sees opportunities and may be able to persuade strong candidates to run and contributors to contribute. It is rare, as can be seen in Table 3.4, for a party to pick up seats in consecutive electoral cycles; double-digit gains like those made by Democrats in House races in 2006 and 2008 are unusual. A successful party is usually busy protecting its vulnerable incumbents and may not have the resources to go after incumbents of the opposing party.

As political operatives and political scientists alike know, the biggest factors in any congressional race are the quality of the candidates running for competitive seats and the candidates' ability to raise the funds to compete effectively. A "high-quality" candidate is usually defined as one who has experience in politics—for example, in state legislative politics, on county commissions, as a mayor—and thus has a network of supporters and knows how to do what needs to be done to put together a campaign.

The lesson is that aspiring politicians think strategically, as the political scientist Gary Jacobson stresses. Talented ones are unlikely to run for office when the prospects do not look good. (Open seats always attract a lot of attention.) Since candidates have to pull the trigger for their campaign effort a year or more before the election, the key is to look at the political environment at that time. If the economy is poor and the president is unpopular a year or more before the election, the party out of the White House will be more successful in persuading ambitious, high-quality, experienced politicians to run. Those politicians know they can raise money and make a good go of it. But if the president is popular and the economy is strong, the prospects for the out-party are not so good, and it will be less successful in recruiting and fund-raising.

In today's congressional election environment, as noted before, national political conditions are a larger factor than they were decades ago. These national factors affect campaigns indirectly through the strategic decisions made by politicians thinking about starting up a campaign. National factors also enter into campaigns more directly through advertisements tying candidates to national political figures, party platforms, or major issues.

CONCLUSION: THE BOARD OF DIRECTORS AND THE CONTINUOUS CAMPAIGN

In Chapter 2, the argument was put forward that senators and representatives are "right-eye-dominant"—meaning that they see their legislative and oversight work as members of the board of directors through the prism of the needs and priorities of their constituents.

The representative role puts pressure on members in other ways as well. Constituent groups constantly demand face time with members. Most members feel very strongly that they need to spend time back in the district or state or risk being portrayed as out of touch and uninterested in the people. Exactly such a charge was largely responsible for bringing down the otherwise popular North Carolina senator Elizabeth Dole in the 2008 elections. She was defeated by state senator Kay Hagan by 53 to 44 percent.

The requirements of running for office in the twenty-first century have their own independent effect on members of Congress. Raising the kind of money it takes to build up a war chest to compete in the next electoral cycle (or to scare away potential competition) is extremely time-consuming, and time spent fund-raising may come at the cost of losing time to work on complex policy issues in Washington. Even while in Washington, some members find themselves shuttling back and forth to party committee offices during the day to make fund-raising calls—some practically camp out at the party offices. (It is illegal for them to make those calls from their congressional offices.)

For those in competitive districts, running for office is nearly a full-time job. The demands for contact back home with constituents are intense. Moreover, the explosion of high-tech media makes members more accessible and more vulnerable to attack than ever. They tread carefully as they carry out their official duties—someone is always watching, recording, or videotaping.

It should be noted that electoral pressures affect different members in different ways. Most have relatively safe seats, but some do not. Although even the members with safe seats expend a great deal of time and effort keeping their seat safe, the pressures on those who come from marginal districts and competitive states can be all-consuming.

All of this effort takes time away from legislative and oversight duties. During the 1960s and 1970s, an average two-year Congress met for 323 days. During the 1980s and 1990s, the average dropped to 278 days. Today the average hovers around 250 days. In addition, the number of committee and subcommittee hearings during a two-year session has declined significantly.[51] As a result, members have less time to examine legislative proposals, less time to look over agency officials' shoulders to make sure they are carrying out the law in the way intended, and less time to forge the difficult and necessary compromises with their colleagues to address pressing national issues.

Representatives and senators have a complex and tremendously difficult task juggling and meshing their twin responsibilities as legislators and representatives in this era of the continuous campaign. The bottom line is this: Fulfilling their representative role, especially as it involves addressing the pressures of the modern campaign, affects everything members do as they direct the work of the federal government.

QUESTIONS FOR DISCUSSION

1. What would be the advantages and disadvantages to having the government finance congressional campaigns? Would it make sense to have federally financed television time for the major party candidates?

2. California governor Arnold Schwarzenegger recently tried (but failed) to take the politics out of drawing congressional and state legislative district lines in his state by giving that power to a board of retired judges. Is this a good idea? How do you think members of Congress view this idea?

SUGGESTIONS FOR FURTHER READING

Currinder, Marian. 2009. *Money in the House.* Boulder, CO: Westview Press.

Erikson, Robert S., and Gerald C. Wright. 2009. "Voters, Candidates, and Issues in Congressional Elections." In *Congress Reconsidered*, 9th ed., edited by Lawrence C. Dodd and Bruce I. Oppenheimer, pp. 71–96. Washington, DC: CQ Press.

Jacobson, Gary. 2009. *The Politics of Congressional Elections*, 7th ed. New York: Longman.

Mellow, Nicole. 2009. "Voting Behavior: A Blue Nation." In *The Elections of 2008*, edited by Michael Nelson, pp. 145–162. Washington, DC: CQ Press.

Pitney, John J., James W. Ceaser, and Andrew E. Busch. 2009. *Epic Journey: The 2008 Elections and American Politics.* Lanham, MD: Rowman and Littlefield.

NOTES

1. John R. Wilke, "Murtha Inc.: How Lawmaker Rebuilt Hometown on Earmarks," *Wall Street Journal*, October 30, 2007.

2. Patrick Yoest, "Katrina vs. Sept. 11: Chairman Opts to Display Both in Homeland Hearing Room," *CQ Today*, September 27, 2007.

3. Wilke, "Murtha Inc."

4. *U.S. Term Limits v. Thornton* (1995). In this case, the Court ruled that an Arkansas term limit law did not create an additional requirement for holding office.

5. Joseph A. Schlesinger, *Ambition and Politics* (Chicago: Rand McNally, 1966).

6. Martin Frost, interview with the author, September 12, 2006.

7. Tim Roemer, interview with the author, March 26, 2009.

8. Robert V. Remini, *The House* (Washington, DC: Smithsonian Books, 2006), pp. 446–447.

9. Alan Ehrenhalt, *The United States of Ambition* (New York: Three Rivers Press, 1992).

10. Gary C. Jacobson, "The Congress: The Structural Basis of Republican Success," in *The Elections of 2004*, edited by Michael Nelson (Washington, DC: CQ Press, 2005), pp. 163–186.

11. Charles Babington and Chris Cilizza, "For GOP, Election Anxiety Mounts," *Washington Post*, October 10, 2005, p. A1.

12. John J. Miller, "Chafee's Challenger: Stephen Laffey Tries to Knock Off the Most Liberal Republican Senator," *National Review*, August 7, 2006.

13. According to statistics compiled by the Committee for the Study of the American Electorate.

14. Charles Mahtesian, interview with the author, October 23, 2007.

15. U.S. Bureau of the Census, "Congressional Apportionment: How It's Calculated," available at: http://www.census.gov/population/www/censusdata/apportionment/calculated.html.

16. For more detail, see *Guide to U.S. Elections*, 5th ed. (Washington, DC: CQ Press), p. 849.

17. Ibid.

18. *Wesberry v. Sanders* (1964).

19. Brenna Findley, chief of staff to Congressman Steve King (R-Iowa), interview with the author, April 5, 2009.

20. Erik Engstrom describes aggressive redistricting efforts in the late nineteenth century in "Stacking the States, Stacking the House," *American Political Science Review* 100, no. 6 (August 2006): 419–427.

21. In 2008 Democrats were able to overcome the Republican advantage in District 1 along Maryland's Eastern Shore by electing Frank Kratovil in an open-seat race.

22. Cracking can also refer to drawing district lines in such a way as to dilute the concentration of a minority group, thereby denying that group a reasonable chance to elect one of its members.

23. *Davis v. Bandemer* (1986).

24. *League of United Latin American Citizens v. Perry* (2006).

25. *Guide to U.S. Elections*, pp. 853–854.

26. Gary C. Jacobson, *The Politics of Congressional Elections*, 6th ed. (New York: Pearson Longman, 2004), p. 12.

27. *Guide to U.S. Elections*, p. 866.

28. See David Lublin, *The Paradox of Representation* (Princeton, NJ: Princeton University Press, 1999); and Carol Swain, *Black Faces, Black Interests* (Oxford: Oxford University Press, 1995). Erik Engstrom has a somewhat different view, suggesting that racial redistricting has not helped the Republican Party as much as some people have asserted; see "Race and Southern Politics: The Special Case of Congressional Redistricting" in *Writing Southern Politics*, edited by Robert P. Steed and Laurence W. Moreland (Lexington: University Press of Kentucky, 2006).

29. Gary Jacobson, "Modern Campaigns and Representation," in *The Legislative Branch*, edited by Paul J. Quirk and Sarah A. Binder (Oxford: Oxford University Press, 2006), p. 113.

30. David Mayhew, *Congress: The Electoral Connection* (New Haven, CT: Yale University Press, 1974), pp. 81–82.

31. See Steven D. Levitt and Catherine D. Wofram, "Decomposing the Sources of Incumbency Advantage in the U.S. House," *Legislative Studies Quarterly* 22 (1997): 45–60.

32. Morris P. Fiorina, *Congress: Keystone of the Washington Establishment*, 2nd ed. (New Haven, CT: Yale University Press, 1989).

33. See Gary Jacobson, *The Politics of Congressional Elections*, 7th ed. (New York: Longman, 2009), ch. 3.

34. Paul S. Herrnson, *Congressional Elections*, 5th ed. (Washington, DC: CQ Press, 2008), p. 246.

35. Marian Currinder, "Campaign Finance: Fundraising and Spending in the 2008 Elections," in *The Elections of 2008*, edited by Michael Nelson (Washington, DC: CQ Press, 2009), p. 179.

36. The law permits candidates to spend an unlimited amount in personal funds on their own campaigns.

37. David E. Price, *The Congressional Experience*, 3rd ed. (Boulder, CO: Westview Press, 2004), p. 16.

38. Marian Currinder, "Campaign Finance: Funding the Presidential and Congressional Elections," in *The Elections of 2004*, edited by Michael Nelson (Washington, DC: CQ Press, 2005), p. 113.

39. Herrnson, *Congressional Elections*, p. 133.

40. David D. Kirkpatrick, "Campaign Funds for Alaskan; Road Aid to Florida," *New York Times*, June 7, 2007, available at: http://www.nytimes.com/2007/06/07/washington/07earmark.html.

41. Most individual "bundlers" are federal lobbyists. Although members of Congress undoubtedly appreciate the fund-raising help that bundlers can provide, they also understand that such relationships between members and lobbyists may be perceived as corrupt. A lobbyist who delivers twenty $1,000 contributions to a candidate might be viewed by some as finding a way around the $2,300 federal contribution limit. To address this potential problem, Congress passed legislation in 2007 requiring the disclosure of bundling activities by registered lobbyists. The law requires candidates to report to the FEC the name and contact information for each registered lobbyist "known (or 'reasonably known') to have made at least two bundled contributions totaling more than $15,000 during specified six-month reporting periods." See Sam R. Garrett, "Campaign Finance Developments in the 110th Congress," Congressional Research Service, September 28, 2007, p. 2.

42. Herrnson, *Congressional Elections*, p. 136.

43. Currinder, "Campaign Finance: Fundraising and Spending in the 2008 Elections," p. 181.

44. This was the cap set by BCRA in 2002.

45. Currinder, "Campaign Finance: Fundraising and Spending in the 2008 Elections," pp. 181–182.

46. Jonathan Degner, Democratic political operative, and The Hotline's Amy Walter, interviews with the author, March 11, 2009 (Degner) and April 19, 2009 (Walter).

47. Though most congressional elections feature a Democrat and a Republican in the general election, third-party candidates can also compete, as long as they qualify for a place on the ballot.

48. See, for example, Anthony Downs, *An Economic Theory of Democracy* (New York: Harper & Row, 1957).

49. Chuck Todd et al., "GOPer Compares Brand to Bad Dog Food," May 14, 2008, available at msnbc.com, "First Read": http://firstread.msnbc.msn.com/archive/2008/05/14/1022156.aspx.

50. Ibid, pp. 167–168.

51. Norman Ornstein, "Part-Time Congress," *Washington Post*, March 7, 2006.

CHAPTER FOUR

CONGRESS AS THE BOARD OF DIRECTORS: AUTHORIZING THE WORK OF GOVERNMENT

The first three chapters set the stage, providing an overview of Congress. We focused in particular on the pressures that members face in the various facets of their representative role. The important takeaway point is that the representative role profoundly affects what Congress does while acting as the board of directors of the federal government.

In this chapter and the next two, we get down to the business of how Congress does its legislative and oversight work. These activities follow a logical progression:

First, Congress passes *authorizing* statutes that establish agencies and federal programs for one year, multiple years, or indefinitely. These statutes detail, with varying levels of specificity, the aim of the programs and the policies that agency officials must follow when implementing the law. In addition, most authorizing statutes set a funding ceiling for the agencies and programs *but do not provide the actual funding* for those programs. (Important exceptions to this last rule are covered later in the chapter.)

Second, Congress passes *appropriations* laws to fund the agencies and programs within the parameters set in the authorizing statutes. Appropriations for the vast majority of government programs are provided on an annual basis. Congress is supposed to appropriate money only for those programs that have a current authorization for appropriation established in law. The appropriations process is covered in Chapter 5.

Third, once programs have been established, funded, and then implemented by the executive branch agencies, members of Congress, usually through the committees of jurisdiction, may choose to check to see whether federal officials are carrying out those programs in the way intended. This is the supervisory power of the Congress, usually called *oversight*. Congress conducts oversight not just to make sure its wishes are being carried out but also to inform the process of reauthorizing (or reconsidering and updating) programs and the next annual round of appropriations. Oversight is the subject of Chapter 6.

The vast majority of bills making their way through Congress at any given time are authorizing bills. These bills may be very long and detailed, establishing policies for enormous government departments such as the Department of Defense. They may cover an important area of policy within a department or agency. For example, the Elementary and Secondary Education Act covers a substantial portion of the activities of the Education Department, but not all of them. A bill may also target a particular program for changes, or even just a particular part of a program.

Through the authorization process, members of Congress are interested in affecting the ongoing work of government by establishing new programs, changing policies, or extending or tinkering with existing programs. Given the size of the government, the possibilities are endless. For a range of reasons, most of these efforts come to nothing—only a small fraction of the thousands of bills introduced every year in Congress make it through the legislative process to become law. In a two-year Congress, about 10,000 bills will be introduced, usually fewer than 5 percent of them will be enacted into law, and many of these will be of little significance—perhaps naming or renaming a post office, for example. For those two years, however, most of the 535 members, all of whom normally serve on one or more committees, will be trying to make a name for themselves through the authorizing power of Congress.

We start the chapter where most of the real work is done. Woodrow Wilson, in his days as a political scientist in the late nineteenth century, once wrote: "It is not far from the truth to say that Congress in session is Congress on public exhibition, whilst Congress in committee rooms is Congress at work."[1] Fundamentally, things have not changed: The serious business is still done in committee and subcommittee. The first section looks at the authorizing committees in Congress, and in particular at how the work of directing the government is divided among them.

We then get into more detail about the policy work of these committees. How do they go about their business? Most importantly, exactly what sort of direction do the authorizing statutes produced by these committees give to executive branch agencies? How does the work of authorizing committees relate to the funding responsibility of Congress? In addition, to get a sense of the lengths to which the board of directors can go in exercising its authorizing power, we examine the case of the recent reorganization of the sixteen government agencies charged with collecting and analyzing foreign intelligence. Congress, with prodding from the 9/11 Commission and the public, passed legislation in 2004 that created the Office of the Director of National Intelligence to oversee and coordinate the intelligence agencies; this reorganization fundamentally changed many of the long-standing roles and relationships among these agencies.

Next we look at the special case of authorizing legislation that results in what is called *direct spending*. Normally, authorizing legislation gives instructions to agencies as to how they will go about their work implementing government programs. The legislation recommends a funding amount for agencies and programs, but does not actually give agencies the authority to get money from the Treasury to conduct their programs. Subsequent appropriations bills provide that authority, thereby enabling the agencies to implement authorized government programs. Direct spending legislation does double duty, in effect doing an end run around the normal process. It both sets agency policy and determines spending levels. Direct spending legislation has become increasingly important in recent decades.

As most people know, authorizing bills (and other kinds of bills for that matter) normally go through a series of steps in order to become law and thus binding on the executive branch agencies. The second section of the chapter covers the fundamentals of the legislative process in the House and Senate. This process differs markedly in the two chambers, particularly when it comes to debate and voting on the floor. We look at the standard "how a bill becomes a law" narrative, but more importantly, we look at how Congress *really* processes legislation. For many important matters, both chambers of the twenty-first-century Congress find themselves veering away from standard procedures in order to get their legislative work done. The aim here is to provide the reader with a real-world sense of the legislative process, which often differs significantly from how it is laid out in the standard textbook.

In authorizing the work of government, Congress is expected to consider carefully what the agencies are doing and to update laws to keep up with changing times and new technologies, revise or eliminate programs that are not fulfilling their original purpose, and create new programs or agencies to address emerging problems. These days Congress is beset with a huge backlog of expired and outdated authorizations. The last section of this chapter considers the impact of the institution's failure to handle its workload in a timely fashion.

Another critical issue examined in the last section is the practice of including direct spending provisions in authorizing legislation. This practice in effect muddies the division of labor in the institution between those committees that write legislation authorizing the work of government and those that handle the bills that determine funding levels for agencies and programs. This trend has had a tremendous impact on how the board of directors handles its budgeting responsibility.

THE AUTHORIZING POWER

The Authorizing Committees

Most committees in Congress are authorizing committees. Each committee has jurisdiction over certain departments and agencies in the executive branch. Listed here are all the House and Senate authorizing committees, together with brief summaries of their jurisdictions. Bills that would affect the work of an agency in a particular committee's jurisdiction are referred to that committee, and often subsequently to one or more subcommittees, for more in-depth consideration. The members of a committee are the ones who work on and frequently develop the legislation that affects the agencies in their purview. Such legislation may do everything from tinker with an individual program to reorganize large swaths of the federal government. The committees also have oversight power over the agencies in their jurisdiction (the subject of Chapter 6). It is important to stress that Congress's ability to look into the work that agencies are doing to implement government programs is closely linked to the authorizing process. Committee members need to know how government programs are working in order to make informed decisions when they update authorizing laws.

House Authorizing Committees and Their Jurisdictions

Committee on Agriculture—The dairy industry; human nutrition; inspection of livestock, poultry, meat produce, seafood, and seafood produce; forestry; rural development; crop insurance

Committee on Armed Services—General defense issues; ongoing military operations; all the armed services; some energy programs

Committee on Education and Labor—All federal education programs, including elementary and secondary education and higher education; school lunch and nutrition programs; pensions and retirements for workers; job training; wages and hours of labor; worker health and safety

Committee on Energy and Commerce—Biomedical research and development; health and health facilities; exploration, production, storage, supply, marketing, pricing, and regulation of energy resources; travel and tourism; public health (including Medicaid)

Committee on Financial Services—Housing and financial services sectors (banking, insurance, real estate, public and assisted housing, and securities); the Federal Reserve System; consumer protection laws

Committee on Foreign Affairs—Foreign affairs, establishment of boundaries; the diplomatic services; UN policy

Committee on Homeland Security—Homeland security issues, including customs

Committee on the Judiciary—Federal judiciary proceedings; civil and criminal law; bankruptcy; counterfeiting; subversive activities affecting the security of the United States; presidential succession

Committee on Natural Resources—Fisheries; wildlife; military parks and battlefields; national cemeteries; national parks; mining interests; petroleum conservation

Committee on Oversight and Government Reform—The federal civil service; federal paperwork reduction; federal holidays and celebrations; oversight and reorganizations of the executive branch

Committee on Science and Technology—Energy research; astronomical research and development; standards; science education

Committee on Small Business—Assistance for and protection of small business, including financial aid and paperwork reduction; small business enterprises and government contracts

Committee on Transportation and Infrastructure—Coast Guard activities; management of emergencies and natural disasters; roads, bridges, and other infrastructure, such as water projects

Committee on Veterans' Affairs—All issues pertaining to veterans; life insurance issued by the federal government for service in the armed forces; service members' civil relief and pensions

Committee on Ways and Means—The tax code; Medicare programs; trade policy; Social Security programs (old age and disability)

Permanent Select Committee on Intelligence—All intelligence-related activities, including the organization of the intelligence-related agencies in several departments

Senate Authorizing Committees and Their Jurisdictions
Committee on Agriculture, Nutrition, and Forestry—Farm programs; forestry and logging; nutrition and health; farm viability; food and agriculture research; inspection of plants, animals, and products

Committee on Armed Services—Aeronautical and space activities related to national defense; the armed services; the benefits and privileges of members of the armed services

Committee on Banking, Housing, and Urban Affairs—Banks and financial institutions; housing; nursing home construction; urban development

Committee on Commerce, Science, and Transportation—The activities of the Coast Guard; fisheries; water projects; aviation; interstate commerce; science, engineering, and technology research and development and policy; highway safety

Committee on Energy and Natural Resources—National energy policy; territorial policy; federal lands issues

Committee on Environment and Public Works—Pollution and other environmental issues; nuclear power; highways and other infrastructure

Committee on Finance—The tax code; Social Security programs; Medicare and Medicaid programs; trade policy

Committee on Foreign Relations—The diplomatic service; the boundaries of the United States; foreign economic, military, technical, and humanitarian assistance; UN policy

Committee on Health, Education, Labor, and Pensions—Federal education policy (elementary, secondary, and higher); U.S. labor policy, including wages, pensions, and work conditions; health policy and public welfare

Committee on Homeland Security and Governmental Affairs—Many homeland security issues; the federal workforce; postal issues; oversight of the executive branch

Committee on Indian Affairs—Matters related to Indian populations and land

Committee on the Judiciary—Bankruptcy; federal penitentiaries; the federal civil and criminal code; the federal judiciary, including nominations

Committee on Small Business and Entrepreneurship—Small business activity

Committee on Veterans' Affairs—Compensation of veterans and other veterans' issues, including vocational rehabilitation; national cemeteries

Select Committee on Intelligence—All intelligence-related activities, including the organization of the intelligence-related agencies in several departments[2]

As noted in Chapter 2, at the beginning of each Congress (in the January immediately after congressional elections), the House and Senate decide how and whether to restructure the committee system that was in place in the previous two years. Each chamber may create new committees, rename existing ones, and change the panels' jurisdictions.

There is a great deal of variety in the workloads and prestige of the committees. But the key to committee power is jurisdiction. How important are the agencies and programs under the panel's control? These jurisdictions have evolved a great deal over the years. The establishment of committee jurisdictions is fundamentally a political decision in the sense that, as noted earlier, the full membership in each chamber votes to establish committee jurisdictions.[3] In the House, the majority leadership controls the process. In the Senate, the minority party may play a major role as well. Any jurisdictional changes reflect some combination of purely political considerations and

BOX 4.1
POLITICS DRIVES CHANGES IN
COMMITTEE JURISDICTIONS

The House of Representatives first established the Committee on Banking and Currency back in 1865. Before that time, the Ways and Means Committee had jurisdiction over banking issues. The committee's jurisdiction was adjusted only incrementally over the years to adjust to changing times. By the mid-1990s, after several name changes but only relatively minor jurisdictional changes, it was called the Committee on Banking and Financial Services.

Bigger changes lay ahead in the 107th Congress in 2001. A fight erupted within the Republican Party over the chairmanship of the powerful Energy and Commerce Committee. Representatives Billy Tauzin of Louisiana and Michael Oxley of Ohio angled for the coveted job. They lobbied the leadership and raised hundreds of thousands of dollars for the Republican Party to prove their loyalty. Each appeared in front of the Republican Steering Committee to make his case. It was a close call for the party. Both Tauzin and Oxley were respected members who had demonstrated knowledge of the issues and a commitment to the party's principles.

Ultimately a deal was struck. Tauzin would get the Energy and Commerce chairmanship, but his committee would lose a key aspect of its jurisdiction—control over securities and exchange issues. Those matters would be handled by the old Banking and Financial Services Committee, which would be renamed the Financial Services Committee. Oxley would get to be chair of that committee.

Thus, a significant change in two committees' jurisdictions was born of a political compromise. Oxley would probably have preferred the Energy and Commerce position, but the leadership settled on giving him the chairmanship of a rival committee with additional policy turf. Committee jurisdictions are as likely to be based on political considerations as on substantive policy questions.

Source: "Tauzin Tapped to Chair House Commerce Panel," *Mediaweek*, January 8, 2001.

policy concerns. Box 4.1 tells the story of significant jurisdictional changes engineered by the House Republican leadership for the Financial Services and Energy and Commerce Committees in the 107th Congress.

One could argue that the most powerful authorizing committee in the Congress—the one with jurisdiction over more important government functions than any other—is the Senate Finance Committee, which has all the major entitlement programs in its jurisdiction, the agencies that administer these programs (the Social Security Administration [SSA] and the Centers for Medicare and Medicaid Services [CMS]), the tax code and the Internal Revenue Service, some energy programs, and trade policy. The House Ways and Means Committee has an almost identical jurisdiction, minus Medicaid. The Commerce, Science, and Transportation Committee in the Senate and the Energy and Commerce Committee in the House also have very broad authority over government agencies and the economy.

Perhaps the busiest authorizing panels are the Armed Services Committees in the House and Senate. Every year the entire Defense Department, an approximately $600 billion organization in 2008, comes under review—its authorizing legislation covers only one year. These committees perennially produce and pass legislation that determines the policies of the Defense Department and the armed services of the United States for the upcoming fiscal year. On the authorizing side of Congress's duties, the work of these committees is probably the most demanding given the scope of the Defense Department and the imperative to produce a product every year.

Other committees have nowhere near the same exacting schedule as the Armed Services Committees or the vast jurisdictions of Ways and Means; Finance; Commerce, Science, and Transportation; and Energy and Commerce. All of the authorizing committees have authority over important parts of the government, but not all committees are created equal.

Authorizing Legislation: Exerting Control over Government Policy

The role of most authorizing legislation is to determine the policies of the U.S. government. Agencies are directed in law to carry out certain programs, abide by certain restrictions, and achieve certain objectives.

In simple terms, what Congress does as a board of directors in authorizing legislation is to codify its thinking as to what the government should do. The staffs and members of these committees are charged with thinking through national policy on controlling immigration, managing fisheries, regulating banks, defending the nation, and so forth. They put together bills designed to carry out their thinking. The members and their staffs are responsible for attempting to shepherd those bills through the legislative process with the aim of delivering a product to the president's desk that he will agree to sign. The realities of legislative politics dictate, however, that the architects of the bills will nearly always have to accept changes and negotiate compromises along the way. Skillful legislators realize, as the saying goes, that "the perfect should not be the enemy of the good." In other words, it is impossible in the legislative process to achieve the ideal, but a good solution is better than no solution at all. Box 4.2 takes a glimpse at the work of committees, and especially the staff, as they research the issues of the day with an eye to creating legislation to direct the work of government agencies.

BOX 4.2
THE INNER WORKINGS OF CONGRESSIONAL COMMITTEES

The serious lawmaking work in the U.S. Congress is usually done by committees and subcommittees. Committees are run by a chairman or chairwoman (or, generically, chair) from the majority party. That person controls the bulk of a committee's resources (in the 111th Congress, it was about two-thirds in the House and three-fifths in the Senate) and sets the committee's agenda. The ranking minority party member controls the remainder of the resources.

These resources enable committee chairs and the ranking members to hire expert staff in their area of jurisdiction. Depending on the committee and the scope and importance of its jurisdiction, the total number of staff ranges from thirty all the way to one hundred or more. (Of course, the chairs can afford to hire many more than the ranking members.) Expert staff on congressional committees go by all sorts of different titles, including *clerk, counsel, staff lead, staff director*, and, most commonly, *professional staff member*.

Professional staff come from a lot of different places. Some have worked on Capitol Hill their entire careers and developed subject matter expertise in a personal office covering issues for a particular member. Some come from academic specialties that relate to particular policy jurisdictions. Others come from the executive branch agencies. Many professional staffers on the Armed Services Committees in the House and Senate are retired military officers.

Although nearly all staff members are hired for their expertise, generally they have ties to one party or the other, and they are certainly expected to be loyal to the chair or ranking member. After all, they can be fired with no notice for insubordination, incompetence, or almost any other reason. They work at the direction and pleasure of the chair or ranking member who hired them.

What do the staff do on a daily basis? That depends. Often they are researching issues of interest to the members of the committee and especially the chair or ranking member or subcommittee chairs or ranking members. They may be working on constructing legislative solutions to new problems, or they may have been asked to put together a bill to update an authorization for an agency and its programs.

Much more than research, however, goes into moving forward on legislation. That process involves constant communication with interested parties among the

The Authorization-Appropriation Connection

For the most part, authorizing bills do not enable agencies to get money from the Treasury to carry out the programs set forth in legislation. It is subsequent appropriations bills that plug money into agency accounts so that they are able to do what is required in authorizing statutes.

---

public as well as executive branch officials. As bills are being prepared, the chair will hold hearings to have key people of interest (from interest groups, agencies, academe) testify in public and take questions on the issues involved. The idea is get certain statements about the issues on the public record that will help the committee as it puts together the bill and moves it through the legislative process. The task of setting up hearings is given to the staff, who find and interview potential witnesses, prepare the members, and craft questions for them to ask.

When a bill has been developed to the chair's liking, it is marked up at the subcommittee and full committee level. The subcommittee stage may be skipped, but for many major bills this is an important part of the process. Subcommittees, which are made up of a subset of the members of the committee, focus on specific areas of the full committee's jurisdiction. House members generally have more time to get into issues at the subcommittee level of specialization than senators do. As a result, the subcommittee stage is more commonly skipped in Senate authorizing committees.

A *markup* is an open meeting of the subcommittee or committee during which the members go through the bill, sometimes line by line. At this stage, the bill is often called the *chairman's mark*—the version crafted by the chair. All members have an opportunity to offer amendments to the chairman's mark, to make any necessary amendments. Ultimately, the bill is voted on and moved along, as amended, to the next stage of the process.

For example, the Armed Services Committees in the House and Senate each begin work on reauthorizing the activities of the Defense Department early each year. They divide this massive undertaking among the committee's six subcommittees. (The House Armed Services Committee has a seventh subcommittee that focuses mostly on oversight.) After holding hearings during the winter—most at the subcommittee level—the subcommittees mark up their portion of the bill in late winter or early spring. At that point, the full Armed Services Committees take up the whole Defense authorization bill and conduct a markup session that can last the better part of a day or sometimes even longer. In a typical year, the bill is reported out of committee after receiving majority support among the committee's membership at a markup. This is called a *favorable report*. Bills that do not receive committee support rarely go any further in the legislative process.

In Congress, *thinking*, in effect, is separated from *spending*.[4] Most members and staff serve on committees that are charged with thinking through what the government does, or should do, in a particular policy domain; others—the Appropriations Committees' members and staff—determine how much money will be available for those aims based on current priorities and the constraints of the overall budget.

From almost the beginning of the republic, Congress has seen merit in the idea of dealing with authorizing and funding in separate bills. This is reflected in the rules of both chambers. There are a few reasons for this separation.

First, merit has been found in the argument that it makes sense to think through what government *should* do before making a decision on what government can *afford* to do. In fact, the nature of many authorizing bills makes it impossible to consider budgetary constraints with any precision. Some authorizing bills are major undertakings, establishing and altering policies in huge government departments. These bills may cover several years, laying out a roadmap for what the government should do, for instance, in higher education, transportation, space exploration, or energy. In effect, for much of the federal government, Congress lays out a plan with projected spending needs but with no idea whether the objectives can be fully funded. The Appropriations Committees follow up every year by looking at budgetary constraints, considering new priorities and unforeseen exigencies, and finally making funding decisions based on these and other criteria. The division of labor makes sense: Make a plan for what Congress would *like* to see done, then follow up by deciding on an annual basis what it is that *can* be done.

Allen Schick, a leading expert on the federal budget process, notes two other reasons Congress decided on this division of labor.[5] If authorizing issues were linked with funding decisions in the same bill, extended debates and intractable disagreements over policy questions would "impede the flow of funds to federal agencies."[6] Or, at the other extreme, Congress might hastily pass unwise policy in its eagerness to make sure that essential government activities were funded and a potential government shutdown was avoided. In short, as a practical matter, the overriding importance of keeping agencies running makes it important to decouple policy decisions from funding decisions. In reality, appropriations bills rarely get passed on time anyway. One of the key reasons is that policy issues have intentionally been injected into (and in fact are very difficult at times to separate from) the appropriations process.

What Authorizing Bills Do
The typical authorizing bill may accomplish one or more of the following:

1. Establish an agency or program
2. Establish or change substantive aspects of a government program and give direction to agency officials
3. Authorize agency funding levels
4. Reorganize an agency or department

Establish an Agency or Program—Authorizing bills are the board of directors' means of establishing programs or creating new agencies to perform certain government functions. In certain periods of our history, Congress has set up myriad programs and agencies to address pressing problems. In the 1930s, Congress, with President Franklin Roosevelt's prodding, established an "alphabet soup" of new agencies to address the immediate needs of the citizenry during the Great Depression as well as to arrest the downward spiral of the economy. The National Recovery Administration (NRA), the Public Works Administration (PWA), the Civilian Conservation Corps (CCC), the Federal Deposit Insurance Corporation (FDIC), the Works Progress Administration (WPA), and many others were created for those purposes.

The years 1964 to 1971 saw another spate of activity inspired initially by President Lyndon Johnson's Great Society agenda. Medicare, Medicaid, the National Endowment for the Arts (NEA), the National Endowment for the Humanities (NEH), and many other agencies and programs were established in 1965. In 1970 the Environmental Protection Agency (EPA) was established on the basis of a proposal by President Richard Nixon that was approved by Congress.

The year 2002 saw the establishment in law of a major new government department. The Department of Homeland Security (DHS) consolidated several existing government agencies to the end of protecting the nation against terrorist attacks. Exhibit 4.1 shows the operative section of the Homeland Security Act, the law passed that year that established the new department.

New government programs that logically would be administered by existing government departments can be created by authorizing legislation as well. The Higher Education Act (HEA), passed by Congress and signed into law by President Johnson in 1965, made the federal government a major player in university and college life in the United States for the first time. It established numerous programs to support certain colleges and universities, and especially individuals who were struggling to be able to afford postsecondary schooling. For the first fifteen years of its existence, HEA programs were administered by the Department of Health, Education, and Welfare (HEW).[7]

EXHIBIT 4.1
CONGRESS ESTABLISHES A NEW
GOVERNMENT DEPARTMENT

Title I—Department of Homeland Security

Sec. 101. Executive Department; Mission

(a) ESTABLISHMENT—There is established a Department of Homeland Security, as an executive department of the United States within the meaning of title 5, United States Code.

(b) MISSION—

(1) IN GENERAL—The primary mission of the Department is to—

(A) prevent terrorist attacks within the United States;

(B) reduce the vulnerability of the United States to terrorism;

(C) minimize the damage, and assist in the recovery, from terrorist attacks that do occur within the United States;

(D) carry out all functions of entities transferred to the Department, including by acting as a focal point regarding natural and manmade crises and emergency planning;

(E) ensure that the functions of the agencies and subdivisions within the Department that are not related directly to securing the homeland are not diminished or neglected except by a specific explicit Act of Congress; and

(F) ensure that the overall economic security of the United States is not diminished by efforts, activities, and programs aimed at securing the homeland.

Source: Homeland Security Act of 2002.

Congress has the power to establish in law a new department or agency of government. In the Homeland Security Act of 2002, Congress brought together several agencies under the new department with the aim of improving the government's ability to prevent terrorist attacks and otherwise protect the homeland.

Establish or Change Substantive Aspects of a Government Program and Give Direction to Agency Officials—Authorizing bills get right to the heart of what the federal government does, setting forth policies that agencies are bound by. The Congress, in its role as the board of directors, may give almost any sort of direction it likes.

Working on an authorizing bill gives Congress the opportunity to reconsider and tinker with existing government programs or establish new ones. The No Child Left Behind Act has been the commonly used name for the extension of the Elementary and Secondary Education Act (ESEA) of 2002, originally passed in 1965. ESEA, like HEA, was authorized for five years. Congress typically revisits major sets of programs like these at about the time the authorization expires.

President George W. Bush saw an opportunity to put his imprint on the federal role at the elementary and secondary levels. The legislation, which was supported by large bipartisan majorities in the House and Senate, added some new programs and instituted new requirements for testing at the state and local levels. Among other things, it instituted the Reading First Program, which provides state-of-the-art reading instruction to needy children in the early grades, and the Charter Schools Program, a competitive grants program designed to provide more school choice for parents. It also recommended increased funding for some existing programs.[8]

Other authorizing bills specify projects that the agency leadership must undertake, often providing explicit instructions. The Water Resources Development Act of 2007 outlines in great detail the navigation, dam, and flood control projects that need to be tackled by the secretary of the Army. A few of the hundreds of projects in the bill are shown in Exhibit 4.2.

Instructions for agencies in authorizing bills vary a great deal and can cover just about anything. Normally they dictate the objectives of a government program, but they may also require the agency to contact Congress on certain matters, to promote and advertise certain programs, to interact with other agencies that have overlapping concerns, and everything in between. The board of directors is in a position to dictate as much or as little as it wishes to federal agencies.

But the fact is that the federal government is involved in such an incredible range of activities, many of which are highly technical, that Congress almost always leaves a great deal to the discretion of agency officials. There is simply too much to keep track of in some areas of government. In effect, Congress frequently delegates authority to executive branch officials. Much like a corporate board of directors, members of Congress commonly defer to the experts in the field—the agency officials who were hired because of their knowledge in a particular area. Of course, Congress, again like a corporate board, retains the ultimate authority to overrule the actions of agency officials by changing the law.

The National Institutes of Health (NIH), an agency within the Department of Health and Human Services, provides a good example of congressional delegation to the experts. The institutes are set up for scientific research on a wide range of health issues, often conducted through grants to scientists at universities or labs. The agency has persuaded Congress to minimize its meddling by arguing that sci-

EXHIBIT 4.2
PROJECT AUTHORIZATIONS FOR THE ARMY CORPS OF ENGINEERS

SEC. 3005. SITKA, ALASKA

The Sitka, Alaska, element of the project for navigation, Southeast Alaska Harbors of Refuge, Alaska, authorized by section 101(1) of the Water Resources Development Act of 1992 (106 Stat. 4801), is modified to direct the Secretary to take such action as is necessary to correct design deficiencies in the Sitka Harbor Breakwater at Federal expense. The estimated cost is $6,300,000.

SEC. 3006. TATITLEK, ALASKA

The maximum amount of Federal funds that may be expended for the project for navigation, Tatitlek, Alaska, being carried out under section 107 of the River and Harbor Act of 1960 (33 U.S.C. 577), shall be $10,000,000.

SEC. 3007. RIO DE FLAG, FLAGSTAFF, ARIZONA

The project for flood damage reduction, Rio De Flag, Flagstaff, Arizona, authorized by section 101(b)(3) of the Water Resources Development Act of 2000 (114 Stat. 2576), is modified to authorize the Secretary to construct the project at a total cost of $54,100,000, with an estimated Federal cost of $35,000,000 and a non-Federal cost of $19,100,000.

SEC. 3008. NOGALES WASH AND TRIBUTARIES FLOOD CONTROL PROJECT, ARIZONA

The project for flood control, Nogales Wash and tributaries, Arizona, authorized by section 101(a)(4) of the Water Resources Development Act of 1990 (104 Stat. 4606) and modified by section 303 of the Water Resources Development Act of 1996 (110 Stat. 3711) and section 302 of the Water Resources Development Act of 2000 (114 Stat. 2600), is modified to authorize the Secretary to construct the project at a total cost of $25,410,000, with an estimated Federal cost of $22,930,000 and an estimated non-Federal cost of $2,480,000.

SEC. 3009. TUCSON DRAINAGE AREA, ARIZONA

The project for flood damage reduction, environmental restoration, and recreation, Tucson drainage area, Arizona, authorized by section 101(a)(5) of the Water Resources Development Act of 1999 (113 Stat. 274), is modified to authorize the Secretary to construct the project at a total cost of $66,700,000, with an estimated Federal cost of $43,350,000 and an estimated non-Federal cost of $23,350,000.

SEC. 3010. OSCEOLA HARBOR, ARKANSAS

(a) In General—The project for navigation, Osceola Harbor, Arkansas, constructed under section 107 of the River and Harbor Act of 1960 (33 U.S.C. 577), is modified to allow non-Federal interests to construct a mooring facility within the existing authorized harbor channel, subject to all necessary permits, certifications, and other requirements.

(b) Limitation on Statutory Construction—Nothing in this section shall be construed as affecting the responsibility of the Secretary to maintain the general navigation features of the project at a bottom width of 250 feet.

Source: Water Resources Development Act of 2007.

In authorizing law, Congress may require specific agency actions, such as the various projects shown here from the Water Resources Development Act of 2007. In this way, Congress leaves no doubt what the agency—in this case, the Army Corps of Engineers—must do.

entific grant decisions should be made strictly on the merits without regard to any political considerations. Even so, agency officials are wise to be wary of awarding grants to controversial entities or for controversial purposes, since members of Congress are well within their rights to restrict the agency's discretion in future legislation.[9]

Authorize Agency Funding Levels—As we have seen, authorizing bills set policy for federal agencies. But they often do another crucial thing: They authorize funding levels for government programs.

Most authorizing bills have an *authorization of appropriations* section. The time frame of an authorization of appropriations may vary widely. Defense Department authorizations cover only one year. Others, such as the authorization for the wide range of programs covered in the Higher Education Act or the Elementary and Secondary Education Act, cover five years. For an example of an authorization of appropriations that was part of a larger reauthorization of the National Aeronautic and Space Administration (NASA), see Exhibit 4.3. This authorization of appropriations covered two years. (When an agency authorization or a set of programs like HEA are said to "expire," that usually means that the authorization of appropriations has reached the end of its time.)

Authorized funding levels do not, however, give an agency the authority to spend the money; rather, the authorization merely reflects the considered view of the policymakers on the relevant committee and the larger Congress about the funding that ought to be provided for a program or an agency. It is more like a hunting license. The license itself does not get a sportsman any game; he has to go find it and kill it. For government programs, the hunting grounds are the Appropriations Committees, and appropriations bills provide the actual game (the money).

Typically the authorization levels in the first year (or the only year in the case of Defense bills) are met or nearly met in appropriations bills because the appropriations decision is made so soon after the authorization decision is made. Similar political circumstances pertain: An overwhelming floor vote for an authorizing bill that contains a particular funding ceiling in the spring or summer will usually be supported by adequate funding later in the year when the appropriations bill is voted on. But when the authorization of appropriations covers multiple years, what the authorizing committee envisions for later years may well not jibe with future political and budgetary realities, many of which cannot be anticipated.

This has been the case for ESEA programs in this decade. As can be seen in Table 4.1, as time passes since the original No Child Left Behind legislation was passed in 2002, the disparity between the authorized funding levels and the actual funding

EXHIBIT 4.3
AUTHORIZATION OF APPROPRIATIONS FOR NASA

Title II—Authorization of Appropriations

SEC. 201. STRUCTURE OF BUDGET ACCOUNTS

Section 313 of the National Aeronautics and Space Act of 1958 (42 U.S.C. 2459f) is amended—

(1) by amending subsection (a) to read as follows:

"(a)(1) Appropriations for the Administration for fiscal year 2007 and thereafter shall be made in three accounts, 'Science, Aeronautics, and Education,' 'Exploration Systems and Space Operations,' and an account for amounts appropriated for the necessary expenses of the Office of the Inspector General.

"(2) Within the Exploration Systems and Space Operations account, no more than 10 percent of the funds for a fiscal year for Exploration Systems may be reprogrammed for Space Operations, and no more than 10 percent of the funds for a fiscal year for Space Operations may be reprogrammed for Exploration Systems. This paragraph shall not apply to reprogramming for the purposes described in subsection (b)(2).

"(3) Appropriations shall remain available for two fiscal years, unless otherwise specified in law. Each account shall include the planned full costs of Administration activities"; and

(2) in subsection (b)—

(A) by inserting "(1)" before "To ensure"; and

(B) by adding at the end the following new paragraph:

"(2) The Administration may also transfer amounts among accounts for the immediate costs of recovering from damage caused by a major disaster (as defined in section 102 of the Robert T. Stafford Disaster Relief and Emergency Assistance Act [42 U.S.C. 5122]) or by an act of terrorism, or for the immediate costs associated with an emergency rescue of astronauts."

SEC. 202. FISCAL YEAR 2007

There are authorized to be appropriated to NASA for fiscal year 2007 $17,932,000,000, as follows:

(1) For Science, Aeronautics, and Education (including amounts for construction of facilities), $7,136,800,000, of which $962,000,000 shall be for Aeronautics.

(2) For Exploration Systems and Space Operations (including amounts for construction of facilities), $10,761,700,000, of which $6,618,600,000 shall be for Space Operations.

(3) For the Office of Inspector General, $33,500,000.

SEC. 203. FISCAL YEAR 2008

There are authorized to be appropriated to NASA for fiscal year 2008 $18,686,300,000 as follows:

(1) For Science, Aeronautics, and Education (including amounts for construction of facilities), $7,747,800,000, of which $990,000,000 shall be for Aeronautics.

(2) For Exploration Systems and Space Operations (including amounts for construction of facilities), $10,903,900,000, of which $6,546,600,000 shall be for Space Operations.

(3) For the Office of Inspector General, $34,600,000.

Source: Reauthorization of the National Aeronautics and Space Administration, 2005.

Most authorizing legislation provides a spending ceiling for the agency in question in the "authorization of appropriations" section of the bill. In this case, NASA was reauthorized for fiscal years 2007 and 2008. This reauthorization did not give the agency money—that came in subsequent annual appropriations law that could not exceed the ceiling in the authorizing bill.

TABLE 4.1   *Appropriations for Elementary and Secondary School Programs Fail to Keep Pace with No Child Left Behind Targets (in millions of dollars)*

FISCAL YEAR	AUTHORIZATION LEVEL	APPROPRIATED FUND	APPROPRIATION AS A PERCENTAGE OF AUTHORIZATION
2003	$18,650	$13,901	75%
2004	21,450	14,435	67
2005	23,750	14,631	62
2006	26,300	14,331	54
2007	28,875	14,358	50

It is not unusual for annual appropriations to fail to match the multiyear spending ceiling in authorizing laws, as shown here for federal elementary and secondary education levels.

Source: *Congressional Research Service.*

provided in the appropriations bill each year for the Education Department to implement the programs becomes greater. Funding levels have increased for the programs, but the generous funding increases envisioned in 2002 for the next several years were by and large unrealized.

It should be noted that authorizations of appropriations frequently expire before Congress can put together and pass into law a comprehensive reauthorization of a program, a set of programs, or an agency. In most cases, Congress still appropriates funds for the programs with the expired authorization of appropriations. Technically this practice violates rules of both chambers of Congress, but the programs may be essential, popular, or both. To members of Congress, the only alternative is to figure out a way to waive the rules against unauthorized appropriations and include funding in the appropriations bills.

Table 4.2 documents the continued funding provided for the Pell Grant Program—which provides aid to needy college students who meet certain criteria—in the HEA after its authorization of appropriations expired. The 1998 HEA authorized funding only through 2003, but the popularity of the program compelled Congress to provide funding in fiscal years 2004 to 2007 until a reauthorization could be completed with new spending targets.

When Congress chooses to fund programs whose authorizations of appropriations have expired, in most cases the substantive policy guidelines for the conduct of those programs as set forth in the authorizing bill are still in effect. In other words, although a program's authorization of appropriations expires, the policy provisions

TABLE 4.2   *Funding for Pell Grants Continues After the Authorization for Appropriations Expires*

FISCAL YEAR	AUTHORIZED MAXIMUM GRANT*	APPROPRIATED MAXIMUM GRANT
1999	$4,500	$3,125
2000	4,800	3,300
2001	5,100	3,750
2002	5,400	4,000
2003	5,800	4,050
2004	—	4,050
2005	—	4,050
2006	—	4,050
2007	—	4,310

* No authorization for appropriations in 2004 through 2007.

The Higher Education Act was reauthorized in 1998, covering fiscal years 1999 to 2003. Congress failed to complete a new reauthorization until 2008. Popular programs such as the Pell Grant Program were funded in yearly appropriations laws even though no authorization for appropriation was in place. The maximum grant award was even increased in 2007. It is a common practice for Congress to continue to fund programs when the authorization for funding has lapsed.

Source: *Congressional Research Service.*

for it usually do not. What happens is that Congress intends to reconsider and update the old legislation—both the substantive provisions and the funding levels—but the members get bogged down by controversies and disagreements about what direction to go with the programs. They fail to pass the legislation on time but want to keep the funding stream going. At the end of the chapter, we look at some of the ramifications of this failure.

Reorganize an Agency or Department—Taking its power to the extreme, Congress may pass authorizing legislation that radically alters the roles and relationships of existing government agencies. As the board of directors, the Congress can restructure and refocus the government in any way it sees fit.

The defense policy expert Charles Cushman calls the reorganizing power Congress's "nuclear weapon."[10] If the members think that agencies are not addressing important matters, they can blow them up and start again from scratch, reshuffling chains of command, creating new entities, and moving authority and power from one position or agency to another. Congress's power to do this stems from the *necessary and proper clause* in Article I, Section 8, of the Constitution. The Congressional Research Service summarizes the authority this clause gives the Congress:

> [Congress] has the power to organize the executive branch. Congress has the authority to create, abolish, reorganize, and fund federal departments. . . . It has the power to assign or reassign functions to departments and agencies, and grant new forms of authority and staff [to executive officials] . . . [and] exercises ultimate authority over executive branch organization and . . . policy.[11]

The most ambitious example of the use of this power was the restructuring of the defense establishment in 1947. Before that, the War Department, consisting of the Army and the Army Air Force, had been completely separate from the Navy and the Marines. The new configuration consolidated all the services (the Air Force was separated from the Army) under the Defense Department. The various rivalries and turf battles among the services made for an awesome bureaucratic task for the department's civilian and military leadership. Most experts believe that major problems in achieving anything resembling a cohesive whole remained until 1986, when new legislation streamlined the chains of command, bridging the service rivalries in a reasonably effective way. It took nearly forty years to make substantial progress in reorganizing the essential government national security function.

A true work in progress is the Department of Homeland Security, created by Congress in 2002 as a response to the September 11, 2001, attacks. It consists of twenty-two federal agencies with a wide range of rather disparate missions, from the Coast Guard to Immigration and Customs Enforcement (ICE) to the Secret Service to the Transportation Safety Administration (TSA). (At least all the major components of the Department of Defense had the same objective: defending the nation and killing adversaries in time of war.[12])

Many observers are not sanguine about the prospects of DHS becoming anything resembling a unified and smoothly functioning whole in the near term given the various potentially incompatible corporate cultures that have been forced together to create a new department. With both Defense and Homeland Security, legislation made wholesale changes in roles and relationships, creating a larger department to focus on a particular objective.

Case Study: Congress Restructures the Intelligence Community

The events of September 11, 2001, were to have yet another major impact on the way the U.S. government does business. As news emerged of lapses within the intelligence agencies leading up to the attacks, Congress created a bipartisan commission, headed by Lee Hamilton, former Democratic congressman from Indiana, and Thomas Kean, former Republican governor of New Jersey, to investigate and make recommendations.

The National Commission on Terrorist Attacks upon the United States—the so-called 9/11 Commission—released its findings in July 2004. Central to these findings was a recommendation to reorganize the way the government collects and analyzes foreign intelligence, a task that had been undertaken by sixteen agencies across the government.[13]

Specifically the 9/11 Commission recommended creating a new position to oversee and direct intelligence activities. Previously the director of the Central Intelligence Agency (DCI), who was responsible for setting intelligence-gathering priorities for the government and bringing together intelligence information for the president, had been what amounted to the head of intelligence. The problem was that most intelligence activities were not housed in the Central Intelligence Agency (CIA), an independent agency, but rather were in the Defense Department.

The Defense Department's intelligence-gathering activities are extensive, constituting about 85 percent of all spending on intelligence. Three agencies within the Department—the National Reconnaissance Office (NRO), the National Security Agency (NSA), and the National Geospatial-Intelligence Agency (NGA)—are involved in gathering information through satellites and communications systems. In addition, the department has extensive intelligence-gathering and -analyzing capabilities that support specific military activities. The CIA is involved only in the gathering and analysis of human intelligence.

The problem was that the DCI would invariably get frustrated in his efforts to direct the actions of Defense Department intelligence agencies. In fact, the CIA director's statutory authorities were vague vis-à-vis Defense agencies.[14] The DCI would end up choosing to focus more of his efforts at the CIA. The bottom line: No one in government had the ability or authority effectively to coordinate and carry out a comprehensive intelligence plan.

A lot of ideas about how to address this problem had been percolating on Capitol Hill, particularly since the attacks. The 9/11 Commission report proved a tremendous catalyst. The commission members fanned out over Congress and, with the help of a group of people who had lost loved ones in the attacks, lobbied the rank-and-file membership hard. In December 2004, the Congress passed and sent to President Bush a bill that he was prepared to sign: the Intelligence Reform and Terrorism Prevention Act, which restructured the community. It passed both chambers with massive bipartisan majorities, in the House 336–75 and in the Senate 89–2.[15]

For the second time in just over two years, Congress had used, in Cushman's term, the nuclear bomb. It created a fully new entity, the Office of the Director of National Intelligence (ODNI), which would be separate from any of the clandestine service agencies. Its job would be to direct all foreign and domestic intelligence operations. Within it would be the National Counterterrorism Center, an agency created by executive order and given the task of supporting ODNI on intelligence coordination.

The person named as director (the DNI) would take over from the CIA director the responsibility of directing the entire intelligence community and would report directly to the president. Unlike the situation that had pertained for the DCI when he headed the larger community, the DNI would have enhanced statutory authority over all the intelligence agencies, including those in the Defense Department.

Most importantly, the Intelligence Reform Act gave the DNI authority over intelligence budgets across the government that the DCI had not had. The DNI is now in a position to exert control over the funds going to all the intelligence agencies in government. (There is one major exception: The agencies involved in providing tactical intelligence for military operations are largely free of the DNI's control.) The DNI also is required by law to set intelligence priorities for the government. The bill says that the DNI shall "manage and direct the tasking of, collection, analysis, production, and dissemination of national intelligence by approving requirements and resolving conflicts."

Whether the DNI can really exert the sort of influence and control envisioned in the law remains to be seen. Government intelligence agencies do a wide range of tasks, and some of the government's intelligence agencies now have multiple masters. Furthermore, the processes set forth in the legislation to give the DNI the power to coordinate intelligence are untested.[16]

One major question involves the three major intelligence-gathering agencies in the Defense Department—the National Reconnaissance Office, the National Security Agency, and the National Geospatial-Intelligence Agency. Many members of Congress wanted to see these agencies remain at least partly under the control of the Defense Department. They made sure to include language in the bill that prohibits the DNI from abrogating existing Defense Department authorities.

The lesson is that even radical legislation like the Intelligence Reform Act is not immune to the congressional tendency to split the difference in order to get a final product. The main thrust of the intelligence bill was to create a workable system of coordination and control over government intelligence activity, but there were people in powerful places on Capitol Hill who believed that some aspects of the status quo should be retained.[17] In the end product, not all of the lines of authority are crystal clear; much depends on the character of the DNI and the secretary of Defense. The president is, of course, the ultimate arbiter.

Another question is how much influence the DNI can have over the proud and insular CIA, an agency with a long history and proven track record in bureaucratic trench warfare.

Nevertheless, the point is that Congress responded to a devastating attack on American soil by reorganizing government functions. In 2002 the board of directors created the Department of Homeland Security in an effort to coordinate a great variety of government activities ranging from border protection to transportation safety to first responders to controlling counterfeiting. Then, two years later, the board restructured the intelligence community. Broad and extensive authorizing statutes were put together and passed with surprising speed, proving that Congress, even in an era of partisan bickering and stalemate on many matters, is capable of carrying out the most far-reaching of its powers. Whether the restructuring will prove both lasting and effective remains to be seen.

Authorizing Direct Spending

Although Congress normally exercises its authorizing power separately from its funding power, there is a major exception to the general rule. Authorizing bills may be written so that they do more than merely authorize programs and subsequent appropriations; they can do double duty by giving an agency, in effect, direct access to the U.S. Treasury.

Direct spending legislation is an authorizing bill that both sets up a program (establishing policies and so forth) and mandates funding without the need for a separate appropriation. Government programs set up in this manner are generically called *mandatory programs* and sometimes *entitlements*. Well-known examples include Medicare programs that provide health care for the elderly and the Department of Agriculture's food stamp program that gives vouchers to the needy for the purchase of groceries.

Unlike programs that arrange to build and buy things (say, a spy plane or a bridge), or clean up a river, or pay civil servants to monitor the nation's borders, a typical mandatory program, such as Medicare and food stamps, sends money directly to individuals or in support of services that benefit those individuals. It should be noted that funding for most programs that provide financial support to individuals—like the Pell Grant Program—cannot be delivered without two legislative decisions, an authorization and an appropriation. Mandatory programs that bypass the appropriation step are the exception—but a few of them are very, very big exceptions.

To get a sense of what Congress is thinking when it sets up a mandatory program, consider the following scenario in which the process of creating a program in the normal two-step way is compared with the direct spending approach.

Addressing Poverty Among the Elderly as a Two-Step Process

Let's imagine that the Congress decides that it needs to write a law to establish an agency and a program to address the problem of rampant poverty among the elderly.

In the normal two-step process, congressional committees would write, and then pass, an authorizing bill that sets forth the objectives and policies of the agency. We can imagine that the agency would be instructed to administer a program to provide financial support, probably at varying levels, to people who meet certain qualifications. This bill would have within it an authorization of appropriations section setting a funding ceiling (probably with a ceiling increase each year) for, say, each of the next five years. Funding for the programs would not be assured but instead would be dependent on subsequent annual action on an appropriations bill. That appropriations bill would determine how much of the authorized funding level is plugged into the agency's accounts for these programs. Full funding might not be forthcoming some years, depending on economic conditions and other national priorities.

Addressing Poverty Among the Elderly with Direct Spending

Alternatively, Congress might structure the legislation to *mandate* a payment to people who qualify based on certain criteria. Instead of leaving the support of the elderly up to the annual discretion of the Appropriations Committees, Congress might deem widespread poverty among the aged as too important a problem to leave to chance. To make the program politically irresistible, members could write legislation to guarantee a monthly check from the government for *any elderly person*, rich or poor, who meets a set of basic criteria—an age threshold, a documentable history of regular employment, and so on.

The level of the payment to each individual would be set in the authorizing statute. Anyone meeting the criteria would be entitled, in law, to receive a payment from the government. He or she would get that money indefinitely, or until Congress chose to rewrite the authorizing statute.

The key differences between direct spending and the normal two-step funding process are that *the precise payment level is set in the authorizing law*—there is no role for the Appropriations Committees to step in and fund below the recommended level—and *the total amount spent on the program is not actually controlled by anyone.* That total is entirely dependent on how many people reach the right age and meet the other criteria. In effect, the authorizing bill would do an end run around appropriators, who write the laws that control the funding for most programs.

———————

Of course, a real-world entitlement, Old Age and Survivors Insurance, administered by the Social Security Administration (SSA), resembles the program in the second scenario. It is the largest single program established and funded in an authorizing statute. The authorizing language puts no end time on the program: Qualifying citizens can continue to collect benefits from the Treasury indefinitely or until Congress acts to end or alter the program.

In the earlier years of the program, the government's year-to-year financial liability was fairly stable and predictable. After all, demographers and statisticians can estimate pretty accurately how many people will qualify and how many will die off. But the program eventually took on a life of its own. First, politicians amended the original legislation that created the program to increase the payment levels, sometimes dramatically; eventually, in the early 1970s, the payments were tied to a cost-of-living index. In years with rampant inflation, overall spending on the program soared uncontrollably.

Medicare programs, administered by the Centers for Medicare and Medicaid Services (CMS), have also grown dramatically. First established in 1965, Medicare has been altered numerous times, most recently in 2003 with the addition of prescription drug coverage for senior citizens. Medicare programs provide medical care for those age sixty-five and older by paying hospitals and other health care providers for services rendered based on criteria set forth in law and in subsequent regulations outlined by the agency—sometimes by assisting seniors with premiums in private plans and also by providing prescription drug coverage. As with Social Security programs, the total money spent in a given year on Medicare is not set in appropriations legislation; instead, it is determined by the number of qualified beneficiaries who submit claims that must be paid out of the Treasury. Total spending may vary unpredictably, depending on inflation in the health care field and other factors.

Nonpermanent Direct Spending

Not all mandatory programs are like Social Security and Medicare programs, which are set to continue on a permanent basis unless altered in the future. Congress may establish a program that goes around the Appropriations Committees while still setting an end time to the program. For example, back in 1965, Congress passed the Food and Agricultural Act, more commonly known as the Farm Bill, which established a subsidy for certain types of commodity farmers. The act required reauthorization in five years or the program would expire. According to the law, government payments to farmers could vary in any given year, and sometimes by a great deal, depending on market conditions.

When the expiration of these programs looms as the five-year period nears an end, the Agriculture Committees go into overdrive to try to update the existing criteria based on new conditions and the policy ideas of the party in power, as well as those of the influential committee members. Farm groups representing the different commodities that receive support are in constant contact with key staffers and members of Congress, offering ideas for enhancing subsidies and improving the processing of payments.

Ideally, Congress accomplishes a comprehensive overhaul of the farm subsidy programs before the five years are up, establishing new and updated payment schedules for the next five-year period. As often as not, however, farming issues are controversial, and the committees are unable to shepherd a new farm bill through the legislative process in time. When that happens, the old criteria are temporarily extended by an act of Congress, usually for a period of a few months, to give Congress time to finish the new bill. It is unthinkable to allow these programs to expire, since that would wreak havoc on local economies across the country and impose debilitating unpredictability on the lives of farmers. The most recent farm bill, for instance, was signed into law in May 2008 and replaced the old bill that expired on September 30, 2007. Eight temporary extensions were passed by Congress between the expiration of the old bill and the enactment of the new one.

There is an important distinction to note here between the funding for the vast majority of government programs that require an appropriation separate from the authorization bill in order to get money from the Treasury and the mandatory programs that give agencies direct access to the Treasury to fund their programs. In the

---

BOX 4.3
A RARE OCCURRENCE: THE TERMINATION
OF AN ENTITLEMENT

Aid to Families with Dependent Children (AFDC) was a mandatory federal program established in 1935 in the Social Security Act. Its purpose was to create a grant program that would allow states to make welfare payments for needy children in one-parent families; in those days a significant portion of the payments went to single mothers whose husbands had died.

Originally states were able to define what constituted a "needy" family and set their own standards for payments. The federal government would reimburse one-third of the cost. By the 1960s, however, the federal government had expanded its role, taking on the program's entire cost and setting the relevant criteria for receiving payments.

By the 1980s, the program had become much more controversial. Instead of widows receiving the bulk of the payments, unwed and often never-wed single mothers were getting most of the money. Some critics alleged that the program was a disincentive to marriage, since intact two-parent families were not eligible for payments. By the 1990s, the cost of the program had skyrocketed to over $6 billion a year.

In 1995 the first Republican Congress in a generation began work on an overhaul of the program. With AFDC, anyone eligible to receive payments could receive them, and could receive them indefinitely as long as they qualified. In bad economic times, mandatory payments to needy families put an additional burden on the federal budget. The solution: Terminate AFDC and replace it with a discretionary program, Temporary Aid to Needy Families (TANF), which would be controlled annually in the appropriations process and which would have guidelines in law making people ineligible for aid after three years. President Clinton signed these changes into law in the summer of 1996, marking the first and only time a major mandatory program has been eliminated.

Source: See Ron Haskins, *Work over Welfare: The Inside Story of the 1996 Welfare Reform Law* (Washington, DC: Brookings Institution Press, 2006).

---

first instance, when the authorization of appropriations expires, the Appropriations Committees, in crafting their annual bills, may go ahead and provide the agencies with funding to keep their programs running. *Budget authority*—the ability to draw money from the Treasury to run a program—is provided to the agencies in that appropriations bill. With nonpermanent mandatory programs, the agency in effect loses its budget authority when the authorization statute expires. For that reason, that statute must be extended.

The bottom line is that mandatory programs are set up to ensure funding based on provisions set forth in authorizing legislation. The vast majority of federal programs are funded only if the Appropriations Committees annually provide for funding in their bills. Programs dependent on action by the Appropriations Committees are called *discretionary programs*. Members of Congress often try to turn discretionary programs subject to appropriations into mandatory programs in order to guarantee their funding. Rarely is there interest in Congress in taking a program in the other direction. In fact, only one major mandatory program has ever been converted into a discretionary program: Aid to Families with Dependent Children (AFDC) was converted into Temporary Assistance to Needy Families (TANF) in 1996 (see Box 4.3).

THE LEGISLATIVE PROCESS

Almost everyone at some point in their lives has been exposed to the "how a bill becomes a law" chart, whether in an American government textbook or on *School House Rock*. The legislative process in the U.S. Congress is a complex system that, if all the stages in the chart are strictly followed, takes about a dozen steps, occurring at different times, and involves different groups of representatives and senators.

Figure 4.1 shows how the process is typically depicted. Note that a bill may start either in the House or in the Senate. The one exception is revenue bills, which the Constitution stipulates must start in the House. It is also possible to have two similar or identical bills start at the same time in both chambers. A bill may make it through the process in one chamber and never receive consideration in the other. Of course, such a bill will never become law.

The process is cumbersome. Following the chart, a bill must first be examined and voted on by the relevant committees in both the House and Senate. (Often subcommittee consideration precedes the full committee stage, especially in the House.) A majority vote of the panel moves the bill along. At that point in the House, most major bills make a stop at the Rules Committee for a rule governing debate on the chamber's floor. Then a vote is taken involving all members on the rule for debate and on the substance of the bill. A floor vote is also required in the Senate on its version of the bill. Normally, with important legislation, the two chambers' versions differ, necessitating negotiations to bridge those differences. A conference committee comprising both a House and Senate contingent may be used to do this, although the conference committee members from each chamber vote separately on

FIGURE 4.1 *The Legislative Process*

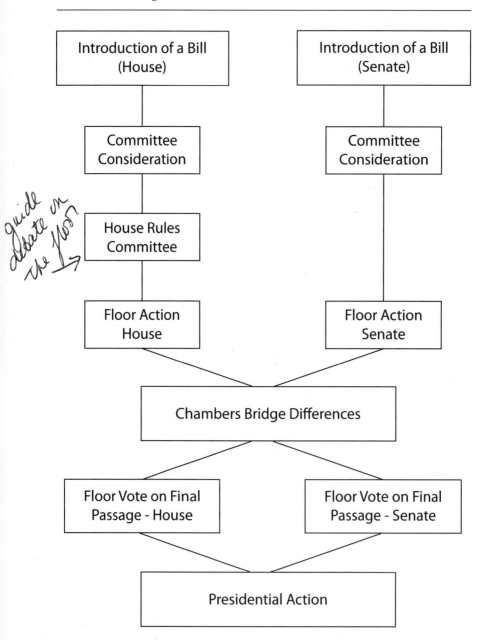

the bill. Finally the House and the Senate must vote on the final version of the bill, however it is arrived at. Another vote may still be required in each chamber if the president decides to veto the bill. A two-thirds vote, not a simple majority, is needed in each chamber to override a presidential veto.

One way to think about the process is to recognize that there are as many as a dozen points at which potential legislation may be killed. Not surprisingly, the legislative process is almost always lengthy and involves considerable negotiation and compromise at most or all of the stages.

To get a real sense of the process and how it actually works, however, it is crucially important to recognize that *almost every stage of the legislative process as it appears on the chart is optional.* In other words, bills do not have to follow the route in the chart. No law—and certainly not the Constitution—requires that the chambers go through all these steps. The steps were devised by members of the two bodies over the last 220 years or so as they settled on rules and precedents based on what they thought was a good way of developing public policy. The idea is that legislation should receive careful consideration by the expert members and staff on the subcommittees and committees, to be followed by a public debate on the floors of the two chambers on its merits. In a republic, the legislative process provides a method by which the elected representatives, coming at the issues from the different perspectives of the House and Senate, carefully and deliberately transform the people's relatively raw opinions and views into public policy that directs the work of the government agencies.

But the only part of the process that is absolutely required is that the House and Senate present to the president a bill that has passed both chambers in identical form. This requirement is based on the presentment clause of the Constitution, which is in Article I, Section 7: "Every Bill which shall have passed the House of Representatives and the Senate, shall, before it become a Law, be presented to the President of the United States."

In other words, only the last stage—the House and Senate voting on identical versions of the bill—must absolutely happen. A majority of both the House and Senate must agree to its passage on the floor—and that's it. All the actions of the authorizing committees and their subcommittees, the Rules Committee, and any conference committee are, in a sense, optional.

As a result, understanding the legislative process in a relevant way begins with *the Rule of 218 and 60.* This means that the legislative process always boils down to the vote on final passage of a bill in the two chambers. Although technically passage requires only the vote of a majority of the members present in both chambers, in the

Senate in this day and age, with the constant threat of a filibuster, 60 votes are almost always required to move significant legislation. In the House, 218 votes constitute a majority if all 435 members are present and voting. Everyone on the Hill knows that if they want to get anything into law, the Rule of 218 and 60 ultimately is the key.

The Legislative Process Resembles Baseball, Not Football

It is important to be familiar with the legislative process as depicted in the chart, but it is not the best way to understand its essence. The Rule of 218 and 60 comes closer. A sports analogy is also helpful for grasping the essence of the legislative process in the modern U.S. Congress.

In a football game, if one team builds an early two-touchdown, fourteen-point lead, maintains that lead, and then extends it by scoring two more touchdowns in the fourth quarter while holding the other team scoreless the whole game, the game is for all intents and purposes over. The reserves come in for both teams, and the fans start heading for the exits. The idea is that at some point it becomes impossible for a team that's four touchdowns behind to catch up.

Baseball is different. No matter how far behind a team falls, it always has the ninth inning. Even with two outs in the ninth and a significant deficit, if a team keeps hitting it has a chance. It is better to be the team that is ahead, of course, whether by one, two, or ten runs, but the trailing team always has a chance.

The legislative process is like baseball, not like football.

Imagine that a member of the House wants to enact a law that will affect an agency's activities. That bill might amount only to a short paragraph that prevents the agency from doing something or that requires the agency to take a particular action, or it might be a full-fledged overhaul of a program or the establishment of a new program. The member's best strategy is to get the desired bill language incorporated into a larger bill on a similar topic that the committee of jurisdiction is working on. (Committees may not have the time to deal with each and every little idea in a piecemeal fashion.) If the regular order of the legislative process is followed, the member will work with the relevant committee to get the language added. If he or she succeeds in getting the language included at the committee stage and the committee approves the bill, the member is probably in good shape, since the committee members are likely to close ranks to protect their legislative product as the process goes along. But there is never any guarantee.

All the way to the very end, at any stage, that provision might be removed. Even toward the end of the game, when the two chambers negotiate to bridge their differences, it is possible to make significant changes to the legislation, even to the point of taking out provisions that were included in both chambers' versions of the bill. If that happens to our representative's favored provision, it will be like losing a baseball game in the bottom of the ninth. By the same token, even if the representative fails to get the language into the committee version and does not succeed in attaching it to the larger bill during floor votes, he or she could be extremely clever and get a colleague to insert the provision in the legislation as late as the conference committee stage (which is analogous to a dramatic, game-ending grand slam home run in the last of the ninth inning).

The bottom line here is that persistent and skilled members know how to exploit the process. Bill language, whether relatively minor and particular or much more substantial, can be attached to legislation that is moving at any stage. As the political scientist Barbara Sinclair has noted, the theoretical process almost seems like a relic of the past. Stages on the "how a bill becomes a law" chart are regularly skipped. Even committee consideration is sometimes circumvented, though traditionally it has been assumed that giving experts a chance to weigh in on legislation is essential. Sometimes one chamber or the other cannot find the time or the political will to take on something controversial at any stage and may, at the end, accept the other chamber's version in a floor vote.

Everyone on Capitol Hill now knows that the "how a bill becomes a law" chart has limited utility. It has been skirted so often that *unorthodox lawmaking*—Sinclair's term—is regarded by some as the norm.[18] It is useful to think of the process as a game in which 535 people are trying to direct the actions of government in law by manipulating procedures so that their favored provisions and legislation are somehow inserted in a larger bill in time for final passage.

It is important to stress, using the baseball analogy, that it is better to build an early lead—that is, to have one's bill language in as early as possible and ideally in both the House and Senate versions. Sometimes, however, that may be neither the best strategy nor even possible, so a representative or senator may have to rely on power hitting in the last of the ninth before the vote on final passage.

We now move to the legislative process in the two chambers. The best way to dive into the particulars of that process is a little counterintuitive. Instead of proceeding chronologically from start to finish, we begin with the way legislation is scheduled for consideration on the floor of the House and Senate. As we shall see, *the decision by party leadership whether to bring a bill to the floor conditions all of the earlier stages of the legislative process.*

Scheduling Legislation

Who determines which bills get a vote on the floor of the House and Senate? And what criteria are used to make that decision? Answering these two questions goes a long way toward gaining a sophisticated understanding of the legislative process in the U.S. Congress.

The answer to the first question is easy: The majority party leadership of the chamber in question determines which bills get to the floor. Specifically, in the House the speaker (Nancy Pelosi of California in the 111th Congress), who is the head of the majority party's leadership team, has the final say on the bills that come up for consideration on the floor. The speaker also has considerable say over the conditions under which bills will be considered. In the Senate, the gatekeeper is the majority leader (Harry Reid of Nevada in the 111th Congress), although the Senate majority leader has considerably less control over the conditions of debate and consideration than the speaker does in the House.

The implications of this authority are tremendously consequential. A great many bills—thousands every Congress—are introduced by the members. Hundreds receive varying levels of consideration at the subcommittee or committee level. But of the ones approved by the committees, it is only those that the leadership wishes to schedule for floor time that have a chance to become law. A great deal of time and effort is expended at earlier stages in the process on legislative proposals that will never see the light of day. All in all, the party leadership has no greater power than that of controlling access to the floor.

The answer to the second question is quite a bit more complicated. What are the criteria that influence the decision to bring bills to the floor?

It stands to reason that the majority party leadership will try to pursue an agenda that promotes the interests of their party. Specifically, they wish to pass laws that will impress the American people enough so that they will remain in power after the next electoral cycle. As strong partisans, the top leaders believe that what their party stands for is good for the country. Thus, the majority leadership has an agenda driven by a desire to do what is best for the country, based on their party's ideological perspective, as well as a desire to pursue this agenda in such a way that the party will be rewarded with two more years in power after the next election. Here is how the leadership attempts to do this, starting with the House.

Scheduling Legislation in the House

As we saw in Chapter 2, the House leadership comprises the speaker, the majority leader, the majority whip, and the caucus chair. (Republicans call this last position the conference chair.) This leadership team enlists the aid of rank-and-file members who are interested in contributing to the party's success. The speaker runs the entire operation, and he or she assigns to the rest of the team particular duties related to running the House and determining the legislative agenda.

First, the party needs to identify a legislative agenda. What issues do party members need to address? How should they address those issues? In what order should they take on these issues? How should these issues be marketed to the larger public and to influential groups? The last question is crucial: A good public relations operation is an important part of passing legislation and maintaining a legislative majority.

The speaker typically names the House majority leader (Steny Hoyer of Maryland in the 111th Congress) as the chief strategist in charge of putting together the agenda. The majority leader consults with a wide range of people and also speaks with the president, if he is of the same party, to see which direction he wants to go on the issues. The majority leader talks to pollsters hired by the party to see what is salient to the public, and why; consults with members of the party in the House to see what they are hearing about the intensity of feeling on certain issues back home in their districts; and keeps tabs on what is percolating up through the various committees.

Numerous meetings are held with other top leaders, key members of the party in the House, and influential people outside the House. Ultimately the speaker and the majority leader settle on an agenda that serves the party and the country in their view. This might mean, for example, scheduling energy independence legislation for floor consideration that week, a tax reform bill the following week, and the budget resolution shortly thereafter.

Lying in wait, however, are some pretty significant stumbling blocks to being able to follow through on the type of energy, tax, and budget bills they want. First, are the relevant committees acting on legislation that fits into the plan? Are bills ready and out of committee? What do they look like? Do they fit with what the leadership deems to be "good for the party and good for the country"?

It is primarily the job of the majority leader to deal with these problems. He is in constant communication with committee chairs and has formulated agenda ideas in a reciprocal process in which they tell him what they want to do and what they can pass out of committee, and he tells them what the leadership would like to see. Ultimately anything at odds with leadership goals is unlikely to be scheduled for floor consideration, and the committee chairs know this. If leadership is desperate to move on a particular area of policy and the relevant committee chair is not cooperating, the leadership may circumvent the committee process and put together a bill by other means. This is not always popular, and it is fairly rare, but it does happen. More often, the committees do what they can or want to do, and then leadership takes over, incorporating their ideas into a bill and making what are called *post-committee adjustments* before the bill is taken to the floor.

The second stumbling block is a purely practical consideration. Do the leaders have the votes to pass the bills on their agenda, in the form they want to pass them and when they want to pass them? The majority whip (James Clyburn of South Carolina in the 111th Congress) is in charge of gathering intelligence. He begins well ahead of the time when the leadership is contemplating having the vote by canvassing members to see whether they will vote for the bills coming up. He asks a variety of questions of the rank and file in the party. Are they firm supporters of this legislation? If not, are there changes they would like to see made? What would it take to change their minds, if anything? If they are undecided, will they hold off their vote to see whether it is needed for passage? The bottom line is that the whip needs to find out whether the majority has the votes—218 to be precise—to pass the legislation on its agenda. If so, they can get anything they want through the chamber. If not, they need to know whether they can change the minds of wavering members by making adjustments in the bill or other changes. The leadership team does have a great deal of leverage; after all, members' legislative goals can only be realized if the leadership schedules a vote on their bills. (Leadership also has considerable control over the committee assignment process.)

The process of establishing the legislative agenda of the House has undergone significant changes in recent decades owing to the increased assertiveness and power of party leadership. Several decades ago, House leadership essentially acted as glorified clerks: They processed legislation as it came from the committee chairs, who were in many respects the real powerhouses in the chamber.[19] Today the leadership in the House really leads. The change began in the 1970s, although the real quantum leap in party leaders' power and assertiveness came with the Republican takeover of the House in 1995. Speakers Newt Gingrich (1995–1998) and Dennis Hastert (1998–2007) asserted their prerogatives successfully, and their Democratic successor, Nancy Pelosi (2007–), has followed suit.

Today leadership in the House is prepared to ignore the process as spelled out in the "how a bill becomes a law" diagram if, in their view, the greater good of the party and the country is at stake. And they have the means to do it. The fact is that the process before floor consideration, especially at the committee and subcommittee stages, is conditioned and driven to a large extent by big-picture agenda concerns as developed by the majority party leadership.

Scheduling Legislation in the Senate

In the Senate, the majority leader has scheduling power, but his situation is much more difficult to manage than the speaker's. The Senate majority leader is limited by

Senate rules and precedents that require sixty votes for most controversial bills (and thus the majority party almost always needs some minority party cooperation to move forward on bills); by the need to move much Senate business by unanimous consent; and by the right each senator has to offer amendments on any bill.

Like his House counterpart, the Senate majority leader would like to move a legislative agenda that enshrines his party's principles in a way that will enhance its chances at maintaining power in the next election cycle. But to move an agenda, the majority leader almost always has to coordinate with the minority party leadership. All senators have the prerogative to hijack the floor for extended periods of time, and as a result, even minority party senators' concerns on almost any significant piece of legislation must be heard.

In the Senate, following any sort of regular procedure is sometimes not an option. Delicate negotiations between Democrats and Republicans are always going on, and all senators, *whether they serve on the committee of jurisdiction or not*, may weigh in on any particular issue. If acrimonious partisanship rules the day, as has sometimes been the case in recent years, virtually nothing can be accomplished. House members and staff sometimes call the Senate the "hospice for legislation"—the place where House-passed bills go to die. Imaginative use of the legislative process in the Senate is often necessary to pass controversial bills.

The point of the foregoing discussion is not to dismiss the early stages of the legislative process. Fortunately, since most of the policy expertise in Congress is with the committee staff, subcommittee and committee consideration of bills is still the norm. But there are many variations on a theme. Committee consideration in one or the other chamber may be short-circuited; bills are often altered in significant ways after committees have had their say; bills that struggle in one chamber or the other may find a place in legislation at the very end of the process (in a conference committee or during informal negotiations between the chambers); and both chambers are extremely imaginative in how they package legislative products for the floor and how they structure debate. All of this unorthodox lawmaking needs to be put in today's context: In this era of partisan politics, party leaders have taken a much more prominent role, especially in the House, in controlling floor access for the greater good of their party, and the committee chairs have had to accommodate the leadership in order to remain relevant. The legislative process is driven by the interests of the majority party, not by adherence to established rules of order.

Key Stages in the Legislative Process: The House

Introducing a Bill

Only members may introduce a bill in Congress, but as mentioned earlier, introducing a bill does not guarantee anything—not even consideration in a committee,
much less consideration on the floor of the chamber.[20] If a bill does not pass into law
in any given two-year Congress, it needs to be reintroduced in the next Congress to
receive consideration.

Members have a lot of different motives in introducing bills. Many times they do
so for strictly political reasons—perhaps as a favor to a group in their constituency—
but do not have the time or even the inclination to do everything possible to move
the bill along in the legislative process. Often members may not be in a position to
move the bill along because they do not serve on the relevant committee or otherwise have the necessary clout. Most members of the minority party in the House, and
even many in the majority party, are not going to get the attention and support of
party leaders, without which their idea stands no chance.

An important but often overlooked aspect of bill introduction is the origin of the
idea for a bill. Interest groups and constituents are sometimes the source, and of course
members and their staff develop bills to address policy concerns and the needs of districts or states. As often as anything else, ideas for legislation come from the government itself—that is, from executive branch agencies. Members of Congress, in their
role as the board of directors, solicit ideas on how to fix problems in the administration and performance of government programs from agency officials, who are often
the ones in the best position to know what will work. Furthermore, many agencies
aggressively push ideas that the administration would like to see implemented and
look for sympathetic members to introduce their bills for them. Ideally, they try to
work with members who are in a better position to move bills through the process,
especially party leaders and committee and subcommittee chairs.

Referring a Bill to a Committee

The first step in the legislative process is committee referral, which is usually a routine step. The committees have established jurisdictions in House rules and precedents; the nonpartisan parliamentarian of the House analyzes the bill in question and
makes the appropriate referral. The situation gets much more complicated—and
much more political—when more complex legislation is introduced that does not
fit neatly into any single existing committee's jurisdiction.

Over the last three decades or so, House leadership has exercised a great deal of power in the referral process when a piece of legislation can be construed as falling under the jurisdiction of more than one committee. Indeed, many of the most important issues of the day do not fit neatly into one or another committee's jurisdiction. In these cases, the referral process may become an important tool for the House leadership in driving its agenda.

House leadership has a few different ways of referring a bill once it is established that the bill does not entirely fit into one committee's jurisdiction. The most common method is probably best described as a type of *split referral*. The leadership identifies the committees that should be involved in considering the bill and refers the bill to them with instructions as to the portion of the bill they should work on and a date when they should finish consideration (also known as *reporting out* the committee's version of that part of the bill). When there is a primary committee of jurisdiction that is instructed to work on the bulk of the bill, as is often the case, that committee is less likely to be given a reporting deadline.

Producing legislation that makes sense for the party in power can be very tricky. The leadership (with the majority leader typically taking the lead) must be very skilled. Committees may have different views on important aspects of a given piece of legislation, and the exact lines of jurisdiction may not be perfectly clear. Committees must work together to produce legislation that makes sense. The majority leader's role is to broker the deal, looking out for the larger interests of the party as important legislation moves through the process. Committee leaders are likely to be the most knowledgeable people in the chamber on the issues in question and may have the best sense of what can be passed. But the leadership has the keys for access to the floor. The negotiations between the leadership and the committee chairs may be intense. Sometimes leadership may need to wrest control of a bill from one or more of the committees if the chairs are not sufficiently cooperative.[21]

In these cases, all or part of a bill may be put together independent of the committee or committees of jurisdiction. This is not a popular move, but issues of particular sensitivity may require such action. More commonly, post-committee adjustments are made to legislation before it makes the floor. Political realities often dictate that bills have to be changed from the version that emerged from committee in order for them to pass on the House floor. Changing circumstances may also make it necessary to adjust a bill. Or the leadership may decide to move a bill forward for floor consideration because there is not enough time to send the bill back through the process again.

The Rules Committee

There are four House of Representatives calendars on which bills are placed to await floor consideration: the House Calendar, the Private Calendar, the Discharge Calendar, and the Union Calendar. But for most consequential matters, the House takes up issues in an order determined by the majority party leadership, paying no heed to the order in which they appear on the relevant calendar.

This is done by securing what is known as a *special rule* from the Rules Committee, which allows bills to, in effect, jump the queue. If leadership thinks it is time to bring up the energy bill, for instance, it requests a special rule. The Rules Committee has thirteen members, nine of whom are selected by the speaker and four of whom are selected by the minority leader, and its importance cannot be overstated: *The Rules Committee provides the means by which the speaker runs the House.*

One way to think about the Rules Committee is to see it as a rule-*waiving* committee. If the standing rules of the House call for a certain order of business or disallow certain types of provisions in a bill that the leadership wants to move, they can ask the Rules Committee to draw up a special rule to have those rules waived.

Here is how it works: The leadership brings a favored bill that has just been reported out of a committee before the Rules Committee. The bill is quite controversial and may even contain provisions unrelated to the bill's main purpose, a violation of the House's *germaneness* rule. The Rules Committee's job is to draw up the guidelines for the consideration of this bill on the House floor. For one thing, since the bill is important to leadership (and since the overwhelming majority of the Rules Committee was handpicked by the speaker), the special rule will prohibit anyone from raising a point of order on the House floor challenging the existence of nongermane provisions in the bill. The special rule will also structure the debate and amendment process on the floor. It may do other things as well.

It was once more common for the special rule to permit unlimited amendments subject to the standing rules of the House. This sort of rule is called an *open rule*. As politics in Congress has become more partisan, open rules are used less and less. It can be seen in Table 4.3 that the use of open rules fell dramatically between the 103rd Congress in 1993–1994 and more recent Congresses.

Ten years ago, open rules were commonly applied to over half of the bills brought before the Rules Committee; more recently, that number has dropped to one-quarter or even less. (The data include the *modified open rule*, which typically either allows any amendments to be offered as long as they have been preprinted in the *Congressional Record* or puts some limit on the time allotted for amendments.)

TABLE 4.3   *The Increase in the Use of Closed and Structured Rules for Consideration of Legislation on the House Floor, 1993–2008 (103rd–110th Congress)*

RULE TYPE	103RD #	103RD %	104TH #	104TH %	105TH #	105TH %	106TH #	106TH %
Open/modified open	46	44%	83	58%	74	53%	91	51%
Structured/modified closed	49	47	40	28	42	30	49	27
Closed	9	9	19	14	24	17	39	22
Total	104	100	142	100	140	100	179	100

RULE TYPE	107TH #	107TH %	108TH #	108TH %	109TH #	109TH %	110TH #	110TH %
Open/modified open	40	37%	34	26%	24	19%	23	14%
Structured/modified closed	44	41	62	47	61	49	81	50
Closed	23	22	37	28	40	32	59	36
Total	107	100	133	101*	125	100	163	100

* Does not total 100 owing to rounding error.

Source: *House Rules Committees and Donald Wolfensberger of the Woodrow Wilson Center.*

Use of the open rule has declined because allowing all members the opportunity to amend a bill leaves open the possibility that the minority party will offer amendments for the sole purpose of embarrassing majority party members, forcing them to make tough votes that weigh party loyalty against their potential electoral interests. Essentially, in this scenario, the majority party leadership loses some control of the agenda, which they are loath to let happen.

On the other hand, as Table 4.3 shows, *closed rules* have become more common. The pure closed rule allows no amendments. Usually, however, the leadership gets the Rules Committee to develop some sort of restrictive rule, often called a *structured* or *modified closed rule.* Such a rule permits only certain types of amendments to be offered (structured rule) or allows only a single substitute amendment (modified closed rule). Members who wish to amend an important bill often appear before the Rules Committee with their amendment in hand to plead their case.

Exhibit 4.4 shows examples of a structured rule and a closed rule from the 110th Congress. The structured rule specifies amendments for the Coast Guard Authorization Act of 2007. The closed rule, forbidding amendments, is for the Renewable Energy and Job Creation Act of 2008.

The leadership cannot always afford to be too restrictive. After all, they need to keep a majority of members happy in order to move their agenda, and rank-and-file members may insist on having a chance to amend some section of a bill.

EXHIBIT 4.4
STRUCTURED AND CLOSED RULES FOR DEBATE ON THE HOUSE FLOOR

Structured Rule: HR 2830—Coast Guard Authorization Act of 2007

1. Provides one hour of general debate, with 40 minutes equally divided and controlled by the chairman and ranking minority member of the Committee on Transportation and Infrastructure and 20 minutes equally divided and controlled by the chairman and ranking minority member of the Committee on Homeland Security.

2. Waives all points of order against consideration of the bill except those arising under clause 9 or 10 of rule XXI.

3. Provides that, in lieu of the amendments in the nature of a substitute recommended by the Committees on Transportation and Infrastructure, Homeland Security, and the Judiciary now printed in the bill, the amendment in the nature of a substitute printed in part A of the Rules Committee report accompanying the resolution shall be considered as an original bill for the purpose of amendment and shall be considered as read.

4. Waives all points of order against the amendment in the nature of a substitute printed in part A of the Rules Committee report accompanying the resolution except those arising under clause 10 of rule XXI. This does not affect the point of order available under clause 9 of rule XXI (regarding earmark disclosure).

5. Makes in order only those further amendments printed in part B of the Rules Committee report accompanying the resolution.

6. Provides that the amendments made in order may be offered only in the order printed in the report, may be offered only by a Member designated in the report, shall be considered as read, shall be debatable for the time specified in the report equally divided and controlled by the proponent and an opponent, shall not be subject to amendment, and shall not be subject to a demand for division of the question in the House or in the Committee of the Whole.

7. Waives all points of order against the amendments printed in part B of the Rules Committee report except for those arising under clause 9 or 10 of rule XXI.

Once the Rules Committee agrees to and reports a special rule, the rule must be adopted by the House by a majority vote. An hour-long debate on the special rule precedes the vote to adopt the rule. In other words, the leadership cannot literally dictate their preferences for the nature of the debate on the floor on the bill itself; they need to gain the assent of a majority of the House. These are usually party line votes. Members of the majority party may need, for political purposes, to vote against a bill. But in the interest of maintaining control over the agenda, the majority party

---

8. Provides one motion to recommit with or without instructions.
9. Provides that in the engrossment of HR 2830, the text of HR 2399, as passed the House, shall be added at the end of HR 2830.
10. Provides that, notwithstanding the operation of the previous question, the Chair may postpone further consideration of the bill to a time designated by the Speaker.
11. Authorizes the chairman of the Committee on the Judiciary to file a supplemental report on HR 2830.

Closed Rule: HR 6049—Renewable Energy and Job Creation Act of 2008

1. Provides one hour of debate equally divided and controlled by the chairman and ranking member of the Committee on Ways and Means.
2. Waives all points of order against consideration of the bill except those arising under clause 9 or 10 of rule XXI.
3. Provides that the amendment in the nature of a substitute recommended by the Committee on Ways and Means now printed in the bill shall be considered as adopted and the bill, as amended, shall be considered as read.
4. Waives all points of order against provisions of the bill, as amended. This waiver does not affect the point of order available under clause 9 or rule XXI.
5. Provides one motion to recommit with or without instructions.
6. Provides that, notwithstanding the operation of the previous question, the Chair may postpone further consideration to a time designated by the Speaker.

Source: House Rules Committee, as suggested by Donald Wolfensberger of the Woodrow Wilson Center.

The House leadership often chooses to limit members' ability to amend legislation that the leaders bring to the floor. With the structured rule, House leadership permits certain amendments, as specified in points 6 and 7. For HR 6049, a closed rule is in place so no amendments are permitted.

leadership will expect its rank and file to support the special rule crafted by the Rules Committee.

One very important tool the majority party leadership sometimes uses is to include a *self-executing provision* in the rule. The special rule says that, upon its adoption by the House, certain legislative provisions will be automatically added to the bill that emerges from the committee or committees of jurisdiction. This is the mechanism by which leadership makes post-committee adjustments to legislation. Such additions do not require a separate vote as amendments to the bill on the House floor, which could jeopardize their inclusion.

But special rules may go even further. The majority party leadership can arrange for the marriage of what are in effect two separate bills in a special rule. This is done when leadership believes that joining the bills before the vote would lead to their defeat. Such a rule stipulates that each bill will get a separate vote but that, by virtue of the adoption of the rule, the bills will then be joined before being sent over to the Senate or to the president for his signature if the Senate version has already passed the Senate as a single measure.

Speaker Pelosi arranged just such a marriage in 2007 when President Bush requested more funding for the Iraq War. The majority of Democrats did not want to give the president the money without a timetable for the withdrawal of U.S. troops—something the president adamantly opposed; in addition, Democrats wanted to add money for domestic priorities, including an increase in the minimum wage.

Any bill requiring the troop withdrawal timetable would have been vetoed, as would also have been the fate of a stand-alone bill that provided funding for domestic priorities opposed by the president. The solution: Bring a war funding bill without the troop withdrawal requirement to the floor, where it would pass with more Republican than Democratic support; then separately bring the domestic spending and minimum wage bill to the floor, where that bill would pass with mostly Democratic support. The rule governing the floor consideration of these bills brought them together as one, which was the version the Senate had already passed, before sending them to the president. The president was happy enough with the war funding that he chose not to veto the entire package even though he opposed the additional domestic spending.

Suspension of the Rules

Another tactic the leadership uses to move legislation is the *suspension procedure*, or the *suspension of the rules*. In this case, the leadership bypasses the Rules Committee in moving bills to the floor. Under the suspension procedure, only forty minutes of debate are permitted (divided equally between supporters and opponents), the bill ordinarily is not amendable, and a two-thirds vote is required for final passage. (Technically that vote does double duty, both suspending the normal rules and passing the bill.)

Historically the suspension procedure has been used primarily for noncontroversial matters, but increasingly the leadership has employed it to pass important matters, including major reauthorizations (NASA's reauthorization was handled this way in 2008), public lands bills, and even some budget legislation. The limited debate and the prohibition on amendments have led to a great deal of criticism of this practice, but its utility is clear. The leadership, provided it can round up the supermajority support, can move things much more quickly and cleanly in this fashion than it can even through the use of special rules. Of course, it should be noted, the two-thirds requirement cannot be met if the leadership does not have support from the minority party, which it must have in order to use suspension procedures successfully.

Floor Consideration

To the best of their ability, the majority leadership tries to make floor consideration of the legislation on their agenda as anticlimactic as possible. But there are too many uncertainties involving wavering members and changing circumstances for them always to know for certain that they can attain the outcome they want if the vote is close.

As we have seen, the main mechanism the leadership uses to structure floor consideration and move their legislative agenda toward the desired result is through the creation and adoption of a special rule. Normally, in fact, the rule is adopted and the majority gets its way. The minority party may try to amend the rule, but such efforts rarely succeed. It does happen, slightly less rarely, that the rule itself is defeated. When that happens, it is a major embarrassment for the leadership, who must go back to the drawing board.

By adopting the rule, the House resolves itself into something called the *Committee of the Whole*. This "committee" includes all the members of the House. In fact, the Committee of the Whole is a parliamentary tactic to facilitate a manageable debating and amending process.

The Committee of the Whole requires that only 100 members be present for a quorum, instead of the 218 required to conduct business when the "actual" House convenes. (In fact, the quorum requirement is enforced only on the infrequent occasions when a member insists upon it.) Also, there are strict limits on debate during the amendment process, including a "five-minute rule" (five minutes for each side to make its case) for each amendment.

Most of the business of the House is conducted in the Committee of the Whole. First, there is general debate on the bill. The member managing the bill on the floor, usually the chair of the committee with preponderant jurisdiction, divvies up the time he or she has been allotted (a half-hour, an hour, or more, as granted by the rule) among those who wish to speak in support of the bill. Opponents of the bill receive an equal amount of time (typically managed by the ranking member of the main committee of jurisdiction) to have their say.

After general debate, the amending process begins as allowed under the special rule. (Of course, no amendments are permitted under a closed rule.) Technically those offering amendments have five minutes to explain them, followed by the floor manager, who has five minutes for rebuttal, unless more time is allowed for that amendment under the provisions of the special rule. Any other member may also speak for five minutes by offering an amendment to "strike the last word [of the amendment]." This is not a change that the member really wishes to enact; rather, the member is complying with a parliamentary requirement in the Committee of the Whole that, once general debate is finished, only those offering amendments may speak. Really, then, what the member is doing is commenting on the substantive amendment in question, not saying that he or she wishes to remove a word from it. (In point of fact, members are rarely permitted to take the full five minutes to comment on the pending amendment. Nor is enough time usually allotted to give anywhere near all the membership the opportunity to speak. With 435 members, the majority feels the need to impose restrictions in order to streamline the process.)

After the debate on the substantive amendment is complete, a recorded vote may be requested. The call is put out to all members, wherever they may be on Capitol Hill, to come to the House chamber. They cast their vote by inserting a card into one of the voting stations on the floor of the chamber, indicating a vote of yea, nay, or present. Members have fifteen minutes to cast their vote. More commonly, the rule stipulates that debates will be held on all the amendments, one after the other, before the call is put out to cast a vote. Fifteen minutes are allotted for members to get to the chamber and vote on the first amendment, after which five minutes are allotted for each of the other amendments. This arrangement is called *stacking* votes. The advantage of stacking is that members do not have to run back and forth from their offices or a hearing all day to vote on each individual amendment.

When the Committee of the Whole finishes up its business, it reports the bill back to the full House, which then convenes to consider that business. Usually the amendments that have been passed in the Committee of the Whole are voted on packaged together, a way of voting referred to as *en bloc*. Ordinarily that package succeeds, since the full House is, after all, the same body of people who voted on the amendments in the first place in the Committee of the Whole. Closely contested amendments may be separated out and voted on individually.

Next, the bill itself, as amended, comes up for a vote. Normally fifteen minutes are allotted for this vote. In particularly contentious matters, the speaker may leave the vote open longer, but doing so invites considerable controversy. Box 4.4 describes an extreme case of leaving the vote open. Obviously the majority would rather have the votes easily in hand and conclude business in a timely fashion. The fact is that the majority controls the House floor and will go to great lengths if necessary, even violating long-established norms of conduct, to move its agenda.

Opponents of a bill have little recourse. If they have been shut out of any opportunity to amend it or to bring their favored approach up for consideration, they may make their point by offering a *motion to recommit*. Such a motion expresses the minority's discontent with what has happened and calls for specific changes in the bill. Usually opponents use a motion to recommit as a last-ditch effort to scuttle the bill, but sometimes a successful motion to recommit effectuates changes in the legislation that the minority favors.

In 2007 Republicans stymied a Democratic agenda item with a cleverly crafted motion to recommit. That year the Democratically controlled U.S. House was poised to pass a bill that would give the residents of the District of Columbia a full-fledged voting House member. (Currently the District has a delegate, who has all the privileges of a member of Congress *except* voting rights on the House floor.) In an effort to score political points at the expense of Democrats representing pro-gun constituencies, the Republicans offered a motion to recommit with instructions to repeal the gun ban in the District. Speaker Pelosi did not want these Democrats to have to vote against the gun ban repeal, so she pulled the DC voting bill from the floor rather than have some of her more vulnerable members cast a controversial vote.[22]

Key Stages in the Legislative Process: The Senate

Bill Introduction and Committee Referral

Although the process for bill introduction is essentially the same in the Senate as it is in the House, the committee referral process is different. According to Senate rules, the majority leader cannot exert the kind of influence over referral that the speaker of the House can through the various types of multiple referrals available in that chamber.

BOX 4.4
PRESCRIPTION DRUG COVERAGE
PASSES IN THE WEE HOURS

One of the most dramatic moments in the recent history of the Congress occurred in the early morning hours of November 22, 2003. President Bush and the Republican Congress were determined to pass their version of a massive new Medicare entitlement program to provide prescription coverage for seniors. They ran into major stumbling blocks on the House floor from Democrats *and* Republicans.

Intent on getting out of town for Thanksgiving, the House was working late to complete important business. Finally, at 3:00 AM, a vote was called on the Medicare prescription drug bill. Members had fifteen minutes to register their votes. The outcome seemed clear: By a 219–215 vote, the plan had failed. But this was an unacceptable outcome for the Republican leadership of the House headed by Speaker Dennis Hastert, as well as for the president, who intended to campaign for reelection in part on the basis of this accomplishment.

It is not uncommon for House votes to be kept open to give members more time to get to the floor, or even to do a little persuading to change what looks like the wrong outcome from the perspective of the majority party. But in this case, the period for voting was taken to extremes. The president got on the phone to talk to some members. He had instructed Secretary of Health and Human Services Tommy Thompson to hang around the Capitol to lobby for the bill. And of course, the House leadership, including the speaker himself and Majority Leader Tom DeLay, were active.

Leaders called the home of one Republican, Jo Ann Emerson of Missouri, whose husband told them that in fact she was still at the Capitol—she was hiding among a group of Democrats on the House floor and had gone unseen after casting a nay vote. Another Republican opponent of the legislation, Nick Smith of Michigan, initially claimed to have been illegally threatened by powerful Republicans for his vote against the legislation. (He later recanted the charge.)

Ultimately, after holding the vote open for a record two hours and fifty-one minutes, the leadership managed to change three minds and the bill was passed. Many Democrats have still not forgotten what they regarded as an abuse of the legislative process—even some Republicans remain bitter at the tough tactics of their party's leadership. In any case, this admittedly extreme case exemplifies the kind of control that the majority party can exert in the House of Representatives.*

---

* A good description of this vote can be found in many journalistic sources. A longer description can be found in Norman Ornstein and Thomas Mann, *The Broken Branch* (Oxford: Oxford University Press, 2006), chs. 1 and 4.

The parliamentarian of the Senate—a nonpartisan office, as it is in the House—refers the entire bill to the committee with preponderant jurisdiction based on the content of the legislation.[23] The rules do not include the option of a multiple referral, as is the case in the House.

The reality, however, is that complex bills often do receive consideration in more than one committee in the Senate. The difference from the House is that consideration of a bill by multiple committees is not handled by a split referral engineered by the majority leadership. Instead, the Senate divides up legislation in its usual way—informally. Committee chairs talk to one another. Often the chair of the committee of jurisdiction agrees to allow other committees to deal with certain provisions of a bill. Chairs do not do this to be magnanimous; they recognize that in the Senate they will need the support of other key members down the line if they want the bill to become law.

As in the House, it is possible for the Senate leadership to bypass the committee process altogether. Then–Senate majority leader Tom Daschle of South Dakota did exactly that with comprehensive energy legislation in 2002. The committee chair handling the bill, Max Baucus of Montana, intended to include a provision permitting drilling for oil in the Arctic National Wildlife Refuge, a policy that Daschle opposed. The leader bypassed the committee and brought the bill to the floor without the drilling provision.

The leadership often works to develop post-committee adjustments to enhance the chances of legislation on the floor and to move forward a favored agenda item. But as with the committee referral process and every other aspect of Senate procedure, the actions of the majority leader in setting and pursuing an agenda are highly constrained compared with what the speaker can do in the House. Assuming the votes are in hand, the speaker may impose his or her agenda, streamlining the committee and floor consideration process to that end. The majority leader of the Senate is in no such position.

The Senate operates under a fundamentally different principle than the House. The Senate leader must respect the rights of the minority because every senator has a wide range of prerogatives that he or she may exercise on the floor. This precludes the kind of tight control over the agenda that is possible in the House. The upshot is that the leadership rarely is able to pursue a partisan agenda with any consistent success. The majority leader must take into account not only the views of the minority party but very often those of every single senator. So engineering post-committee adjustments on legislation, for example, must to a significant degree be a cooperative activity.

Floor Consideration

In the Senate every member has equal stature and thus every member has an equal right to recognition on the Senate floor. The majority leader, however, is slightly "more equal." If the majority leader asks to be recognized, he or she may trump the rest of the membership of the body. It is this simple right of first recognition that gives the majority leader the ability, by tradition, to establish the agenda of the body.

The majority leader's agenda-setting power, however, is much more constrained than the House speaker's. Not only may any of the other senators take the floor, but they may hold the floor for as long as they want (often called a *filibuster*), raise any issues they want, and offer any amendments they want.[24] By contrast, members of the House must stay on topic, have a limited time to speak, and are almost always restricted in how they may offer amendments.

The implication of these differences with the House is that the agenda of the Senate can become very fluid. The leader has great difficulty moving legislation in a timely fashion, and since members can offer any amendments they wish, the very nature of the agenda can very easily be turned on its head. Whole bills that the leader wants to see disappear may reappear on the floor at any time in the form of an amendment. A bill instituting a 10 percent tax cut can become a 10 percent tax increase with a successful amendment.

How can the leader move his agenda, serving the interests of his party and the country? Only with the greatest difficulty.

Ultimately what the majority leader is doing is trying to achieve *unanimous consent* to move forward with the consideration of a bill. Most of the business on the Senate floor is conducted only after *every member* agrees to proceed. That does not mean that all members *support* the legislation in question; it does mean that they agree to permit debate to move forward without engaging in a filibuster or other delaying tactic.

Members will agree to let the majority leader go forward, even if they oppose the bill, for a lot of reasons. They may simply wish to have their say and get on the record as opposing the bill. They may want the opportunity to bring up an amendment for a vote. They may want a concession or two or a provision added to another bill later in the year. They may just want to have some predictability in their schedules, which can be facilitated only by conceding some control over the agenda to the majority leader. All members recognize that the leader can be helpful in the future with some matter of particular importance to them.

For complex legislation, the majority leader negotiates something called a *unanimous consent agreement*, or a *time limitation agreement* (sometimes referred to as a *UC* or *UC agreement*). Getting to a UC agreement is a very delicate matter. Getting one hundred strong-willed individuals to agree to anything is always going to be difficult.

The UC agreement is basically a version of a House special rule, with the obvious exception that it needs to have everyone on board, not just the support of a majority. The UC agreement structures floor consideration, perhaps by limiting amendments and debate time. Usually many amendments have to be permitted in the Senate, and much more time for debate allowed, than in the House, since all members are in a position to negotiate.

In fact, much of the Senate floor workload is *passed* by unanimous consent without a vote after little or no debate. The Senate simply does not have time to handle everything on the docket with a complex UC agreement, which normally must allow for days of debating and amending. The Senate docket is considerably longer than the House's. The Senate, unlike the House, must approve of judicial nominations as well as hundreds of nominations to high-level executive branch positions. And the Senate cannot streamline debate the way the House can. So it is commonplace for noncontroversial (although important) nominations or noncontroversial legislation to be passed by unanimous consent with little or no debate. Sometimes potentially more controversial matters are handled in this way as well.

The leader often uses a technique called *hotlining* to deal with the heavy Senate workload. What happens is that, at some point when the Senate is in session, the majority leader and the minority leader send a special message to their respective senators, delivered to a dedicated phone and e-mail account in each office. The message says that the majority leadership intends to pass by unanimous consent certain bills or nominations for executive branch positions or district court nominations at some point—say, the next day. Any senator who objects is expected to notify his or her leadership. If no senator communicates an objection, the leader can anticipate that no opposition will arise when he or she makes a unanimous consent request to pass the measures or approve the nominations put forth.

This process has occasionally become controversial in recent years when leadership has included more substantial legislation in the hotline message and given only a short time frame for objections. Senators who felt that they did not have a fair opportunity to object have voiced their frustration and sometimes retaliated by attempting to undermine other leadership agenda items.

The catch is that any one senator, by objecting, derails the process. By objecting to the unanimous consent request, a senator places a *hold* on legislation or on a nomination. It is then necessary to invoke something called *cloture* in order to bring the bill or nomination to the floor. Invoking cloture is the forceful way, as opposed to

---

BOX 4.5
THE FEDERAL ELECTION COMMISSION IS PUT ON ICE

As of December 31, 2007, the Federal Election Commission (FEC) was forced by the U.S. Senate, for all intents and purposes, to close its doors. The independent agency, charged with enforcing the federal election and financing laws, is governed by a six-member commission. A vote of at least four commissioners is required to enforce the complex and controversial campaign laws. As the 2008 campaign got into full swing, three openings on the commission—positions that required Senate confirmation—were unfilled. Unfortunately, some senators objected to one of the president's nominees. As a result, through much of the 2008 election cycle the commission failed to have a quorum and was unable to rule on important campaign financing matters, including one especially sticky matter involving Senator John McCain's decision to opt out of public financing for his campaign for the Republican nomination.

Source: Martin Kady II, "FEC Nominations on Hold Until After Memorial Day," *Politico*, May 21, 2008, available at: http://www.politico.com/blogs/thecrypt/0508/FEC _nominees_on_hold_until_after_Memorial_Day_.html.

---

getting unanimous agreement, to put a limit on debate in the Senate. Because cloture requires sixty votes, however, it almost always involves members of both parties. (Even when a party has sixty senators, rarely can all sixty be held together on almost anything.) After cloture is invoked, consideration is limited to thirty hours and all amendments must be prefiled and germane to the subject of the bill.

The problem is that invoking cloture can take up hours or days (theoretically even weeks) of precious time, because Senate rules give individual members the prerogative to slow the process even when sixty or more members want to move forward.[25] As a result, cloture is rarely used for less substantial matters. The Senate simply cannot afford the time it would take to invoke it on everything. The leader, then, when confronted with a hold, needs to consult with the objecting senator. (Senators from the minority party may further complicate efforts to move forward by not divulging their identity to the majority leader.) Since the leader knows he cannot invoke cloture on everything, he either has to give in to the senator's demand or, in the case of a nomination for a federal position, allow the position to go unfilled. As can be seen in Box 4.5, in 2008 the Federal Election Commission was rendered powerless by just such a hold.

The hold process gives each member tremendous leverage. A clever member can often find something essential to hold up that will force the majority leader to come calling. In this way, every member is in a position to bargain with the leadership and can exert influence on almost any legislation he or she wants.

On major issues—let's say comprehensive energy legislation or an overhaul of defense policy—the leadership will go ahead and take the time to break a hold by invoking cloture. After all, even with a UC agreement, debate may go on for days in the Senate on major bills, so holds are not really a factor for them.

These days, for significant bills, sixty votes are required for passage for another reason: By successfully invoking cloture, only germane amendments to a bill are permitted. This tactic subverts the tendency of some senators to try to add amendments to a bill on extraneous matters, which would tend, if passed, to undermine support for the legislation.

Since gaining sixty votes requires the cooperation of some minority party members, the Senate majority leader and minority leader routinely communicate almost every day. This distinguishes the Senate from the House in a critical way. The House majority leadership may move an agenda as quickly as they would like without consulting the minority (as long as they have the votes). In the Senate, when the majority leader indicates a readiness to move forward with a particular bill, he or she needs to know who from the rank and file *of both parties* might have objections. The majority party members communicate with the majority leader, and the minority party members communicate with their leader.

In sum, even if the majority leader is assured of the sixty votes needed to put a limit to debate, the opportunities for delaying tactics are so extensive that he or she ordinarily wants to be as accommodating as possible to all the members, in the interest of time. This is because each member is in a position to demand time on the floor and has the right to offer amendments. The Senate has a lot of business to attend to and not much time.

The Senate is characterized by seemingly endless deliberation and delay and almost always by compromise on substance. It is certainly in the interest of all the members to complete important business; however, nearly all senators have strong feelings on certain issues, and all resolutely defend the interests of their state. Negotiations can thus be slow and painstaking, and often it is impossible, given the time constraints, to move an ambitious agenda. Certainly the Senate tends to lag behind the House.

In the end, the majority leader usually feels his or her way along on the floor. The negotiated UC agreement may not cover the whole bill, and the leader gets agreement, tacit or otherwise, to move forward with a bill, negotiating along the way. As the bill proceeds, members may insist on more floor time or more amendments. Members and the majority leader rely on each other's good faith. The aim is to get something passed and to move forward to reconcile the Senate version of a bill with what may already have passed the House.

Reconciling the Differences

As we have seen, the presentment clause of the Constitution requires that legislation sent to the president be passed in identical form in each chamber. This is no easy task, as senators and members of the House almost always have very different perspectives on issues. As a result, the versions of a bill that emerge from each chamber—whether it is an appropriations bill, the defense authorization bill, a bill to authorize funding for roads and bridges, or what have you—will differ, usually in significant ways, even when the same party controls the House and Senate.

It is important to point out that the two chambers do not always strike a deal, and lack of a deal means the death of a bill. But it is also true that once the two chambers have passed complex legislation, there is a great deal of buy-in, and many members do not want to see all the effort they have put in wasted. Having said that, important matters have in fact languished in limbo—sometimes for years—as the chambers tried to hammer out a compromise. Recently legislation to reform the credit industry took several years of negotiation stretching over more than two Congresses to be finalized. The most recent comprehensive energy legislation, signed into law in 2005, followed a similar years-long path to final passage and law. Sometimes the sticking point is the president, whose veto threat can complicate the process. Because the president is a player in the legislative process, it is necessary to consider his concerns on major legislation.

There are three ways in which the chambers can come to an agreement on legislation. The easy way is for one chamber simply to pick up what has passed the other and then pass that bill unaltered. This is rare for consequential matters, but quite common for less controversial ones. Alternatively, in a process often called *amendments between the chambers*, the chambers may pass legislation back and forth, amending the legislation as they go along until both sides' needs are met and one chamber adopts whatever the other chamber has passed. The third option is to form a *conference committee*, an ad hoc panel made up of the relevant players in the House and Senate, to hammer out the differences. We focus on the latter two approaches since they are the ones normally used for important legislation.

Conference Committee

One common way to bridge the differences between bills passed by the House and Senate is to form a conference committee (or simply a *conference*) made up of members from each chamber. One chamber or the other requests a conference, and the other may follow up by agreeing to the request. The speaker is in charge of appointing the House conferees. He or she is bound by what are fairly flexible rules in making these appointments. At least a majority of members must be supportive of the House version of the bill, and there must be minority party representation. Typically the speaker appoints members from the committee or committees who worked on the bill from the beginning, on the theory that they are the most qualified to deal with the complex questions that will come up in negotiations with the other chamber.

In the Senate, the committee chair or chairs who worked on the bill and the majority leader choose their party's delegation to the conference, and the minority leader and the committee's ranking member choose the remainder of the conferees. It is most important to note that the Senate process of agreeing to go to conference with the House is complex, requiring three steps. Because it is relatively easy for determined senators to block the effort with dilatory tactics, amendments between the chambers is used more often than a conference committee as the method of bridging differences on major legislation by a ratio of about two-to-one.[26]

The conference committee approach to bridging differences is logical for complex legislation, on which there are often many differences between the two chambers' versions, some of them even fundamental differences. Difficult negotiations are required to handle all the problem areas in the bill. On appropriations bills, for example, there are often hundreds of differences between the two versions. (Appropriations bills are almost always handled in conference committee.) Complex energy legislation or an overhaul of the banking system will have involved multiple committees in each chamber.

Often the thinking is that the best way to handle the negotiations is behind closed doors, where hard decisions can be made more easily and simple "split the difference" compromises can be hidden from view. In addition, conference committees are made up of those members who are most knowledgeable on the particular issues in question.

Technically, conference committees meet in public; in reality, they hold very few public sessions—usually only one pro forma session—while handling the real work behind the scenes. The public session is often reserved for officially ratifying the work done behind closed doors. The final version of the bill agreed to in the conference committee is called the *conference report.*

Conference committees are required by the rules of both chambers to keep the negotiations within the scope of the bills as passed by the two chambers. Thus, new items that were not in the House or Senate bill are not allowed to appear magically in the final version; negotiations must stay within the parameters of the two bills. (If one bills says the government should buy fifty missiles and the other says one hundred, the final version must have a number somewhere between fifty and one hundred.) Moreover, items that appeared in both the House and Senate versions must stay in the final version.

In the real world, members frequently stray from these rules (which are treated more like guidelines). Each chamber has methods that can be used to get around the rules prohibiting extraneous provisions, staying within the parameters of the two bills, and removing agreed-to items in the final product. The decisions in conference are not always premised on abiding by the technical rules of the chambers.

Instead, conference negotiations are premised on the Rule of 218 and 60. What really guides behavior is the question: What do we need to do to put together a conference report that can pass both chambers? If new provisions need to be added, given changing views or changing circumstances, then new language is inserted. If the president threatens a veto based on something he opposes that is in both versions, then every effort is made to find a way to waive the relevant chamber's rule once the conference report is sent back to the House and Senate floor. The larger point is that so much is at stake at this point, so many members have put in so much time and effort, that everything possible will be done to produce a final version that can pass both chambers.

When the final version is completed, the delegation from the House and the delegation from the Senate vote separately. If both chambers' delegations vote in favor by a majority vote, the conference report is sent back to the House and Senate for a vote on final passage. Typically the conference report may not be amended on the House or Senate floor, but it may be filibustered in the Senate. Thus, sixty votes are often required to get a vote on final passage in the Senate.

Amendments Between the Chambers

Sometimes it is impossible to form a conference committee, particularly if senators block the formation of one. Or it may be easier, or deemed preferable, to avoid a conference. In these cases, differences can be resolved by sending a bill back and forth in the process called amendments between the chambers, with each chamber making changes until one chamber agrees with the whole version as sent to it from the other.

Although it is true that amendments between the chambers may sometimes be the only option for arriving at agreement, it is also the case that the majority party leadership in the two chambers may prefer this method. The reason: It can give them more control over the process than a conference committee.

Conference committees bring into the same room many of the committee members who have worked on the bill in both chambers—with complex legislation, these are often members from three or more congressional committees. Although leadership is almost always asked to help broker the negotiations in these cases, the fact is that a conference committee is run by one of the committee chairs and the work is driven to a great degree by the interests of the committee members. The bottom line is that the leadership may lose control over the final legislative product to committee chairs who do not necessarily see eye to eye with them on all the major substantive issues involved.

By ping-ponging the bill back and forth between the chambers, the leadership retains control over the negotiations and scheduling. Unlike in a conference committee, where rank-and-file congressional negotiators make the changes, the leaders determine the parameters for changes in the bill through the amendment process on the floor of the two chambers. These negotiations between the top leaders of the two chambers can be highly delicate, as one would imagine, especially in the Senate, where leadership operates under more constraints than House leadership.

Negotiations using the amendments between the chambers method are entirely informal and can be limited to just a few prominent players, all to the benefit of leadership trying to push through an agenda advantageous to their party. Still, the complexity of the issues at stake on many bills and the desire of the rank and file to have a conference committee can trump the leadership's desire for more control.

The End of the Process: The White House

With most major legislation, the president and his closest aides and cabinet members have been involved in the negotiations on Capitol Hill. The administration is likely to have an interest in every major piece of legislation that affects the work of the executive branch of government. If Congress wants the final version of a piece of legislation to become law, and the members cannot override a presidential veto, they will have to address the president's concerns. In effect, the administration becomes part of the legislative process to the point of lobbying aggressively for its viewpoint.

Of course, if the president does not like the final product, he may also veto it. When he does that, he explains his reasons and sends the bill back to Congress. Both houses must muster a two-thirds vote to override a veto and make a bill law over the president's objection.

The president may also allow a bill to become law without his signature. If he does not act on a bill within ten days, it becomes law. He may also "pocket veto" a bill by refusing to sign it in the last ten days of a two-year Congress. In this way, Congress has no opportunity to override the veto, and the bill does not become law.

But ordinarily, as already mentioned, Congress wants a result for all the hard work that went into navigating the legislative process and so compromises with the president to produce a bill he will sign. Sometimes, however, Congress passes legislation, knowing the president will veto it and knowing it cannot override that veto, simply to make a point. This is most common when the government is divided and Congress is intent on demonstrating what it could pass into law if a president of the other party were elected. Democrats did this in the 1980s and early 1990s with the Family and Medical Leave Act, which was passed three times in that period, but the Congress was unable to override presidential vetoes. Finally, in 1993, Democratic president Bill Clinton signed it into law.

CONGRESS AND THE AUTHORIZING POWER

The State of the Authorization Process: The Spending Continues— Sometimes Without the Thinking

In directing the work of the government, Congress relies heavily on the expertise of its authorizing committees. The staff and members of these committees are among the top "policy wonks" on Capitol Hill in each jurisdiction. Congress can direct the agencies to do its bidding, at whatever level of specificity it wants, by passing authorizing bills. These bills bind the agencies to the will of Congress as expressed in law. Congress normally plans to revisit agency and program authorizations on a regular basis—to "reauthorize" those functions, in the parlance of Capitol Hill. Times change, circumstances change, new issues arise, and congressional committees invariably wish to leave their mark on the government in a timely fashion by updating existing laws governing programs and agencies.

But as a general rule, these committees have been getting a bad reputation. One congressman put it this way: "Most authorizing committees are just debating societies; they rarely put in the serious work and effort required to pass legislation."[27] (This member excluded the Armed Services Committees and the House Transportation and Infrastructure Committee from his analysis.) He pointed to the frequency with which Congress fails to complete timely reauthorizations for agencies and programs for which the authorization to appropriate has expired. He rued the fact that authorizing committees are losing stature to the Appropriations Committees, which *must* finish bills to keep the government funded and functioning.

What seems to happen is that agencies and outside groups with an interest in a particular policy end up focusing some of their attention away from the authorizing committee of jurisdiction if that committee cannot come together to pass a bill updating an agency or programs. Some agencies report that they focus almost all of their attention on the Appropriations Committees if they need a change in law to enable them to do their work more effectively in a changing world.

Why do the authorizing committees often fail to complete the essential work of reconsidering government programs in a timely manner? After all, there is a reason the Congress includes in, for example, its NASA authorizing bill a two-year authorization to appropriate: It believes that NASA programs need to be comprehensively reevaluated on a biennial basis.

First, many sticky, controversial, or politically charged issues come up when a congressional committee takes up a major overhaul of an agency, such as NASA, or a set of programs within an agency, such as the farm program. Simply put, it can be difficult or impossible to come to the agreements necessary to move the bill through the legislative process in a timely fashion. As we have seen, the process is complex and time-consuming: Sometimes it is impossible to get 218 House members and 60 senators to agree on something.

Second, the congressional calendar is jammed, especially in the Senate, where the rules permit unrestricted debate and amendments and, with the responsibility of approving hundreds of presidential nominations, the docket is longer than in the House.

The Root of the Problem

The historical roots of the problem explain a great deal. Prior to the 1960s, not only was the government smaller, but there was a much more trusting relationship between the executive and legislative branches than there is now. This was reflected in the fact that in decades past Congress tended to give very broad statutory discretion to the agencies when it set up programs. Congress basically trusted the bureaucrats to do what was laid out in law and to exercise their discretion in a reasonable way. And many of the authorizing laws were open-ended, with indefinite authorizations of appropriation and no so-called sunset provisions that could effectively close down programs after a certain time. Congress had far fewer staff, and many members did not think they needed more. If they wanted to redirect the work of the agencies by changing an existing authorization, they could, but they felt no urgency about it. As a result, the calendar for legislative activity was nowhere near as overwhelming as it is today.

Then, in the 1960s, as we have seen, a spasm of legislation stemming from the social and political upheaval of the era greatly expanded the scope of government. The period from 1964 to 1971 was especially intense. A lot of these new programs were experimental and controversial. At the same time, Congress was becoming more professionalized as it acquired many more expert staff and a generally more sophisticated membership. Many people on the Hill believed that too much discretion had been given over the years to unelected executive branch agency officials. The upshot was that Congress, in creating new programs, often established sunset dates for agency and program authorizations.

As Congress "bulked up" even more in the 1970s—more staff, a new support agency with the establishment of the Congressional Budget Office (CBO), new self-imposed oversight requirements—it became increasingly willing to meddle in areas that it had delegated to agency officials in the past. Legislatively, Congress wanted to keep the agencies on a short leash. Government programs and federal money touched every constituent and practically every entity in society by this time, and members were eager to exercise their authority over the government's work in order to serve the people in their districts or states.

The problem was that there just wasn't time to do everything they needed to do. Congress found itself unable to keep up with many of the authorizing responsibilities it had given itself, despite its good intentions. The situation was made worse by an increase in the level of partisanship. Ironically, just as Congress decided that it was best to keep the government on a short leash, either the politics were too contentious or they simply did not have the time to update authorizations as needed or required.

As noted earlier, it was not that programs were unable to get money appropriated for their continuation. It is relatively easy to get around the rules of the House and Senate prohibiting unauthorized appropriations. Even if Congress could not update the authorization for NASA, for instance, it surely was going to keep the agency going. Jobs at the agency and government contracts were at stake, and the agency was doing vital and popular work.

The upshot of all these changes was that the authorizing committees that could not update the laws affecting their areas of jurisdiction became less relevant. If a change in law needed to happen, the most effective tactic was to turn to the Appropriations Committees and get something inserted in a bill there. The budget experts at Appropriations ended up being the gatekeepers for important policy changes—a situation that was not what Congress intended with the division of labor between authorizers, who are supposed to think through policy issues, and appropriators, who are meant to consider the budgetary implications of government program spending.

Ultimately we get back to the congressman's comment noted earlier. Many authorizing committees do not wield the same kind of power they did in the past. They conduct oversight, and they try to do the authorization updates, but if no one is confident that they can produce a passable final product, the authorizing committees lose the attention of their stakeholders and the public. Conversely, the appropriators gain in power and prestige.

In today's Congress, observers know that the Armed Services Committees in both chambers are relevant; they reauthorize the work of the *entire Defense Department every year*. All the other authorizing committees could be that relevant, so no one with something at stake can safely ignore them. But they are inconsistent, making progress on legislative changes some years, but not in others. Many do finish reauthorizations, but quite often this happens years behind schedule.

Most programs and agencies should be carefully reevaluated and reauthorized on a regular basis—and the failure to do so has real costs. The experts on the authorizing committees, both members and staff, do the important thinking about what the federal government should do. This thinking is translated into law through the authorization process, which is meant to update and improve what the government does. Since the programs are mostly either essential or popular or both, Congress goes ahead and funds their continuation without the kind of thorough examination needed.

Authorizers Usurp Their Rivals: The Increase in Mandatory Spending

While the foregoing discussion might lead one to believe that the Appropriations Committees have the clear upper hand over the authorizing committees, this is not entirely the case. Appropriators *have* usurped authorizers when authorizers have let their bills lapse, since appropriators have been more than willing to be the gatekeepers for policy language to guide agency behavior in their bills. But it is also true, as we saw earlier in the chapter, that authorizers have managed to undermine appropriators' control of the purse strings by including the legal authority for agencies to get money from the Treasury in their authorizing legislation.

Over the last forty years, the amount of federal money spent directly through authorizing legislation has outstripped that controlled by the appropriators in their bills. The spending on the big entitlements, such as Social Security and Medicare—which are put on automatic pilot for all intents and purposes—does an end run around the Appropriations Committees.

Members of Congress, in an effort to establish a program that the appropriators cannot touch, can offer legislation to fund a program by direct spending in authorization legislation. Naturally, appropriators resist this, pointing out that direct spending programs put more of the budget outside of the annual control of the Congress. They say that these programs often become sacrosanct and in lean times have put an incredible burden on the budget. Furthermore, with the retirement of the baby boom generation beginning in the 2010s, entitlement programs are already set to put almost unbearable stress on the nation's finances. The appropriators argue that it is better for Congress to keep as much of the government under control as possible by subjecting it to yearly review.

In recent years a few members of Congress have made a big push to turn federal support for students with learning disabilities (a program established by the Individuals with Disabilities Education Act in 1975) into a mandatory program, protecting it from the yearly whims of appropriators.[28] So far the Appropriations Committees have successfully resisted this gambit, preserving their influence over the funding of the program. But it is a classic example of a struggle, four decades in the making, that pits budget watchers on the Appropriations Committees against policy experts on the authorizing committees who want to make sure that more resources are guaranteed for their favored programs.

—————

In sum, the influence of the authorizing committees is in flux. Their failure to complete timely updates of agencies and programs has left an opening for appropriators to exploit. The Appropriations Committees are happy to decide what changes will be made in agency policy in the funding bills they write.

On the other hand, in the last few decades authorizers have succeeded at funding programs outside of the appropriations process. Programs whose funding is for all intents and purposes on automatic pilot have proven hard to control. They tend to grow in popularity and often are enhanced over the years. Nonetheless, the direct spending strategy has allowed authorizers to regain some of the power they lost to the appropriators.

CONCLUSION

A great deal of legislative activity revolves around the authorizing process. Thousands of bills are introduced every year aimed at changing, enhancing, or creating government programs, sometimes altering the roles, relationships, and responsibilities of government agencies and even on occasion establishing entirely new departments. In 2009 alone, Congress evaluated authorizing bills to address global warming and other aspects of the nation's energy policy, the health care system, federal involvement in student loans, policies on the procurement of weapons, the regulatory structure of the financial system, and a great many other issues.

In this chapter, we looked at the scope of Congress's power to authorize the work of government, as well as the process by which authorizing legislation moves through the two chambers. As we saw, though the two bodies handle legislation in very different ways, they must in the end come to agreement for law to be made. In the twenty-first century, the House and Senate party leaders play crucial roles in determining the agenda for their respective bodies. Nevertheless, most of the serious policy work happens in the committees and subcommittees, where the specialized expertise resides. In the end, the interaction between the leadership and the committees determines what the board of directors authorizes the government agencies to do on the people's behalf.

QUESTIONS FOR DISCUSSION

1. Does it make sense to have mandatory funding for certain government programs? If so, what kind of programs should be handled this way? Which ones should not be mandatory? What is the downside to making program funding mandatory?

2. What are the potential problems that come up when Congress engages in wholesale reorganization of agencies or departments? How might these problems be avoided? Are there any advantages to giving the president the power to organize departments and agencies as he sees fit?

3. What would be gained if the Senate were to streamline its procedures by removing the possibility of the filibuster? What would be lost, if anything?

SUGGESTIONS FOR FURTHER READING

King, David C. 1997. *Turf Wars: How Congressional Committees Claim Jurisdiction.* Chicago: University of Chicago Press.

Oleszek, Walter. 2007. *Congressional Procedures and the Policy Process,* 7th ed. Washington, DC: CQ Press.

Sinclair, Barbara. 2008. *Unorthodox Lawmaking: New Legislative Processes in the U.S. Congress,* 3rd ed. Washington, DC: CQ Press.

Wawro, Gregory John, and Eric Schickler. 2006. *Filibuster: Obstruction and Lawmaking in the U.S. Senate*. Princeton, NJ: Princeton University Press.

NOTES

1. Quoted in Jean Reith Schroedel, *Congress, the President, and Policymaking* (New York: M. E. Sharpe, 1994), p. 121.

2. All of the committee websites, most with complete descriptions of their jurisdictions, can be found at www.house.gov and www.senate.gov.

3. See David C. King, *Turf Wars: How Congressional Committees Claim Jurisdiction* (Chicago: University of Chicago Press, 1997).

4. The idea of calling the authorizing committees the "thinking committees" and the appropriations committees the "spending committees" comes from Michael Robinson, former professor of government at Georgetown University and currently a scholar at the Pew Research Center for the People and the Press.

5. Allen Schick, *The Federal Budget*, 3rd ed. (Washington, DC: Brookings Institution Press, 2007), pp. 191–194.

6. Ibid., p. 194.

7. In 1980 the name of the department was changed to Health and Human Services (HHS). The Education Department was created to administer HEA programs and other programs in the education area that had been handled by HEW.

8. Wayne C. Riddle, "CRS Report for Congress: No Child Left Behind: An Overview of Reauthorization Issues for the 110th Congress," Congressional Research Service, December 14, 2006.

9. One example of politics entering into the realm of government grants for scientific research was noted by Christine M. Marra, "Syphilis and Human Immunodeficiency Virus," *Archives of Neurology* 61 (2004): 1505–1508: "In 2003 . . . Representatives Patrick Toomey (R, Pa) and Chris Chocola (R, Ind) proposed an amendment to defund five peer-reviewed, approved NIH grants. Four of these grants had sexual themes as determined by their 'key words,' such as 'abortion,' 'condom effectiveness,' 'commercial sex workers,' and 'men who have sex with men.' The measure was defeated by only 2 votes (212 to 210). Subsequently, Congress directed NIH to defend 190 funded studies that dealt with human sexuality."

10. Charles Cushman, interview with the author, September 8, 2008.

11. Frederick M. Kaiser et al., "CRS Report for Congress: Congressional Oversight Manual," Congressional Research Service, October 21, 2004, p. 5.

12. Cushman, interview with the author, September 8, 2008.

13. See the 9/11 Commission website at: http://www.911commission.gov/. The complete report is available at: http://govinfo.library.unt.edu/911/report/index.htm.

14. Richard A. Best Jr. et al., "CRS Report for Congress: Director of National Intelligence: Statutory Authorities," Congressional Research Service, April 11, 2005, p. 2.

15. Charles Babington, "Senate Passes Intelligence Reform Bill," *Washington Post*, December 8, 2004, p. A4.

16. Best et al., "CRS Report for Congress," p. 5.

17. Babington, "Senate Passes Intelligence Reform Bill," p. A4.

18. Barbara Sinclair, *Unorthodox Lawmaking: New Legislative Processes in the U.S. Congress*, 3rd ed. (Washington, DC: CQ Press, 2008).

19. An excellent resource on the evolution of Congress, covering the changing role of committee chairs, their relationship to party leadership, and other related matters, is Nelson Polsby, *How Congress Evolves: Social Bases of Institutional Change* (Oxford: Oxford University Press, 2004). See also John H. Aldrich and David W. Rohde, "Congressional Committees in a Continuing Partisan Era," in *Congress Reconsidered*, 9th ed. (Washington, DC: CQ Press, 2009), pp. 217–239.

20. This summary of the legislative process in the House and Senate draws from three principal published sources: Sinclair, *Unorthodox Lawmaking*; Walter Oleszek, *Congressional Procedures and the Policy Process*, 7th ed. (Washington, DC: CQ Press, 2007); and Valerie Heitshusen, "The Legislative Process on the Senate Floor," in *The Senate of the United States: Committees, Rules, and Procedures* (Hauppauge, NY: Nova, 2008), pp. 153–168. It also draws from numerous e-mail correspondences and in-person interviews with Valerie Heitshusen of the Congressional Research Service.

21. In the 110th Congress, Speaker Pelosi found herself at odds on important matters of policy with Energy and Commerce Committee chair John Dingell. Because he was unwilling to move legislation of the sort the party leadership preferred, Dingell's committee was frequently bypassed and legislation was brought to the floor without his having weighed in. Dingell was challenged for the committee chair post by Henry Waxman of California at the beginning of the 111th Congress, and Waxman won a close vote in the Democratic caucus.

22. Don Wolfensberger, "Democrats' DC Vote Fix Backfires in Gun Law Blowup," *Roll Call*, April 9, 2007.

23. There is an exception to this in Senate rules. Any bill with tax provisions is referred to the Senate Finance Committee regardless of whether Finance is the committee of preponderant jurisdiction.

24. The Senate, unlike the House and most other legislative bodies around the world, has no means to "call the question"—that is, make a motion to end debate and bring a bill or amendment to a vote. Essentially, then, a debate has to run its course before a matter can be voted on. As a practical matter, informal agreements are made to limit debate in the

Senate. Invoking cloture on a lengthy debate has the effect of limiting debate but does not bring the bill or amendment to an immediate vote. See Gregory John Wawro and Eric Schickler, *Filibuster: Obstruction and Lawmaking in the U.S. Senate* (Princeton, NJ: Princeton University Press, 2006).

25. A particularly obstinate member willing to use all tactics available in Senate rules may filibuster three times (or even more) on the same bill, thus multiplying the thirty-hour debate limit.

26. Oleszek, *Congressional Procedures and the Policy Process*, ch. 8.

27. Congressman Mark Kirk (R-IL), speech, March 18, 2004.

28. A description and criticism of congressional efforts to make the Individuals with Disabilities Act a mandatory program is Krista Kafer and Brian Riedl, "Comments on the Harkin Amendment to the Elementary and Secondary Education Act," Heritage Foundation, November 30, 2001, available at: http://www.heritage.org/research/education/WM61.cfm.

CHAPTER FIVE

CONGRESS AS THE BOARD
OF DIRECTORS: FUNDING
THE GOVERNMENT

For the board of directors of the federal government, no power is more crucial than the so-called power of the purse. Needless to say, the agencies cannot function without money—they cannot fight wars, build bridges, patrol borders, or anything else.

The vast majority of government programs (which have been established in authorizing statutes) require an appropriation in order to be implemented. In simple terms, what happens when an appropriations bill becomes law is that Congress gives the executive branch agencies the legal authority to spend money—that is, *budget authority*. To draw an analogy, budget authority puts money in a given agency's "bank account," which enables it to draw funds from the U.S. Treasury and commit those funds for a particular purpose. Committing to spend money is called *obligating* funds, which might entail, for example, entering into a contractual arrangement with a construction company to build an interstate highway or repair a bridge. Payments made to a contractor in exchange for work that is completed are called *outlays*.

The appropriations process is tremendously important just by virtue of the fact that it funds most of what government does. After all, holding the purse strings gives Congress a lot of leverage to force an agency to do one thing or not to do another.

The board of directors determines which of the authorized programs receive funding and how much they get. But that is only part of the picture.

In the last chapter, we saw that agency authorizations are not always updated on schedule. Congress cannot keep up with its workload because government has gotten so big and the policy issues that come up during the authorizing process are usually too complex and controversial to resolve easily. But an agency does not necessarily shut down if its authorizing legislation is not passed on time. As long as the agency receives funding, its programs will continue functioning.

So what can the board of directors do if it wants to change the policies of agencies that do not have an updated authorization? One common method is through the oversight process. But congressional oversight of agency performance, as we shall see in the next chapter, has limitations. First, it is not systematically performed, and second, it can be used only as a means to *persuade* agency officials to do things as certain members of Congress would want them done. As a tool of the legislative branch, it cannot *compel* action in the same way that a law can, whether an authorizing or an appropriations statute.

Invariably, members of the board look to the appropriations process when they wish to force agencies to do certain things or prohibit them from doing certain other things. Appropriations bills are *must-pass legislation*—these bills need to be completed every year to keep the essential functions of the federal government up and running. While appropriations bills are meant only to provide funding and not to establish policy, members of Congress attach provisions to appropriations bills telling agencies what they can and cannot do. In many years, the appropriations process is the primary way in which Congress flexes its muscle in directing the actions of the federal agencies.

Although the funding role is Congress's most important function, it is probably also the least understood of congressional processes. People with experience in the intricate ways of the appropriations process are highly valued on the Hill and in Washington. The aim in this chapter is to give the student a working grasp of how Congress directs the actions of the federal government through its power of the purse.

The first step in understanding the budget process on Capitol Hill is to get a sense of the tremendous scope of the federal budget and the different categories of spending—the subject of the first section. After taking this bird's-eye look at the federal budget, the next step is to look at how that budget is developed. The order of events for the budget process, beginning with the presidential budget submission and ending with the completion of appropriations legislation, is depicted here. For the purposes of this example, the dates are for the fiscal year 2011 (FY 2011) federal budget. The federal fiscal year starts on October 1 (for FY 2011, October 1, 2010) and ends on September 30 of the following year.

The Formulation of the Fiscal Year 2011 (FY 2011) Budget

March 2009 through January 2010—Federal agencies and departments formulate the president's budget under the guidance of the Office of Management and Budget (OMB).

First Monday in February 2010—OMB delivers the president's budget (also known as the "budget request") to Congress.

Winter and early spring 2010—Congressional committees examine the president's budget request.

April 15, 2010—Congress passes the Concurrent Budget Resolution to set forth its budgetary priorities.

May through the end of September 2010—Congress begins and completes work on appropriations bills and other budget-related legislation.

We begin by looking at how the president's budget is developed. When it is delivered to Congress, the president's budget effectively kicks off the budget process on Capitol Hill. It is his request for what he would like to see passed into law, in terms of both spending and taxes, in the coming year. (Congress refers to the president's budget as the *budget request*.)

The next section covers the board of directors' initial response to the president. The staff and members of Congress immediately begin digesting the president's comprehensive budget request with an eye to the impact of what the president wants on both the economy and their own particular priorities that may differ from the president's. Their aim is to produce their own budget blueprint by April 15 each year. This blueprint is called the *Concurrent Budget Resolution*. It presents Congress's big-picture goals, but it is not law and thus does not commit the government to any actions.

The appropriations process begins in earnest after the budget resolution is passed, which is the subject of the next section. We look first at how the appropriations bills are put together and passed. The Appropriations Committees in the two chambers, primarily at the subcommittee level, assess carefully, through hearings and other means, what the executive branch agencies are requesting in terms of funding for the coming fiscal year. On the basis of input from the agencies and many other sources, the subcommittees then begin the process of writing appropriations bills and moving them through the legislative process.

The second part of this section looks at the appropriations bills themselves. We cover the meaning of the different sections of the bills and, most importantly, how the board of directors uses these bills in various ways to direct the work of the agencies. As we saw in Chapter 4, the theory is that the authorizing committees, which are staffed by policy experts, decide in the legislation they write what it is that the government ideally should be doing to address the needs of the nation, and then the appropriators follow up by funding authorized programs as close to the maximum level allowable given budget constraints and other factors of their choosing. The reality is that authorizations frequently lapse or are extended without a thorough examination of the programs and agency policy. In these instances, appropriators "fill the gap" by including policy provisions in the funding bills. As we shall see, the board of directors is more than willing to meddle in agency affairs in the appropriations process, both by specifying what agencies must do with their funds as well as by limiting what they may do.

In recent years, the appropriations process has not proceeded smoothly, to say the least. In fact, from 1997 to 2008, it did not once do its work on time—and most years it was not even close. This has led to charges that the congressional budget process has "broken down," which may not be far from the truth. In the next section, we look at why Congress has failed in recent years to complete arguably its most essential function and what it does to avoid the catastrophe of a government shutdown.

The chapter concludes with an examination of the major challenges that Congress faces in dealing with the federal budget. First, we consider the larger question of whether Congress budgets responsibly. Then we look at two specific problems facing the board in the twenty-first century: chronic deficits and a growing national debt.

THE BUDGET PIE

The federal government is a massive entity; in fact, it is the single largest entity on the face of the earth. In fiscal year 2009, the government spent about $3.5 trillion, an amount that constitutes nearly 25 percent of the entire U.S. economy and is larger than the economies of all but a few countries in the world. The actions of something as big as the federal government, then, not only affect every American individually in terms of the reach of government programs and policies, but also can significantly affect the overall performance of the economy. Economists acknowledge that the impact of something so large is often unpredictable, but there is no denying its significance.

There are a lot of ways to break down federal spending, but if the goal is to understand how Congress directs the actions of the government, the most useful way is to look at it the way the board of directors does. On Capitol Hill, spending is usually broken down into three broad categories, discretionary spending, mandatory spending or direct spending, and spending to pay for the interest on the accumulated national debt:

Discretionary spending—This category refers to spending on government programs (known as *discretionary programs*) that are dependent on budget authority in yearly appropriations acts for their funding. Discretionary spending is often called *controllable* spending, because appropriations acts are in effect for only a single year, so Congress retains more control over agency programs that are covered in these acts. Most of what the government does fits into this category—including providing for the defense of the nation, protecting the homeland, funding most education and research programs, providing foreign aid, caring for the national parks, tracking infectious diseases, inspecting the food supply, regulating the nuclear industry, implementing environmental laws, and on and on. The operating budgets of all the agencies are included in the discretionary spending category, including those that administer mandatory programs.[1]

Mandatory spending, or direct spending—This category refers to spending on programs that is determined by formulas or criteria set forth in authorizing legislation. This sort of spending is often referred to as *uncontrollable* because the spending levels are not set from year to year in appropriations bills, as with discretionary programs, but rather depend in most cases on the number of people who meet eligibility criteria for the subsidies or payments. If the economy takes an unexpected downturn, more people will qualify for Medicaid (medical assistance to the poor) and unemployment insurance—both mandatory programs—and federal spending will increase in ways sometimes not anticipated by economists and budget experts. Many mandatory programs are called *entitlements* because citizens who qualify through age, disability, employment status, poverty, or other criteria are *entitled* to payments from the government by law. The biggest mandatory programs include those administered by the Social Security Administration (SSA), especially old-age and survivors' insurance, the Medicare programs, and Medicaid; others include unemployment insurance and food stamps.[2]

FIGURE 5.1   *Mandatory Spending Consumes a Growing Share of the Federal Budget*

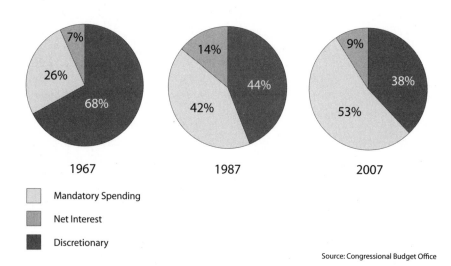

☐	Mandatory Spending
☐	Net Interest
■	Discretionary

Source: Congressional Budget Office

Interest on the national debt—This category is exactly what it sounds like: Congress authorizes the Treasury Department to borrow to finance the activities of the government that are not covered by taxes and other revenue sources. Ordinary citizens, banks, and foreign governments in effect lend the Treasury money by buying U.S. bonds. Like any credit account, this debt must be serviced. Sometimes people confuse the national debt with the *deficit*. The deficit is any annual shortfall, which will add to the nation's total accumulated debt. In 2009 about 60 percent of the total debt of over $11 trillion was owed "publicly," that is, to citizens, banks, and foreign governments; the remainder was owed internally to government trust funds, mostly the Social Security trust fund.

The breakdown of the federal budget has changed dramatically over the last forty years. Figure 5.1 shows the changes in the proportion of spending on discretionary programs and mandatory programs in 1967, 1987, and 2007. Obviously, mandatory spending has grown dramatically relative to discretionary spending.

The discretionary part of the federal government is, however, tremendously important; as mentioned earlier, it includes most of the essential government services that Americans rely on every day. But in sheer dollar terms, the major mandatory

TABLE 5.1   *Spending by Agency, Fiscal Year 2008 (in millions of dollars)*

AGENCY OR DEPARTMENT	OUTLAYS	% OF TOTAL[a]
Agriculture[b]	$90,796	2.75%
Commerce	7,222	0.21
Defense (military)	594,686	18.50
Education	65,960	2.06
Energy	21,400	0.66
Health and Human Services[c]	700,489	21.88
Homeland Security	40,684	1.25
Housing and Urban Development	49,088	1.50
Interior	9,875	0.32
Justice	26,545	0.83
Labor[d]	58,838	1.82
State	17,506	0.51
Transportation	64,944	1.88
Treasury[e]	548,813	17.06
Veterans Affairs	84,786	2.61
Corps of Engineers	5,075	0.16
Other Defense (civil programs)	45,785	1.39
Environmental Protection Agency	7,939	0.25
Executive Office of the President	1,173	0.35
General Services Administration	343	0.08
International assistance programs	11,405	0.35
National Aeronautics and Space Administration	17,833	0.56
National Science Foundation	5,847	0.18
Office of Personnel Management	64,393	2.00
Small Business Administration	528	0.14
Social Security Administration	646,423	20.11
Other independent agencies	49,643	1.51
Total	3,056,427	100.92

a. Total does not equal 100 percent owing to rounding.

b. Includes mandatory spending on farm subsidies and food stamps.

c. Includes mandatory spending on Medicare and Medicaid programs.

d. Includes mandatory spending on unemployment insurance and other outlays.

e. Outlays to service the national debt constitute most of the total.

Source: *Office of Management and Budget.*

programs have swamped the discretionary side of the budget. Most of the change is due to the growth of Medicare, Medicaid, and Social Security. As can be seen in the more detailed agency-by-agency breakdown of federal spending in Table 5.1, the amount of money spent by the Social Security Administration in fiscal year 2008 was greater than that spent by the Defense Department. (About $600 billion of SSA spending was on mandatory programs.) In addition, almost 85 percent of the spending at the U.S. Department of Health and Human Services (HHS) is for mandatory Medicare and Medicaid programs.

THE PRESIDENT'S BUDGET: KICKING OFF THE CONGRESSIONAL BUDGET PROCESS

Each year Congress eagerly awaits the delivery of the president's budget on the first Monday in February. Its arrival serves as the kickoff for the congressional budget season.

In a nutshell, the president's budget is a detailed description of the president's agenda for the coming fiscal year beginning on October 1. It also tracks the long-term implications of that agenda. After all, presidents often propose new programs and changes in tax law that would take years to implement. The budget includes exactly what the president wants each and every agency of the government to do, how much money the executive branch would need appropriated to carry out its agenda, and any tax laws the president would like to see enacted or changed.

A lot of work goes into this document. Budget offices in every federal agency and department, together with the Office of Management and Budget (OMB), an agency in the Executive Office of the President, spend a good part of the year putting together the documents. Literally thousands of federal workers spend a major part of their day on the details of the president's budget.

It is not uncommon for congressional leaders to declare the president's budget "dead on arrival" the moment it arrives in February, especially if the presidency and the Congress are controlled by different parties. Members of Congress invariably point out that it is the legislative branch that decides in law what the government will do and, more to the point, how much it will spend.

But the president's budget request *does* matter, regardless of which party is in control or if control is divided. The claim that the comprehensive presentation of the president's vision for the upcoming year is irrelevant—or "dead on arrival"—is just political rhetoric. There are two reasons why the president's budget matters when the final policies are put into law.

First of all, the president has the power to veto laws passed by Congress, which, as we have seen, makes the president a player in the legislative process. It is a rare day when Congress overrides a presidential veto. If Congress wants to put something into law, the president's preferences almost always have to be a part of the equation. Since the president's budget is, in effect, the official statement of his agenda, it is a consequential document, and Congress invariably must incorporate at least some of the president's priorities into appropriations law. The separated system of government is a power-*sharing* arrangement, and it applies to the budget as much as anywhere else.

Second, the federal government is an incredibly vast entity with an incredibly complex budget. It is literally impossible for the relatively limited congressional staff to have intricate, detailed knowledge of the vast range of government programs. There are thousands of employees in the budget offices of the federal government putting together the president's budget, yet there are only a couple of hundred professional staff on the congressional Appropriations Committees. Congressional staff rely on the experts in the executive branch to a significant degree. As a practical matter, Congress uses the president's budget request as a starting point each year when putting the budget into law in the appropriations acts. The federal budget is simply too big for Congress to start from scratch each year in deciding what to fund.

Putting the President's Budget Together

Putting together the president's budget is a fairly orderly process that takes place in the year before the budget is presented to Congress on the first Monday in February. The following is the timetable followed most years in the executive branch.

Timetable for the Preparation of the President's FY 2011 Budget

March 2009—Agencies begin formulating budgets with guidance from the parent departments.

June 2009—Agencies submit budgets to the departments. (Independent agencies such as the National Aeronautic and Space Administration [NASA] and the National Endowment for the Humanities [NEH] do not have parent departments and thus do not follow this step.)

July 2009—OMB Circular A-11, which provides guidance on budget development, is issued to the departments.

September 2009—The departments and independent agencies submit budgets to OMB.

November 2009—OMB gives the *passback* to the departments around Thanksgiving.

December 2009—The departments and independent agencies may appeal the funding levels and allocations through OMB all the way to the president.

February 2010—The president submits his budget to Congress on the first Monday of the month.

The Office of Management and Budget supervises this process for the president.[3] OMB is his main management tool as he copes with the responsibility of running (or trying to run) the federal government. It is staffed by about five hundred highly trained civil servants, with a thin layer of political appointees at the top designated by the president to make sure the agency does his bidding. The OMB director is subject to Senate approval and is one of the most important positions in any administration. OMB does not itself run any federal programs; instead, it has the task of managing the process of putting together the president's budget, managing executive branch budget implementation, and monitoring the progress of the president's budgetary priorities on Capitol Hill.

OMB sets guidelines for each department and agency to follow in constructing its budget, according to the priorities and instructions of the president. As indicated earlier, agencies begin work on a particular fiscal year budget about eighteen months before the relevant fiscal year begins, usually in March of the previous calendar year. Through the spring and summer, agencies work with their parent departments (for example, the U.S. Fish and Wildlife Service [FWS] and the Bureau of Land Management [BLM] are part of the Interior Department, and each branch of the armed services works with the Defense Department) to put together a detailed budget, which they submit to OMB around Labor Day. Independent agencies, such as NASA, NEH, and many regulatory agencies, work directly with OMB without the supervision of a parent department.

OMB then goes through a comprehensive review of the submissions of the various departments and independent agencies of government, checking carefully to see whether they are staying within the OMB budgetary guidelines reflecting the priorities of the president. During the fall, OMB is in constant contact with officials at the departments and agencies. Ultimately OMB completes a full draft of the president's budget by around Thanksgiving and returns the relevant portions to the departments and independent agencies. This is called the *passback*. If the departments and agencies do not like what they see in the passback, they may appeal the decisions made by OMB up the executive branch chain of command all the way to the president himself. In practice, the president usually hears only a few appeals; top-ranking White House officials handle most of the work for him. This practice can differ a great deal, however, from one president to the next.

Ultimately OMB and the agency and department budget offices throughout the government work through the holidays and into January finishing up the complex

FIGURE 5.2   *Congressional Budget and Appropriations Process*

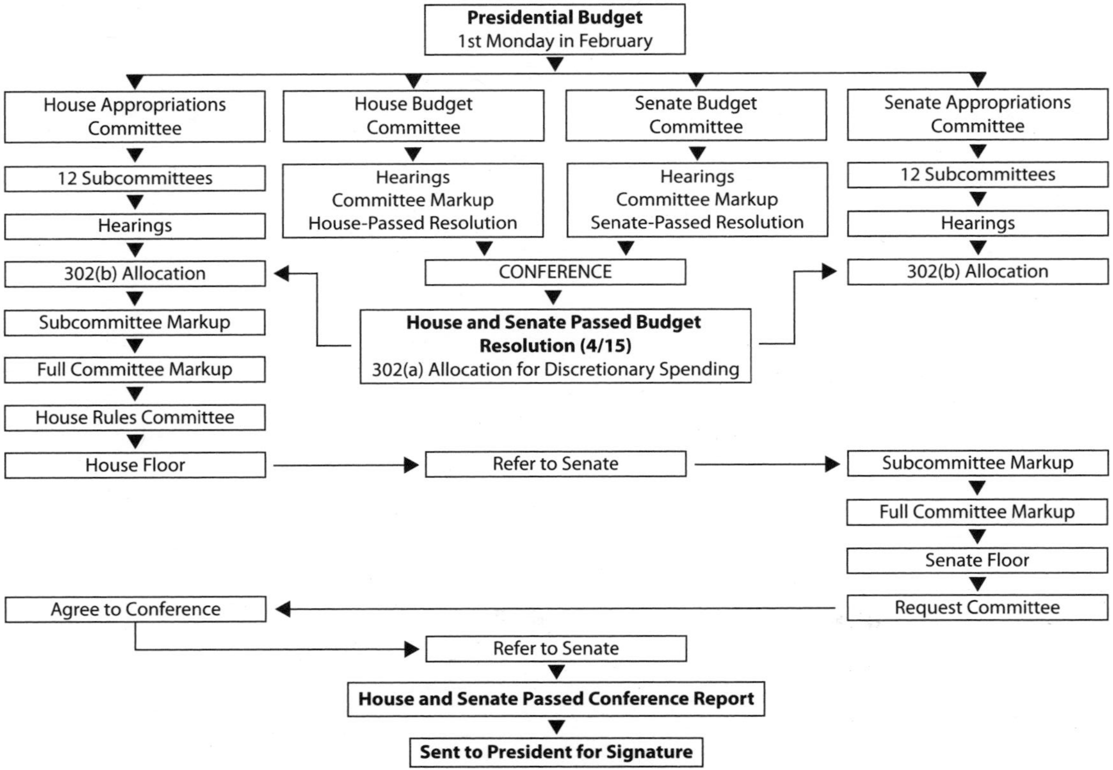

budget documents that will be transmitted to the Congress. OMB also writes descriptive material providing an overview of the president's goals and priorities, which is intended to sell the budget to the board of directors and the American people. Finally the president, as tradition dictates, delivers a prime-time address on the State of the Union in late January, which is in many ways a preview of and initial sales pitch for his comprehensive budget request.

OMB stays very busy the rest of the year monitoring the progress of the president's agenda on Capitol Hill and submitting official statements—called *statements of administration policy* (SAPs)[4]—on the president's position on bills as they make their way through the legislative process. At the same time, OMB must manage the whole budget preparation process all over again for the next fiscal year.

CONGRESS RESPONDS:
THE CONCURRENT BUDGET RESOLUTION

Congress's first order of business, once it receives the president's budget on the first Monday in February, is to establish its own priorities. That is what the Concurrent Budget Resolution (or the *budget resolution*) is meant to do.

The budget resolution establishes the priorities of the majority party in the Congress—or in the case of a House and Senate controlled by opposing parties, a compromise set of priorities. It is meant to put in place the framework for building the federal budget for the next fiscal year on the spending and revenue side, setting budget rules to guide the work of Congress in the ensuing several months as it attempts to pass appropriations bills, authorizing bills that affect mandatory programs, and tax bills on the revenue side before the new fiscal year starts on October 1. In and of itself the budget resolution is not law and never goes to the president. As can be seen in the congressional budget process chart in Figure 5.2, it is supposed to pass both houses of Congress in identical form by April 15.

What Does the Budget Resolution Do?

Putting together the budget resolution is rather like sitting down at the kitchen table on January 1 and trying to establish a reasonable framework for your personal or family budget for the next twelve months. You would probably estimate what your income will be and decide what sorts of expenditures you are stuck with (rent or the mortgage, student loan payments, and the like) and what other expenditures you would have more control over (vacations and travel, new clothes, eating out, and so on). In the more controllable area, you would decide whether you could spend more or whether it would be wise to cut back. You might consider whether you would like to take on any more long-term obligations, such as purchasing a new car or buying a first home if you are a renter. You would also decide what kind of additional debt, if any, you can afford to incur; you might entertain the idea of increasing your revenue stream by working harder, taking on a second job, or trying to find a new, more remunerative, one.

Setting out a personal budget like this is, in many respects, a goal. You might aim to cut back on spending, or you might aim to work harder and make more money, but you would have to take real, concrete actions during the year to accomplish those things. Similarly, Congress's budget resolution puts it on record for a set of priorities on spending and taxes, but it does not actually accomplish those goals. You probably would hope that your actions during the year will closely coincide with the personal or family budget you established on the first day of the year; in the same way, the majority party in Congress would like for the bills it passes during the year establishing the actual federal budget and revenue stream to resemble its budget framework as voted on in the budget resolution.

In our personal or family budget, many of us do relatively little tinkering with big, fixed expenses (often because we cannot), such as the mortgage, college tuition for the children, insurance costs, and health care premiums. And increasing the revenue stream by taking another job, working harder, or getting a new job might not be feasible either. As a result, in most years our most important financial decisions boil down to the ones we have more control over. Will we cut back on controllable spending—by spending fewer nights out, taking a less extravagant vacation, and buying fewer clothes—or will we leave room in our budget to increase those discretionary types of expenditures?

The same is usually true for Congress. The members often leave the revenue stream alone, making no major changes in the tax code. And typically they leave in place long-term obligations such as mandatory spending for Social Security and Medicare programs, which take up so much of the budget (much as your personal budget may be dominated by mortgage, tuition, and car payments). Attention ends up being focused on the controllable part of the budget, the part Congress has to look at every year—the discretionary spending accounts. These costs happen to be extremely important (national defense, research, border security, among many others) but are less expensive in terms of sheer dollar amounts than mandatory programs, as we have seen. The congressional budget resolution always establishes an allotment for discretionary spending, which becomes the focus of a great deal of attention every year.

The Budget Process Is Created

The budget resolution and the Budget Committees were a creation of the 93rd Congress in 1974. Up until that time, Congress had no institutionalized way to look at and coordinate taxing and spending policy—in other words, *to budget*. The Ways and Means (House) and Finance (Senate) Committees set tax policy, and the Appropriations Committees took care of spending policy. The problem was that by this time the appropriators were rapidly losing control of much federal spending, entitlement programs having been dramatically expanded and enhanced in the mid-1960s and early 1970s. As large deficits were becoming chronic, the federal budget seemed to be out of control.

The Budget and Impoundment Act of 1974 was passed to remedy the problem. One committee, the Budget Committee (each chamber would have one), would look at both sides of the ledger—taxing and spending—and develop a blueprint to guide lawmaking in those areas. This would be the Concurrent Budget Resolution.

The idea was to have members of the Budget Committees take a big-picture view of the federal budget that would not be linked to arbitrary jurisdictional categories as reflected in the congressional committee structure and the departments and agencies of the government. The new law broke down federal spending into twenty-one functional categories or areas of government activity not strictly tied to those jurisdictions. The committee members would recommend how much money needed to be spent on health, or on education, training and employment, or on science and technology, and so on, given existing federal programs. They might envision new programs as well. They would add up that spending and then be in a position to compare it to revenue as received by the Treasury, based on current tax law. Or alternatively, the committee could envision tax cuts to boost the economy or tax increases to balance the budget or for other purposes.

Functional Categories of the Budget Resolution

1. National defense (military)
2. National defense (other)
3. International affairs
4. General science, space, and technology
5. Energy
6. Natural resources and environment
7. Agriculture
8. Commerce and housing credit

9. Transportation
10. Community and regional development
11. Education, training, employment, and social services
12. Health
13. Medicare
14. Income security
15. Social Security
16. Veterans' benefits and services
17. Administration of justice
18. General government
19. Net interest
20. Allowances
21. Undistributed offsetting receipts

The budget resolution coming out of committee would, in effect, be a recommendation on spending and taxing priorities for the next fiscal year (and usually projected out for five years) to the rest of the Congress. It would also provide information on the deficit or surplus situation, frequently offering the committee's judgment on what kind of deficit the government could prudently handle. Although not legally binding, the concurrent passage in the two chambers of the resolution would put Congress—or at least the majority party, which normally dictates the terms of the resolution—on record as keeping to a certain level of overall spending and a specific deficit figure. It could also, in certain circumstances, provide a special streamlined process to make it less difficult for Congress to do unpopular but necessary things, such as raising taxes or cutting spending on mandatory programs.

It is most important to stress the political implications of the budget resolution. It is not binding, but it does represent a public statement by the majority party of its priorities in the federal budget—essentially what the majority party in Congress wants the government to spend and what tax levels and deficit it deems appropriate. Failing to follow through with legislation consistent with those goals can have political repercussions.

The reason the budget resolution can be a relatively pure expression of the majority's preferences is that by law it cannot be filibustered in the Senate, unlike almost every other kind of bill. Thus, the majority in the Senate does not need to consult and compromise with the minority, as it normally must do with other legislation. When the same party controls both chambers, the resolution usually passes with little or no minority party support.

The Early Stages of the Process

Immediately upon receipt of the president's budget in early February, the Budget Committees in the House and Senate commence with hearings to examine the president's request. These usually take the form of looking at the president's big-picture goals as laid out in his spending and taxing priorities.

Budget Committee hearings are often high-profile affairs, with members of the Committee grilling the chairman of the Federal Reserve, the secretary of the Treasury Department, the secretary of the Defense Department, and the president's chief budget adviser, the OMB director. If the party in control of the Congress is different from the president's party, nationally known experts outside of government who will take the side of the congressional majority are called on to highlight the differences between the two parties.

Ultimately each Budget Committee chair in the House and Senate will direct his or her staff to write up the resolution itself. The chair normally does not consult very much with the minority party in the development of the resolution. If the presidency and Congress are controlled by the same party, there is considerable cross-fertilization between the branches, and the resolution is likely to enshrine most of the president's priorities. But even in the case of unified government, it can be difficult at the end of the process for the House and Senate to agree to the same blueprint. Twice during the two-term administration of George W. Bush, when Republicans controlled the levers of power in Congress, House and Senate negotiators were unable to agree on a budget blueprint.[5] The perspectives of the two chambers can be so different as to preclude agreement, even with unified party control.

The Components of the Budget Resolution

The budget resolution is essentially a big-picture view of what the majority party thinks the government should do in the next fiscal year. Normally it has five key components:

1. It adds up the total spending envisioned by the majority party, including the discretionary area, mandatory programs, and anticipated debt service.
2. It establishes a target for all tax revenues.
3. It divides all spending into functional categories in order to inform the debate about budgetary priorities on the floor of each chamber.
4. It establishes spending limits, the so-called 302(a) allocations, for congressional committees—most importantly for the Appropriations Committees, which handle the discretionary part of the federal budget.

5. It calculates the expected deficit (or surplus) in the coming fiscal year.

The budget resolution *may* have the following additional component:

6. If the majority party wishes to make significant changes to a tax law or mandatory program, the resolution may include *reconciliation instructions*. These instructions are the means by which the Budget Committees expedite the consideration of such changes. The reconciliation instructions give broad guidance to the authorizing committees that deal with tax matters or mandatory programs. When those committees finish their work (and they are given a target date), they send the results to the Budget Committee in their chamber. The Budget Committee packages all the component parts into a *reconciliation bill* for floor consideration. *That bill may not be filibustered on the Senate floor.* The term "reconciliation" is used because the budget resolution gives instructions to the relevant committees to *reconcile* current tax law with the revenue target set forth in the budget resolution, or to *reconcile* the law governing mandatory programs with the spending totals in the budget resolution.

The budget resolution covers all aspects of the federal budget. In looking at the tax side, it may call for changes or it may merely calculate revenue based on existing law and economic conditions. The resolution looks at the spending side and always sets the level of the more controllable discretionary spending for the next fiscal year, the 302(a) allocation, which is then parceled out to government agencies by the Appropriations Committees in appropriations laws. It may merely calculate mandatory spending based on current law, or it may call for changes. It calculates the expected debt service based on the yearly deficit projected to be added to the national debt. (Of course, if the resolution anticipates a budget surplus, the debt service may well decrease as the national debt decreases.)

The more ambitious budget resolution that calls for tax and/or mandatory program changes may handle these in one of two ways. It may simply put forth a budget that calls for, let's say, a new Medicare prescription drug program or tax increases to close the deficit, and then allow the relevant committees to go about their work putting the change into effect through the normal legislative process. Or the resolution may use reconciliation instructions that require authorizing committees to send their tax or mandatory program changes back to the Budget Committee for approval and packaging for floor consideration. Reconciliation instructions can work to streamline the legislative process in the Senate, but as we shall see shortly, they have certain disadvantages.

FIGURE 5.3   *Budget Reconciliation Process*

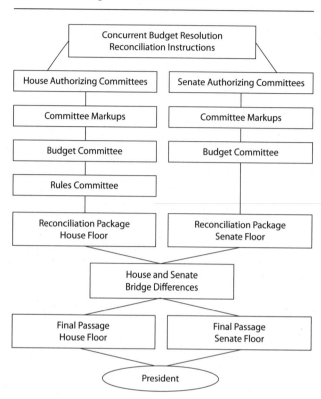

Passing the Budget Resolution

The budget resolution is typically rammed through the House and Senate committees on party line votes. On the floors of the respective bodies, however, the process
differs in significant ways.

In the House, the minority party is not permitted to amend the majority's budget resolution on the floor, but it is typically allowed a full-fledged alternative resolution to be brought up for consideration (technically called an *amendment in the
nature of a substitute*, or simply a *substitute*). It is normally voted down on a party line
vote, followed by the affirmative vote, also party line, for the majority's resolution.
Occasionally a rump group from one or the other party is permitted to offer a full
alternative resolution. In recent years the Republican Study Committee (a conservative caucus within the party), the Blue Dog Coalition (a group of moderate Democrats interested in deficit reduction), and the Congressional Black Caucus have
been allowed to offer alternatives.[6]

In the more freewheeling Senate, no filibuster is permitted (and in a rare departure in Senate procedure, debate is limited to twenty hours), but amendments are allowed. Within the debate time limit set in law, dozens of amendments are brought up, often on specific spending proposals that are not usually a part of the original resolution document. Some of these pass; most do not. Those that do pass usually do not survive the subsequent conference negotiations to produce a Concurrent Budget Resolution. More often than not, senators offer amendments in order to appease certain interested parties and to indicate publicly their support for a particular program or agency. In other words, most of these amendments are for political consumption only and have little or no effect on subsequent spending or tax legislation.

In the end, a relatively simple and clean resolution is usually agreed to by the bodies after the conference committee meets. It states the spending and revenue levels for the government in the coming year, sets the discretionary allotment for the Appropriations Committees, calculates whatever deficit or surplus is likely to result, and sometimes includes reconciliation instructions for any controversial and high-priority matters for the majority party.

The agreement is not usually made by the April 15 deadline—the resolution falls behind schedule by a month or more in most years. This has the effect of delaying the processing of appropriations bills and any other budget-related legislation contemplated by the resolution in the mandatory or tax areas.

The Reconciliation Process

In 2003, when the Republican Congress wished to institute several tax cuts, including a large reduction in the capital gains tax rate, it chose to go the reconciliation route. The reason? If a tax bill is produced pursuant to reconciliation instructions in the budget resolution, that bill, like the resolution itself, may not be filibustered in the Senate. As we saw in the last chapter, the Senate usually requires sixty votes to pass consequential legislation; with reconciliation, the tax bill would be *fast-tracked* and require only fifty-one votes. This worked to the Republicans' advantage because there was substantial Democratic opposition to this particular provision and the GOP did not have the working sixty-vote margin to pass the bill in the normal way.

As can be seen in Figure 5.3, a separate procedure is followed when reconciliation instructions are included in the budget resolution.

As noted earlier, these instructions may only pertain to tax law and mandatory programs. (Discretionary spending is covered by the 302[a] allocation.) The relevant authorizing committees are given instructions to produce tax or mandatory program changes to meet certain revenue or spending targets. When these committees have completed their work, it is packaged together by the Budget Committees before floor consideration.

For the Republicans in 2003, the downside was that, according to Senate rules, if a reconciliation bill will increase the deficit or reduce the surplus after a five-year period, its provisions must expire at that point.[7] So the capital gains provision, as well as several others passed with it, had to be set to expire at the end of the five-year period. This would not have been the case if the bill had passed in the normal legislative process without the filibuster protections afforded by reconciliation.

Contrast that to the Medicare prescription drug plan, a mandatory spending program that Republicans budgeted for and that passed the same year. It, too, would have tended to increase the deficit after five years, but Republicans chose to pass it in the normal way, unprotected from the filibuster by reconciliation procedures. They calculated that they could probably quash any attempted filibusters by picking up some Democratic votes. As a result, when the Medicare prescription drug plan passed, it was not set to expire in five years.

It should be noted that changes put into effect by reconciliation procedures—specifically, cuts in mandatory programs and tax increases—do *not* have to expire after five years, since such changes would tend to *decrease* the deficit. The reconciliation process was put in place to make it somewhat easier to do unpopular things that go against the grain in Congress—namely, tax more and cut popular mandatory programs. Sometimes these sorts of actions are needed if deficits threaten economic growth. In 2007 Democrats moved to prohibit the use of reconciliation for legislation that would increase the deficit.

The budget resolution expresses the agenda of the majority party for the coming fiscal year. Failure to pass such a resolution is not the end of the world, but it does indicate serious divisions within the congressional majority party in terms of priorities and emphasis. The resolution is often criticized as toothless—as a "New Year's resolution"—and easily ignored once Congress gets down to the real business of passing laws. But in fact the resolution does put constraints on discretionary spending in the form of the 302(a) allocation, an important part of fiscal discipline, and has been the vehicle, through reconciliation, for putting into place most of the major changes in tax law in the last thirty years, as well as many significant reductions in mandatory spending. It was also used to pass legislation in 1996 that ended the federal welfare entitlement.

THE APPROPRIATIONS PROCESS

From year to year, no committees direct government action more than the Appropriations Committees. These panels have funding jurisdiction over the operations of the entire government and most government programs. (The only exceptions are the mandatory programs, the funding levels for which are determined in authorizing legislation.) From the moment the president's budget request arrives on Capitol Hill the first Monday in February, the Appropriations Committees are hard at work examining the funding that the agencies want in the coming fiscal year and developing the legislation that they believe will enable the agencies to serve their missions. This is the so-called power of the purse, the board of directors' most important tool in directing the work of government.

There are twelve appropriations bills that determine discretionary spending levels for the next fiscal year, and all are truly "must-pass" legislation. In fact, the U.S. government could operate satisfactorily if Congress did nothing more in a given year than pass these twelve bills. Because of the centrality of these bills, the appropriations process typically becomes the center of attention for the Congress. As efforts by authorizing committees to create new programs or make changes in existing ones are either passed into law or, more commonly, run into insuperable obstacles in the legislative process, the focus turns to the appropriations bills.

The fact that these bills must be passed does not make them *easy* to pass; in fact, the opposite is true. Appropriations bills can be extremely difficult to complete and often require highly creative approaches to the legislative process in order to become law.

The Appropriations Committees

The Appropriations Committees first came into existence in the 1860s. Before that time, spending and taxes were handled by the Ways and Means and Finance Committees. The two responsibilities were separated in 1865, leaving Ways and Means and Finance with jurisdiction over the tax code and giving the new Appropriations Committees control over funding legislation.[8]

For much of the history of the Appropriations Committees, nearly all federal spending was discretionary, and thus under their control. Beginning in the 1930s and especially in the 1960s, the tide began to turn with the creation of mandatory programs through authorizing legislation. Still, to this day, even though only about 38 percent of federal spending is discretionary, this category includes most of the essential work of the government. These committees do not have quite the overarching control they had in their heyday, but they remain the most important committees on the Hill year in and year out—largely because they must act to keep the government operating.

Today, in both chambers, the Appropriations Committees have twelve subcommittees, as listed here. Funding jurisdiction over the executive branch of the federal government is divided among eleven of them. One subcommittee handles funding for the legislative branch.

Appropriations Subcommittees (both House and Senate)
1. Agriculture, Rural Development, Food and Drug Administration, and Related Agencies
2. Commerce, Justice, Science, and Related Agencies
3. Defense
4. Energy and Water Development and Related Agencies
5. Financial Services and General Government
6. Homeland Security
7. Interior, Environment, and Related Agencies
8. Labor, Health and Human Services, Education, and Related Agencies
9. Legislative Branch
10. Military Construction, Veterans' Affairs, and Related Agencies
11. State, Foreign Operations, and Related Agencies
12. Transportation, Housing and Urban Development, and Related Agencies

Each of the fifty-nine House members who serve on the committee gets two or three subcommittee assignments. Most of these members serve only on the Appropriations Committee. The importance and power associated with the committee make it an exclusive one by the rules of both parties—its members need to get a rules waiver from their party in order to receive other committee assignments. Members clamor to get on Appropriations because it deals with "real money"; authorizing committees, on the other hand, may be relatively less appealing because they do not actually dole out money in most cases.

In the Senate, the thirty members of the Appropriations Committee may have as many as six subcommittee assignments, but unlike in the House, all Senate appropriators have other committee assignments.

Not only does the majority party control the chair position for the full committee, but all the subcommittees are chaired by majority party members as well. These twelve slots are some of the most sought-after positions in the Congress—the group of subcommittee chairs is sometimes called the "college of cardinals." The cardinals write the first drafts of appropriations bills, a task that effectively gives them substantial influence over billions of dollars of federal spending each year. The majority leadership of the committees also hires the bulk of the expert committee staff, many of whom have been with the committee for a long time and have far more detailed knowledge of the federal budget than the members themselves. Of the approximately 240 staffers on Appropriations in the House and Senate, about two-thirds are hired by the majority. Having said that, Appropriations staff operate in a more bipartisan fashion than those on most other committees.

The Subcommittee Hearings

Much like the members of the Budget Committees, who begin examining the president's budget the moment it reaches Capitol Hill, the Appropriations subcommittees begin holding hearings and initiating meetings with executive branch agency officials in early February. But unlike the Budget Committees, with their bird's-eye view of the federal budget, the Appropriations Committees—especially at the subcommittee level—get into the specific details of government programs at all government agencies.

From February through April every year, a parade of agency heads and other high-ranking officials, as well as the top brass in the armed services, march up to Capitol Hill for formal and informal meetings with Appropriations staff and members. The agency personnel have one task: to defend the president's budget request to their congressional overseers. Although agency officials might have had bitter disagreements with OMB and the president over funding matters and other policies, once the president's budget is delivered, they all must be on the same page. Disagreements within the executive branch are regarded as internal matters, and all executive branch personnel are required to support the final decision as handed down by OMB for the president.[9]

Subcommittee hearings are the most public of the interactions between appropriators and the agencies. While Appropriations staff have done in-depth research into the agency budget requests and have usually been in constant contact with top agency personnel throughout the year, hearings are the opportunity to get high-ranking officials on the public record on the key issues facing the agency and its funding levels.

Often agency heads and the members of the subcommittee understand each other well and have long-established relationships. They may collaborate on the questions to be asked and the answers to be tendered during the hearings in order to advance common goals. Sometimes members of Congress try to get agency people to admit that they disagree with the president's spending priorities. Such prodding can lead to very uncomfortable moments for high-ranking people, who must stay true to the president's priorities as expressed in the president's budget in all official interactions. Politics and opposing priorities in the two branches or between the two parties are almost always behind these sorts of clashes. Agency officials need to be on their toes while testifying. A well-stated case in public may make it tougher for members to cut agency funding or otherwise tie agency officials' hands if they are so inclined.

In the larger picture, hearings are a chance for any interested group to gauge what is happening with the federal budget in a given year (in fact, many nongovernmental groups are brought in to testify at hearings) and for members of Congress to advance a case for their priorities. Hearings amount to a public vetting of the views of the relevant parties.

The All-Important 302(a) and 302(b) Allocations

The day the Congress passes the Concurrent Budget Resolution is a big one for appropriators. The resolution contains the 302(a) allocation, which represents the total sum of funds that Congress intends to allocate to discretionary spending for the next fiscal year. The appropriators take over from there.

It is up to the Appropriations Committees in the two chambers, in internal deliberations controlled by the respective full committee chairs, to divide the 302(a) allocation among the twelve subcommittees. This subdivision of the larger pot of money is called the 302(b) allocation. Each subcommittee gets one. Ideally the budget resolution passes by April 15, giving the committees ample time to set the 302(b) allocations and the subcommittees time to complete their bills. But with the budget resolution more commonly being tardy, the appropriations process begins to fall behind schedule.

Typically the House Appropriations chair moves more quickly than the Senate chair in establishing 302(b) allocations for each subcommittee. Table 5.2 shows the 302(b) allocations in the House and Senate for fiscal year 2009.

Senators on Appropriations are stretched so thin that it is harder for them to find the time to come to a speedy agreement. They serve on other committees, and some have twice as many subcommittee assignments as House appropriators. Some senators are also chairs of both an Appropriations subcommittee and another full authorizing committee. This amounts to two full-time jobs! Most House appropriators have the advantage of being able to focus exclusively on their committee work while doing legislative business in Washington.

TABLE 5.2   *302(b) Allocations for Fiscal Year 2009 (in millions of dollars)*

APPROPRIATIONS SUBCOMMITTEES	HOUSE ALLOCATION	SENATE ALLOCATION
Agriculture	$20,623	$20,435
Commerce, Justice, Science	56,858	57,900
Defense	487,740	487,740
Energy and Water	33,265	33,258
Financial Services and		
General Government	22,390	22,870
Homeland Security	42,075*	42,252*
Interior and Environment	27,867	27,750
Labor, HHS, and Education	153,121	153,139
Legislative Branch	4,404	4,400
Military Construction/VA	72,729	73,000
State and Foreign Operations	36,620	36,620
Transportation and HUD	54,997	53,325
Total	1,012,690	1,012,690

* The Homeland Security allocation includes $2,175,000 for BioShield, a program that the department administers in conjunction with Health and Human Services. BioShield stockpiles medical countermeasures for biological, chemical, nuclear, and radiological agents.

Source: *CongressDaily and the Appropriations Committees.*

The 302(b) allocation determines, for example, how much money the Subcommittee on Homeland Security has to distribute in its bill to the twenty-two agencies in the Department of Homeland Security. The chair of the Subcommittee on the Interior, Environment, and Related Agencies finds out the total sum he has to work with for the Interior Department and its agencies, the Environmental Protection Agency (EPA), and related smaller agencies. As can be seen in Table 5.2, the Senate 302(b) allocations are usually slightly different from the House ones, since senators are bound to have some different priorities in the distribution of discretionary spending even if the two chambers are controlled by the same party.

One cannot exaggerate the importance of the 302(b) allocations. It is at this stage that the relative priority of defense spending versus social spending—or more specifically, for example, spending on the Commerce Department, science, and space (the Subcommittee on Commerce, Justice, Science, and Related Agencies) versus spending on foreign aid and diplomacy (the Subcommittee on State and Foreign Operations)—is determined. This sets up potentially bitter zero-sum games among the agencies covered in the same appropriations bill. The Interior Department is pitted against the EPA in their bill, the Defense bill pits the armed services against one another, and the Homeland Security bill forces Customs and Border Protection, the Secret Service, and twenty other agencies to squabble over the same pot of money.

Marking Up the Appropriations Bills

The appropriations subcommittee chairs have one job: to write a bill to fund the agencies in their jurisdiction that can ultimately pass into law after the legislative process runs its course. Ideally that final bill, with all the inevitable changes and compromises along the way, will resemble the priorities of the chair and his or her party. The first task is to get the subcommittee members to go along.

The bills almost always move first in the House since, again, Senate appropriators have trouble focusing the way House members can because of the multiplicity of their legislative duties.[10] The goal in the House, in keeping with the chamber's rules, is to get all twelve appropriations bills passed on the floor and sent to the Senate before the July 4 holiday break. In recent years the House has sometimes done this, but more often a few of the bills are not passed until mid to late July.

The Appropriations Committees are under more pressure than many other committees to produce a product that can make it through the process and become law. After all, the functioning of the federal government depends on the successful completion of the appropriations bills. Subcommittee chairs, as a result, are carefully attuned to the legislative realities, especially the need for bipartisanship due to the ability of the minority party to block action in the Senate. It is for this reason that the Appropriations Committees are characterized by more bipartisanship than almost all other congressional committees.

House subcommittee chairs schedule a markup as soon as they and their staff put together a bill. Most chairs consult carefully with all subcommittee members, including minority party members, and try to assemble a consensus product—that is, one that is more likely to make it through the entire legislative process and to the president's desk relatively intact.

As soon as the bill passes the House subcommittee—there is often a unanimous bipartisan vote at this stage—it is scheduled by the full committee chair for a markup involving the entire committee. Although it is relatively easy to get a consensus among the twelve to fifteen subcommittee members, the full committee can be a different matter. The hearing room is jammed during the markup with members, staff, and a standing-room-only crowd of interest group representatives who have a stake in the particular government funding decisions being made. The chair goes through the bill line by line, with committee members offering amendments that change wording or funding levels. Eventually a vote is taken on the bill as amended, and it is then in a position to move toward floor consideration in the full House.

The completion of the bill at the committee stage in the House is a key point in the funding process for agencies and government programs. House Appropriations Committee members and their staff are among the most knowledgeable people on the Hill regarding the particulars of agency funding. They not only establish a benchmark for the rest of the appropriations process but produce a report explaining in plain language what they want the agencies to do to comply with the committee in the next fiscal year. This so-called *report language* is not statutory, but as a clear statement of the wishes of the appropriators, it is closely followed by agency heads. Even if Congress does not put something into law, it is wise for the agency heads to abide by committee report language—after all, they have to come before the committee members each and every year to plead their case for more funding or different priorities. There is no point in needlessly irritating these key players and their staff.

The Rules Committee and the House Floor

As can be seen in Figure 5.2, appropriations bills, like other legislation, make a stop at the Rules Committee before going to the House floor. Technically this step is unnecessary. House rules give appropriations bills privileged status, which means that they may move to the head of the queue for consideration on the floor and do not require a special rule to structure debate. In reality, however, appropriations bills always make the obligatory stop at the Rules Committee before being scheduled for the floor by leadership.

The reason is simple: Although appropriations bills are traditionally kept open to amendment on the floor of the House (unlike almost all other controversial and important measures) and thus do not require a closed rule, they always run afoul of at least a couple of House rules. The Appropriations Committee, as a result, needs protections for its bill on the floor that can only be granted by the Rules Committee. Two House rules in particular are always violated in appropriations legislation as it emerges from the committee.

First, in theory, appropriations bills are supposed to provide funding only for programs that have current authorization of appropriations. But authorizing committees often fail to update authorizations, for the reasons discussed in Chapter 4. However, members of Congress (and the public for that matter) insist that key government programs continue operating, whether or not they have a current authorization for appropriations. Every year hundreds of billions of dollars are appropriated

TABLE 5.3   *Fiscal Year 2008 Appropriations with Expired Authorizations, by Senate Authorizing Committee (in millions of dollars)*

SENATE COMMITTEE	NUMBER OF LAWS*	AMOUNT APPROPRIATED
Agriculture	10	$120
Armed Services	4	581,410
Banking	16	32, 888
Commerce	34	14, 839
Energy and National Resources	21	5,104
Environment and Public Works	33	2,478
Finance	5	177
Foreign Relations	20	27,984
Health, Education, Labor, and Pensions	33	35,772
Homeland Security and Governmental Affairs	13	206
Indian Affairs	10	3,420
Judiciary	18	6,109
Rules and Administration	4	191
Small Business	2	1
Veterans' Affairs	7	37,791
Total	220	748,490

* The number of laws under the jurisdiction of the committee with expired authorization of appropriations.

Source: *Congressional Budget Office.*

for programs whose authorizations have expired. The high-water mark was in fiscal year 2008. As indicated in Table 5.3, over $748 billion of discretionary spending—nearly three-quarters of the total—was for programs whose authorization of appropriations had expired. The figure was particularly high that year because the Defense Department appropriation preceded the authorization (which followed several weeks later).

In addition, because of Congress's difficulty in reauthorizing agencies and programs, some policies on the books are out of date. As a result, members of authorizing committees often request that key provisions they were unable to pass as part of a larger authorization be included in the appropriations bill as considered in the Appropriations Committee. If they really want their pet provisions in law, the appropriations bill is a good vehicle to achieve that end, since those eventually must pass. This practice also violates a House rule—appropriations bills are only supposed to provide funding and are not supposed to establish agency policy. It should be noted, however, that appropriators are willing to serve as the gatekeepers for changes in agency policies and sometimes inject favored provisions of their own.

The upshot is that appropriations bills almost always violate the prohibitions against unauthorized appropriations and policy language in an appropriations bill. Violation of these rules may make a bill subject to a point of order on the floor. The enforcement of a point of order for a rules violation strips the offending provision from the bill. To avoid that, the Rules Committee must be consulted to obtain a waiver. If the special rule passes containing that waiver, the bill may not be challenged on the floor based on those rule violations.

That special rule, while permitting unauthorized appropriations and policy language in the underlying bill, *will not permit amendments on the floor that violate those rules*. So even though the bill that comes out of committee is always considered under some version of an open rule, amendments must abide by the rules of the House regardless of the fact that the bill itself does not.

One type of amendment that is permissible is one that increases or decreases funding for an agency. However, appropriations bills must stay within the 302(b) allocations given to each subcommittee. The bill reported from the committee is almost always at the 302(b) limit. If a member wishes to offer an amendment giving more money to a particular agency or program, that amendment must have an offset within the bill that cuts funding for something else. It is difficult for members to get support for amendments of this nature because they irritate other members who support the agency that would receive the cut. These amendments fail more often than they pass.

The other sort of amendment that is allowable on the House floor contains what is called *limitation language*, which restricts what an agency may do with appropriated funds. (Appropriations bills are loaded with limitation language even before they make it to the floor.) Limitation language is one of Congress's favorite tools for meddling with federal agencies. Telling an agency what it *cannot do* with its funds may be just as effective as telling the agency in an affirmative way what it must do. Limitation language has been used in recent years to prevent agencies from implementing regulations on the concentration of media ownership (the Federal Communications Commission), enforcing environmental standards (the EPA), and other matters. (Examples of limitation language can be seen in Exhibit 5.2.)

Although limitation language can have a significant impact on an agency, it is technically not a violation of the House rules that prohibit policy language. Policy language is defined as wording that affirmatively directs an agency to do something, as opposed to wording that prohibits a particular activity.

Appropriations Bills in the Senate

As one would expect, the Senate process is less structured and more haphazard. The Senate lags behind the House most years, owing to an overloaded schedule, the tradition of extended debate, and the overburdened membership. With appropriations legislation, the Senate normally waits for the House to pass a bill before it marks up its version. When the House begins passing bills in May and June, the markup process in Senate subcommittees is effectively jump-started.

For example, let's say that a House-passed appropriations bill—call it HR 2000, "Appropriations for the Department of Homeland Security"—is referred to the Senate Subcommittee on Homeland Security. As the Senate subcommittee chair and his staff prepare for markup, they retain the House number (HR 2000) but remove all House-passed language (with policy provisions and dollar figures for the agencies) and substitute their own version of the bill that they have been working on through the winter and spring. Ten or fifteen years ago, it was common for the Senate subcommittee to leave all the House policy and funding language intact and to amend it as bills went through the different stages of the process. That approach is no longer used.[11]

After the subcommittee marks up and passes its version of the Homeland Security funding bill, the bill moves to the full committee for a typically more contentious markup, just as in the House. The Senate Appropriations Committee will produce its own version of the report language for the bill, expressing its instructions for the department in plain language.

The Senate floor amendment procedure for appropriations legislation is more freewheeling than in the House. The majority leader in the Senate usually tries to negotiate a unanimous consent agreement (UC) so that there will be an end time to debate on this must-pass legislation. But to get such an agreement he has to make time for dozens of amendments. Senators will offer amendments that change funding levels (they, too, have to find offsets to stay within the 302[b] limits, just as House members do) and they are more easily able to inject policy matters into these bills, even though doing so also technically breaks Senate rules.

The Senate has a germaneness rule that applies only to appropriations legislation. The rule disallows any but funding-related amendments. Senators know that this rule is not always enforced, however, because the germaneness rule for appropriations requires only a bare majority vote to waive, rather than the supermajority sixty-vote requirement of many Senate rules, including the rule prohibiting funding in excess of the 302(b) allocation. So even as the Senate's presiding officer rules that a policy amendment is out of order, the senator offering the amendment can usually get a vote on the ruling. Members may not vote to enforce the rule but rather may vote based on their views on the substance of their colleague's amendment. Because policy amendments can be added to appropriations legislation with relative ease in the Senate, more controversial provisions are added to these bills on the floor than in the House.

When all goes smoothly in the Senate, the subcommittees and the full Appropriations Committee move bills along as soon as the House sends its finished product over, so that many appropriations bills will get to the Senate floor in July. Ideally, more than half are finished and moved on to conference committee before the traditional August recess, when subcommittee staff from the two chambers try to iron out the differences between the two versions of the bill in question. The aim is to have the remaining bills move through the Senate in September. The reality is that the process rarely proceeds on schedule—a problem we look into later in the chapter.

The Conference Committee Stage

Appropriations bills are complex and detailed pieces of legislation and, as such, always require lengthy and intense negotiations to resolve the substantial differences between the two chambers' versions of a bill. (The chambers are technically working on the same bill—HR 2000 in our example—although the language of each bill differs.) Unlike with other types of legislation, conference committees are overwhelmingly the method of choice for bridging the differences.

The conference committee comprises the relevant subcommittee members as well as the full committee chair and ranking member. Subcommittee staff from the two chambers meet for hours at a time to iron out the differences in dollar amounts and substantive policy language. The idea is to produce one consensus product. Staff resolve the vast majority of these differences in ways they are confident will satisfy the subcommittee leadership, the committee leadership, and the party leadership. They consult with the committee chair, the ranking member, the subcommittee chair, and the ranking subcommittee member on any controversial sticking points.

The finished version, the *conference report*, is agreed to by the majority of the senators and representatives in the conference and returned to the chambers for final approval. At that point the bills are normally not amendable on the floor of either chamber.[12] In the House, to the extent that standing rules have been violated, a

EXHIBIT 5.1
ACCOUNTS IN THE APPROPRIATIONS LAW FROM "FISCAL YEAR 2007 APPROPRIATION FOR THE DEPARTMENT OF DEFENSE"

Division A—Department of Defense Appropriations Act, 2007

That the following sums are appropriated, out of any money in the Treasury not otherwise appropriated, for the fiscal year ending September 30, 2007, for military functions administered by the Department of Defense and for other purposes, namely:

Title I: Military Personnel

MILITARY PERSONNEL, ARMY

For pay, allowances, individual clothing, subsistence, interest on deposits, gratuities, permanent change of station travel (including all expenses thereof for organizational movements), and expenses of temporary duty travel between permanent duty stations, for members of the Army on active duty (except members of reserve components provided for elsewhere), cadets, and aviation cadets; for members of the Reserve Officers' Training Corps; and for payments pursuant to section 156 of Public Law 97-377, as amended (42 U.S.C. 402 note), and to the Department of Defense Military Retirement Fund, $25,911,349,000.

MILITARY PERSONNEL, NAVY

For pay, allowances, individual clothing, subsistence, interest on deposits, gratuities, permanent change of station travel (including all expenses thereof for organizational movements), and expenses of temporary duty travel between permanent duty stations, for members of the Navy on active duty (except members of the Reserve provided for elsewhere), midshipmen, and aviation cadets; for members of the Reserve Officers' Training Corps; and for payments pursuant to section 156 of Public Law 97-377, as amended (42 U.S.C. 402 note), and to the Department of Defense Military Retirement Fund, $19,049,454,000.

MILITARY PERSONNEL, MARINE CORPS

For pay, allowances, individual clothing, subsistence, interest on deposits, gratuities, permanent change of station travel (including all expenses thereof for organizational movements), and expenses of temporary duty travel between permanent duty stations, for members of the Marine Corps on active duty (except members of the Reserve provided for elsewhere); and for payments pursuant to section 156 of Public Law 97-377, as amended (42 U.S.C. 402 note), and to the Department of Defense Military Retirement Fund, $7,932,749,000.

MILITARY PERSONNEL, AIR FORCE

For pay, allowances, individual clothing, subsistence, interest on deposits, gratuities, permanent change of station travel (including all expenses thereof for organizational movements), and expenses of temporary duty travel between permanent duty stations, for members of the Air Force on active duty (except members of reserve components provided for elsewhere), cadets, and aviation cadets; for members of the Reserve Officers' Training Corps; and for payments pursuant to section 156 of Public Law 97-377, as amended (42 U.S.C. 402 note), and to the Department of Defense Military Retirement Fund, $20,285,871,000.

Each of these paragraphs effectively plugs money into the account of one of the armed services. The money is for the coming fiscal year and must be spent according to existing authorizing law (cited near the end of each paragraph—42 U.S.C. 402 note). Other stipulations may be placed on the use of the money later in other parts of the bill.

special rule may be needed to protect the bill from points of order. In the Senate, cloture may occasionally need to be invoked. Naturally, since these are must-pass bills, the president's strongly felt views have to have been considered in the negotiations in order to stave off the possibility of a veto.

Looking at Appropriations Bills

Appropriations bills are detailed pieces of legislation, but their structure is surprisingly simple and straightforward. This is not the case with some of the vocabulary used to describe parts of the bill.

An appropriations law has only two major components, but the terms used to describe the bill and its accompanying documents can be confusing. In this section, some of the key terms are clarified.

The *conference report* is the final version of the bill plus nonstatutory *report language* (technically known at this stage as the *joint explanatory statement*). The term "conference report" encompasses the whole package—the bill and the accompanying report language.

Accounts are the main units of appropriations law. There are about two hundred accounts in the twelve appropriations bills that encompass broad categories of activities in the agencies or departments. Some agencies have numerous accounts; smaller agencies may have only one account. The account is recognizable as an unnumbered paragraph containing dollar amounts and giving an agency budget authority. The paragraph usually includes only a very general and broad description of the purpose for the money, and it cites the relevant authorizing statute that governs the use of the funds. Examples of accounts from the fiscal year 2007 appropriation for the Defense Department are shown in Exhibit 5.1, including military personnel funding for the different armed services.

General or *administrative provisions* are the second and last of the major components of appropriations bills. General provisions are located at the end of the accounts for a particular agency or department and at the end of each bill. They are consecutively numbered, as can be seen in Exhibit 5.2. General provisions most commonly take the form of so-called limitation language, which restricts how money in the accounts may be spent. It is often stated: "None of the funds made available in this act may be used [for a particular purpose]." But general provisions also frequently involve a requirement for reporting back to the Congress on the status of a program (known as *report requirements*); some include *earmarks*, which direct money to be spent in a particular congressional district or state; and sometimes they contain policy prescriptions. As with accounts, general provisions are

EXHIBIT 5.2
GENERAL PROVISIONS IN THE APPROPRIATIONS LAW FROM "FISCAL YEAR 2004 APPROPRIATION FOR MILITARY CONSTRUCTION"

General Provisions

SEC. 101. None of the funds appropriated in Military Construction Appropriations Acts shall be expended for payments under a cost-plus-a-fixed-fee contract for construction, where cost estimates exceed $25,000, to be performed within the United States, except Alaska, without the specific approval in writing of the Secretary of Defense setting forth the reasons therefor.

SEC. 102. Funds appropriated to the Department of Defense for construction shall be available for hire of passenger motor vehicles.

SEC. 103. Funds appropriated to the Department of Defense for construction may be used for advances to the Federal Highway Administration, Department of Transportation, for the construction of access roads as authorized by section 210 of title 23, United States Code, when projects authorized therein are certified as important to the national defense by the Secretary of Defense.

SEC. 104. None of the funds appropriated in this Act may be used to begin construction of new bases inside the continental United States for which specific appropriations have not been made.

SEC. 105. No part of the funds provided in Military Construction Appropriations Acts shall be used for purchase of land or land easements in excess of 100 percent of the value as determined by the Army Corps of Engineers or the Naval Facilities Engineering Command, except: (1) where there is a determination of value by a Federal court; (2) purchases negotiated by the Attorney General or his designee; (3) where the estimated value is less than $25,000; or (4) as otherwise determined by the Secretary of Defense to be in the public interest.

SEC. 106. None of the funds appropriated in Military Construction Appropriations Acts shall be used to: (1) acquire land; (2) provide for site preparation; or (3) install utilities for any family housing, except housing for which funds have been made available in annual Military Construction Appropriations Acts.

SEC. 107. None of the funds appropriated in Military Construction Appropriations Acts for minor construction may be used to transfer or relocate any activity from one base or installation to another, without prior notification to the Committees on Appropriations.

SEC. 108. No part of the funds appropriated in Military Construction Appropriations Acts may be used for the procurement of steel for any construction project or activity for which American steel producers, fabricators, and manufacturers have been denied the opportunity to compete for such steel procurement.

SEC. 109. None of the funds available to the Department of Defense for military construction or family housing during the current fiscal year may be used to pay real property taxes in any foreign nation.

SEC. 110. None of the funds appropriated in Military Construction Appropriations Acts may be used to initiate a new installation overseas without prior notification to the Committees on Appropriations.

SEC. 111. None of the funds appropriated in Military Construction Appropriations Acts may be obligated for architect and engineer contracts estimated by the Government to exceed $500,000 for projects to be accomplished in Japan, in any NATO member country, or in countries bordering the Arabian Sea, unless such contracts are awarded to United States firms or United States firms in joint venture with host nation firms.

SEC. 112. None of the funds appropriated in Military Construction Appropriations Acts for military construction in the United States territories and possessions in the Pacific and on Kwajalein Atoll, or in countries bordering the Arabian Sea, may be used to award any contract estimated by the Government to exceed $1,000,000 to a foreign contractor: Provided, That this section shall not be applicable to contract awards for which the lowest responsive and responsible bid of a United States contractor exceeds the lowest responsive and responsible bid of a foreign contractor by greater than 20 percent: Provided further, That this section shall not apply to contract awards for military construction on Kwajalein Atoll for which the lowest responsive and responsible bid is submitted by a Marshallese contractor.

SEC. 113. The Secretary of Defense is to inform the appropriate committees of Congress, including the Committees on Appropriations, of the plans and scope of any proposed military exercise involving United States personnel 30 days prior to its occurring, if amounts expended for construction, either temporary or permanent, are anticipated to exceed $100,000.

SEC. 114. Not more than 20 percent of the appropriations in Military Construction Appropriations Acts which are limited for obligation during the current fiscal year shall be obligated during the last 2 months of the fiscal year.

In this bill, many general provisions limit the use of funds. All those from sections 101 to 112 fit into the category of so-called limitation language. The highlighted portions provide other sorts of specific guidance to the department. In section 113, the Appropriations Committees require notification in the case of deployment of military personnel requiring the use of $100,000 or more of construction funds. In section 114, the committees are stipulating that the department may not spend a disproportionate part of the appropriation in the last part of the fiscal year.

law. In effect, general provisions are used by Congress to manage—some critics would say "micromanage"—the agencies. Report requirements in particular serve Congress as a means of supervising or conducting oversight of the executive branch. In recent years there have been somewhere between 1,100 and 1,200 general provisions in all the appropriations bills—a dramatic increase from the congressional practice a generation ago.[13]

EXHIBIT 5.3
EXCERPT FROM THE JOINT EXPLANATORY STATEMENT IN "FISCAL YEAR 2005 APPROPRIATION FOR HOMELAND SECURITY CONFERENCE REPORT"

Financial Management of the Department

The conferees are concerned with the Department's execution of its financial responsibilities after numerous budgetary and management crises over the 18 months of the Department's existence, notably with the Bureau of Immigration and Customs Enforcement and the Transportation Security Administration. The Department and senior agency management are coping with major changes in the organizational environment, resources, and communication networks of new and radically expanding or changing agencies. It is, therefore, to be expected that the Department will experience direct and indirect costs and management problems as it integrates its agencies. The conferees also acknowledge that reconciling different systems and legacy accounting bureaucracies is difficult. Nonetheless, the conferees will not assent to a repeat of recent experience of shifting and multiple, last minute requests for funding relief, particularly when the Department and agencies can neither explain nor even fully understand their own financial condition. Such a level of uncertainty is inexplicable, and adversely affects the Department's ability to fulfill its missions and carry out Administration and Congressional policy.

The conferees direct the Secretary and Department agency heads to devote the resources and managerial energy required to ensure that basic financial control and transparency in accounting are achieved, and avoid the waste and disruption caused by failure to carry out this fundamental management function. The conferees expect that agencies will establish baseline budgets and reconcile their financial records and accounting systems to provide sufficient information to the Department's Chief Financial Officer (CFO) to permit a clear understanding of financial resources available as well as existing and upcoming liabilities. The conferees further direct that the CFO include in the monthly budget execution report an update on the status of steps underway to improve financial management in critical agencies. Finally, the conferees expect that the Secretary and CFO will

The *joint explanatory statement* (JES) is the last of three versions of report language for the bills. (We have seen that the Appropriations Committees in each chamber attach *report language*, sometimes called the *committee report*, to the bills when they emerge from full committee markup.) At the end of the process, the conferees attach the nonstatutory JES to the bill to explain how the two chambers reconciled their differences; more importantly, the JES also reiterates various suggestions that the House and Senate Appropriations Committees made in their committee reports.

---

strive to ensure that required financial audits of the Department's components are conducted in a timely fashion and with full cooperation of agency personnel.

Transportation Security Administration Reprogrammings

The conferees are concerned that the Department of Homeland Security has submitted numerous reprogramming for the Transportation Security Administration (TSA) to the House and Senate Committees on Appropriations that TSA cannot fully explain and justify. In fiscal year 2004, three TSA reprogrammings were submitted. For each of these reprogrammings, TSA was unable to provide timely and consistent data to answer specific questions about the need for these actions. For instance, when the Department's reprogramming letter states that " . . . $42,200,000 will be used to fund screener professional development to increase retention, and to cover higher benefit costs and increased supervision costs," the conferees expect TSA to readily explain the dollars for each of these three items. Similarly, TSA has been unable to provide an accurate annual estimate for a variety of requirements, such as maintenance costs, and salaries and expenses, which has led to repeated reprogramming requests for additional funds to cover these activities throughout the year, at the expense of other TSA or Department programs. This causes the conferees to question the competency of TSA's estimating capabilities. Therefore, the conferees direct that the Department institute financial controls to enable TSA to live within its resource limitations to negate or minimize the need for reprogrammings. If a reprogramming is necessary for fiscal year 2005, it should provide sufficient basic information for it to be properly considered by the Committees and each specific funding increase and decrease should be fully explained and justified.

The highlighted portions indicate Congress's views of the management of the Department of Homeland Security and the Transportation Safety Administration (an agency within the department). Congress's pointed views as expressed in nonstatutory language are usually carefully considered by the agencies. The board of directors' leverage over the agencies derives in large measure from its power over funding levels. Failure to follow explicit guidelines set forth in the JES can have dire consequences for an agency in future legislation.

These suggestions frequently involve criticism of agency management practices, as can be seen in the sharp language directed at the Department of Homeland Security and the Transportation Security Administration in Exhibit 5.3.

The JES also gives specific earmarked instructions to agencies on how to spend the money in an account. Exhibit 5.4 contains a few of the hundreds of earmarks for the Justice Department's Edward Byrne Discretionary Grants in the "Fiscal Year 2005 Appropriation for Commerce, Justice, and Science." (As of 2007, the sponsors of earmarks are now listed in the JES.)

The JES also often includes the procedures by which the agencies should contact the Appropriations Committees in order to receive permission to move money around within an account or transfer money between accounts.

Appropriations bills have many purposes. The most obvious is to dictate how much money agencies are going to get for particular purposes. Accounts determine

---

EXHIBIT 5.4
EARMARKS IN THE JOINT EXPLANATORY STATEMENT FOR THE EDWARD BYRNE DISCRETIONARY GRANTS

The conference agreement includes $170,027,000 for discretionary grants under this account.

Within the amounts provided, [the Office of Justice Programs] is expected to review the following proposals, provide grants if warranted, and report to the Committees on Appropriations regarding its intentions:

$4,500,000 for the National Citizens Crime Prevention Campaign;

$1,750,000 for continued support for the expansion of SEARCH Group, Inc. and the National Technical Assistance and Training Program to assist States, such as West Virginia and Alabama, to accelerate the automation of the fingerprint identification process;

$350,000 for the Turtle Mountain Community College, ND, Project Peacemaker;

$1,000,000 for the Indigenous Peoples Law & Policy Project at the University of Arizona;

$1,700,000 for the Drug Abuse Resistance Education (DARE) program;

$8,000,000 for Operation UNITE for a drug enforcement, treatment and education program;

$700,000 for the New Orleans, LA, Police Department for crime fighting initiatives;

$200,000 for the Orleans Parish, LA, District Attorney's Office for crime fighting initiatives;

the amounts of money that agencies will have with which to work. Sometimes within the accounts and more commonly in the general provisions and the report language (or JES), Congress may specify how some of the money it gives the agencies should be spent. When Congress does this, in effect it is telling the agencies what they should do *that differs from what the agencies stated they would like to do in the president's budget documents.* Congressional specifications in the accounts and the general provisions are legally binding on the agencies.

Specifications in report language—the JES and the committee reports—are not legally binding, but agencies almost always do Congress's bidding as expressed there for fear of biting the hand that feeds them.[14] Agencies are mindful that they have to plead their case every year before the appropriators. Failure to abide by suggestions in report language may result in unpleasant public hearings, less money in future bills, or more restrictive requirements in those bills.

$500,000 for the Paul and Lisa Foundation;

$2,000,000 for the Northern Virginia Regional Gang Task Force;

$587,000 for the Northwest Virginia Regional Drug Task Force;

$3,000,000 for the State of Virginia for anti-gang coordination;

$2,500,000 for Mothers Against Drunk Driving including the continuation of Spanish language public service announcements;

$1,500,000 for the National Institute of Justice and Bureau of Justice Statistics to conduct a study of conditions of confinement in Indian country correctional facilities and the factors that exacerbate those conditions;

$150,000 for the Obscenity Crimes Project to provide citizens with an online tool to report Internet obscenity crimes;

$350,000 for Gospel Rescue Ministries;

$300,000 for The Women's Center in Vienna, VA.

Source: "Fiscal Year 2005 Commerce, Justice, and Science Appropriations Conference Report—Joint Explanatory Statement."

In this case, the account providing the funds for the Edward Byrne Discretionary Grants gave no specific instructions to the agency as to the use of the money. Nor did the general provisions in the law. But the report language (JES) we see here did so. In fact, the list of earmarks went on for several pages and proposed to use all of the appropriated funds ($170,027,000). The highlighted portion seems to show that Congress was only suggesting that the agency fund the entities listed, but like most agencies, the Office of Justice Programs took these "suggestions" very seriously and proceeded to fund them all.

Instructions in report language have one key advantage for the agencies: Since they are not in law, agencies have the flexibility to make their case to Appropriations Committee staff and members that following certain suggestions would have adverse consequences. Agencies develop relationships with the appropriators and staff in order to be able to have these kinds of discussions. If they can persuasively argue that the agency mission will be best served by giving them more flexibility, members and staff may well relent.[15]

Supplemental Appropriations

Every year the government runs into some unexpected and unaccounted-for expense. Massive flooding in the Midwest cannot be anticipated, and when it occurs, government agencies such as the Federal Emergency Management Agency (FEMA) will not have enough money to respond effectively. Jet fuel prices can be so volatile that the Air Force and the Navy may be unable to afford to fly their planes with the money they were provided in the regular appropriations process. The president may intervene in an escalating international crisis, as President Clinton did in Bosnia in the 1990s. Extra money that was not provided in the regular appropriations process the previous year is needed in the current fiscal year.

Almost every year Congress receives a request from the president for supplemental appropriations for emergencies like these. Because time is often of the essence, the Appropriations Committees will drop everything to consider the request and, if warranted, report out legislation. In the past the amounts were not too large—historically in the neighborhood of $5 billion or less.

Supplemental appropriations became more controversial when they were used to fund not just the first year or two of the wars in Afghanistan and Iraq in the early 2000s but throughout the lengthy conflicts to date.[16] Eventually, as war costs escalated, supplemental appropriations of nearly $200 billion had been used by decade's end—roughly 20 percent of the entire discretionary budget of the United States. (The aftermath of Hurricane Katrina in 2005 in the Gulf region also required massive supplemental spending.)

This use of supplemental appropriations had two negative ramifications. One was that the budget resolution, which is meant to address the question of how much money it is wise for the government to spend in the upcoming fiscal year, was not really taking into consideration the impact of the whole of what the government was doing. Essentially it was ignoring the massive costs of the wars. Second, the appropriations process was gamed. Eventually everyone knew that a massive supplemental bill (or two in some years) would be coming down the pike. In the Defense Department, additional non-war-related items would be added to the supplemental request

TABLE 5.4 *Earmarks: Fiscal Year 1991 to Fiscal Year 2008*

FISCAL YEAR	EARMARKS (IN BILLIONS OF DOLLARS)	NUMBER OF EARMARKS
1991	$ 3.1	546
1992	2.6	892
1993	6.6	1,712
1994	7.8	1,318
1995	10.0	1,439
1996	12.5	958
1997	14.5	1,596
1998	13.2	2,143
1999	12.0	2,839
2000	17.7	4,326
2001	18.5	6,333
2002	20.1	8,341
2003	22.5	9,362
2004	22.9	10,656
2005	27.3	13,997
2006	29.0	9,963
2007	13.2	2,658
2008	17.2	11,610

Source: *Citizens Against Government Waste.*

that the president submitted to Congress. In the Congress supplemental appropriations became a vehicle on which to attach favored domestic spending items that had not made it under the 302(a) and 302(b) limitations imposed by the regular budget process in the previous year.

Earmarks in Appropriations Bills

The most controversial area in appropriations bills in recent years has been earmarks. And for good reason: As can be seen in Table 5.4, earmarks in appropriations and other bills have increased by 400 percent in the last fifteen years and by approximately 2,000 percent since 1991.

But this subject is a little slippery, since there is no universally agreed upon definition of an earmark, and there is certainly little agreement on what constitutes a "good" earmark, if such a thing exists. The following definition is based on the one used by the House of Representatives:

When the Congress, usually in an appropriations bill or report language attached to an appropriations bill (although earmarks are also common in transportation and water project authorizing legislation), specifies the location or recipient of federal funding circumventing otherwise established merit-based formulas or competitive allocation processes handled by the executive branch.[17]

Senator John McCain (R-AZ), a longtime opponent of most earmarking, maintains that meeting the "earmark" designation also means that the provision in question did not receive sufficient vetting in the legislative process.[18] He believes that Congress acts inappropriately in directing funds to a particular district or state if the directing provision has not had a hearing or received other consideration at the subcommittee or committee level.

Going back to the middle decades of the twentieth century, Appropriations Committee leadership in the House and Senate rejected earmarking, fearing that once some members were able to direct funds to the districts or states, the remaining members would clamor for earmarks of their own and the situation would get out of control, leading to irresponsible spending.

The practice of discouraging this sort of targeted spending began to break down in the 1980s after Democrats instituted rules that subjected Appropriations subcommittee chairs in the House to approval from the full Democratic caucus. (Before that they had been determined by the Appropriations Committee chair.) Gradually rank-and-file members were able to prevail on some of these newly accountable subcommittee chairs to direct funding to their districts. The amount of money was not that huge considering how big the federal government had become, but the precedent was significant.

Most subcommittee chairs resisted, however, and Democratic Party leadership never attempted to force them to earmark money for rank-and-file members. This was probably because the Democrats' majority was so huge from the late 1950s into the early 1990s that they never feared losing power because of a failure to provide vulnerable newer members with earmarked projects they could point to as evidence of their effectiveness. Instead, the earmarked spending that did happen was disproportionately awarded to more senior members who had paid their dues. (It should be noted that senior members of Congress, especially those on the Appropriations Committees, had always leaned on agencies in informal ways to spend money as they directed; this sort of pressure just wasn't always in writing.[19])

All of this changed when the Republicans shocked Washington by taking over the Congress in 1994. Speaker Newt Gingrich immediately recognized, as did his Republican successor Dennis Hastert, that the slim Republican majority might not hold. Gingrich's plan for keeping the majority included targeting federal funds via earmarks to newly elected members' districts, particularly those who had won by slim margins. This opened the floodgates as all members of both parties saw what was happening and wanted to get in on it.

Although Republicans reserved the bulk of the earmarks for their own in both the House and Senate, they did not shut out the Democrats entirely—the breakdown was usually about 60–40—probably because they feared that, if they did shut out the minority, the Democrats might publicize some of the more questionable earmarks and bring public wrath down on the majority. It was thought that it was better to spread the wealth around in order to avoid unnecessary scrutiny.

In any case, earmarks proliferated. Although some critics allege that earmarking funds is a major contributor to deficit spending, in fact the total money involved is not so large—less than 5 percent of all discretionary spending—as to constitute a major burden on the budget. Even that figure exaggerates the impact of this sort of spending, because earmarked funds are normally carved out of agency budgets rather than added to those budgets.

But there are other criticisms of the practice. Some earmarks have been exposed as boondoggles that seem to go for projects that are not worthy of federal funding. Presidents and some good government watchdog groups say that the decisions to allocate funds are better left to formulas or criteria established by government agencies that are based on national needs rather than on particular district needs identified by members of Congress. Members of Congress counter that (a) they have the power of the purse and thus every right to direct funding, and that furthermore, (b) they understand the needs of the people better than anyone—certainly better than executive branch bureaucrats—and consequently are in the best position to make specific spending decisions.

The only thing that can be said for certain is that earmarks remain wildly popular with almost every member of Congress. Only a handful make no earmark requests in each budget cycle. And despite recent reform efforts requiring that members who request earmarks be identified in report language, earmarks are not going away anytime soon.

The Power of the Purse

The appropriations process serves a crucial function for Congress. Appropriations bills decide which programs get funded and at what levels. But the committees go much further than that, sometimes by stepping in for authorizers to specify agency policy formally in appropriations law. The power of the purse also gives the committees the leverage to exert influence in nonstatutory report language. Rarely are the suggestions found in the joint explanatory statements ignored by the agencies; in fact, they are usually followed to the letter. Agency officials know that it is unwise to get on the wrong side of the people who hold the purse strings. Agencies are given a whole range of instructions in report language, from earmarked projects to reporting requirements to ways they can better manage their affairs. Appropriators may also influence agencies in much less formal ways through letters, phone calls, or other communications. In addition, they conduct investigations and hold hearings that shine a spotlight on agency actions, whether strictly related to funding or not.

The power of the purse comes down to this: *The appropriations process involves all three of Congress's powers—authorizing, funding, and supervising.* And it takes place every year, unlike most agency reauthorizations. Year in and year out the appropriations process is the principal way in which Congress directs the work of the federal government.

THE BREAKDOWN OF THE BUDGET PROCESS

No description of the congressional budget process would be complete without noting that, even though appropriations bills fall into the category of must-pass legislation, they rarely pass on schedule. Figure 5.4 documents the recent history of Congress's efforts to fund the federal government in a timely fashion. In the twelve years from fiscal year 1998 through fiscal year 2009 (fiscal year 1997 was the last time all the bills passed on time), an average of one and a half appropriations bills have passed before the beginning of the new fiscal year.

Obviously this dysfunction has become chronic. It is very instructive to see why the board of directors fails to accomplish in a timely fashion its most essential function—funding the government—year after year, and what it must do to keep the government running on a stopgap basis.

Efficiency in processing legislation was never meant to be Congress's hallmark. As we have seen, the Senate was set up more for delay than for action, and it is always going to be difficult for the two chambers to come to a meeting of the minds given their different perspectives. Divided government can throw another wrench in the works, making agreement on controversial matters harder still. And Congress's legislative workload is tremendous. All of these factors, together with the demands of constant campaigning and fund-raising, trips home, shortened schedules, and other factors, sometimes make it difficult to find floor time—especially in the Senate—to deal with legislation, even must-pass legislation.

FIGURE 5.4   *Appropriations Bills Approved On Time by Fiscal Year*

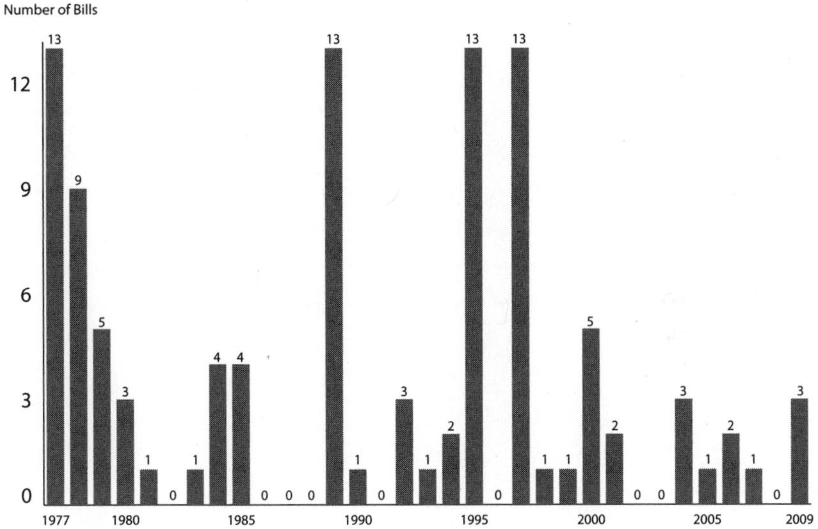

Note: There were 13 appropriations subcommittees from 1977-2005. There were 11 bills in 2007 and 2008. The House had 11 subcommittees and the Senate had 12. Both chambers have had 12 subcommittees since FY 2008.

In the case of appropriations bills, two specific factors impede the process: scarce funds and policy debates.

Not Enough Money

Members of Congress are invariably under political pressure to keep spending down as a general principle, and that is especially true in the one area that is more controllable: discretionary spending in appropriations bills. As spending soars on the major "untouchable" mandatory programs like Social Security and Medicare, pressures to control spending and reduce deficits are greater in the discretionary areas.

Early in the year, as we have seen, the party in power sets a top-line number for discretionary spending in the budget resolution. Although party leaders pay lip service to funding all their key priorities in the resolution, there is usually movement among key players on the Budget Committees and the party leadership (who want to portray their party as "fiscally responsible" in preparation for the next election cycle) to limit the growth of spending in the 302(a) allocation.

Problems arise when the appropriations subcommittees find out what this tight figure means for their 302(b) allocations. If the country is at war, spending on defense will be up, so subcommittees that cover domestic spending will often get little or no increase to fund health, education, environmental cleanup, and other popular priorities. Unfortunately the full consequences of the "fiscal conservatism" message are not internalized by all members of the Congress, most of whom, regardless of party, clamor for more spending for the programs that are important in their districts or states.

The upshot is that the subcommittee chairs often have trouble putting together bills that can move quickly through their chamber because, when it comes to voting, members invariably object to belt-tightening for popular government programs, especially those that serve the people in their districts or states. This is more of a problem in the Senate. Since the House moves first on appropriations, members usually decide to pass something that is not perfect, knowing that corrections can be made later. And House rules permit streamlined debate, thus limiting the amount of time it takes to pass the bills. In the Senate, streamlining debate is next to impossible, so there is often resistance to moving bills to the floor that might not pass and that will crowd other matters off the agenda.

In recent years, in fact, Senate subcommittee chairs have had a great deal of trouble getting their bills adopted by the full committee, much less by the full Senate. In 2006, 2007, and 2008, under both Republican and Democratic leadership, only one or two of the twelve appropriations bills were brought up individually on the Senate floor before the beginning of the new fiscal year. Obviously the appropriations process bogs down when this happens. Many bills never reach the conference stage, and certainly, as Figure 5.4 indicates, most bills are not passed by the beginning of the fiscal year.

Policy and Politics

In addition to money woes, appropriations bills become magnets for controversial policy provisions. Many members view must-pass bills as a great opportunity to raise controversial issues that are not being addressed to their satisfaction in the normal authorization process. Although appropriations bills are not supposed to have policy language in them to start with, and policy amendments are not technically permitted in either chamber, it is easy to get around those restrictions in the Senate (as noted earlier) and even doable in the much more restrictive House.

For example, in 2005 Senator John McCain held up the defense appropriations bill—a bill that had enough funding to gain the support of the overwhelming majority of members—for three months, going well into the new fiscal year, because he was not satisfied with the pace of negotiations on a detainee treatment bill he wanted in law. McCain threatened to amend the defense funding bill with his version of revised detainee treatment policies until the president and congressional leaders would work with him. Finally, nearly three months into fiscal year 2006, President Bush and the Senate leadership relented and came to the table to negotiate. At that point the senator allowed the defense funding bill to go forward.

One of the most common ways of introducing policy into appropriations legislation is to offer an amendment to prohibit spending funds for a particular purpose—the so-called limitation language that appears in general provisions. The bill provides the agency with the funds it requested, but ties its hands by specifying what it may *not* spend money on. This is a handy way to set agency policy, because telling an agency what it *cannot* do usually does not run afoul of rules restricting the addition of policy language for technical reasons. In recent years, immigration policy, abortion, and offshore drilling restrictions have been brought into the debates about funding government agencies. Abortion was once debated on a defense spending bill when a member offered an amendment to prohibit that procedure at army hospitals.

Appropriations decisions have always been separated from authorizing decisions to the extent possible (see Chapter 4) to keep the process of funding the government on track. The fear was that contentious policy debates would hamper the flow of money for essential government programs. As it has turned out, that fear has been realized.[20] As the authorizing process has proven unable to resolve key policy debates, those debates have increasingly moved to the appropriations process, slowing down the processing of those bills.

The Specter of a Government Shutdown

The consequences of an unfinished appropriations bill can be catastrophic. If funding for the operations and programs of an agency is not signed into law by the time the new fiscal year starts on October 1, the agency has to shut its doors. National parks will close if the Interior Department spending bill is not passed. Border security will go unstaffed if DHS does not get its funding.

In the winter of 1995–1996, the government did shut down for about three weeks. President Clinton and the Republican Congress were at loggerheads on spending priorities, and neither side would give in. All they could agree on was to fund critical functions such as defense, border security, the Social Security Administration, and a few other areas. Much of government was allowed to shut down, including hundreds of programs affecting the lives of millions of Americans. The failure of the two sides to reach a timely compromise was decidedly unpopular.

Continuing Resolutions and Omnibus Appropriations

What they did not do that year was pass a *continuing resolution* (CR). A CR is a simple piece of legislation that serves as a stopgap to fund the functioning of the government at the previous year's level for a specified period into the new fiscal year. The CR may be set to fund the government for any length of time, from a day to a year. Typically no changes are made from the previous fiscal year in the distribution of money and no major changes to existing programs are permitted, but at least the government agencies can continue operating until a new appropriations bill is finally agreed to, however late that happens. Sometimes several CRs are required before bills can be completed. The average in recent years has been over five CRs. In 2003 most of the government was on continuing resolution five months into the new fiscal year before a massive bill was passed that joined together the eleven bills that had not passed. For fiscal year 2009, nine of the twelve bills were joined together in mid-March—more than five months into the fiscal year.

These massive pieces of legislation are called *omnibus appropriations*. They are the vehicles used when individual bills are too controversial or do not have enough funding in them to pass on their own. House and Senate leadership package two, three, on up to twelve bills together and bring them up for a vote. The advantage is that members can usually find something they desperately want in the huge package, thus justifying a vote even though they may think a program here or an account there is underfunded. The disadvantage is that an omnibus conference report does not permit amendments and is too large for members to be able to digest in a short period of time. It undercuts the responsibility of all the membership to consider with some care what they are funding the government to do. Despite those problems, Congress now regularly relies on an omnibus appropriation, often months into the new fiscal year, to finish its work.

CONGRESS AND THE FUNDING POWER

Does Congress Budget Responsibly?

Several criticisms of the congressional budget process have been mentioned in this chapter. Three are particularly noteworthy.

First of all, many observers believe that the budget process has broken down. The theory behind the budget process on the Hill is simple: The Budget Committees put together a blueprint for a budget—the Concurrent Budget Resolution—that is economically sound and addresses the priorities of the majority, after which the

Appropriations Committees in particular and some other committees move bills through the legislative process to fill in the details. In recent years Congress has found a huge loophole to exploit—the supplemental appropriations bills for the Iraq and Afghanistan wars—with spending that dramatically exceeds the amount deemed prudent in the budget resolution. The supplemental vehicle has been used to attach spending in defense and other areas that had not been budgeted for and that was unrelated to war costs. Although supplemental bills had been subject to this sort of gaming for more than a decade before the invasion of Afghanistan in 2002, the amounts had been relatively small.

Furthermore, the lateness of the appropriations bills creates a host of problems for the functioning of the government. Members of Congress do not want to leave large swaths of the federal government on a continuing resolution months into the fiscal year, hampering the operations of agencies that need new budget authority to make critical hires, enter into contracts for services, and put in place needed programs. But as we have seen, bills are delayed when policy debates get injected into the process. Members want to show themselves to be wise stewards of the taxpayers' money in the larger picture, but it does not always add up when nearly all of them fight hard for more money for programs affecting their own constituencies. These fights over scarce resources also make it very hard to move bills through the process.

In 2007 the situation became so dire that the Congress ended up putting most of the federal government on a continuing resolution for the whole fiscal year. Agencies had to spend countless staff hours looking into what they could legally do with the minimal money they had, since no full-fledged appropriations bill had been passed to make clear what new priorities could be addressed. New circumstances call for reallocations of funds, but continuing resolutions do not normally include anything but the authority to spend for ongoing programs at the previous year's level. Americans complain about inefficient practices at government agencies, but some of them are surely caused by Congress's failure to get the funding bills done on time.

Third is the question of earmarks. Many of the criticisms of earmarks miss the mark. For one thing, earmarks are certainly *not* what is causing deficits to be so large, nor are earmarks a significant part of the long-term budget problems the government faces. Also, many earmarks are for valuable and deserving projects that most people would support. Most members of Congress are unabashedly proud of most or all of their earmarks and are more than happy to publicize them. Furthermore, as we saw earlier, earmarks are usually not add-ons to agency budgets; rather, they represent "carve-outs" from the budgets. In other words, the president and Congress have agreed on an appropriate dollar figure for an agency to do its mission, then Congress spells out district- or state-specific instructions as to how the money should be spent.

This creates a problem that goes less recognized by the public. Agency officials' hands are tied by congressional earmarks that may not in all cases be decided with the national interest in mind. Perhaps even more important, because earmarks are often carved out of the budgets of core governmental functions—including, for instance, national defense, infrastructure, and airport safety programs—vital government services may be affected. For example, a member may successfully earmark funds for improvements at an airport in his district. This may appear entirely justified; after all, what airport cannot stand to be made safer? But with scarce funds, the agency administering the program might have allotted that money differently, perhaps to airports facing far more severe traffic and safety problems.

In the final analysis, members of Congress are acting within their rights to earmark funds as they see fit. After all, the Constitution gives them the power of the purse. Whether their earmarking decisions for worthwhile projects are wise, given funding constraints and the established missions of the agencies, may be a different matter.

Does Congress Need to Start Balancing the Budget?

The most common complaint about the federal budget from informed observers is concern about the persistent and potentially destabilizing deficits the government runs. Nearly every year the president proposes a budget that assumes insufficient revenue to pay for what the government does, and nearly every year Congress, while changing the president's request at the margins, goes along. Ambitious proposals to upset the status quo by cutting or eliminating major programs or raising taxes in order to balance the budget rarely see the light of day.

There is a lot of debate and disagreement about the wisdom of deficit spending, but one thing can be said for sure: Deficit spending adds to the accumulated national debt, which puts a burden on the federal budget in terms of debt service. The question is whether the government can sustain the debt it is accumulating without causing an increase in inflation and interest rates.

Most economists think that deficit spending is not necessarily bad. For instance, it may be wise policy to spend more or cut taxes in order to reinvigorate the economy in times of recession. In the fall of 2008, economists of all stripes agreed that the government needed to borrow large sums of money to stave off a potentially disastrous meltdown in the credit markets. In addition, just as with one's household budget, government does make some productive investments. (Going into debt to pay for college tuition will pay off, one hopes, in the long run.) Up to a point, deficit spending can be defended in the interest of long-term productivity. Improved roads and waterways help commerce, funding research can lead to important innovations, and spending on education to better equip the workforce can have a positive effect on the economy and, ultimately, living standards.

But just as it is not wise for a person to go into debt for immediate gratification (more clothes, another car, an expensive vacation), the government places a burden on future generations when it runs a deficit to fund unproductive programs. And no one seriously questions the fact that the government's current deficit spending is largely focused on addressing the immediate needs and desires of the population rather than on productive investments.

A Time of Surpluses

From fiscal year 1998 to fiscal year 2001, the government escaped the chronic cycle of deficits it had been in for the previous thirty years. The budget was balanced in 1998, and we enjoyed large surpluses, well in excess of $100 billion, the next three years. A confluence of factors produced this happy result. Defense spending had dropped dramatically since the beginning of the end of the Cold War in the late 1980s.[21] Medical inflation, which affects two of the largest mandatory programs, Medicare and Medicaid, had unexpectedly declined during the 1990s. And tax revenues practically flooded the Treasury, owing to a robust economy and other factors.

But the situation changed in the new century. For one thing, the attacks on America on September 11, 2001, led to a sharp spike in defense and homeland security spending. In addition, education and agriculture programs were enhanced. And tax cuts implemented in 2001 and 2003 led to a large relative decrease in revenues.[22] The government ledger was plunged back into deficit in 2002 and has remained that way.

This development is of particular concern to economists and other budget watchers for a simple reason: The government's liabilities for retirement and medical expenses are about to skyrocket as the baby boom generation (people born between 1946 and 1964) begins to retire in earnest with full benefits in the 2010s. That fact, coupled with increased life expectancies, will lead to much higher deficits and debt, with debt service payments beginning to outstrip discretionary spending within a few decades and eventually exploding out of control by the middle of the twenty-first century. The forecast by economists and public policy experts from across the ideological spectrum is for much higher interest rates, a much less stable economic environment for investment, and potentially devastating recessions, with global consequences, if no changes are made.

What Is So Hard About Balancing the Budget?

Budget decisions in Washington—as reflected in the actions of both the president and the Congress—are driven by politics. This should not surprise anyone—we are after all talking about politicians! And politics makes balancing the budget difficult for a simple reason: Voters like more government services and prefer to pay less in taxes. And the politicians are nothing if not responsive to voters.

As we have seen, influential interest groups are important to politicians in myriad ways, from providing helpful advice on legislative strategy and public policy to funding campaigns to getting out the vote. As the journalist Jeffrey Birnbaum points out, interest groups, among other things, are organized around the goal of channeling the views of the public in an effective way to Washington policymakers. This usually involves advocating for more spending on government programs or for tax breaks that benefit particular groups of citizens. Of course, industry is also heavily invested in lobbying for tax breaks and subsidies. And companies always make the case that tax breaks are necessary in order to maintain productivity and jobs. To say it is difficult for politicians to resist the force of the lobbyists when they speak for the strongly held views of their constituents and the job-creating industries in their districts is a great understatement.

Dealing with budget deficits involves some combination of cutting spending and raising taxes. Invariably, cutting spending for almost any program raises the ire of some interested party that represents real flesh-and-blood voters. Increasing taxes does the same thing, sometimes for a much broader segment of the electorate. No wonder the president and members of Congress find it hard to balance the budget!

Politicians who go against the grain and try to address deficits in a serious way rarely get any traction. And if they do, they often pay a big price. President George H. W. Bush agreed to discretionary spending caps (not cuts) and, more importantly, substantial tax increases in a controversial 1990 deal with the Democratic congressional leadership. In 1992, despite having led the country to a decisive and highly popular victory in the first Persian Gulf War, presiding over a rebounding economy, and having a spotless reputation, Bush garnered only 38 percent of the vote against then-governor Bill Clinton and the independent candidate, Ross Perot. Republicans believe strongly that his willingness to raise taxes doomed him, and the party has taken a consistent position resisting any tax increases (and normally advocating tax cuts) ever since.

The 1990 Bush deal did not produce immediate results in terms of the federal budget picture. President Clinton faced an even more dire deficit predicament when he took office in 1993. He proposed still more tax increases and actual spending cuts. He could only get Democrats to go along with his plan, with just enough votes to pass it. Then the party paid a heavy price in 1994 (Clinton was probably lucky he was not up for reelection), and Congress went to the Republicans for the first time in forty years in a landslide. Just as it was for the Republicans, the prevailing view among many Democrats was that taking responsibility for dealing with the deficit by raising taxes and cutting spending was a huge political loser.

The Growing Entitlement Programs

Although government revenue is clearly not keeping up with current demands for government services, the single most important long-term problem is the virtually uncontrollable growth of the mandatory programs that provide services and benefits mostly to the large and growing group of elderly voters. The popularity of these programs makes addressing the problem all the more difficult. They are often called the "third rail of American politics," a reference to the electrified rail that powers trains and subways. Anyone who touches that rail will almost certainly die. Many politicians fear a career-ending electoral defeat if they propose cuts in Medicare or Social Security. Tax increases may also have to be a part of the solution to the problem, but according to the Government Accountability Office, taxes literally cannot be raised enough to cover the long-term Social Security and Medicare liabilities. David Walker, former comptroller general of GAO, sees a "fiscal train wreck" on the horizon.[23]

The important thing is that these programs are not only wildly popular but set on "automatic pilot"—they will grow in perpetuity unless Congress and the president act to cut them. The fact is that politicians find it a lot easier to leave these programs alone (or even to enhance them, as was done in 2003 with the addition of prescription drug coverage to Medicare) than to cut them back in some way. In this sense the mandatory programs are very different from discretionary programs, which come under scrutiny every year and thus are not on automatic pilot.

Mandatory programs did not always take up so much room in the budget. As we have seen, discretionary spending used to dominate the federal budget. Before new major mandatory programs were adopted in the 1960s, most federal spending was addressed every year in appropriations bills. Congress had much smaller appropriations committees, and the few members lucky enough to be on them were usually fiscal conservatives who were determined to come as close to balancing the budget every year as was possible given economic conditions. And these members were in a good position to exercise influence since almost all federal spending had to be approved by them. In those days, appropriators were known as the "watchdogs of the Treasury" and accorded prestige and respect for taming the irresponsible and free-spending habits of the rest of the membership. In effect, leadership made sure that someone minded the store while the rest of the members went their merry way proposing this or that new program.

Everything changed in the 1970s. The new Medicare system began to grow and expand, and Social Security payments, once adjusted on a yearly basis, were first increased dramatically by bipartisan agreement, and then tagged to inflation automatically. Suddenly the federal budget was under no one's control. Furthermore, a movement by young Democrats took hold in the House to expand and democratize the Appropriations Committee so as to make it responsive to the spendthrift larger membership of the party and the whole House.

As deficits soared, Congress, recognizing rather quickly that it had no watchdog anymore, created the Budget Committees to produce a budget resolution to inform the rest of the membership of the budgetary consequences of their taxing and spending decisions. The problem was that the popularity of the mandatory programs was too great to confront, and to complicate matters, a tax revolt was brewing in the country. Republicans, joined by many prominent Democrats, supported and put in place tax relief and turned a blind eye to the situation with the mandatory programs.

To the extent that there are still "watchdogs of the Treasury" in Congress, they are usually to be found on the Budget Committee. But the Budget Committee only has the authority to bring nonbinding resolutions to the floor. These can include reconciliation instructions, which were meant to make the hard decisions (increasing taxes and cutting spending) easier to pass by prohibiting the filibuster in the Senate. But the reconciliation process has been used more often in recent years to put in place tax cuts than to reduce deficits.

Is There Any Hope?

There is no denying the obvious: Addressing the government's long-term budget problem is very difficult. It is not easy to get politicians to raise taxes or cut spending. But a great deal is at stake. Economic growth is affected by chronic deficits, and the situation will get much more serious in future years. Increasing expenditures on retirement programs will also crowd out spending for other crucial government activities, including national defense, infrastructure, research and development, and education.

The politics of the situation does not seem to hold much promise. Republicans believe strongly in cutting taxes and oppose any efforts to raise more revenue. At the same time, while they might be inclined to support cuts in the major mandatory programs, they live in fear of what Democrats will do to them if they propose changes in Medicare or Social Security. Democrats, for their part, believe in the major mandatory programs and will abide no substantial changes in them. They would be willing to think about increasing revenues through the tax code, but are terrified of the "tax-and-spend" label that Republicans would hit them with during the election season.

Some encouragement can be found in some tough decisions that were made in the not too distant past. From about 1983 through the 1990s, it was not at all uncommon for serious proposals to be put forward to cut spending, raise taxes, or do both. Sometimes bills were enacted to do these things—as with President Bush in 1990 and President Clinton in 1993—although the political consequences of these actions tended to depress any enthusiasm for belt-tightening.

Two of the most dramatic instances were in 1983 and 1997. In 1983 Social Security was bankrupt; incoming payroll taxes could not cover the growing commitment for old-age insurance payments. Congress and the president were at a loss. What to do? A bipartisan commission was formed. Headed by Alan Greenspan (before he became chair of the Federal Reserve) and including leading players in Congress and outside of it, the commission was charged with coming up with a consensus solution.[24]

The solution would guarantee a funding stream for the program for at least fifty years. It was strong medicine, with a major tax increase and some benefits made taxable for the first time, as well as a benefit cut in the form of increasing the retirement age. Congress, with Democrats in charge of the House and Republicans controlling the Senate, adopted the proposal. Republican president Ronald Reagan signed on.

In 1997 it looked like a balanced budget was in sight—if only entitlements and discretionary spending could be brought under control. President Clinton and Speaker Gingrich provided the impetus, and the Congress put together a plan that extended and tightened statutory caps on discretionary spending over the next five years and found roughly $250 billion of savings in Medicare. The Balanced Budget Act of 1997 was passed. It aimed to balance the budget by 2002. As we saw, the budget achieved balance ahead of schedule, in 1998, owing to an unexpected flood of tax revenues.

These two landmark agreements are instructive in a couple of ways. In 1983 Congress and the president decided that it would be politically wise to charter a commission, which would meet largely out of the public eye, to work on the details of a plan rather than to have Congress do it out in the open. If wise old hands struck a reasonable deal that both parties in Congress agreed could not be picked apart, then it would have a better chance of passing.

Congress often deals with sticky issues this way: Let someone else come up with a plan, and we will decide whether to accept it. Making deals in secret makes it a little less clear exactly who is to blame for the controversial or unpopular aspects of a plan.

Maybe more important is that in each case government was divided, with Democrats and Republicans alike having some control over the levers of power. In 1983 it was a Democratic House and a Republican-controlled Senate and White House. In 1997, Clinton, a Democrat, was dealing with Majority Leader Trent Lott and Speaker Gingrich representing the Republican Congress. It is likely that neither side, if they had been in control of both branches, would have wanted to face the voters to accept full accountability for the unpopular aspects of these bills. As noted, both sides believe they will get killed at the polls when they advocate tax increases or spending cuts, especially in popular mandatory programs.

But if responsibility for the needed actions can be shared, there may be room for agreement. In 1997 the bill was sweetened by including some tax cuts to appease Republicans and some social spending for Democrats. This might be the model for addressing the difficult budget issues facing the country.

CONCLUSION

Congress's funding power is without a doubt its most important tool in directing the work of the federal government. The power of the purse gives it the leverage to get agencies to do things, or not do things, as key members and the institution as a whole see fit.

In the budget process, Congress looks at what the government does both in the big picture and at a more granular level. The Concurrent Budget Resolution is the board of directors' way of setting forth priorities for the government. It is passed as an answer to the chief executive's statement of priorities, as detailed in the president's budget. But the budget resolution is only a broad brushstroke. If Congress is particularly ambitious and resolves to make major changes in the tax code or the mandatory spending programs, the relevant authorizing committees get to work to put those goals into effect.

Every year Congress must work on appropriations bills to fund the vast majority of programs that fit into the discretionary spending category. It is in these bills, and in the appropriations process more broadly, that Congress regularly does the bulk of its most important work directing government agencies and programs. In appropriations bills, agencies are given budget authority to operate, and they are often given explicit instructions as to how to manage and implement government programs. More often than not, these instructions appear in nonstatutory report language, which agencies normally choose to follow given the annual leverage that Congress has over their budgets.

In the coming years, Congress faces great challenges in exercising its power over the federal budget. A "fiscal train wreck"—the term used by the nonpartisan Government Accountability Office—is visible on the horizon. Many observers believe that the institution is not well equipped to make the hard decisions necessary to rein in spending on entitlement programs for seniors and pay for all the government services the public demands. In the past Congress has found a way to address difficult fiscal issues, sometimes by circumventing the regular legislative process. At this point the political will has not been found to address the impending crisis.

QUESTIONS FOR DISCUSSION

1. Both a corporate board and the Congress have the responsibility to budget. What makes it harder for Congress to perform this task efficiently than it might be for a corporate board?
2. What are the drawbacks of Congress's common practice of using the appropriations process to set agency policy?
3. Where does the blame lie for the chronic deficits faced by the federal government? Is there any particular culprit, or is the blame widely shared?
4. What are the pluses and minuses of using the reconciliation process to pass legislation through the Senate?

SUGGESTIONS FOR FURTHER READING

Government Accountability Office. 2008. "The Federal Government's Financial Health." Available at: http://www.gao.gov/financial/citizensguide2008.pdf.

Palazzolo, Daniel J. 1999. *Done Deal: The Politics of the 1997 Budget Agreement.* Chatham, NJ: Chatham House.

Rauch, Jonathan. 2009. "Earmarks Are a Model, Not a Menace." *National Journal,* March 14, 2009.

Schick, Allen. 2007. *The Federal Budget,* 3rd ed. Washington, DC: Brookings Institution Press.

NOTES

1. This definition is drawn from that used by Allen Schick in *The Federal Budget,* 3rd ed. (Washington, DC: Brookings Institution Press, 2007), p. 327.

2. Ibid.

3. For a description of the process by which the agencies put together their budgets, see http://www.whitehouse.gov/omb/. In particular, the A-11 Circular details what the agencies and departments must do; see http://www.whitehouse.gov/omb/circulars/a11/current _year/a11_toc.html.

4. For examples of SAPs, see http://www.whitehouse.gov/omb/legislative/sap/ index.html.

5. The budget resolutions for fiscal years 2005 and 2007 were not adopted by Congress in 2004 and 2006, respectively.

6. More information on the Republican Study Committee can be found at http://john shadegg.house.gov/rsc/about.htm. The Blue Dog Coalition website and the Congressional Black Caucus website are found, respectively, at: http://www.house.gov/ross/BlueDogs/ and http://www.thecongressionalblackcaucus.com/.

7. The Senate's so-called Byrd Rule applies to this situation and puts other stipulations on what may be in a reconciliation bill; for example, it forbids cuts in Social Security programs. More on the Byrd Rule can be found in Robert Keith, "CRS Report for Congress: The Budget Reconciliation Process: The Senate's Byrd Rule," Congressional Research Service, April 7, 2005.

8. See Charles H. Stewart, *Budget Reform Politics: The Design of the Appropriations Process, 1865–1921* (Cambridge: Cambridge University Press, 1989).

9. See the A-11 Circular at: http://www.whitehouse.gov/omb/circulars/a11/current _year/a11_toc.html.

10. House Appropriations Committee staff and members often claim that the Constitution requires that appropriations bills move first in the House. The Constitution says that *revenue* bills must move first through the House. This stipulation obviously applies to tax bills and probably does not apply to spending bills. In addition, the Senate did in fact pass an appropriations bill before the House a few times as recently as the late 1990s. This very rare event has not happened again since.

11. It has been about ten years, at this writing, since the Senate left a House-passed appropriations bill intact and then amended it. The Senate has essentially chosen instead to start from scratch. This has ramifications in conference committee, since the old method identified a discrete number of differences (the Senate amendments) between the bills, and the newer method leaves the entire bill open to negotiation.

12. The Senate added a rule in 2007 that makes it easier to strip provisions in the conference report that were added during the conference committee deliberations. This was to prevent so-called air-dropped earmarks that were not considered earlier in the process.

13. Schick, *The Federal Budget*, p. 266.

14. Some Appropriations Committee members and staff assert that some report language in the JES is legally binding. They say this is the case when the bill itself, in either the account paragraph or the general provisions, refers to sections of the JES. This assertion has not been tested in court. Suffice it to say that, whether technically binding or not, JES provisions are almost always followed by agency officials. OMB officials generally agree with appropriations staff to the extent that, if the reference in the account to the JES is specific, it is incumbent upon agencies to do what is in the report language.

15. It is also the case that some report language provisions amount to "throwaway" language that is inserted to assuage certain constituencies but is of no real concern to members.

16. By comparison, in America's last extended conflict, in Vietnam, supplemental appropriations accounted for the bulk of war costs only in the first two years (fiscal years 1966 and 1967). Subsequently, they were used sparingly or not at all through the end of U.S. involvement in 1975. See Stephen Daggett, "CRS Report for Congress: Military Operations: Precedents for Funding Contingency Operations in Regular or in Supplemental Appropriations Bills," Congressional Research Service, June 13, 2006.

17. For the House and Senate definitions, see http://earmarks.omb.gov/house_and_senate _earmarks_definition.html. The House definition is in section 404(d).

18. Senator McCain's website goes into more detail.

19. Jonathan Rauch makes this point and takes some other rather contrarian views on earmarking in "Earmarks Are a Model, Not a Menace," *National Journal*, March 14, 2009.

20. Schick, *The Federal Budget*, p. 194.

21. Ibid., pp. 27–31.

22. Ibid., ch. 3.

23. Walker starkly laid out the situation on *60 Minutes* on March 4, 2007. The interview can be read and seen at Daniel Schorn, "U.S. Heading for Financial Trouble?" July 8, 2007, *60 Minutes*, CBSNews.com, http://www.cbsnews.com/stories/2007/03/01/60minutes/ main2528226.shtml.

24. See Paul Light, *Artful Work: The Politics of Social Security Reform* (New York: Mc-Graw-Hill, 1985).

CHAPTER SIX

Congress as the Board of Directors: Oversight of the Executive Branch

In the previous two chapters, we looked at how Congress establishes and funds government agencies and programs in authorizing and appropriations law. Once programs are established and funded, it is up to the executive branch agencies to implement the law. But that does not mean the board of directors loses interest.

Quite to the contrary—Congress has a legitimate interest in how the laws it passes are executed by government agencies, and members are well within their rights to look into how programs are administered. After all, what use would the legislative power be if the chief executive—the president—or the head of an agency or department could administer a program and spend federal funds in ways that contradicted what was set in law? (In fact, executive branch officials run the risk of impeachment, a lawsuit, jail time, or some combination of these sanctions if they contravene the law.)

Furthermore, as Congress begins the annual appropriations process and the periodic reauthorizations of government programs and agencies, it needs a great deal of information in order to make considered decisions. Much of that information must come from the agencies. The board looks into what is working and what is not working to see whether changes in the law need to be made. The board also needs to see whether funds are being put to good use, whether funds should be shifted to other priorities, or perhaps whether more money might be required for an agency to serve its mission effectively. In short, conducting oversight— looking into how agencies carry out programs—is an integral part of the legislative process. Oversight or supervision is every bit as much the regular business of Congress as actual legislating; neither can be done effectively without the other.

Oversight is a tough job for members of Congress and their staff. The government is huge and complex, and agencies do not always make it easy to get information. Presidents, cabinet secretaries, and agency heads have an interest in protecting their prerogatives and running programs in ways that they feel reflect well on their stewardship of the government. Congress can seem, from the executive perspective, to be meddling when members ask for information—and sometimes only to advance a cause that matters to a particular district or state or the interests of one political party.

The board of directors has a very different perspective. It sees an executive branch run largely by unelected people—cabinet secretaries, agency heads, and other high-ranking officials. (The president and the vice president are the only elected officials in the executive branch.) As the representatives of the people, members of Congress see oversight as a key means to hold powerful officials accountable for government activities that were put in place and funded through legislation by Congress.

The idea of the U.S. government as a codependent system is most evident in the area of congressional oversight of government agencies and programs. Every day the executive branch agencies communicate with the legislative branch to report on the progress they are making on important issues and problems of the day and to respond to inquiries initiated by Congress. Often the communication is an effort to influence the legislative process. And every day the legislative branch initiates inquiries into program performance, calls powerful cabinet secretaries and agency heads to Capitol Hill for public hearings on major issues, and sits down with agency policy experts to work on legislation solutions. It is a wary interaction, but the constant is negotiation. Each side has leverage, and each side has a distinct role. In fact, neither can perform its duties without the other.

In covering the sources of the board of directors' authority to monitor the executive branch, the first section of this chapter looks at the theoretical and constitutional underpinnings of the oversight power, the statutory bases of oversight, and the congressional rules that require committees to conduct oversight in their areas of jurisdiction.

The second section surveys the many formal and informal methods that Congress uses to look into the actions of executive branch agencies. Most oversight is conducted by committees. Committees and subcommittees hold hearings to highlight their oversight work, but members of Congress use hearings for a range of other purposes as well. Commonly, hearings are part of a process to nudge executive branch officials in a certain direction—that is, to get them to change the way they are implementing government programs. Essentially, hearings are often used by committees and subcommittees in lieu of actual legislation that would compel agency actions. The legislative process can be extremely difficult to navigate, so the board of directors may decide that hearings and other forms of oversight will achieve the results they want more quickly.

Congressional investigations are another form of oversight. We look at a specific case in the late 1990s when congressional committees investigated the Internal Revenue Service (IRS). High-profile hearings forced the IRS commissioner to change some agency policies immediately and eventually led to a full-fledged reform bill that was signed into law by President Clinton in 1998.

The board of directors also may oversee the executive branch by putting into law, or in accompanying report language, explicit directions for agency officials to follow. Sometimes this takes the form of a *legislative veto*, an approach that has been ruled unconstitutional but, curiously, is still very much in use.

Congress also relies on so-called extra-congressional sources for some of its oversight. In particular, the Government Accountability Office (GAO), a support agency for the legislative branch, acts on congressional requests to look into the performance of government programs. GAO's nonpartisan stature and its experienced and professional staff lend credibility to its findings. In addition, in the 1970s Congress established inspector general (IG) offices in most government agencies. IGs perform a unique role in the American system. Although housed in the executive branch, the IG offices report directly to Congress and sometimes respond to congressional requests for investigations.

The last section looks at the politics of congressional oversight. Congress is often criticized for failing to conduct oversight in a comprehensive and systematic manner, a charge that undoubtedly is true. It is also true, however, that a great deal of oversight does indeed go on every year, but that there are too few members and not enough resources to conduct truly thorough oversight of the activities of a government that is simply too big. Ultimately the key questions are: Why do members of Congress not make a higher priority of their crucial responsibility to make sure government programs are run effectively and efficiently? Do they care about "good government"? Is there a pattern to the conduct of oversight, and if so, what is that pattern?

CONGRESSIONAL OVERSIGHT AUTHORITY

The Two Central Purposes of Oversight

In creating separate branches of government, the Framers of the Constitution put in place instruments for each branch to check the others. One of the most influential of the *Federalist Papers* states that "the constant aim is to divide and arrange [the branches of government] in such a manner that each may be a check on the other."[1] The notion that one branch needs to be able to dip into the territory of another was thought to be a key, if not *the* key, to ensuring that the people's liberties would not be trampled on by a central government that was being given substantial powers.[2]

James Madison, who wrote the *Federalist Papers* just quoted, did not think that the act of writing down the essential liberties—freedom of speech, freedom of the press, freedom of religion, right to jury trial, and so on—in what became the Bill of Rights would be nearly sufficient to protect them. In his view, a carefully structured government was the only hope for securing the people's freedoms. A threat to liberty could certainly arise from an executive branch that wielded unchecked authority under the control of the president. Administering the laws of the land could be done in capricious and dangerous ways. Keep in mind that the president was to be the one who could call the state militias into service and otherwise have the responsibility of maintaining domestic tranquillity. The executive had "the sword," in the manner of speaking at the time, and thus was a potential threat to the people's liberties.

To keep the executive from running wild, Congress, which contained the true representatives of the people, would need to be able to check up on the executive. First and foremost, this would be done by *monitoring executive actions to make sure that the laws were obeyed and the liberties of the people were not infringed upon.*

As noted in Chapter 4, Congress was given the power to "create, abolish, reorganize, and fund federal departments."[3] Congress, then, as the representative of the people, needed to be able to protect these prerogatives in the separated system; only by being able to "look over the shoulder" of executive branch officials could it do this. How else could Congress make sure that the president was spending money in accordance with law? How else could it make sure that legally required programs to give educational grants to the needy were being administered properly? After all, Congress had been given the legislative power, which the Constitution spelled out as the power of the purse and the authority to establish federal program guidelines.

The executive would be required to follow clearly stated legislative intent, and Congress would be entitled to make sure it was doing so.

Congress's other main objective in pursuing oversight is *to ensure good government*. The power of the purse carries with it a tremendous responsibility: the efficient, wise, and honest stewardship of taxpayers' money. The U.S. government has become, as we have seen, the single largest entity in the world, spending well over $3 trillion yearly on everything from spy satellites to farm subsidies to social work. It is a big job to make sure that this kind of money is being spent wisely.

The executive branch has some mechanisms in place to do its part. It has monitors in every department and agency charged with ferreting out waste, fraud, and abuse (the IG offices, for example). The Office of Management and Budget (OMB) has the responsibility to manage budget activity throughout the government. Under the George W. Bush administration, OMB evaluated every government program to see whether it was being carried out efficiently and whether it addressed the intended problems or achieved the intended results.[4] This evaluation was such an ambitious undertaking that it took much of Bush's two terms in office to complete.

But ultimately it is Congress, as the people's elected representative, that is responsible for evaluating government activities, and in this capacity Congress is often wary of the messages coming from the president or top department and agency officials appointed by the president. Executive branch leaders may have a political motivation to downplay internal management problems, and they may not want malfeasance to come to light. As a result, Congress has a responsibility to make its own judgments as to the efficiency or effectiveness of any given program. And members and staff on Capitol Hill try to be particularly attuned to waste, fraud, and abuse in a program or in the contracting process. In a forward-looking sense, Congress needs information about current programs in order to inform the legislative process as to changes and enhancements that may need to be made in law to meet new circumstances.

The Statutory Bases of Oversight

Though the Constitution grants Congress the power to "create, abolish, reorganize, and fund federal departments," it does not spell out exactly how Congress should do this, or how it should make sure that these agencies remain responsive to the needs of the American public. To fill in these gaps, Congress has passed legislation over the years to codify and institutionalize these processes. Some of this legislation created legislative branch agencies that are responsible, in whole or in part, for augmenting Congress's ability to supervise the executive:

1. In 1921 Congress created the General Accounting Office, later renamed the *Government Accountability Office (GAO)*, which was given the power to investigate agencies' use of funds. We look at its role in more depth later in the chapter.

2. In 1946 Congress established the Legislative Reference Service, now the *Congressional Research Service (CRS)*, which has access to executive branch documents in order to inform the policymaking process.

3. In 1974 Congress created the *Congressional Budget Office (CBO)*, which can "secure information . . . directly from various departments" to aid Congress in understanding the budgetary implications of legislation it is contemplating.[5]

Congressional staff conducting oversight often rely on information they receive directly from the civil servants who run government programs. Because the executive branch has prerogatives of its own that it feels it must protect, it sometimes resists congressional meddling in executive affairs. It is not always sure of members' motivations, which could be driven by narrow, district-specific interests or by partisan politics. As a result, agency heads and presidents have tried to close the lines of communication from executive branch personnel to the Congress, putting up a wall between the branches even though the divide between them must be permeable in order for the system to function. To combat this, legislation introduced over the years has provided legal protections for executive branch personnel who pass information to members of Congress. These so-called *whistleblower* laws are meant to shield executive branch officials who believe they have information about a violation of law or other abuse and who communicate such concerns to Congress.[6]

Congress has also put into law provisions that require committees to be watchful of agencies in their areas of jurisdiction. Of particular note was legislation in 1946 that authorized staff for the committees. Before that time, work on the Hill was handled by members and a staffer or two in their personal office. By the 1940s, after the expansion of government in the New Deal, the growth of the defense establishment during World War II, and the need to maintain a large military after the war, Congress was overwhelmed. Washington was not a sleepy little town anymore, and the board of directors needed some help. As seen in Box 6.1, then-senator Harry S Truman showed what a senator fortified by strong staff support could do in the public interest.

In recent decades, particularly since the explosion in government programs in the 1960s and early 1970s, the House and Senate have gone further by putting in place explicit oversight responsibilities in their respective bodies of rules. In the House, the Oversight and Government Reform Committee takes the lead in supervising

BOX 6.1
SENATOR TRUMAN SHOWS THE VALUE
OF CONGRESSIONAL STAFF

As a member of the Senate in the 1930s and into the early 1940s, Harry Truman had the typical skeletal staff for that time consisting of clerical assistance plus one or two professionals to help him handle his legislative duties.

After getting reelected in 1940, Truman set his sights on the government contracting process in the defense area as the nation geared up for the massive rearmament required to fight a world war. He had received considerable correspondence in his Senate office alleging widespread "waste and favoritism" in government contracts.

In March 1941, the Special Committee Investigating National Defense, which came to be known as the Truman Committee, was established. Its charge was to look into the methods by which contracts were awarded, the geographic distribution of contracts, the effect of the rearmament program on labor, the accounting practices of contractors, and other matters. Initially President Franklin Roosevelt opposed the investigation, alleging that it would undermine morale for the war effort. Truman assured the president that his aim was not to criticize the military but rather to focus on contracting and contracting alone. Ultimately the Truman Committee was credited with uncovering considerable waste and saving the government billions of dollars.

How did Truman do it? Initially the committee was given only $15,000 to conduct its business. This enabled Truman to hire a full-time investigator and relatively little else. In the end Truman was able to prevail upon the Senate to give him far more resources—at its height, the committee had eighteen investigators and other support.

The Truman Committee was a precursor to the greater expansion of congressional staff in 1946 and in later years. Congress came to recognize that, after the tremendous growth of government in the 1930s and 1940s in response to the Depression and to World War II, it needed to bulk up in order to be able to keep up with everything going on in the executive branch.

Source: Donald H. Riddle, *The Truman Committee* (New Brunswick, NJ: Rutgers University Press, 1964).

government agencies and programs. In the Senate, the Homeland Security and Governmental Affairs Committee has that responsibility. The authorizing committees in both chambers, as well as the Appropriations Committees, are given specific responsibilities to conduct oversight in their jurisdictions. In the House, each authorizing committee must establish an oversight subcommittee to keep tabs on the agencies in its jurisdiction.

METHODS OF CONGRESSIONAL OVERSIGHT

Although individual members of Congress are well within their rights to make inquiries about the conduct of government programs, it is the committees and subcommittees of Congress, as suggested earlier, that are officially sanctioned by House and Senate rules to supervise the vast federal bureaucracy. Members acting on their own may be able to focus attention on problem areas in the government, but it is the committees and subcommittees that have the expertise and the wherewithal to be the most aggressive and effective overseers of the agencies.

Most committees in Congress have fully sanctioned oversight responsibilities. Two committees in particular are intended primarily to conduct oversight:

House Committee on Oversight and Government Reform
Subcommittees on:
1. Domestic Policy
2. Federal Workforce, Postal Service, and the District of Columbia
3. Government Management, Organization, and Procurement
4. Information Policy, Census, and National Archives
5. National Security and Foreign Affairs

Senate Committee on Homeland Security and Governmental Affairs
Subcommittees on:
1. Disaster Recovery
2. Federal Financial Management, Government Information, Federal Services, and International Security
3. Oversight of Government Management, the Federal Workforce, and the District of Columbia
4. Investigations (Permanent Subcommittee on Investigations)
5. State, Local, and Private-Sector Preparedness and Integration

These committees and their subcommittees are intended, among other things, to look into the effectiveness of government programs as well as to investigate potential malfeasance in the agencies. Their jurisdiction is the *entire government*. House rules require the Oversight and Government Reform Committee to provide the information it collects from the agencies to the relevant authorizing committees. In the Senate committee, the Permanent Subcommittee on Investigations was created to look into criminal matters and abuse of power in the executive branch. Both of these committees take their mandate quite a bit further than just looking into executive branch activities; sometimes they look into malfeasance in the corporate world, professional sports, and other areas. These efforts are justifiable given Congress's extensive power to regulate commerce. (The House Oversight and Government Reform Committee has taken a special interest in recent years in the use of steroids in major league baseball. Some performance-enhancing drugs are federally controlled substances and thus subject to congressional scrutiny; in addition, baseball has an antitrust exemption in federal law.)

To aid in looking into executive branch activities, these two committees have also been accorded enhanced subpoena power. Congress may subpoena government witnesses and documents; there are substantial risks to ignoring or snubbing a congressional subpoena. Most congressional subpoenas require a majority vote to be enforced by the committee making the request for information. Only the Oversight and Government Reform Committee and the Homeland Security and Governmental Affairs Committee may issue a subpoena based on the decision of only the committee chair. (The chair of the Oversight and Government Reform Committee in the 110th Congress, Henry Waxman of California, chose not to exercise this power unilaterally. He issued numerous subpoenas, but only with the support of a majority of the committee.) In the case of the Permanent Subcommittee on Investigations, the subcommittee chair may issue the subpoena.

Authorizing committees also have oversight responsibilities in their areas of jurisdiction and thus, in effect, have two roles: they authorize the existence of government programs in law, and they are responsible for looking into whether these programs are being carried out according to congressional intent. Their oversight function is meant primarily to inform the development of new authorizing legislation.

The Appropriations Committees in the House and Senate also get into the act. They are expressly responsible for looking into how government monies are being spent as a means of informing the annual appropriations process. The House

Appropriations Committee has a special investigations unit to look into potential illegalities in the expenditure of government funds.

Congressional Hearings

Congressional hearings are probably the most pervasive method of conducting oversight on Capitol Hill. Many hearings serve both to probe the conduct of government
programs and to inform Congress about pending authorizing or appropriations legislation. They may serve other purposes as well. Here are descriptions of the different types of congressional hearings.[7]

Types of Congressional Hearings

Legislative hearings—The purpose of legislative hearings is to look into legislation
that a committee is considering. A legislative hearing typically involves testimony
from some combination of executive branch officials, interest group leaders, and
outside experts with an interest in the legislation.

Oversight hearings—Oversight hearings primarily involve testimony from executive
officials about the conduct of government programs. Other people representing
groups with a stake in the programs may also be asked to testify. Oversight hearings
often serve the dual role of informing the reauthorization process for agencies and
programs.

Investigatory hearings—In investigatory hearings, which are often a type of oversight
hearing, the committee or subcommittee is looking to expose improper conduct on
the part of government officials in the implementation of government programs.
Some investigatory hearings probe into private-sector activities, sometimes with an
eye toward enhancing the regulatory role of the government.

Confirmation hearings—Only the Senate conducts confirmation hearings. The Senate has the responsibility to consider and then vote to approve or reject presidential nominees—in other words, provide advice and consent—for high-ranking
executive branch positions and federal judgeships. Hearings are often held to question nominees.[8]

Hearings are meetings of a congressional committee or subcommittee that are
called by the chair of that panel for a specific purpose. They are almost always held
in public, with the exception of hearings that involve classified information. (The

House and Senate Intelligence Committees, for example, usually conduct their hearings in closed session in a special room in the Capitol that is regularly swept for listening devices.) Hearings bring government officials, interest group representatives, and other private citizens to Capitol Hill to answer questions from the members of the committee or subcommittee. Occasionally members of Congress request a chance to give testimony—or are asked to—and to take questions from members of a committee on which they do not serve.

Oversight hearings are rarely called to pat agency officials on the back for a job well done. Often the committee members are at odds with the agency representative and trying to press their case as to how things should, in their view, be done in the implementation of a government program. An implicit or sometimes explicit threat may hang in the air: *If you do not accede to our wishes, we will begin work on requiring you by law to do things our way. Perhaps you can make it easier for everybody by simply changing how you implement this program.*

There are literally hundreds of these types of hearings every year. Why is it so common that Congress and the executive branch are at odds about the conduct of government programs?

First of all, those who are asked to carry out the law—the government bureaucrats—frequently have a different view on how to do their work than the elected representatives who wrote the law. At one level the clash between the branches boils down to a difference of perspective. Members of Congress answer to their constituents; they are driven by reelection concerns as well as the needs of their party. Executive branch officials, on the other hand, receive direction from the president and view themselves as working for the nation as a whole. Divergent perspectives may lead to different interpretations of the same law.

This is especially apparent when one understands something about the ambiguity that is intentionally built into most major legislation. The board of directors passes laws that leave a great deal to the discretion of the experts in the agencies. It is also true that no law can anticipate the future events to which those carrying out the law may have to respond. In some cases ambiguous legal language may have been necessary to gloss over strong differences of opinion among members and enable the leadership of the Congress to secure the necessary majorities for final passage.

The bottom line is that there is a lot of potential for disagreement in the implementation of a federal program. Hearings provide a convenient public venue for the Congress to publicize and hash out these differences of opinion. This venue is particularly convenient for Congress because members stage the hearings to put the agency officials at a distinct disadvantage. Of course, sometimes differences can be negotiated in private, but even then Congress may see some advantage in bringing a matter to the public's attention by conducting a hearing.

The Way to Think About Hearings

Anytime a member of Congress goes public in official proceedings, it is safe to assume that the event or the speech is scripted, or at the very least that the member intends to influence the course of events in a particular way. This is certainly true with hearings.

To develop an analogy, hearings may resemble election campaigning in that they often boil down to a question of marketing.

When influential people in a political party decide that they want to field their most qualified candidate in a race that looks promising for their party—say, the incumbent candidate of the other party has been involved in a scandal, or a retirement opens up a seat—they usually begin by doing what they can to market their candidate. Marketing congressional candidates involves, more than anything else, advertising in a variety of media, including television, the Internet, radio, newspapers, and billboards. Marketing experts, or campaign consultants, do a tremendous amount of research on behalf of political candidates to determine what to say in the advertising and how to describe and depict the candidate on billboards and other public places. Candidates prepare speeches, use teleprompters, carefully stage backdrops, and of course, depict themselves in strategic ways in ads. Experts recognize that a good advertising campaign is crucial to winning votes. This is true even though voters recognize that there is nothing spontaneous about advertising or even about most campaign appearances.

These same marketing elements of political campaigning apply to hearings. Committee chairs direct congressional committee staff to research the issues and programs to which they want to draw attention. The staff find witnesses inside and outside of government who will help the chair make his or her case in public session. The staff also come up with questions and other preparatory material for the members of the committee. In other words, members hold hearings in order to advance a particular agenda. Often they are trying to expose a poorly functioning government program, while trying to persuade agency officials to change their behavior. Or in a legislative hearing, they are trying to put a good first foot forward in selling a pending piece of legislation to the public and to other members of Congress. Even the most brilliant piece of legislation starts the legislative process with far fewer than the 218 (in the House) and 60 (in the Senate) committed supporters it ultimately needs.

Hearings are essentially the public face of a great deal of research that has been done ahead of time to advance the committee chair's agenda. They are only *ostensibly* fact-finding exercises. In reality, the facts have been found; committee and subcommittee chairs are trying to place those facts in the context that best serves their interests and the interests of their party. They are using the public forum of the hearing as a way to *market* their legislative and oversight agendas, just as campaign advertising serves to market candidates.

Bringing Attention to Issues

If hearings are not fact-finding exercises, but rather are fact-*exposing* exercises, how do members of Congress set up hearings to maximize this role?

As their first and most important goal, members want to gain the attention of the target audience, which may be a specific interest group or groups; other members of Congress; the general public or some targeted segment of it; or some combination of these. There are different ways for hearings to find their audience, but in all cases publicity—through the mass media, specific media outlets, or trade publications— is the key. The target audience has to be drawn in. For example, if a hearing is meant to criticize administration policy regarding funding research on Parkinson's disease, will more media attend if the committee brings in major university researchers who can explain in scientific detail why more money is needed, or if a movie and television star like Michael J. Fox, who suffers from the disease, appears in a public session? Asking the question itself almost serves to answer it.

Congressional committee staff will have talked to scientists and are likely to have one or two testify at some point in order to get their views on the record, but the main thrust of the hearing is bringing in the celebrity so that the media will cover it more broadly and people—members of Congress as well as the general public—will be aware of the issue. In this way the chair hopes public pressure will be brought to bear to rally support for his or her objective.

Congressional committees have brought in Elizabeth Taylor to advocate for more AIDS research money, Christie Brinkley to talk about the dangers of nuclear power technology, and Sissy Spacek to inform them about the plight of the family farmer. Each of these celebrities had an interest in the issue at hand, even if they were not technically experts. And in all these cases, the portion of the hearing that featured them got a great deal more attention than the testimony from subsequent panels of witnesses that included scientists, farm economists, interest group advocates, and technical experts from the agencies.

The same principles apply when committee chairs request the testimony, even on fairly technical matters, of a cabinet official—say, the secretary of Defense—or a well-known agency head who oversees a vast bureaucracy with a multibillion-dollar budget and thousands of employees. The well-known cabinet secretary will garner far more attention from the media, and in turn shine a light on the issue in question, than the anonymous technical experts in the agency. The technical person will certainly have been consulted or even deposed, but he or she may not be valuable as a witness. If technical matters come up in the hearing that the top official cannot answer, he or she is required to provide the committee with answers within a short period of time. The committee can thus add technical details to the record without necessarily having to summon the experts in person.

The idea is to draw attention and advance an agenda, and actors, athletes, models, and cabinet officials usually seem to do this better than experts. It is not always necessary to have a celebrity witness, especially if the target audience is narrow and requires only local or specialized coverage. But in any case, hearings may have little more substance than most election campaign advertising, and they are often almost as scripted. The simple lesson is that public relations and marketing are every bit as important in moving policy priorities forward in the U.S. Congress as they are in winning over voters in an election campaign or selling beer to consumers.

Scheduling Hearings

It is up to the discretion of the committee or subcommittee chair to decide when and whether to hold hearings. Having said that, certain hearings are scheduled on a fairly predictable and regular basis every year, although their content varies depending on circumstances. As we saw in Chapter 5, the Appropriations subcommittees in the two chambers must work on funding bills each and every year. A given subcommittee may handle the funding for two or three cabinet-level departments and a dozen or more agencies. Invariably, from February to May every year, agency heads and other important officials march up to the Hill to appear in front of the subcommittees to defend the president's budget request and answer questions about how they are implementing existing programs.

In the defense world, not only must the armed services defend their budgets to the appropriators on Capitol Hill, but the top brass are subjected each year to authorization hearings. The Armed Services Committees on the Hill work on annual comprehensive authorizing legislation; Army, Air Force, Navy, and Marine leadership expect to appear in front of the Armed Services subcommittees (and often the full committee) every year. Similarly, departments or agencies whose multi-year authorizations expire in a given year can also plan on being summoned to appear at hearings to have their work examined. In all these cases, the specific issues in which Congress takes an interest vary from year to year.

On any given day, however, many of the hearings on Capitol Hill are much more discretionary. All agencies have to be on their toes, particularly when things go awry with their programs, because the committees with jurisdiction are likely to be interested in bringing problems to light. The article reproduced in Box 6.2 provides a good example of a congressional response to headline-making news that affected a federal agency—the Consumer Product Safety Commission. In this case we can see Congress using oversight as a way to inform both its authorizing and appropriations processes.

An agency head knows that an article in the *Washington Post* exposing wasteful spending or malfeasance of some sort in his agency is likely to elicit an invitation to appear in front of a congressional committee. Problems in Iraq almost always lead to a call to the Defense Department requesting one of the service chiefs to appear in open session to explain what is happening and what the administration is doing about it. The breakout of hostilities between the Taliban and government forces in Pakistan has a congressional response, usually a request to have the secretary of State or other high-ranking official explain the administration policy. The aftermath of Hurricane Katrina led to more hearings than anyone could count, most involving an almost inquisition-like atmosphere for the top officials at the Federal Emergency Management Agency (FEMA) whose responses were considered insufficient.

So, as we have seen, hearings are often held in response to events, but they may also simply be driven by the whims of the chairs. If an issue interests a chair, he or she will try to draw attention to it. Hearings are a good way to accomplish that end. Chairs who do not like administration policy or program implementation in their area of jurisdiction—often because of adverse affects on their district or state—can call a hearing.

What Do Hearings Look Like?

A great deal may be at stake for an agency at a committee or subcommittee hearing. In probing into a program, Congress may be contemplating a funding cut or other restrictions on agency actions in law. Members may also be intent on embarrassing witnesses in order to get them to change their behavior. It is a high-pressure environment, and the playing field is not level.

"The witness is not in the driver's seat at a hearing," one committee staffer said.[9] Although agency people have an opportunity to share what they know, the hearing

BOX 6.2
CPSC HEAD GETS GRILLED

Members of Congress almost always demand to hear from an agency head when things go wrong—especially when the issue hits home with constituents, as in this case concerning the safety of children's toys. This article, published on the ombwatch.org website on September 25, 2007, provides a good description of how hearings can fit into all facets of the board of directors' activities—funding, authorizing, and oversight. And in this case, committees in both chambers got into the act.

Congress Hears Pleas for Expanded Authority and Resources at CPSC

A proliferation of children's product recalls due to potentially dangerous exposure to lead has left many turning to the federal government for answers. The Consumer Product Safety Commission (CPSC) has borne much of the brunt for the regulatory failures. Congress is considering solutions including new federal standards for lead, expanding the agency's regulatory authority and increasing agency resources.

Currently, CPSC regulations ban the use of lead paint in many products, including toys. Children may also be exposed to lead in jewelry. CPSC has initiated a rulemaking which would ban lead in jewelry. While that rule moves through the regulatory pipeline, CPSC has begun a campaign of voluntary recalls focusing on reducing lead exposure in children's products.

However, neither CPSC regulations nor enforcement practices have kept up with a changing marketplace dominated by Chinese imports. Subsequently, a large number of children's products containing lead have found their way into American households. In these cases, CPSC has had to resort to voluntary recalls, in which the agency works with toy manufacturers and distributors in order to publicize a recall and work to remove tainted products from the market.

In 2007, CPSC has negotiated at least 43 recalls of children's products—from toys to school supplies to jewelry—containing lead, according to CPSC recall announcements. Those 43 recalls have involved approximately 10.8 million products, 84 percent of which were manufactured in China.

The product failures have spurred congressional oversight. Both the House and the Senate have held hearings focusing on children's exposure to lead from toys, jewelry and other products.

The Senate Appropriations Committee Subcommittee on Financial Services and General Government held a hearing on Sept. 12. One panel of witnesses included CPSC Acting Chairman Nancy Nord. Subcommittee members questioned Nord on a new agreement CPSC has negotiated with its Chinese counterpart. Under the agreement, the Chinese agency, the General Administration of Quality Supervision, Inspection and Quarantine, has pledged to work to eliminate lead in toys manufactured in China.

Senators inquired as to whether the agreement would yield actual benefits in the form of safer toys. Nord could not provide a straightforward answer. On multiple occasions, Nord instructed the subcommittee to "ask the Chinese."

Another panel included Mattel chairman Robert Eckert, Toy Industry Association president Carter Keithley, and Consumers Union counsel Sally Greenberg. Eckert was forthright in acknowledging his company had allowed lead-tainted products on the market and apologized for the mistakes. All witnesses expressed full-throated support for a strong and well-resourced CPSC.

During the hearing, ranking member Sam Brownback (R-KS) urged CPSC to "pull out the heavy club" and do a better job enforcing current regulations. Sen. Richard Durbin (D-IL), chairman of the subcommittee, closed the hearing by saying that China, the CPSC and Congress had failed, and he encouraged greater federal involvement: "There are moments when we need government, when we need someone to make certain that the products on the shelves are always going to be safe for our families and our kids. We need to step up to that responsibility."

On Sept. 19 and 20, the House Energy and Commerce Committee Subcommittee on Commerce, Trade and Consumer Protection held a two-day hearing on lead paint in children's toys. Congressmen from both parties were critical of CPSC and the toy industry. Committee Chair John Dingell (D-MI) scolded Nord for being too trustworthy of China, saying, "We have a fistful of promises from China."

Congressmen and witnesses also discussed legislative solutions. One proposed solution would require toys be certified for safety by an independent third party before the products could be sold. Gary Knell, president of the Sesame Workshop, announced his company would begin the process voluntarily.

Sen. Mark Pryor (D-AR) has introduced the CPSC Reform Act of 2007 (S. 2045). The bill would mandate third-party certification for children's products. It would also ban the presence of lead in children's products and tighten the standard for lead in all paints to 0.009 percent from the current 0.06 percent standard. The legislation goes beyond children's products and lead issues and addresses some of the broader problems plaguing CPSC. Pryor's legislation would also provide CPSC expanded ability to assess civil penalties for parties in violation of CPSC standards. The legislation would also mandate an expansion in appropriations for CPSC.

CPSC's eroding resources have been cited as a reason for the agency's inability to properly ensure product safety. The agency's budget is half of what it was in the 1970s when accounting for inflation. CPSC's staff, once near 1,000, is now 420.

President George W. Bush's proposed budget for FY 2008 would exacerbate this problem. CPSC's budget for FY 2007 was $62,728,000. Bush has proposed a new funding level of $63,250,000 for FY 2008, a cut when taking inflation into account. Bush's budget proposes a cut in staff down to 401.

Congress is attempting to counter the president on his proposed cuts. In their respective versions of the Financial Services and General Government Appropriations bills, the House proposed $66,838,000 for CPSC, and the Senate proposed $70,000,000 for FY 2008. Bush has repeatedly indicated he will veto appropriations bills exceeding his requests.

Pryor's legislation would mandate an increase in staff to at least 500 full-time employees by the beginning of FY 2014. It would also mandate an increase in appropriations to $141,725,000 by FY 2015. The legislation has not yet been considered by the Senate Commerce, Science and Transportation Committee.

is really not about the witnesses; it is about what the members of the committee want and what they have to say, whether in prodding the witness or in acting on behalf of constituents. Remember, the point of the hearing is to promote the agenda of the chair and often the interests of his or her party.

Given all of this, it is surprising that hearings often have a fairly informal flavor. Most hearings do not have Elizabeth Taylor or Michael J. Fox or Condoleezza Rice testifying; more often a lesser-known agency official or interest group representative is testifying. As a result, even though every hearing is tremendously important to some members of Congress or some agency or some group in society affected by a government program, most hearings do not attract the attention of the general public or the mass media.

Members stroll into and out of hearings. Sometimes they ask a question and then leave before the answer is completed. Or they ask a question and turn to whisper to a staff member sitting behind them or another member while the witness nervously responds. The attending public must be quiet, but people do shuffle in and out of hearings whenever they want. This environment can be rather unnerving for the inexperienced witness.

It should be noted that the absence of members from hearings does not mean they are being lazy. In fact, the opposite is usually true. Their schedules are chock-a-block with fund-raising events and meetings with key constituent groups, administration officials, and congressional leaders—and other hearings. Sometimes a member has two hearings to go to *at the same time*. Not every hearing rises to the top of the priority list, and sometimes it can be impossible for a member to stay for the whole hearing.

Hearing procedures vary from committee to committee, but they tend to be fairly uniform in the House and to follow a similar overall framework. The committee or subcommittee chair opens the proceedings by announcing the purpose of the hearing, after which the witness delivers his or her testimony, usually a summary of detailed testimony submitted to the committee before the hearing. Sometimes several witnesses appear at one time—a "panel." These witnesses all briefly summarize their testimony. Members then have the opportunity to ask questions.

The chair starts, often with a statement followed by questions for the witness or witnesses. The ranking member follows. After that, each member, either in order of seniority alternating between parties or in order of attendance at the hearing if some members arrive late, are given five minutes to ask questions. In the Senate, some committees have slightly different rules, and the enforcement of the time limits is often more relaxed.

Most hearings last only two or three hours, with one or two panels of witnesses. Some that deal with more controversial topics and more complex issues require more witnesses and last longer. Some hearings may go on for days or weeks. Extended hearings are usually the result of investigations into major scandals or allegations of extensive malfeasance. Occasionally, controversial nominations to the Supreme Court or to cabinet-level positions result in multi-day confirmation hearings.

Testifying at Hearings

As suggested earlier, hearings are important regardless of the surrounding atmosphere. Of course, some attract worldwide attention, such as the hearings into the Watergate break-in in the 1970s, the Iran-Contra scandal in the 1980s, or the impeachment of President Clinton in the 1990s, but even relatively casual and ill-attended hearings are likely to be very significant to particular groups or agencies.

For a given agency, *every* hearing involving its business is momentous. Certainly if the hearing is about an agency's budget or a pending reauthorization bill, anything is fair game and the agency officials who testify need to be thoroughly briefed. Funding levels and key provisions in the authorization law may hang in the balance. Preparation for a hearing is a significant undertaking at an agency. The witness, either the agency head or other supervisory personnel, does not necessarily know every detail of the programs under examination. As a result, the briefing process spearheaded by the agency's congressional affairs staff is often intense.

Furthermore, and most important, because hearings are a stage for the representatives or senators, witnesses need to be mindful of the political climate. Members may be examining programs for a host of reasons. Though issues may be technical in nature, members are more often interested in programs that affect their constituents or have larger political ramifications. Remember: The chair is calling the hearing for a reason. Even hearings that are conducted regularly, such as those by appropriations subcommittees, go in the directions that the chair and other members want. Witnesses need to be aware of issues such as what is going on with each member on the committee or subcommittee, what the two parties are fighting about at the time, and what kinds of questions each member tends to ask.

Ideally, experienced agency heads and their congressional affairs staffs have developed good relations with key congressmen and staffers that enable them to anticipate better the line of questioning. Often friendly staffers alert witnesses to the sort of questions that will be asked or even solicit potential questions from the agency. Although most oversight hearings are not particularly friendly confrontations between the branches, good relationship-building with staff and members can help an agency mitigate congressional criticism and possible negative legislative ramifications down the road.

The Many Faces of Hearings

The bottom line is that hearings are an important part of all three of Congress's main responsibilities—funding, authorizing, and oversight. Even though most hearings are carefully structured and orchestrated by the committee staff, the performance of the witnesses is crucial. The chair is trying to advance a legislative or oversight agenda by shining a light on a particular agency activity. As a result, government officials need to be aware of what is going on and be ready to defend their position or offer possible solutions to problems that Congress identifies.

In effect, hearings are a way for the people's elected representatives to hold powerful *unelected* people—cabinet secretaries, agency heads, top military brass—accountable to the public. Because of the complex nature of so much of what government does, Congress gives the executive branch tremendous discretion. One way for Congress to try to change how agencies exercise their discretion is to hold a hearing that puts their decision-making in a bad light. Public embarrassment can be enough to force an agency to change its ways or to be more careful about consulting with Congress in the future before moving forward on major initiatives.

Hearing transcripts—the verbatim record of what officials say in response to congressional questions—are very useful for Congress as well. Congressional staff report that they sometimes consult hearing transcripts and other official agency documents to see what the experts wish to see in law as they put legislation together in committee or later in the legislative process.[10]

Congressional committee staff who become interested in addressing certain aspects of government programs often work hard to persuade their boss to hold a hearing on the subject. This is how they force at least some members of the committee or subcommittee to focus on the matter. (No members want to look ill informed in a public setting like a hearing, so they will agree to spend time learning the issue.) Getting members to focus on something is very important—it puts agency officials and other interested parties on the alert and can pay real dividends in terms of good public policy and legislative changes down the road.

———

Hearings should be thought of as part of the ongoing communication between the executive and legislative branches. Congress directs the executive through legislation, but in so doing must give it a great deal of leeway. It has an interest in checking up on the agencies, just as the agencies have an interest in checking in with the legislative branch. Agencies would like to stave off unfriendly hearings so that their funds will not be cut or their hands will not be tied in restrictive legislation. Disagreements inevitably arise, and Congress will wish to dig deeper and use hearings to publicize its findings. Good relations with Congress can help agencies reduce the frequency and impact of the often adversarial and unfriendly hearing environment.

Congressional Investigations

The last section on hearings covered largely run-of-the-mill oversight of ongoing government programs and agency actions. There is little or no debate regarding Congress's right to check to see how programs are running, particularly when Congress is considering pending legislation in conjunction with conducting oversight. With appropriations, of course, Congress is annually looking into how agencies are spending money and determining what funding levels should be provided for the next fiscal year. The administration recognizes that when Congress requests information in the course of exercising its legislative duties, those requests must be answered. It is unusual for agency witnesses to refuse to testify or fail to produce at least some of the requested documents.

It has historically been more controversial for Congress to request documents or testimony from agencies if there is only the *potential* for legislation. In 1927 the Supreme Court seemed to suggest that Congress could investigate executive branch activity for just about any purpose, even if there was no pending legislation.[11] This notion was challenged by the Reagan administration, but the Congress, in general, has the upper hand, because a member may at any time introduce legislation bolstering the legitimacy of a request for information.

The greater sticking point today between the branches involves the doctrine of *executive privilege*. The following is a common working definition:

> The doctrine that allows the president and other high officials of the executive branch to keep certain communications private if disclosing those communications would disrupt the functions or decision-making processes of the executive branch.

The very first president, George Washington, maintained that the executive should "communicate [to Congress] such papers as the public good would permit."[12]

He seemed to imply that, for the executive to function effectively within the constitutional framework, he needed space for privileged internal deliberations.

In today's parlance, the president is likely to assert his prerogatives regarding so-called *pre-decisional deliberations*. The view is that the White House and the agencies should be able to shield from view the decision-making process that goes into the use of their executive authority.

Even so, over the course of history there has often been considerable overlap between what presidents regard as privileged and what Congress believes it should have access to in disposing of its legislative and oversight responsibilities. No hard and fast rule has ever been laid down by the courts; they much prefer to stay out of the issue of exactly which internal deliberations in the executive branch can be made public and which cannot. They regard these disputes as "political questions" that are better left to the political branches to work out.

In controversial areas, Congress may issue a *subpoena* to top executive branch officials, requesting documents and perhaps their testimony. As mentioned before, subpoenas are issued by committees in their oversight capacity over agencies in their jurisdiction.

But the president may claim executive privilege to deny access to documents or refuse testimony. Congress may go so far as to issue a citation of contempt (requiring the vote of one of the houses of Congress) against the official who is holding back. The case is then referred to the Justice Department for potential prosecution. A conviction for contempt of Congress may lead to fines or imprisonment.

In cases involving executive privilege claims, it is much more common for the two sides to reach reasonable accommodations that respect the prerogatives of both branches. Congress usually gets the information it is seeking from the executive, but not always everything and not always in open proceedings or in sworn testimony. Congress is generally successful because of the leverage it can wield, particularly its power of the purse.

The courts have not resolved—and probably never will—the limits of executive privilege, on the one hand, and congressional investigatory power, on the other. As a general rule, according to Duke University's Chris Schroeder, Congress wins out when the information in question is needed for a specific legislative decision, but if, for example, "national security is directly implicated," then the balance tips in favor of the executive branch's desire not to disclose the information.[13]

The George W. Bush administration attempted to push the limits of executive privilege to the point of asserting that presidential advisers and agency officials have absolute immunity from congressional subpoenas. But in August 2008, a federal district court disagreed with the administration, ruling that former White House counsel Harriet Miers would in fact have to appear in front of the House Judiciary Committee to entertain questions concerning her role in the controversial firings of several U.S. attorneys.[14]

Case Study: Congress Investigates: The Senate and the IRS

In the fall of 1997 and spring of 1998, the Senate Finance Committee conducted an aggressive investigation of the Internal Revenue Service, the largest agency in the Treasury Department, and that investigation culminated in a series of hearings. It is instructive to look at Congress's actions at this time, since these hearings exemplify the range of motivations that drive congressional oversight.

Congress has always had a complicated relationship with the IRS. On the one hand, the agency's tax-collecting responsibility gives it one of the most essential of government functions. After all, the government cannot provide the services it does without revenue from individual income taxes, corporate levies, and other forms of taxation. Since the overwhelming majority of Americans faithfully pay their taxes, Congress is motivated to give the IRS the authority to track down those companies and individuals who cheat. On the other hand, no one likes to pay taxes, so complaints from constituents about overzealous IRS agents resonate with the board of directors. The result is that Congress wavers between pushing for more aggressive enforcement of tax laws and pressuring the agency to take it easy on taxpayers when complaints of IRS abuses are frequent.

In 1997 the pendulum seemed to have swung far over to the side of taxpayers and against the IRS. Conservative Republicans were feeling their oats after having taken over the Congress in the 1994 elections. It was time, in their view, to show that they were serious about radical reform of the tax code, which they criticized as a drag on economic efficiency for being overly complex and much too burdensome and costly to comply with.[15]

It had come to the Senate Finance Committee's attention through complaints from private citizens and from agency whistleblowers—employees who, even though many feared for their jobs, could attest to abuses of authority from within the agency—that the agency was too often heavy-handed in its tax collection practices.[16] The Finance Committee's chairman, Senator William Roth of Delaware, thought it was about time to hold some hearings exposing what his staff had found. This would be good politics, he felt, for Republicans (the administration was Democratic at the time, and the IRS commissioner was a Clinton appointee), it might motivate better behavior on the part of agency officials, and it might lay the groundwork for a larger legislative overhaul of the agency and the tax code in the long run. There were even some prominent Republicans, including then–House majority leader Dick Armey of Texas and House Commerce Committee chair Billy Tauzin of Louisiana, who were trying to generate interest in a movement to eliminate the IRS and replace the existing tax code wholesale.

September 1997: The Hearings Begin

> It was, as theater, reminiscent of those great old mob trials—back when the mob really meant something. Wearing black cotton hoods, six witnesses filed into a Senate chamber last week to tell an astonishing tale of corruption and abuse of power. But this wasn't about the Mafia; this was about mainstream America. It was all the more frightening that the witnesses weren't colorful thugs like Jimmy the Weasel or Sammy the Bull, but solid citizens who, acting as Internal Revenue Service agents across the nation, had wives, kids, well-tended yards. And, it seems, scruples. Seated behind a screen, their voices altered electronically—most sounded like Munchkins with Deep South accents—the whistle-blowers heaped dirt on their employer. They told of an IRS that is a virtual police state within a democracy, a Borgia-like fiefdom of tax terror at the heart of the U.S. economy.[17]

This was how *Newsweek* magazine reported the proceedings. Agency witnesses went on at length about IRS agents framing innocent taxpayers in order to meet "production" quotas. They talked about supervisors waiving multimillion-dollar tax liabilities for companies they hoped would hire them at lucrative salaries when they left the agency. The whistleblowers told of the agency policy of hounding poorer taxpayers while auditing only a tiny percentage of wealthier people. These witnesses were concerned for their own safety.

Ordinary citizens testified too. They told of being hounded for a decade or more to pay taxes that they did not actually owe. One woman told of being forced into bankruptcy and divorce. Tom Savage, a Delaware builder, had an illegal lien placed on his property by the IRS, which ultimately cost him hundreds of thousands of dollars.[18]

The acting IRS commissioner at the time, Michael Dolan, was placed on the stand as well, and he had no defense.[19] He apologized effusively and immediately communicated his displeasure to agency supervisors in IRS offices around the country. According to contemporaneous reporting, he suspended several managers the day the hearings ended. The agency acknowledged that the quota system in place in some offices (with supervisors receiving bonuses for tax collections) was against the law and promised to correct its procedures.

Some congressional critics noted that the Finance Committee was not able to document with any precision how widespread the abuses were.[20] Were these isolated instances? Or was this behavior epidemic in the agency? No one kept or could find complete statistics. In any case, the effect was immediate. Aggressive congressional oversight based on more than a year of investigations by committee staff yielded an immediate response from the agency. But the committee was far from done.

Spring 1998: More Hearings and Legislative Action

In the winter a new IRS commissioner, Charles Rossotti, was installed, replacing acting head Dolan. Drawn from the business world, Rossotti promised a new, updated, consumer-friendly approach to tax collection. He said he wanted the public to believe that the IRS took seriously the word "Service" in its name.[21]

But Senator Roth's staff had done a lot more digging, and the goals of the chairman and other top Republicans, including Majority Leader Trent Lott, were far from realized. As the *Washington Post* reported:

> Some Republicans apparently hope to parlay voter dislike of the tax agency
> into support for an entirely new tax system, and in the meantime are finding
> bashing it a helpful campaign tool. House Majority Leader Richard K. Armey
> (R-TX) and the National Republican Senatorial Committee say last fall's hear
> ings boosted contributions.[22]

A week of hearings was scheduled for late April 1998.

More whistleblowers came forward. This time Yvonne D. DesJardins, chief of employee and labor relations at the agency, testified openly. She said executives at the agency broke the rules and protected each other. The agency's director of equal employment opportunity had pending sexual harassment claims against him. In one case, an agent had threatened a state trooper with an audit when subjected to a routine traffic stop.[23]

Numerous tales of gun-toting agents, sometimes in groups of a half-dozen or more, were related, suggesting that the agency used the most severe form of physical intimidation. Democratic senator Patrick Moynihan of New York said: "We have to be much concerned about the paramilitary performance of the IRS."[24] Tax preparers and other small businesspeople told of being targeted by the IRS because of complaints apparently lodged by competitors and vengeance-seekers.

In the most dramatic testimony of the week, former Senate majority leader Howard Baker (R-TN) was brought forward to tell of how a rogue IRS agent tried to frame him and other Tennessee politicians on money-laundering and bribery charges. That agent did not lose his job initially—he was relieved of his duties only after an arrest for suspected possession of cocaine years later.[25]

The hearings were handled with "gotcha" tactics. Normally, congressional committees inform an agency ahead of time who its witnesses will be in oversight hearings; in this case, no heads-up was given. The agency was left scrambling. Commissioner Rossotti held an impromptu press conference after the second day of hearings, promising to get to the bottom of some of the allegations.[26] He immediately formed an independent task force to look into agency procedure and protocols. At the end of the hearings, he asked Congress for new laws giving him more authority over agency personnel.

Legislative Action

The impact of the hearings was considerable. In 1997 the House had passed reform legislation, but it had not been acted on by the full Senate. In 1998, after the second round of hearings, impetus developed for much wider-ranging reforms. The *Washington Post* reported: "Using uncommonly derisive language against an agency run by his own administration, [President] Clinton showed in his weekly radio address that he is determined not to be outdone by Republicans in voicing scorn for out-of-bounds tax collectors."[27] Clinton had originally opposed Republican reform efforts; the hearings seemed to bring him into the negotiations on the Hill.

The bill did not do everything some Republicans had wanted; certainly it did not abolish the agency and the tax code along with it. But those who wanted those sorts of changes cited progress toward their goal. The reform law, signed by President Clinton on July 22, 1998, contained several service-related changes, including bolstering the Office of the Taxpayer Advocate, limiting interest charges on outstanding tax liability (which some believed to be exorbitant), changing the burden-of-proof standard in some court cases, and establishing an independent agency oversight board.[28]

In the end, Senator Roth was able to bring about some significant changes at the IRS. The committee continued to receive a great deal of criticism for its selective use of witnesses and its inability to substantiate every charge with accuracy or to demonstrate the pervasiveness of the abuses it alleged were happening. But no one doubted the brilliance or effectiveness of the political theatrics. The senator had a story to tell, and he told it well. He believed that the culture of the agency needed an overhaul, and the point was well taken. The agency took some voluntary actions to address committee concerns, and it asked for certain legislative remedies. The theatrics helped to jump-start the legislative process, with the president signing on to the most far-reaching legislation affecting the agency in decades.

Oversight in Legislation and Report Language

If the board of directors wants to make sure that government programs are carried out the way they want, they can make administrative details clear in law. Although presidents often bristle at what they regard as infringements on the flexibility they claim to need to carry out laws in the most effective and efficient manner, if they sign a law that includes specific instructions, they are left with little choice but to do what Congress says.[29]

Exhibit 6.1 shows a provision in appropriations legislation for fiscal year 2009 in which Congress stipulates in exhaustive detail the steps that Customs and Border Protection (CBP), an agency within the Department of Homeland Security, must go through in planning for and implementing border fencing. This is a classic example of the legislative branch delving into details of the execution of law that it normally would leave to the agencies. At the time the Department of Homeland Security had been under heavy fire for its unresponsiveness to congressional criticisms of the way it was administering its programs, and it was in this climate that the requirements seen in Exhibit 6.1 were put on it.

Usually Congress's actions in this area are relatively mundane, as shown in Exhibit 6.2, taken from the fiscal year 2008 appropriation for the National Endowment for the Arts. It contains administrative detail, to be sure, but not a full-fledged blueprint for a major program, as with CBP and the border fencing plan.

Far more often, Congress relies on nonstatutory suggestions in report language attached to legislation to influence the administration of the law. Exhibit 6.3, pertaining to the National Marine Fisheries Service (NMFS, sometimes called NOAA Fisheries), shows Congress (specifically the Appropriations Committees) to have been highly critical of Bush administration policies that, in Congress's view, undercut NMFS's ability to perform its core mission by requiring the agency to spend money on costly projects that were not its responsibility.

When agencies resist the instructions in report language, the committee sometimes comes back the next year and makes the requirements statutory, leaving no room for the flexibility or dialogue between the agency and Congress that can arise from nonstatutory provisions.

EXHIBIT 6.1
OVERSIGHT IN LEGISLATION: INSTRUCTIONS TO
CUSTOMS AND BORDER PROTECTION

Border Security Fencing, Infrastructure, and Technology

For expenses for customs and border protection fencing, infrastructure, and technology, $775,000,000, to remain available until expended: *Provided,* That of the amount provided under this heading, $400,000,000 shall not be obligated until the Committees on Appropriations of the Senate and the House of Representatives receive and approve a plan for expenditure, prepared by the Secretary of Homeland Security and submitted not later than 90 days after the date of the enactment of this Act, for a program to establish and maintain a security barrier along the borders of the United States of fencing and vehicle barriers, where practicable, and other forms of tactical infrastructure and technology, that includes the following—

(1) a detailed accounting of the program's implementation to date for all investments, including technology and tactical infrastructure, for funding already expended relative to system capabilities or services, system performance levels, mission benefits and outcomes, milestones, cost targets, program management capabilities, identification of the maximum investment, including life cycle costs, related to the Secure Border Initiative program or any successor program, and description of the methodology used to obtain these cost figures;

(2) a description of how specific projects will further the objectives of the Secure Border Initiative, as defined in the Department of Homeland Security Secure Border Plan, and how the expenditure plan allocates funding to the highest priority border security needs;

(3) an explicit plan of action defining how all funds are to be obligated to meet future program commitments, with the planned expenditure of funds linked to the milestone-based delivery of specific capabilities, services, performance levels, mission benefits and outcomes, and program management capabilities;

(4) an identification of staffing, including full-time equivalents, contractors, and detailees, by program office;

(5) a description of how the plan addresses security needs at the Northern border and ports of entry, including infrastructure, technology, design and operations requirements, specific locations where funding would be used, and priorities for Northern border activities;

(6) a report on budget, obligations and expenditures, the activities completed, and the progress made by the program in terms of obtaining operational control of the entire border of the United States;

(7) a listing of all open Government Accountability Office and the Office of Inspector General recommendations related to the program and the status of Department of Homeland Security actions to address the recommendations, including milestones to fully address such recommendations.

Source: "FY 2009 Appropriations Act for Homeland Security."

The list of requirements for the plan (see highlighted portion) to be submitted to the Appropriations Committees goes on for several pages. Seven requirements are listed here. The committees put more teeth in their request for administrative details by "fencing off" more than half the money ($400,000,000) pending approval of the plan for the border fencing. This sort of arrangement constituted an unconstitutional legislative veto but was unlikely to be challenged by the agency or the department.

The Legislative Veto

The micromanagement of CBP shown in Exhibit 6.1 is an example of a legislative veto. Congress put into law provisions that gave the Appropriations Committees the ability to reject the administrative actions proposed or taken by the agency. The legislative veto is used when Congress acknowledges an agency's prerogative to run government programs, but retains the power to veto the actions taken by the agency. The veto may be exercised by a committee or by one or both of the houses of Congress (depending on how the legislation is written). The political scientist Michael John Berry describes three types of legislative vetoes:

> The legislature empowers an executive agency with certain discretionary policy-making responsibilities. Following this legislative authorization, the agency has latitude in terms of how it chooses to implement policies within its jurisdiction. Negative legislative vetoes allow the policies delegated to administrative agencies to be implemented unless Congress takes some action to veto a specific action. . . . Affirmative legislative vetoes require certain administrative actions or decisions to be first submitted to Congress for congressional approval. Absent the approval of Congress, administrative agencies are not permitted to continue making policy with respect to the functions requiring congressional consent. . . . Deliberative legislative vetoes require congressional notification of proposed administrative actions . . . prior to their execution.[30]

Legislative vetoes were commonly put into legislation in the middle decades of the twentieth century and generally served the interests of both branches. The executive got the delegated authority it wanted, and the Congress had a relatively easy way, if so inclined, to meddle with subsequent agency policymaking.

The problem was that the legislative veto was ruled unconstitutional in 1983 (*Chadha v. U.S.*). The Supreme Court said that when Congress delegates authority in law to the agencies, it must go through the full-fledged legislative process (passage in both houses and the president's signature) to retract that delegation of power. It cannot "veto" executive actions just by a vote of the House or Senate or a single committee.

Still, Congress continues to put legislative vetoes into law—more frequently than ever before, in fact.[31] Probably the most common sort of legislative veto in the twenty-first century appears in appropriations bills. Typically the wording is like that seen in the first paragraph of Exhibit 6.1:

EXHIBIT 6.2
OVERSIGHT IN THE APPROPRIATIONS LAW
FOR THE NATIONAL ENDOWMENT FOR THE ARTS

Administrative Provisions

None of the funds appropriated to the National Foundation on the Arts and the Humanities may be used to process any grant or contract documents which do not include the text of 18 U.S.C. 1913: *Provided,* That none of the funds appropriated to the National Foundation on the Arts and the Humanities may be used for official reception and representation expenses: *Provided further,* That funds from non-appropriated sources may be used as necessary for official reception and representation expenses: *Provided further,* That the Chairperson of the National Endowment for the Arts may approve grants of up to $10,000, if in the aggregate this amount does not exceed 5 percent of the sums appropriated for grant-making purposes per year: *Provided further,* That such small grant actions are taken pursuant to the terms of an expressed and direct delegation of authority from the National Council on the Arts to the Chairperson: *Provided further,* That section 309(1) of division E, Public Law 108-447, is amended by inserting "National Opera Fellowship," after "National Heritage Fellowship."

Source: "FY 2008 Interior, Environment, and Related Agencies Appropriation."

The highlighted area shows typical oversight instructions given to agencies in appropriations law. Most administrative detail is left to the agency.

For expenses for customs and border protection fencing, infrastructure, and technology, $775,000,000, to remain available until expended: *Provided, That of the amount provided under this heading, $400,000,000 shall not be obligated until the Committees on Appropriations of the Senate and the House of Representatives receive and approve a plan* for expenditure, prepared by the Secretary of Homeland Security and submitted not later than 90 days after the date of the enactment of this Act. . . . (emphasis added)

The aim of the italicized section is to accomplish what appropriators describe as "fencing off" funds. Congress is, in law, providing the agency with $775 million, but giving itself the ability to deny $400 million of that amount simply by a decision of the Appropriations Committees to reject the agency's administrative plan of action.

EXHIBIT 6.3
OVERSIGHT IN REPORT LANGUAGE

National Marine Fisheries Service Operations, Research, and Facilities (continued)

The amended bill provides $25,379,000 for Fisheries Habitat Restoration, which is $5,893,000 below the President's requested level. The Appropriations Committees recognize that significant administration priorities are embedded in this account and direct NOAA to determine the level of funding necessary for each of those priorities within the funding provided, without cutting into base program funding. The Committees further understand that the Penobscot River Habitat Restoration project is a timely opportunity to leverage current regional resources to revitalize this large-scale marine and estuarine habitat. However, the Committees have strong concerns about NOAA taking the full, long term financial lead in such a large, cross-agency project, especially since a majority of the requested funds will be spent purchasing privately-owned dams. Though the Committees recognize NOAA's expertise in smaller dam removal and fish passageway projects, this project is an order of magnitude larger than any previous project undertaken by the agency, and pushes the limits of the agency's authority to use funds from NMFS's operations account to purchase multi-million dollar facilities. The Appropriations Committees admonish the administration for carelessly exposing NMFS's base funding to future large-scale, redevelopment projects that would jeopardize the agency's financial support for standard national fisheries activities and responsibilities. Given that this is a multi-year project, NOAA is directed to coordinate with the Departments of the Interior and Energy, and the U.S. Army Corps of Engineers to determine an appropriate role for the agency solely as a habitat restoration advisor to its Federal and State partners, and eliminate the agency's questionable role as a broker for future large-scale, riverine construction projects. In future years, the Appropriations Committees will support NOAA's participation in habitat restoration projects, which is an on-going, environmental assessment process, but will no longer appropriate funds from the [Operations, Research, and Facilities] accounts to purchase costly, private dams.

Source: "FY 2008 Appropriation for Commerce, Justice, and Science—Joint Explanatory Statement."

Congressional oversight instructions are more commonly found in report language attached to appropriations bills than in the bills themselves. In this case, the highlighted area shows the Appropriations Committees' displeasure in particular with an expanded role for NMFS in large-scale redevelopment projects.

As noted, this is unconstitutional—technically the Congress needs to go through the legislative process in order to reject an administrative plan. But in reality the agency has little choice.[32] It must square its plan with a particular subset of the Congress or risk losing a great deal of its funding.

The Government Accountability Office and Oversight

Congress needs help—lots of help—in trying to keep tabs on everything it is supposed to oversee in government. To that end, as noted earlier, it has created three independent legislative branch support agencies. The Congressional Budget Office provides help for Congress in its funding responsibilities. The Congressional Research Service, part of the Library of Congress, is staffed with about 750 people with expertise on a range of issues, legal matters, government programs, and congressional processes. The Government Accountability Office was created back in 1921 (it was called the General Accounting Office until early this century) to help inform Congress, principally in its oversight and authorizing duties.

GAO describes its responsibilities this way:

> [GAO's] work is done at the request of congressional committees or subcommittees or is mandated by public laws or committee reports. [The agency] also undertake[s] research under the authority of the Comptroller General [the director of GAO]. [GAO] support[s] congressional oversight by
>
> - auditing agency operations to determine whether federal funds are being spent efficiently and effectively;
> - investigating allegations of illegal and improper activities;
> - reporting on how well government programs and policies are meeting their objectives;
> - performing policy analyses and outlining options for congressional consideration; and
> - issuing legal decisions and opinions, such as bid protest rulings and reports on agency rules.
>
> [GAO] advises Congress and the heads of executive agencies about ways to make government more efficient, effective, ethical, equitable and responsive.[33]

The agency has about 3,200 employees and is headed by the comptroller general, who is insulated from political pressures by a fourteen-year term of office. (He may only be removed for cause.) GAO's investigations into government programs are respected as fair and impartial, even if the objects of the investigations are not always happy with the conclusions.

GAO takes requests for investigations into federal programs from any member of Congress, but in practice it is usually only able to handle higher-priority matters coming from party leaders and committee and subcommittee chairs and ranking members. Members of Congress know that to get a GAO investigation into a program of interest they need to go through the committee with jurisdiction over the agency in question. As mentioned earlier, the comptroller general also has the authority to initiate investigations into matters of pressing importance without a specific congressional request.

GAO investigators write up a report of their findings after completing an investigation. The investigations may take anywhere from months to a year or more to complete. The agency gets a chance to see the report and comment on it before it is made public. (The report may include a rejoinder from the agency in question.) All reports on nonclassified matters are immediately made public via the GAO website.

Sometimes these reports can be tremendously embarrassing to federal agencies, creating major publicity problems. In 2005, GAO was made aware of lapses in the process by which the Nuclear Regulatory Commission (NRC) awarded licenses to companies to purchase radioactive materials for legitimate scientific or medical purposes.[34] In 2006, GAO investigators created two fictitious companies, both of which were able to obtain licenses from the NRC without much difficulty. The agency never checked to see whether the companies had a legitimate purpose or even whether they actually existed. (Of course, they did not.) No site visits were made to check whether the material could be safely stored. Not only that but the GAO investigators found that the licenses the agencies gave the GAO investigators (posing as fictitious company executives) were so unsophisticated that they could be tampered with to enable the "companies" to buy almost unlimited quantities of radioactive material.

Members of Congress may do what they wish with a GAO report. A report may be ignored if the results do not square with the agenda of the requester, or it may end up being the focus of hearings to further publicize the issues it highlights. Congressional staff regularly use GAO reports in their oversight efforts, and GAO investigators and agency officials are frequently asked to testify about their findings.

If GAO finds problems in the conduct of a program, it makes recommendations to the agency and keeps track of agency compliance in order to inform the Congress. In the long run, some reports influence changes in law and funding priorities. In the nuclear materials case, the GAO report prompted major changes in the licensing processes at the agency.

Box 6.3 provides another good example of GAO work having an impact on agency operations—this time with management practices at the Federal Aviation Administration (FAA).

The Inspectors General

As the federal government expanded in the 1960s and 1970s and instances of malfeasance came to light in the conduct of federal programs, Congress decided to institutionalize internal controls in the agencies. The Inspector General Act of 1978, as amended in 1988, created offices ("the IGs," for short) across the government in almost every agency and department. (A few government departments already had an IG.) They were given a mandate to ferret out waste, fraud, and abuse in the conduct of government programs.[35]

IGs for all the government departments and most major subcabinet-level agencies are appointed by the president and must receive Senate approval. IGs at some smaller agencies as well as at independent agencies are appointed by the agency head. The law requires that IGs be chosen based on experience in auditing and investigations and without regard to political affiliation. This requirement is not always adhered to.[36] Presidentially appointed IGs may be removed by the president for cause; others may be removed by an agency head.

The idea was that these offices, though situated within the agencies and hence part of the executive branch, would be given a measure of statutory independence by being required to report directly to the legislative branch on a regular basis. Congress felt that it could not trust the president to make internal investigations a high priority, owing to the potential political fallout for the president from the exposure of illegal or wasteful activities by his appointees in executive branch agencies.

The law gives IGs a great deal of latitude in looking into agency business. They have access to agency records and can exercise subpoena power. In addition, the law provides some protection to any agency employee who comes to the IG with a complaint involving mismanagement of funds or other illegalities (a whistleblower).

IGs refer suspected violations of federal law to the attorney general of the United States. They also submit reports of their activities twice a year, both to their agency head or department secretary and directly to the congressional committees of jurisdiction for the agency. These reports typically highlight programs that the IG believes are wasting taxpayer money and often include recommendations to improve program performance. The purpose is to gain the attention of the agency head, who may implement changes to remedy the situation, and Congress, which may hold hearings or act through legislation to improve program performance.

BOX 6.3
THE GOVERNMENT ACCOUNTABILITY OFFICE
AND THE FEDERAL AVIATION ADMINISTRATION

GAO uses its investigatory authority to shine a spotlight on government programs that are underperforming. The agency is limited, however, in its ability to effect change. Although GAO reports are in the public domain, normally congressional hearings are required to draw attention to the problem areas in government detailed in a report. A good example of the results of GAO investigations being addressed by Congress involved the Federal Aviation Administration (FAA) in the 1990s and the first part of this decade.

In 1995, GAO placed the FAA's air traffic control (ATC) modernization program on its "high-risk" list of federal programs, which indicates major problems in the administration of a program. This designation is for programs that GAO believes have egregious inefficiencies that are resulting in a misuse of taxpayer money. The ATC modernization effort was an attempt to update the existing system with new equipment and methods of ensuring safety at the nation's airports. But the program had experienced cost overruns, schedule delays, and performance shortfalls.

Congress began to focus on the problems shortly after the 1995 report was issued, but it really got into gear after the crashes of ValuJet Flight 592 on May 11, 1996, and TWA Flight 800 on July 17, 1996. This represents a typical congressional pattern of behavior: increased responsiveness in the aftermath of high-profile events. The Senate Commerce Committee's Subcommittee on Aviation and the House Transportation and Infrastructure Committee scheduled hearings to assess airline safety and the status of ATC modernization in the summer and fall of that year. Among other things, members of Congress discovered that many of the problems with the modernization effort stemmed from shortcomings in the agency's financial management practices.

Congressional committees gradually began pressing the agency, a process that was aided by a 1999 GAO report placing FAA's financial management system in that high-risk category along with ATC modernization. GAO said that "serious financial management weaknesses" existed at the agency and were affecting many programs, including ATC modernization.

By 2003, significant improvements had been made by the agency in its financial management practices, to the point where, in 2004, GAO's director of physical infrastructure, JayEtta Hecker, could report major improvements at the agency. That report led to the removal of the financial management system from the list of high-risk programs in 2005. The ATC modernization effort did not lose its high-risk designation, but considerable progress was noted in the most recent GAO report released in January 2007.

Sources: U.S. Government Accountability Office, "High-Risk Series: An Update" (2005), and "Major Management Challenges and Program Risks: Department of Transportation" (GAO report 99–13); JayEtta Z. Hecker, "Federal Aviation Administration: Challenges for Transforming into a High-Performing Organization," testimony before 108th Congress.

The Government Performance and Results Act

In 1993 Congress passed into law the Government Performance and Results Act (GPRA). The purpose of the law was to institute a new regime of strategic planning in federal agencies. Drawing from the business world, Congress required the agencies to assess every program they run by stating the program's purpose and the results the agency expects it to achieve and to provide a method to measure those results. Regular reporting to Congress in all of these areas is required.

These expectations sound good, but the scope of what Congress required in the act has proved too much for it to handle. In fact, most of the members and staff who were dedicated to the GPRA regime are no longer serving there, and no one seems to have taken up the flag. It is not that Congress is uninterested in program performance (a subject we return to at the end of the chapter), but that this exhaustive method of keeping tabs on all government activities through strategic planning proved to be unrealistic for Congress—it simply can't keep up with the work.

Any strategic planning that is implemented in government is much more likely to be done by the president. Presidents often have an interest in streamlining government; after all, it is good politics for the president to show (or claim) that more is being done on his watch with fewer government workers and less taxpayer money. In fact, as noted earlier in the chapter, President George W. Bush took particular interest in measuring performance and pushing agencies to assess programs from top to bottom. He instituted a thorough examination of every program as part of his management agenda, which took years to complete. These evaluations had a significant impact on the funding requests he made to Congress.

Informal Methods of Oversight

Members of Congress use many means to try to influence executive branch agencies as they go about their business of implementing government programs. Naturally, putting requirements into law is most effective, but that is not always possible for all sorts of reasons; first and foremost among these reasons is that the legislative process is often too cumbersome to navigate. Nonstatutory report language in an appropriations bill also sends a very clear message to the agencies: If you do not do what we say, we may cut your funding or tie your hands in law next year. And as we have seen, hearings can be effective in getting agencies to change policy without having to "go the distance" and produce legislation, which would not be able to anticipate all eventualities anyway. But members have all sorts of policy preferences, receive an enormous number of requests from constituents, and are always trying to get agencies to do more for their districts and states. Even hearings involve a great deal of heavy lifting, and often members' needs cannot wait. If this is the case, they may try more informal means of moving things along in an agency.

Iowa Republican senator Charles Grassley's office focuses on oversight like no other personal office on Capitol Hill. When the senator catches wind of what he regards as poor program implementation, a waste of taxpayer dollars, or shoddy regulatory practices, he does everything he can to shine a light on the problem, even if he is not on the committee of jurisdiction. He is famous for his efforts to ferret out waste and fraud at the Defense Department, for instance, even though he is not a member of the Armed Services Committee. For much of the first decade of this century, Grassley has focused attention on the Food and Drug Administration (FDA), the agency responsible for approving drugs and keeping the food supply safe; its chief overseer in the Senate is the Health, Education, Labor, and Pensions Committee—a panel, once again, on which Grassley does not serve.

Grassley relied on whistleblowers at the FDA who shared with his staff internal memos that appeared to show efforts at the agency to stifle internal dissent on important scientific matters. He followed up with a "flurry of letters, press conferences, and congressional hearings" to publicize his findings.[37] The purpose of all this activity was to put enough pressure on the agency to get it to address matters of concern to the senator. Underlying all such activity is the implicit or explicit threat that Grassley is more than willing to propose legislation to deal with the problem.

In their efforts to direct funds to fulfill needs in their districts, members sometimes engage in *phone-marking*.[38] This practice became especially prevalent in 2007, when most of the government functioned on a yearlong continuing resolution. Since Congress did not do most of the appropriations bills, earmark instructions for the agencies were largely absent from legislation, and there was no committee report language in some cases. But members were certainly not content to sit idly by and hope that agencies would direct money as the members saw fit for key programs. It was reported that many members contacted agency officials hoping to convince them that it was in their best interest to consider the needs of the member's district or state when determining where to spend federal funds. It was no mystery to anyone that the implied threat was potentially unpleasant hearings or even cuts in the next year's appropriations process.

CONCLUSION: THE POLITICS OF CONGRESSIONAL OVERSIGHT

Of the three ways in which Congress wields influence in its role as the board of directors, oversight is certainly the most contentious. For one thing, Congress has the responsibility to make sure that programs are executed as intended, but it does not always make its intentions clear in legislation. For another, Congress has a legitimate need to look into how laws are being administered, although the line where Congress is inappropriately encroaching on executive prerogatives has never been defined precisely. And Congress, when exercising oversight, often uses imprecise and blunt nonstatutory methods—hearings, informal communications, report language, and so on—that leave a lot of wiggle room for executive discretion and interpretation and ongoing disagreement. Of course, it is also often the case that different members of Congress send conflicting signals to federal agencies.

But oversight is a crucial function of the Congress, and for several reasons it is not only pervasive but often the most effective of the three ways in which Congress can get the executive branch to do what it wants. First, it is not practical, or even possible, for Congress to write laws that are precise enough to direct the executive in every detail, and members certainly cannot anticipate future events when passing a bill. As a result, Congress always gives the executive branch a measure of leeway to carry out a program as it sees fit. If Congress is unhappy with how that delegation of authority is managed, it may use its oversight tools to try to redirect executive action.

Second, and perhaps most importantly, the members of the board are faced with a profound conundrum: Congress is not a fast-moving institution by its nature, *but the public still expects the members to respond effectively and quickly to events.* Often the only feasible way for Congress to respond is to communicate its concerns to the relevant agency handling an immediate crisis, such as a natural disaster, by means of hearings, letters, and floor speeches and in this way pressure the agency to do what Congress wants in response to the event.

And third, following from the second point, it is very difficult and sometimes nearly impossible for Congress to come to an agreement on important bills, to overcome a presidential veto, or even to find time to schedule floor consideration. In lieu of legislation, Congress may only be able to resort to its ability to shine a spotlight on a program in a hearing in order to effect policy change and direct the work of government. Often there is an implied or even explicit threat that the agency may face more restrictive legislation or a funding cut down the line if it does not heed the members' wishes. In other words, oversight can be a substitute for legislative solutions when the legislative process proves too difficult to negotiate.

Members and Program Efficiency

Everyone has an interest in the efficient operation of government programs. After all, who wants to see their tax money wasted? That goes for members of Congress too, especially if they can take some credit for the streamlining of a program or for improved agency responsiveness to citizen complaints and needs.

But program efficiency is not priority number one for most members. Watchdog groups in Washington as well as GAO and the inspectors general may regard it as their primary duty to monitor government programs for waste, fraud, and abuse. (In fact, this is the primary *statutory* duty of IGs and GAO.) But members of Congress have other concerns. First and foremost is the reason they were sent to Washington in the first place: to look after the needs of their constituents. Most of them are making a career out of politics, and that requires getting reelected every two years in the House or every six years in the Senate.

As the congressional scholar David Mayhew has noted, spending time looking over the shoulder of government bureaucrats and getting into the mind-numbing details of the operations of specific government programs are not tasks that usually contribute very much to the members' goal of reelection.[39] Of course, exposing egregious waste and malfeasance is good for a member's reputation and can enhance his or her prospects of reelection, but these sorts of opportunities are not that common. The fact is that most voters are not interested in the detailed workings of government programs.

The bottom line is that members' precious time, as well as the time of their staff, is better spent communicating directly with voters, working on high-profile issues and issues of particular salience in the district or state, and ensuring the district's or state's fair share of earmarks and government spending on infrastructure. Auditing government programs does not usually provide the same kind of political reward.[40]

It is important to note that advocating for more resources for a district or state, as almost all members do, is not necessarily consistent with the drive to ensure the most efficient conduct of government programs. If studies indicate that the addition of one lane to a highway bypass will alleviate traffic congestion in a particular city, a member of Congress may still argue for federal funds to build *two* lanes; after all, adding two lanes would provide twice as many good-paying jobs for his or her constituents, even though the second lane would be unnecessary and would cost the taxpayer a good deal more money.

Discerning a Pattern to Congressional Oversight

The bottom line is that focused oversight of government programs is sporadic. But there are some discernible patterns.

- If a program touches a member's district or state, he or she is much more likely to keep tabs on it. The member will try to be absolutely sure that the agency is responsive to the needs of his or her constituents and that money is going where it needs to go. As we have seen, this member will not necessarily be concerned about the program's efficiency. If jobs are involved, the member may want to see more money funneled in, even if the project could be completed with a lower expenditure.

- Major events in the world or the nation prompt congressional oversight. Political scientists say that more oversight is done by members in response to a "fire alarm" indicating an emergency than is done on the basis of careful analysis of ongoing assessments of agency performance conducted by GAO or committee staff.[41] The Federal Emergency Management Agency came under intense scrutiny in the aftermath of Hurricane Katrina in 2005 and in the years following. Citizens and members were appalled at the agency response. Members score political points when they respond with hearings that put an agency on the hot seat, as well as when they propose legislation that addresses the weaknesses that are exposed.

- If oversight can enhance the stature of a member's party, he or she will be more aggressive in pursuing it. In times of unified government, there is typically less oversight and many fewer hearings investigating agency business. But in times of divided government, oversight increases. In 2007, when Democrats took over Congress, they dramatically bolstered the oversight capacity of key committees, especially the Oversight and Reform Committee in the House, the Armed Services Committees in both chambers, and the Appropriations Committee in the House. Democratic members believed that President Bush had gotten a free ride from his partisans, and they wanted to settle some scores by exposing agency misdeeds that had been ignored in previous years and win political points at the Republicans' expense in the process.

Ultimately it is impossible for Congress to supervise every government program and uncover every instance of agency mismanagement. Having said that, a great deal of very careful and systematic oversight is done by congressional staff and GAO, often behind the scenes and out of the limelight. This kind of oversight is institutionalized: It is carried out yearly by appropriations staff as they work on their annual bills, by the oversight committees' staff, and at the subcommittee level in many committees. But much of what they do fails to rise to the surface. It is hard to get the attention of members of Congress.

Our elected representatives have complicated jobs, incredibly crowded schedules, and dozens of issues to keep track of. Frankly, it is hard even for some of their staffers to get their attention. Members have to pick and choose what to give highest priority. Getting into the details of most programs to save a few dollars or to make minor improvements is not on the top of the list for most of them. What does make it to the top of their list, however, is oversight to highlight major failures, particularly of the opposing party. Oversight in response to constituent complaints about agency responsiveness or overbearing IRS agents also rises to the top. The key when it comes to oversight, according to Mayhew, is whether members can claim credit for better program performance in a way that resonates with their constituents. For better or worse, most members find their time better spent in other ways.

QUESTIONS FOR DISCUSSION

1. Do you think the Framers' main purposes for congressional oversight are being realized? Why or why not?
2. What would it take to get Congress to do oversight more systematically? Why has it become so much rarer for a member to conduct oversight of a president of his or her own party, as Harry Truman did back in the 1940s?
3. Why must the board of directors rely so heavily on oversight to get the agencies to do what it wants them to do?

SUGGESTIONS FOR FURTHER READING

Henderson, Diedtra. 2006. "Watching the Watchdog." *Boston Globe*, June 8. Available at: http://www.boston.com/business/globe/articles/2006/06/08/watching_the_watchdog/.
McCubbins, Matthew, and Thomas Schwartz. 1984. "Congressional Oversight Overlooked: Police Patrol Versus Fire Alarms." *American Journal of Political Science* 28, no. 1 (February): 165–179.
Oleszek, Walter. 2007. *Congressional Procedures and the Policy Process*, 7th ed., ch. 3. Washington, DC: CQ Press.

NOTES

1. James Madison, *The Federalist Papers*, No. 51.
2. Frederick M. Kaiser, "CRS Report for Congress: Congressional Oversight," Congressional Research Service, January 3, 2006, p. 2.
3. Frederick M. Kaiser et al., "CRS Report for Congress: Oversight Manual," Congressional Research Service, May 1, 2007, p. 5.
4. The Bush administration conducted the Program Assessment Rating Tool (PART) to evaluate government programs. For more information on this initiative, see http://www.whitehouse.gov/omb/part/.
5. Kaiser et al., "Oversight Manual," pp. 7–10.
6. Ibid., pp. 6–7.

7. For an excellent overview of the role of hearings, see Walter Oleszek, *Congressional Procedures and the Policy Process*, 7th ed. (Washington, DC: CQ Press, 2007), ch. 3.

8. Richard Sachs, "CRS Report for Congress: Types of Committee Hearings," Congressional Research Service, March 8, 2001.

9. Paul M. Feeney, "Crouching Hearing, Hidden Legislation," *Journal of Public Inquiry* (Spring–Summer 2002): 29.

10. Jonathan Etherton, former professional staff member on the Senate Armed Services Committee, interview with the author, April 19, 2007.

11. *McGrain v. Daugherty* (1927), as noted in Kaiser et al., "Oversight Manual," p. 6.

12. Quoted in Louis Fisher, "CRS Report for Congress: Congressional Investigations: Subpoenas and Contempt Power," Congressional Research Service, April 2, 2003, p. 2.

13. Chris Schroeder, "*Cheney v. United States District Court*: Liberal Civil Discovery Rules Versus the Separation of Powers," Supreme Court Online (Duke Law), available at: http://www.law.duke.edu/publiclaw/supremecourtonline/commentary/chevuni.

14. Jon Ward, "Federal Judge Rejects Executive Privilege for Miers, Bolten," *Washington Times*, July 31, 2008, available at: http://www.washingtontimes.com/news/2008/jul/31/federal-judge-rejects-executive-privilege-two-whit/.

15. David Cay Johnston, "Behind IRS Hearings, a GOP Plan to End the Tax Code," *New York Times*, May 4, 1998.

16. Thomas H. Moore, "IRS Nightmares Get Senate Hearings," CNN, September 24, 1997, available at: http://www.cnn.com/ALLPOLITICS/1997/09/24/irs.hearing/; and Albert B. Crenshaw, "IRS Hearings to Focus on Alleged Improper Conduct," *Washington Post*, April 28, 1998, p. A4.

17. Michael Hirsch, "Behind the IRS Curtain," *Newsweek*, October 6, 1997, available at: http://www.newsweek.com/id/97087/.

18. Ibid.

19. Ibid.

20. "Phantom Rogues at the IRS" (editorial), *New York Times*, August 19, 2000, available at: http://query.nytimes.com/gst/fullpage.html?res=9E0DE5DD133EF93AA2575BC0A9669C8B63; and Albert B. Crenshaw, "An IRS Under Siege Walks a Fine Dotted Line," *Washington Post*, February 6, 1998, p. A1.

21. Crenshaw, "An IRS Under Siege Walks a Fine Dotted Line."

22. Crenshaw, "IRS Hearings to Focus on Alleged Improper Conduct."

23. Albert B. Crenshaw and Stephen Barr, "IRS Official Reports Agency Double Standard," *Washington Post*, April 29, 1998, p. A4.

24. Albert B. Crenshaw, "Alleged Victims Tell of IRS Raids That Hurt Businesses," *Washington Post*, April 30, 1998, p. A4.

25. Albert B. Crenshaw, "Witnesses Say IRS Agent Tried to Frame Ex-Senator," *Washington Post*, May 1, 1998, p. A1.

26. Crenshaw, "Alleged Victims Tell of IRS Raids That Hurt Businesses."

27. John F. Harris, "'Outraged' Clinton Vows IRS Overhaul," *Washington Post*, May 3, 1998, p. A1.

28. Peter Baker, "Clinton Signs IRS Overhaul into Law," *Washington Post*, July 23, 1998, p. A1.

29. The George W. Bush administration instigated a firestorm when it began aggressively using the presidential signing statement to assert the right to ignore parts of laws that the president believed encroached on his executive prerogatives. (Signing statements, which are commonly issued by the White House after signing a bill into law, had most frequently been used in previous administrations to explain, for example, how a president planned to implement the legislation.) Although Bush attracted a great deal of attention with his claim that he did not need to abide by everything in the laws he was signing, neither the GAO nor the CRS has found evidence that he followed through on the more controversial of his threats. The GAO's views can be found in Gary Kepplinger, "Presidential Signing Statements: Agency Implementation of Select Provisions of Law," testimony before the House Subcommittee on Oversight and Investigations, March 11, 2008, available at: http://www.gao.gov/new.items/do8553t.pdf. The CRS's T. J. Halstead wrote about them in "Presidential Signing Statements: Constitutional and Institutional Implications," Congressional Research Service, September 20, 2006.

30. Michael John Berry, "Beyond Chadha: The Modern Legislative Veto as Macropolitical Conflict," paper delivered at the annual meeting of the American Political Science Association, September 2007, p. 11.

31. Louis Fisher, "CRS Report for Congress: Committee Controls of Agency Decisions," Congressional Research Service, November 16, 2005.

32. The House Appropriations Committee staff aided in the development of the CBP legislative veto example.

33. See U.S. Government Accountability Office, "About GAO," available at: http://gao.gov/about/index.html.

34. David de Sola, "Government Investigators Smuggled Radioactive Materials into U.S.," CNN, March 27, 2006, available at: http://www.cnn.com/2006/US/03/27/radioactive.smuggling/.

35. Frederick M. Kaiser, "CRS Report for Congress: Statutory Offices of Inspector General: Establishment and Evolution," Congressional Research Service, July 1, 2003.

36. For a summary, see Oversight and Government Reform Committee chair Henry Waxman's study on the politicization of the inspector general's office, "The Politicization

of Inspectors General," October 21, 2004, available at: http://oversight.house.gov/story
.asp?ID=726. Waxman found that some IGs chosen by President Clinton did not have the
requisite background, but that a far greater percentage of Bush appointees did not.

37. Diedtra Henderson, "Watching the Watchdog," *Boston Globe*, June 8, 2006, available at: http://www.boston.com/business/globe/articles/2006/06/08/watching_the_watch
dog/.

38. John Solomon and Jeffrey H. Birnbaum, "In the Democratic Congress, Pork Still
Gets Served," *Washington Post*, May 24, 2007, p. A1.

39. David Mayhew, *Congress: The Electoral Connection* (New Haven, CT: Yale University Press, 1974), pp. 110–140.

40. See Terry Moe, "The Politics of Bureaucratic Structure," in *Can the Government
Govern?* edited by Jon E. Chubb and Paul E. Peterson (Washington, DC: Brookings Institution Press, 1989), esp. p. 278.

41. See Matthew McCubbins and Thomas Schwartz, "Congressional Oversight Overlooked: Police Patrol Versus Fire Alarms," *American Journal of Political Science* 28, no. 1
(February 1984): 165–179.

CHAPTER SEVEN

THE BOARD OF DIRECTORS
MEETS ITS MATCH:
WAR POWERS

Just three days after the September 11, 2001, attacks on the World Trade Center and the Pentagon, Congress passed into law, by votes of 420–1 in the House and 98–0 in the Senate, the "Authorization for Use of Military Force" against those responsible. Less than a month later, on October 9, President George W. Bush reported in a letter to Congress that U.S. forces had commenced combat operations in Afghanistan against Al Qaeda and the Taliban, stating that he took these actions "pursuant to my constitutional authority to conduct U.S. foreign relations as Commander in Chief and Chief Executive." The president's letter stated that he "appreciated the continuing support of Congress" but was not acting based on any authority given to him by Congress.[1]

Although the Constitution seems to give the Congress the power to commit U.S. troops to battle (Article I, Section 8: "Congress shall have the power . . . to declare war"), what is interesting is that even though Congress authorized the use of military force against Al Qaeda in Afghanistan, *President Bush indicated that he did not need an authorization from Congress to act and had the power unilaterally to commit the nation to war.* He explicitly relied on Article II, which spells out the executive branch powers given to the president, to justify the actions he took, not the legal authorization given to him by the board of directors.

In claiming this authority, the president was certainly not setting a precedent; his two immediate predecessors had operated under similar assumptions. President Clinton did not ask for and did not receive authorization from Congress when he ordered the bombing of what was then Yugoslavia in 1999 during the Kosovo War. President George H. W. Bush did receive authorization to drive Iraq from Kuwait (Iraq had invaded Kuwait and was occupying the country) in the first Persian Gulf War in 1991, but he, like his son, maintained that he did not need that authorization—that he had only gone to Congress to receive an authorization "as a courtesy."[2] Going much further back, President Truman did not receive congressional authorization to commit American forces to war in Korea in 1950.

In 2002, President Bush did seek authorization from Congress to invade Iraq, based in large part on the claim that it had acquired, or was in the process of acquiring, weapons of mass destruction. Although Congress was considerably more divided on authorizing a war with Iraq than it had been on authorizing the removal of Al Qaeda from Afghanistan immediately following the September 11, 2001, attacks, it did end up granting the president the authority to conduct the war. With congressional elections less than one month away, Congress passed the bill by margins of 77–23 in the Senate and 296–133 in the House.

Evidence that Iraq had acquired weapons of mass destruction was never found, and the war proved much lengthier and more costly than had been predicted by most analysts, as well as by the administration. Even after a majority of the American public had come to oppose the war, Congress seemed unwilling or unable to change the course of U.S. involvement. Congressional oversight of the conduct of the war was sporadic and usually not focused on the larger issues. President Bush would turn to Congress only to provide the funding for the war, which Congress would continue to provide, sometimes with relatively little debate despite the sizable sums involved.

In the November 2006 midterm elections, three and a half years after the war in Iraq began, the Democrats took control of the Congress from Republicans based in part on public dissatisfaction with the conduct of the war. The newly elected Democrats in the 110th Congress believed that they had a mandate to begin winding down American involvement in the war in Iraq. This objective was bolstered by public opinion polls at the time indicating that close to 70 percent of the public opposed the war. Nonetheless, Democrats failed in every attempt they made to influence the course of the war in 2007 and 2008, and it was this failure, more than anything else, that would define the powerlessness of Congress in the realm of war powers in the modern era.

Why does the president have such a distinct upper hand when it comes to war powers—an advantage not held in domestic policy? What has happened to enable presidents who commit the country to war to go nearly unchallenged in the last sixty years or so when a reasonable reading of the Constitution seems to give that power to Congress and Congress alone?

The chapter starts with an overview and comparison of the current relationship between the branches in the spheres of domestic policy and war powers. In the domestic arena, there is a rough consensus that the branches have coequal constitutional roles, even though ample room remains for disagreement and dispute as to exactly where one branch's prerogatives end and the other's begin. But no consensus exists concerning the authority of each branch with respect to war powers, and the relationship has been at times extraordinarily contentious.

The next section looks in much more depth at the constitutional debate concerning war powers. We review the arguments of both those who maintain that Congress's rightful constitutional powers have been improperly usurped in recent decades and those who claim that a proper reading of the relevant constitutional provisions— particularly in a changing world—clearly favors presidential prerogatives.

Ultimately we find that the executive has the upper hand for *political* and *informational* reasons. The politics of the decision to go to war and especially the subsequent actions required to fund that effort tend to work to the advantage of the president—to a significant degree because, in the areas of foreign affairs and intelligence, presidents have much more control over the flow of information than they do in other areas of public policy. The president may, in short, be the only one with the ability to see the big picture.

But in the following section, we see that the board of directors has not always stood idly by as authorities it has long cherished have seemingly been trumped. In 1973 Congress asserted itself by dramatically overriding a presidential veto with the enactment of the War Powers Act, an effort to curb presidents' ability to conduct war indefinitely without congressional input. And in the 1980s, Congress attempted to use the power of the purse to rein in covert operations undertaken by the Reagan administration. Neither effort was successful in controlling presidential actions, although the latter case highlights the potential for constitutional conflict when the aggressive assertion of presidential national security prerogatives is challenged by legislative actions to cut off funding for ongoing operations.

We then explore in depth in two case studies the scope and limits of the board of directors' war powers in the twenty-first century. In the decisions to commit troops to Afghanistan in response to the 9/11 attacks and to topple Saddam Hussein's regime in Iraq in 2003, Congress's relative impotence in this important area of public policy was on full display.

The chapter closes with a summary and some thoughts on why the branches need to come together to cooperate on the decision to go to war. On the one hand, it is important to note that Congress has frequently and willingly abdicated any role in war powers to the president. Members often find that their time is better spent on matters—usually domestic—that are more directly related to their constituents and their own reelection prospects. On the other hand, presidents in recent decades have found themselves in some very difficult spots when they have gone it alone in exercising war powers—to the point of undermining their political effectiveness and even destroying their presidency.

THE BOARD OF DIRECTORS:
DOMESTIC POWERS AND WAR POWERS

In Chapters 4 through 6, we have detailed the various ways in which Congress directs the work of government—through statute (both authorizing and appropriations), strong suggestions in report language, and various forms of oversight. As we have seen, there are often serious disagreements between the branches because of their different outlooks and perspectives. When one branch is charged with *directing* the work of government, and the other charged with *doing* the work of government, there are bound to be differences of opinion in the interpretation of congressional intent, as expressed in law or otherwise. This tension was built into our system quite intentionally to serve as a check on the power of the federal government; it could be described as part of the normal relationship between the branches. And each branch was given the ability to invade, as it were, the sphere of the other branch in order to serve as a check on its power.

In national security policy and especially war powers, however, the system of checks and balances does not work in anywhere near the same way. Presidents have resisted efforts by Congress to intervene in policy decisions in this realm (especially those involving the commitment of troops to battle); in fact, presidents are frequently downright dismissive of legislative branch efforts in ways rarely seen on the domestic side of policy.

It is difficult to say whether this situation is due more to the actions of assertive and activist presidents in the last several decades or to the passivity of weak Congresses. It is probably some combination of the two, but this is much more than a question of process. The last half-century and more has been a period of existential threat and vigorous activism by the United States in world affairs. The nation faced the possibility of full-scale nuclear war and attempted to contain the spread of Soviet-style communism; promoted democracy, human rights, and capitalism around the globe; and shouldered the host of responsibilities that went along with its position as, eventually, the world's only superpower.

Every post–World War II president has initiated or overseen some form of American military action abroad. In a number of administrations, foreign wars have been the dominant focus of attention, the most recent case being the George W. Bush administration. Over the same period in this area of policy, Congress appears to have become increasingly less effective, sometimes to the point of complete subordination.

One reason for the change in the attention that Congress gives to foreign affairs and national security is simply the increasing preoccupation of its membership with their representative role. As we saw in Chapters 2 and 3, there are more and more demands on members to address local issues, provide constituent services, and raise money for reelection. Congress meets for fewer days, there are fewer and shorter hearings, and the members spend more time in their states and districts.

Perhaps the last member of Congress to engage a president in a genuine long-term debate over a war was J. William Fulbright of Arkansas. Senator Fulbright served as the chairman of the Foreign Relations Committee from 1959 to 1974 and became Congress's leading opponent of how Presidents Johnson and Nixon conducted the Vietnam War.[3] Fulbright was a Democrat, so it is particularly noteworthy that he tangled with Johnson, also a Democrat.

The Fulbright exception serves to prove the rule. The senator paid a heavy price for his active Vietnam War oversight: He was defeated for reelection in 1974 owing to a combination of the unpopularity of his views in some quarters of his state and his failure to stay sufficiently abreast of local issues and concerns.

The relationship between the branches is extraordinary in the area of war powers in part because there is no consensus over the meaning and implications of the relevant constitutional language. What are Congress's prerogatives? What exactly are the president's? The debate has gone on without interruption ever since World War II, with no end in sight in the twenty-first century. In fact, the Iraq War has highlighted the clash between the branches. Senator Robert Byrd of West Virginia, a vigorous proponent of congressional prerogatives, succinctly summarized the presidential position on the matter in the days leading up to the beginning of that conflict:

> The Bush Administration thinks that the Constitution, with its inefficient separation of powers and its cumbersome checks and balances, has become an anachronism in a world of international terrorism and weapons of mass destruction.[4]

CONGRESS VERSUS THE PRESIDENT

The Constitutional Provisions

Congress has essentially the same sources of power in determining the national security policy of the nation that it has in all other policy areas—those provisions in Article I that give the institution the power to authorize and fund the actions of the government. However, there are four constitutional provisions that are at the heart of the continuing debate over the two branches' prerogatives in the specific realm of war powers.

The first is the power to declare war, granted, in Article I, Section 8, to the Congress:

> Congress has the power . . . to declare war, grant letters of marque and reprisal, and make rules concerning captures on land and water; to raise and support armies, but no appropriation of money to that use shall be for a longer term than two years; to provide and maintain a navy; to make rules for the government and regulation of the land and naval forces.

The second provision, in Article II, Section 1, refers to the general grant of executive power to the president:

> The executive power shall be vested in a president of the United States of America.

The third, in Article II, Section 2, gives the president the commander-in-chief power:

> The president shall be commander in chief of the army and navy of the United States, and of the militia of the several states, when called in the actual service of the United States.

The fourth, also in Article II, Section 2, confers a more general power over foreign affairs to the president:

> [The president] shall have power, by and with the advice and consent of the Senate, to make treaties, provided two thirds of the senators present concur; and he shall nominate, and by and with the advice and consent of the Senate, shall appoint ambassadors.

As noted earlier, there is no consensus as to the exact meaning, scope, and implications of these provisions. The views of those who claim a congressional prerogative to commit the country to war are developed in the next section. Then we look at the presidential view.

The Case for Congress

Many scholars and politicians believe that the Framers of the Constitution placed the power to commit the country to war in the hands of Congress and Congress alone. They see this as the most logical reading of Article I, Section 8. This perspective maintains that the president's commander-in-chief power, or any other constitutionally granted executive powers, cannot usurp Congress's authority to decide whether to go to war. As such, the power to declare war is not a shared power except insofar as a declaration of war, to be legally in effect, requires the president's signature.

Those in favor of congressional prerogatives say that the Framers of the Constitution placed the war power exclusively in the hands of Congress in direct reaction to the existing European model, which placed the war power exclusively with the monarch. According to Louis Fisher of the Congressional Research Service:

> The framers broke decisively with that tradition. Drawing on lessons learned at home in the American colonies and the Continental Congress, they deliberately transferred the power to initiate war from the executive to the legislature. The framers, aspiring to achieve the ideal of republican government, drafted a Constitution "that allowed only Congress to loose the military forces of the United States on other nations."[5]

Following this line of thinking, some Congress partisans suggest that the president's commander-in-chief power does not kick in until war is declared. This idea is backed up by a literal reading of the Article II, Section 2, provision stating that "the president shall be Commander in Chief of the Army and Navy of the United States, and of the militia of the several States, *when called into the actual service of the United States*" (emphasis added). A declaration of war would constitute the most obvious "call into the actual service of the United States." Presumably this interpretation might also mean that the president has to relinquish the commander-in-chief power when the war is over.

But declarations of war have gone out of fashion. The United States has had dozens of military engagements, both major and minor, since the last congressional declaration of war in 1942. Is Congress's constitutional claim on the power to commit the nation to war even relevant anymore?

"Perfect" and "Imperfect" Wars

Before the Constitution, the Articles of Confederation (1777–1788) deliberately vested the war power in Congress. Article 9 of the Articles stated: "The United States, in Congress assembled, shall have the sole and exclusive right and power of determining on peace and war." In addition, and importantly, as Fisher points out, the Continental Congress (the governing legislature at the time) intended that authority to include both

> "perfect" and "imperfect" wars . . . wars that were formally declared by Congress and those that were merely authorized. . . . The power over perfect and imperfect wars lay with the Continental Congress *and would remain with the U.S. Congress.*[6]

Some modern-day proponents of presidential war prerogatives mistakenly maintain that the Framers failed to anticipate undeclared wars. In fact, Alexander Hamilton made mention of them and suggested that, even in those days, declared wars were beginning to fall out of favor. All in all, Fisher contends, the only reasonable reading of the intent of the Framers is to recognize that Congress has the power to commit the nation to war, whether by declaration or by authorizing statute.

In the modern context, perhaps the key reason declarations of war are avoided is that they have various legal—both international and domestic—ramifications. For example, on the domestic side, a formal declaration of war, according to Jennifer Elsea and Richard Grimmett of the Congressional Research Service, "automatically triggers many standby statutory authorities conferring special powers on the president with respect to the military, foreign trade, transportation, communications, manufacturing, alien enemies, etc."[7] On the international front, a nation has more flexibility with less formal mechanisms of committing its military to war—specifically, statutes authorizing the use of force.

Congress's authority to "grant letters of marque and reprisal," in Article I, Section 8, sounds quaint to us today. There is little debate that this originally involved the government's power to authorize private citizens to retaliate against piracy, for example, without running afoul of international law. The legal scholar Kathryn Einspanier contends that such letters encompass any sort of limited military activity authorized by the government—perhaps a covert operation or a retaliatory air strike—and that, again, Congress was explicitly given the authority over such matters.[8]

Some advocates of congressional prerogatives also claim that, by giving the Congress the power to declare war, the Framers did not necessarily intend for the president to have free rein in the conduct of the war, in his capacity as commander in chief, from the time of the declaration. In the eighteenth century, declarations of war were often very specific and limited in scope. In giving Congress the power to declare war, many of the Framers believed that they gave Congress the authority to make decisions about a war's scope and duration.[9]

Having said all of this, there is a broad consensus that the Framers intended to give the president the ability to repel sudden attacks and recognized that the legislature was ill equipped to make decisions that might be required in a genuine emergency, given the state of technology and modes of transportation in the eighteenth century. It took days or weeks to get to the nation's capital, and no one could just pick up a phone. It was initially expected that Congress would convene only once a year for a limited duration, which would have made it impossible for the members to weigh in during an emergency that did not coincide with a congressional session.

Congress partisans maintain that today the president's responsibility to repel attacks has been used as a cover for all sorts of executive actions committing the nation to armed conflict when in fact no genuine emergency has existed. (Abraham Lincoln warned of exactly this possibility more than 150 years ago.[10]) In fact, this argument is at the crux of much of the contemporary debate over war powers, as we shall see shortly.

The Power of the Purse and Congressional Prerogatives

The Framers were concerned about the British monarchy's common practice of financing military activities with monies from outside sources, including funds from foreign governments. James Madison was quite explicit in his aim to keep the power of the purse lodged in the legislative branch and apart from the commander-in-chief power. To his way of thinking, this was the key to ensuring that the people's liberties would not be infringed upon by an overzealous executive. The idea of separating "the purse" and "the sword" was the fundamental reason why Congress was given the funding power.[11]

When it comes to war powers, however, the power of the purse gives Congress much less leverage than one might think. Consider first that some foreign engagements in the last sixty years have been initiated by the president. At the point when troops have been placed in harm's way, it is extremely difficult for Congress to deny funding for the operation; exercising the power of the purse is usually not an option by that time. The fact is that members of the House and Senate are loath to be accused of not supporting the troops or of undermining America's prestige abroad.

Basically the same principle applies to other military actions that have received congressional authorization. The Congress finds it difficult to limit funding after a commitment has been made, even if members have had a change of heart or the president is conducting the war in a way that the majority of Congress opposes.

Furthermore, attempts by Congress to legislate limits on military operations during a conflict may not always be constitutionally permissible. Even those who favor congressional prerogatives acknowledge that Congress may not use provisions in appropriations legislation like a "scalpel," dictating the details of military policy to the president.[12] The idea is that, once a war is declared or authorized, there are limits to how far Congress may infringe upon the president's prerogatives as commander in chief to conduct that war as he sees fit.

Still, it is widely agreed that Congress is within its constitutional authority to cut off funding for a military operation. For those who support congressional war power prerogatives, the power of the purse is the backstop. If all else fails, refuse to fund the war.

But, in reality, this is a move born of desperation. And from a political perspective, it is basically a hollow threat; as noted, most members of Congress support the troops in the field even if they disagree with the direction of the war. When all is said and done, it is *the decision to go to war* that matters. To the extent that the president has usurped Congress's prerogative to commit the nation to war, the political reality is that the power of the purse loses a good deal of its punch.

The Case for Presidential Prerogative

By designating the president the "commander in chief," in Article II, Section 2, the Framers empowered him to do at least two things: one, to conduct military operations pursuant to declared or authorized wars; and two, to repel attacks on the homeland. Beyond that, there is no consensus as to what, if anything, the Framers intended.

Recent presidents and some scholars certainly do wish to extend the president's powers beyond those basics. They believe that the commander-in-chief power requires no trigger from a congressional authorization or declaration of war to take effect—instead, they maintain, it is always in place. Furthermore, although no president has attempted to lay claim to the power to declare war, numerous presidents and proponents of presidential war power have pointed to the commander-in-chief clause in the Constitution as, at least in part, a legitimate basis for sending U.S. forces into battle irrespective of any action by Congress.

The most expansive interpretations of presidential power in the last sixty years include the contention that the Constitution gives the president the authority to commence and conduct virtually any military action that he sees as being in the interest of the nation.[13] As we saw at the beginning of the chapter, *presidents of both parties, even when they have received or sought congressional authorization, now maintain that they do not need that congressionally granted authority to commit American troops.* What has caused this rather dramatic and consequential change from an often restricted view of the president's prerogatives to a greatly expanded view of his commander-in-chief role? And how is it justified? A little historical background is helpful in setting the stage for understanding the dramatic change in the relationship between the branches in this area of policy.

World War II, Communists, and the Standing Army

World War II saw a massive mobilization of the nation's industry and populace for war. The nation, together with its allies, fought the three notorious dictators from Japan, Italy, and Germany on multiple fronts around the globe. The scale of it even exceeded the mobilization efforts required for World War I.

For the Second World War, American forces were based on multiple continents, as they had been for World War I, but there was a major difference in the American posture in the years after the war. Instead of "standing down"—dramatically scaling back the armed forces at the end of a war—the United States retained an international posture by maintaining bases all over the world and, in effect, keeping all the branches of the armed services on ready alert.

The reason? It was recognized very soon after the end of the war that a U.S. ally in World War II, the Soviet Union, might constitute a threat to the western European allies, and perhaps even the homeland. The Soviets had rapidly solidified their position by exerting control over much of eastern and central Europe. This development—the establishment of what were called the Warsaw Pact nations—concerned western Europeans, who feared further Soviet expansion into their countries. With the prodding of Britain's Winston Churchill and under the leadership of President Harry Truman, a bipartisan consensus developed in the United States around the idea that the Soviet Union needed to be contained within its sphere of influence.

The Soviets, for their part, made little effort to hide their intention to exert influence on other continents. It appeared that the Soviet Communists were on the move, and the only conceivable obstacle to them would be the United States, which, despite the considerable sacrifice of its citizens during the war, was relatively intact and economically vital compared to its other allies. Politically, the containment of the Soviets became an imperative supported enthusiastically by most Democrats and Republicans alike. The forty-five-year Cold War had begun.

This only became more of an imperative when the Soviet Union tested its first atom bomb in 1949. The United States no longer had a monopoly on nuclear weapons. The race to build more and more lethal bombs began in earnest. By the mid-1950s, the Soviets had tested a single nuclear weapon with more destructive potential than all the munitions used in World War II combined.

The competition with the Soviet Union affected American politics and its institutions profoundly. By the late 1940s, covert operations to counter Soviet influence in Europe and, in fairly short order, across the globe had escalated. The United States did not dare scale back its military posture for fear of encouraging the Soviets' ambitions. American interests were considered threatened in Asia, the Middle East, Africa, Central and South America, and, of course, Europe.

Post–World War II America and the Commander in Chief
In earlier times, American presidents, even if they had wanted to, would have had a great deal of difficulty unilaterally and precipitously committing the nation to a major foreign entanglement. The nation did not maintain the type of military posture necessary for sustained, large-scale military ventures. Considerable mobilization, necessitating appropriations for the armed services and other actions of Congress to harness industry, would have been required.

After World War II, the president had a lot more to work with. As noted, he had armed forces positioned at far-flung bases who were easily deployable anywhere around the world. It would take longer to mobilize a force for a large-scale war, but such a force was available at bases in the United States. The president also had the ability to inflict massive damage anywhere on earth with the rapidly growing nuclear arsenal, over which he had unquestioned authority. Most importantly perhaps, post-war presidents had what amounted to explicit bipartisan support to do what needed to be done—to contain the spread of communism by any means necessary.

It was not a huge stretch for presidents to conclude that they could get away with acting unilaterally to engage American troops whenever and wherever American interests were threatened. In fact, every single president since the end of World War II, Democrats and Republicans alike, has claimed the authority to do so. But how did presidents justify this rather radical departure from the long-established constitutional interpretation that Congress has control over the decision to commit troops to battle?[14]

Truman's 1950 decision to send troops without congressional authorization into the Korean conflict, a major front in the Cold War, precipitated a series of justifications. In 1951 Secretary of State Dean Acheson, testifying before the Senate Foreign Relations and Armed Services Committees, said, "Not only has the president the authority to use the armed forces in carrying out the broad foreign policy of the United States and implementing treaties, but it is equally clear that this authority may not be interfered with by the Congress in the exercise of power which it has in the Constitution."[15] Notably, some years later, a Johnson administration State Department official, Leonard Meeker, stated: "The grant of authority to the president in Article II of the Constitution extends to the actions of the United States currently undertaken in Vietnam."[16]

Practically speaking, the argument was that the Congress had spent the money to put the armed forces on ready alert all over the globe for a reason. And that reason was that our interests and our very existence were perceived to be threatened in the Cold War. To presidents, there was no longer any debate: The nation was in a precarious situation that constituted something like a permanent emergency. The commander in chief had the authority unilaterally to commit troops to war if need be.

Advocates of presidential prerogatives have grounded this power in more than the commander-in-chief clause in Article II. Rather, they put forth a much broader argument rooted in all three of the Article II provisions noted earlier, including the commander-in-chief clause.[17] The president is said to be solely responsible for representing the nation in foreign relations based on the primary role that presidents are given in the Constitution in treaty negotiations and the receiving of ambassadors. The Supreme Court essentially took this position in 1936.[18] The Court has also cooperated by not standing in the way of executive agreements and other unilateral diplomatic actions taken by presidents. And most broadly, the executive power vested in the president in the very first words of Article II is said to give him the exclusive

BOX 7.1
THE CURIOUS CASE OF EXECUTIVE POWER

One of the most intriguing and controversial passages in the Constitution of the United States is the one right at the beginning of Article II: "The executive power shall be vested in a president of the United States of America." Perhaps intentionally, the Framers did not define fully what they meant by that sentence. After all, they were dipping their toes into a touchy subject so soon after the nation had escaped the yoke of the English monarch, and they needed to tamp down controversy in order to get the Constitution ratified.

Many of the Framers believed that the executive, while kept in check for obvious reasons, needed to have much more power to act decisively and make the government work than the impotent executive that had been set up in the ill-fated Articles of Confederation. The Articles were an overreaction, they thought. The Constitution would put in place checks, but the executive needed "energy"—it needed to be able to act with "dispatch" and authority. It was partly in the interest of "energy" and "dispatch" that the Framers settled on establishing a single executive instead of an executive council.[1]

But the executive's powers were not defined in Article II at anywhere near the level of specificity that Congress's were in Article I. What were the limits of this "executive power"? The legislative powers "herein granted" were exhaustively listed, especially in Article I, Section 8. The executive power seemed to be a more general grant of authority. (It is widely believed that the delegate who penned the document, Gouverneur Morris, was responsible, given his sentiments on the matter of executive authority, for making sure that executive powers were not circumscribed in the way legislative powers were by the inclusion of the words "herein granted" in the first sentence of Article II.)

The issue of the meaning of executive power became a political football. An entire political party movement, the Whigs, was organized around the idea that the president should limit himself to simply executing Congress's wishes (except in the most dire emergency) so that the office would not endanger the liberties of the people. Others, especially Thomas Jefferson and Andrew Jackson, felt that the Constitution permitted them to exercise more discretion if their actions were taken in the interests of the nation. Teddy Roosevelt in particular was famous for asserting that the president should act aggressively in the national interest as the "steward" of the nation, as long as he did not run afoul of the Constitution or the laws passed by Congress. There were plenty of gray areas for presidents to exploit, he said, and he meant to do so.

But since the beginning an even more expansive interpretation of executive power has been used to bolster controversial unilateral presidential actions. John Locke, a seventeenth-century English philosopher, was the source of what is called the *prerogative view of executive power*. Locke wrote that the executive needed "to act according to [his] discretion for the public good, without the prescription of the law, and *sometimes even against it*" (emphasis added).[2] What he meant was that the executive can or even should break the law if doing so is necessary to serve the public in a crisis.

Abraham Lincoln seemed to have Locke's view in mind when he wrote a famous letter to A. G. Hodges in 1864 defending some of the actions he had taken as president in the period leading up to and during the Civil War.

Was it possible to lose the nation, and yet preserve the Constitution? By general law life and limb must be protected; yet often a limb must be amputated to save a life; but a life is never wisely given to save a limb. I felt that measures, otherwise unconstitutional, might become lawful, by becoming indispensable to the preservation of the nation. Right or wrong, I assumed this ground, and now avow it.[3]

President Nixon used the same justification, citing Lincoln's letter, in defense of some of his actions—many of which were plainly illegal—to quell protests and infiltrate what he regarded as potentially subversive domestic groups during the Vietnam War.[4] Thomas Jefferson was familiar with Locke's arguments and seemed to subscribe to them as well.[5]

President George W. Bush was extremely assertive regarding the president's executive prerogatives. His administration put forth the *unitary theory of executive power*, which argues for strict limits on Congress's power to encroach on the president's turf.[6] Specifically, adherents of this view maintain that the president must have full control over subordinate officers in the executive branch and that the Constitution, through the commander-in-chief and foreign relations clauses as well as executive power, gives the president the authority to move unilaterally in the realm of foreign and military affairs. (One former high-ranking Bush administration official suggested that the president's assertions of prerogative provoked such a fierce reaction from the other branches that, ironically, the institution of the presidency was weakened while he was still in office.[7])

The exact meaning of "executive power" will never be established to everyone's satisfaction. The Constitution is far too opaque on the subject for a final answer to be discerned. But certainly presidents have occasionally relied on the idea of an "undefined residuum" of executive power to bolster their case for an expanded interpretation of the commander-in-chief role.[8]

1. Alexander Hamilton, *The Federalist Papers*, No. 70.

2. John Locke, *Second Treatise of Government* (1690).

3. For the full text of Lincoln's letter, see Abraham Lincoln Online, "Speeches and Writings," available at: http://showcase.netins.net/web/creative/lincoln/speeches/hodges.htm.

4. Nixon publicly espoused this position in the famous Nixon-Frost interviews of 1977. The relevant passages can be found at Landmark Supreme Court Cases, "*United States v. Nixon* (1974)," available at: http://www.landmarkcases.org/nixon/nixonview.html.

5. Jack L. Goldsmith, *The Terror Presidency* (New York: Norton, 2007), pp. 80–83.

6. A full examination of the unitary executive theory can be found in Stephen G. Calabresi and Christopher S. Yoo, *The Unitary Executive* (New Haven, CT: Yale University Press, 2008).

7. Goldsmith, *The Terror Presidency*.

8. William Howard Taft used the term "undefined residuum." He was an opponent of the expansion of presidential prerogatives advocated by his contemporaries, Teddy Roosevelt and Woodrow Wilson.

power to act in the interest of the nation during a time of crisis. The centuries-long debate over the interpretation of "executive power" is described in Box 7.1.

The argument from this perspective is that the modern-day need for quick action (or "dispatch," in the words of the Framers) necessitates a change in the way we should think about the constitutional provisions affecting presidential power. In the Cold War period from the late 1940s to 1991, when the Soviet Union collapsed, the Soviets' intercontinental nuclear capability, as well as their incursions and influence around the world affecting American interests, put the nation's security permanently at risk.

After the Cold War, Presidents George H. W. Bush and Bill Clinton still viewed the world as a dangerous place for American interests. Bush, in particular, identified American economic and strategic interests in the Middle East as a reasonable justification for unilateral presidential action in the First Gulf War. (He got the authority in law to remove Iraq from Kuwait, but claimed that he did not need it to act, given the UN resolutions and the clear threat to American interests.) And Clinton went further, arguing that instability and human rights violations in south-central Europe, as well as North Atlantic Treaty Organization (NATO) commitments, justified unilateral presidential actions in the Kosovo conflict. It is interesting that U.S. membership in NATO and the United Nations explicitly *does not* legally commit it (or any other nation for that matter) to war. The charters of the organizations leave it up to member states to make that determination. Having said that, these two presidents' political case for committing American troops was surely bolstered by our participation in those bodies.

Clinton and his successor, George W. Bush, also faced the threat of international terrorism. Again, the need for speed was used to justify presidential action, even to the point of committing the nation to war.

Ultimately the consensus view among presidents, if not among scholars or members of Congress, is that waiting for Congress to weigh in before any commitment of American troops is an antiquated and downright dangerous idea in this day and age. The view is that, unlike in previous eras, the nation's vital interests are so extensive and, in many cases, vulnerable, and the capabilities of America's enemies so diabolical and sophisticated, that the requirement of dispatch legitimizes the invocation of, in effect, an umbrella of constitutional authority (encompassing the commander-in-chief clause, executive power, and the Article II, Section 2, provisions covering foreign relations) to commit the country to military action irrespective of congressional authorization.

Two Key Dimensions of the Presidential Advantage

There is no doubt about who the winner is in the struggle between the branches over war powers: It's the executive in a landslide. Simply put, over the last several decades Congress has not exerted the same kind of influence over national security policy, especially committing the country to war, as it has over domestic policy. Even its vaunted "power of the purse" has a diminished impact when it comes to influencing the president in the conduct of war. There are a couple of principal, overarching reasons for the ascendancy of the executive branch with respect to war powers.

First, there is a very strong *political dimension* to Congress's inability to weigh in on foreign or military affairs as it does on domestic policy. A long tradition of depoliticizing foreign and defense policy is encapsulated in the saying that "politics stops at the water's edge." This notion, articulated by Republican senator Arthur Vandenberg in 1952, meant, in his words, that it is important "to unite our official voice at the water's edge so that America speaks with maximum authority against those who would divide and conquer us."[19] He said this in the particular context of the Cold War at a time when he and some other Republicans were working with Democratic president Harry Truman to present a united front. Such a viewpoint gives the president extra leverage, as he always speaks with one voice—something that is virtually impossible for the Congress to do. Presidents become much harder for other politicians to challenge when they are understood to be speaking for the interests of the nation in foreign relations.

The president's political advantage has not, however, enabled him always to dictate what America's proper role in world politics will be. In fact, during the Vietnam War era the debate about war and foreign policy was extremely heated, and during the Reagan years Congress was unusually assertive in opposing the president's policies in Latin America. That said, in the spirit of Arthur Vandenberg, a tradition of bipartisanship and unity in support of the president generally dominates in the most relevant congressional committees (the Senate Foreign Relations Committee and the Armed Services Committees in both chambers).

Also in the political realm, Republican presidents have been able to exploit a perceived weakness on the part of Democrats in the area of national defense. Going back to Vietnam and the Cold War, some Democrats were charged with failing to understand the dangers of Soviet-style imperialism and accused of naïveté and weakness in world affairs. The party's fate in this regard was sealed in 1972 when its presidential candidate, South Dakota senator George McGovern, said he would "beg

Hanoi" for the return of prisoners of war.[20] Ever since then, the burden of proof has been on Democrats to show that they are tough enough to deal with a dangerous world. This has made it politically difficult for Democrats to challenge the aggressive assertion of presidential prerogatives in committing troops to combat. And certainly, as discussed earlier, it is politically difficult or impossible for members of either party to support pulling the plug on funding for an ongoing military operation.

The second reason Congress has become weak on national security policy is the *informational dimension.* Although it is true that Congress depends on information from the executive branch to exercise its authorizing, appropriations, and oversight powers in the domestic arena, the situation is more problematic in the defense sphere. Information related to national security is controlled to a greater degree by the executive branch. The president has a tremendous built-in advantage vis-à-vis Congress when troops are stationed in or patrolling potentially hostile territory or seas. Presidents are able to use their access to military intelligence to portray events in such a way as to make it very difficult for Congress to oppose the march to war when time is of the essence.

Perhaps the most famous example of this sort of information management was the controversial Gulf of Tonkin incident, which led to Congress passing a resolution that granted a broad authorization for military activity in Southeast Asia. Two ambiguous engagements in Southeast Asian waters in 1964 between American destroyers and North Vietnamese torpedo boats were portrayed by the Johnson administration as unprovoked attacks on the American ships. Congress had no ability in this time of crisis to gain access to all the available information (in fact, it took decades for all of it to become public) and had little recourse other than to respond affirmatively and quickly to the president's request for action. The resulting authorization for war was, as Johnson said privately, "like grandmother's nightshirt; it covers everything."[21] It should be noted that only two members of Congress opposed that authorization, and they were both defeated for reelection in the next electoral cycle.

President George W. Bush's administration has also been criticized for how it managed ambiguous information in 2002 and 2003 concerning Iraq's program for developing and acquiring weapons of mass destruction. Ultimately, Secretary of State Colin Powell made the case to the United Nations in early 2003 that the United States had irrefutable evidence of the program. The closely controlled information— much of it highly classified—was nearly impossible to challenge, giving a decided advantage to the administration in its case for war.

In a broader sense, access to information related to defense and national security is limited by the sheer volume generated by the Department of Defense, the armed services, the intelligence agencies, the Department of State, and all the other departments and agencies that have some level of involvement with national security policy (including the FBI, the Department of Homeland Security, and the Energy Department). Members of Congress, their staffs, and the institution's support arms—the Congressional Budget Office, the Government Accountability Office, and the Congressional Research Service—simply do not have the staffing and other resources to access or analyze the vast quantity of information in a systematic way. The Congress is at a distinct disadvantage.

Although there are areas of domestic policy where the sheer volume of information presents problems, there are some important differences in the national security area. First, much of the information is collected outside the United States. Second, information related to national security is analyzed, cataloged, and stored by the defense and intelligence agencies and is often not available in the public domain. And last, a significant portion of that information is always going to be classified or sensitive and therefore may not be shared on a regular basis with the Congress. Although members of Congress automatically have top security clearance, most congressional staff do not, and practical limitations are placed on sharing classified or sensitive information even with the members themselves.

In fact, through a combination of laws, report language, and interbranch understandings, the president shares some intelligence information with just the so-called Gang of Eight, a group that includes the speaker of the House, the House minority leader, the Senate majority and minority leaders, and the chairs and ranking members of the two chambers' Intelligence Committees.[22] Gang of Eight notifications are supposed to be limited to covert operations—an area where information is held especially tightly by presidents for fear of leaks or the exposure of potentially risky activities. Such exposure could put operatives overseas in immediate mortal danger and could also be highly embarrassing, both diplomatically and politically.

One example of an operation that came to light and created political fallout is the National Security Agency (NSA) surveillance program, which stirred great controversy in 2006. NSA, an intelligence agency under the auspices of the Defense Department, was collecting information on terror suspects via wiretapping and other methods. The program's legality was dubious, and its existence was shared only with the Gang of Eight. When a few details of the program were leaked, some in Congress asserted that its existence should have been shared with a much broader range of members.[23]

In general, Congress's efforts to assert its oversight authority over covert operations have been sporadic and often thwarted. And despite the establishment of a congressional oversight regime beginning in 1976 with the creation of the House Intelligence Committee—the first systematic congressional oversight of the intelligence agencies in the nation's history—it took only a few years before Congress was again left out of the loop by the president and the CIA director regarding important covert operations.[24] In such matters, *sharing information with Congress always depends on the cooperation and good faith of the president.* Congress has a great deal of difficulty locating or gaining access to information it might want in a timely fashion if the president chooses not to share it.

The result of both the political and informational dimensions is that Congress tends to give a great deal of leeway to the president in the conduct of foreign and military affairs. Presidents have the upper hand, given their control of the flow of information, and the political dynamics militate strongly in favor of congressional deference. Members of Congress do not necessarily dislike this arrangement—after all, when left out of the loop, they may be in a position to avoid accountability for botched intelligence or military ventures that bog down and may even score political points at the president's expense.

Whether such an arrangement is good for the country and contributes to better policy is an open question, one that is addressed at the end of the chapter. First, however, we consider a couple of dramatic instances in which Congress attempted to assert its prerogatives in war policy. In one case, the institution's ineffectuality was on stark display; in the other, the result was a dramatic constitutional confrontation.

CONGRESS ATTEMPTS TO FLEX ITS MUSCLES

The 1973 War Powers Act

U.S. efforts in Vietnam to discourage and roll back Communist influence, constituting at first just a few hundred military advisers, began in the 1950s. Eventually, by the mid-1960s, the nation had become fully engaged in all-out war in an effort to save non-Communist South Vietnam. Presidents Johnson and Nixon continued the effort all the way until 1973, when a peace treaty was signed that effectively terminated offensive efforts by the United States.

By that time, the nearly decade-long war had taken its toll. Fierce opposition to the policies of the two presidents and a raging debate in Congress had torn apart the country. Over fifty thousand Americans had died in what many felt was either an unnecessary war or one that ultimately was not fought with the clear intention of winning.

In retrospect, despite having authorized actions in Vietnam with the aforementioned Gulf of Tonkin Resolution, a strong majority of Congress believed it had effectively abdicated its authority to the president, both in the decision to go to war and in the conduct of the war. On November 7, 1973, Congress took decisive action, passing the War Powers Act into law over President Nixon's veto.

Some of the key provisions of the bill, Sections 1 through 5, can be seen in Exhibit 7.1. The purpose of the act, as expressed in Section 2, was to ensure that Congress and the president share in making decisions that involve committing U.S. forces to military action. It requires in Section 3 that the president consult with Congress before introducing U.S. forces into hostile or potentially hostile situations, and when that is not possible, to report to Congress (see Section 4) as soon as possible after doing so. Once a report is submitted or required to be submitted, Section 5(b) of the law says that Congress must authorize the use of the armed forces within sixty days *or those forces must be withdrawn* within thirty days.[25]

Although presidents have submitted more than one hundred reports to Congress on military activities consistent with the War Powers Act, it is interesting that only one of those was under the specific section of the act, 5(b), that starts the sixty-day clock ticking, and that one was submitted only after U.S. forces had already been withdrawn. (In the 1975 *Mayaguez* incident, President Ford ordered military action after a U.S. merchant marine vessel had been seized by Cambodian forces.) The reason? Every president since Richard Nixon has taken the position that the War Powers Act (especially Section 5) is an unconstitutional infringement by Congress on the president's authority as commander in chief.[26] The War Powers Act thus has done little to change the board of directors' role with respect to war powers. In fact, there is a nearly universal consensus that it has been at best ineffective, and at worst damaging, to Congress's quest to reestablish a meaningful role in decisions to commit forces to combat.

The act is worth noting because of what it indicates about the state of the relationship between the branches in the area of war powers. After the debacle of the Vietnam War, Congress felt that it needed to salvage some role in the decision to go to war. In reality, in view of the fact that presidents refuse to recognize the constitutionality of Section 5, it may have only salvaged the right to be consulted. The fact is that the act legitimized what Congress partisans believe is the ultimate usurpation of legislative branch prerogatives—the power to make the decision to go to war. The act clearly gives the president the right to make the first move to put troops in harm's

EXHIBIT 7.1
SECTIONS 1 THROUGH 5 OF THE WAR POWERS ACT OF 1973

Public Law 93-148, 93rd Congress, House Joint Resolution 542, November 7, 1973, Concerning the War Powers of Congress and the President

Resolved by the Senate and the House of Representatives of the United States of America in Congress assembled,

SHORT TITLE

Section 1

This joint resolution may be cited as the "War Powers Resolution."

PURPOSE AND POLICY

Section 2(a)

It is the purpose of this joint resolution to fulfill the intent of the framers of the Constitution of the United States and insure that the collective judgement of both the Congress and the President will apply to the introduction of United States Armed Forces into hostilities, or into situations where imminent involvement in hostilities is clearly indicated by the circumstances, and to the continued use of such forces in hostilities or in such situations.

Section 2(b)

Under article I, section 8, of the Constitution, it is specifically provided that the Congress shall have the power to make all laws necessary and proper for carrying into execution, not only its own powers but also all other powers vested by the Constitution in the Government of the United States, or in any department or officer thereof.

Section 2(c)

The constitutional powers of the President as Commander-in-Chief to introduce United States Armed Forces into hostilities, or into situations where imminent involvement in hostilities is clearly indicated by the circumstances, are exercised only pursuant to (1) a declaration of war, (2) specific statutory authorization, or (3) a national emergency created by attack upon the United States, its territories or possessions, or its armed forces.

CONSULTATION

Section 3

The President in every possible instance shall consult with Congress before introducing United States Armed Forces into hostilities or into situations where imminent involvement in hostilities is clearly indicated by the circumstances, and after every such introduction shall consult regularly with the Congress until United States Armed Forces are no longer engaged in hostilities or have been removed from such situations.

REPORTING

Section 4(a)

In the absence of a declaration of war, in any case in which United States Armed Forces are introduced—

(1)

into hostilities or into situations where imminent involvement in hostilities is clearly indicated by the circumstances;

(2)

into the territory, airspace or waters of a foreign nation, while equipped for combat, except for deployments which relate solely to supply, replacement, repair, or training of such forces; or

(3)

(A) the circumstances necessitating the introduction of United States Armed Forces;

(B) the constitutional and legislative authority under which such introduction took place; and

(C) the estimated scope and duration of the hostilities or involvement.

Section 4(b)

The President shall provide such other information as the Congress may request in the fulfillment of its constitutional responsibilities with respect to committing the Nation to war and to the use of United States Armed Forces abroad.

Section 4(c)

Whenever United States Armed Forces are introduced into hostilities or into any situation described in subsection (a) of this section, the President shall, so long as such armed forces continue to be engaged in such hostilities or situation, report to the Congress periodically on the status of such hostilities or situation as well as on the scope and duration of such hostilities or situation, but in no event shall he report to the Congress less often than once every six months.

CONGRESSIONAL ACTION

Section 5(a)

Each report submitted pursuant to section 4(a)(1) shall be transmitted to the Speaker of the House of Representatives and to the President pro tempore of the Senate on the same calendar day. Each report so transmitted shall be referred to the Committee on Foreign Affairs of the House of Representatives and to the Committee on Foreign Relations of the Senate for appropriate action. If, when the report is transmitted, the Congress has adjourned sine die or has adjourned for any period in excess of three calendar days, the Speaker of the House of Representatives and the President pro tempore of the Senate, if they deem it advisable (or if petitioned by at least 30 percent of the membership of their respective Houses), shall jointly request the President to convene Congress in order that it may consider the report and take appropriate action pursuant to this section.

Section 5(b)

Within sixty calendar days after a report is submitted or is required to be submitted pursuant to section 4(a)(1), whichever is earlier, the President shall terminate any use of United States Armed Forces with respect to which such report was submitted (or required to be submitted), unless the Congress (1) has declared war or has enacted a specific authorization for such use of United States Armed Forces, (2) has extended by law such sixty-day period, or (3) is physically unable to meet as a result of an armed attack upon the United States. Such sixty-day period shall be extended for not more than an additional thirty days if the President determines and certifies to the Congress in writing that unavoidable military necessity respecting the safety of United States Armed Forces requires the continued use of such armed forces in the course of bringing about a prompt removal of such forces.

Section 5(c)

Notwithstanding subsection (b), at any time that United States Armed Forces are engaged in hostilities outside the territory of the United States, its possessions and territories without a declaration of war or specific statutory authorization, such forces shall be removed by the President if the Congress so directs by concurrent resolution.

way *without even statutory authorization*, and certainly without a full-fledged declaration of war. Simply put, the War Powers Act was the acknowledgment by Congress,
in the immediate aftermath of the Vietnam War, that it had lost control of the war
power and that presidentially initiated war had become the reality.

Exercising the Power of the Purse: The Iran-Contra Affair

Congress has not proven entirely toothless in this era, however. As mentioned before,
the power of the purse is Congress's ultimate backstop. It may not be the most effective tool in the case of war powers, for both political and legal reasons (there are
constitutional limits to Congress's ability to micromanage a war through appropriations legislation once that war has been declared or authorized), but it has occasionally been used to some effect. In particular, in 1982 the Boland Amendment
to an appropriations bill, named after its sponsor, Representative Edward Boland
(D-MA), cut off funding for covert military assistance in Nicaragua.

The Boland case, as we shall see, points up the potential for a profound clash between the branches—a potential that, in effect, is embedded in the Constitution. On
the one hand, a lot of people support the notion that presidents in the modern day
have the prerogative to act swiftly and unilaterally to commit troops or otherwise act
to protect American interests. At the same time, no one doubts Congress's right to
cut off funds (or simply refuse to provide them) for military actions through its
power of the purse. But what happens when Congress forbids funding for military
action that the president claims is in the nation's interests to carry out? There is no
simple resolution. If each side pushes its prerogatives to the limit, there may be no
room for compromise, and a dramatic confrontation can result.

This is exactly what happened when, in 1982, Congress used an appropriations
act to prohibit the Reagan administration from providing any military support for
the antigovernment forces—the Contras—in Nicaragua, where a civil war raged.
President Reagan believed that the Sandinista government of Nicaragua was a threat
to the United States owing to its close ties to Cuba and the Soviet Union. He had
been pursuing a covert strategy to overthrow the government, a strategy that had
been made public through leaks and aggressive reporting.[27] Many in Congress found
the Sandinistas less threatening than Reagan did and, furthermore, were appalled
by some of the tactics and associations of the Contras.

When Congress passed the prohibition on the use of government funds for the
purpose of overthrowing the government of Nicaragua, the administration went
about finding other sources of funding for the rebels. As these alternative efforts to
fund the Contras came to light (part of a convoluted set of weapons deals known as

the Iran-Contra Affair), Congress investigated. Dramatic hearings were held in the summer of 1987, involving a select committee created for the purpose of looking into the affair. Top administration officials, including national security adviser John Poindexter and his subordinate, Oliver North, were accused of subverting the Constitution and federal law by organizing the scheme to fund the Contras. Ultimately, several officials were convicted of felonies, including lying to Congress and obstructing justice, in connection with the affair.

What was not resolved, and may never be, was the question of whether the president has the right to find other sources of funding in the service of his foreign policy objectives when Congress restricts the use of appropriated monies. The Reagan administration suggested that the president had this right, but was determined to conceal its controversial efforts—to the point of lying to Congress—in order to do so. What we are left with is the continuing potential for constitutional clashes between the legislative power of the purse and the executive's claims for expansive unilateral authority in foreign and military affairs.

CASE STUDIES OF WAR IN THE TWENTY-FIRST CENTURY

The new century offers two vivid examples of the current relationship between the branches regarding the decision to commit the nation to war. They illustrate well the tensions in that relationship, the presidential perspective, and the impediments encountered by Congress in effectively asserting its prerogatives.

Authorizing Action Against the Perpetrators of 9/11

On September 11, 2001, Islamic terrorists linked to Al Qaeda leader Osama bin Laden hijacked four U.S. commercial airliners and crashed two of them into the Twin Towers of the World Trade Center in New York City and one into the Pentagon. The fourth airliner went down in rural Pennsylvania after passengers attempted to gain control of the plane. Nearly three thousand people died as a result of these attacks. The following day, President Bush described the so-called 9/11 attacks as acts of war: "They were acts of war . . . freedom and democracy are under attack," and stated that the United States would use "all of our resources to conquer this enemy."[28]

The politics of the situation militated in favor of immediate action. The United States had not seen anything resembling these attacks in its history. Nineteen men with, as it turned out, only about a half-million dollars destroyed landmarks, killed thousands, and sent shock waves through the nation and its economy. It was impossible for most members of Congress to contemplate anything less than a broad grant of authority to the president enabling him to respond swiftly and decisively against the perpetrators. On the morning of September 14, 2001, just three days after the attacks, the Senate passed Senate Joint Resolution 23 under a unanimous consent agreement by a vote of 98–0. Later that evening, it passed the House by a vote of 420–1. Only Representative Barbara Lee, Democrat from northern California, was in opposition. The bill, as seen in Exhibit 7.2, was signed into law by President Bush on September 18.

The so-called Use of Force Resolution was unusual in that it authorized military action not only against a nation or nations but also against organizations and persons who had been involved in the 9/11 attacks. It is notable that the document seemed to give the president the sole responsibility to determine who or what countries were involved. Congress would, it seems, have no role—not even a joint role—in that determination.

Details of the negotiation of the agreement, however, reveal an important assertion of congressional prerogatives. Just one day after the attacks, the administration privately presented congressional leadership with a draft resolution that included Section 2(a) (the part that gave the president the authority to determine what entities were responsible), but also included a clause authorizing the president "to *deter and preempt* any future acts of terrorism or aggression against the United States" (emphasis added). Congress balked at this unprecedented grant of power and, on a bipartisan basis, insisted that it be removed from the final version. Congress also insisted on the inclusion of Section 2(b), which invoked the War Powers Act. Congress was maintaining its commitment to that legislation, although no sitting president had ever acknowledged its constitutionality.

Of course, Congress had to give something to get those concessions. What Congress gave was the last "Whereas" clause in the preamble of the bill that said that the president has the authority to, in effect, act preemptively ("deter and prevent") to thwart terrorism. Although this concession might seem to vitiate Congress's assertions of prerogative, giving in with almost identical wording to the president's original proposed resolution, in fact, *preambles to bills are not legally binding.* From a legal standpoint, Congress had actually asserted itself in a meaningful way.[29]

Nonetheless, the president restated his prerogatives in his signing statement, a nonbinding document that accompanies the bill and expresses the president's interpretation of the legislation he is signing into law. He claimed to have the exclusive power over the decision to use military force, which would include that force necessary to counter threats to American interests and security, and went on to reassert the executive branch's continued view that the War Powers Act is unconstitutional.[30]

EXHIBIT 7.2
POST-9/11 AUTHORIZATION FOR ACTION AGAINST THE PERPETRATORS OF THE 9/11 ATTACKS
Authorization for Use of Military Force, September 18, 2001,
Public Law 107-40 (Senate Joint Resolution 23), 107th Congress

Joint Resolution

To authorize the use of United States Armed Forces against those responsible for the recent attacks launched against the United States.

Whereas, on September 11, 2001, acts of treacherous violence were committed against the United States and its citizens; and

Whereas, such acts render it both necessary and appropriate that the United States exercise its rights to self-defense and to protect United States citizens both at home and abroad; and

Whereas, in light of the threat to the national security and foreign policy of the United States posed by these grave acts of violence; and

Whereas, such acts continue to pose an unusual and extraordinary threat to the national security and foreign policy of the United States; and

Whereas, the President has authority under the Constitution to take action to deter and prevent acts of international terrorism against the United States: Now, therefore, be it

Resolved by the Senate and House of Representatives of the United States of America in Congress assembled,

SECTION 1. SHORT TITLE

This joint resolution may be cited as the "Authorization for Use of Military Force."

SECTION 2. AUTHORIZATION FOR USE OF UNITED STATES ARMED FORCES

(a) IN GENERAL—That the President is authorized to use all necessary and appropriate force against those nations, organizations, or persons he determines planned, authorized, committed, or aided the terrorist attacks that occurred on September 11, 2001, or harbored such organizations or persons, in order to prevent any future acts of international terrorism against the United States by such nations, organizations or persons.

(b) War Powers Resolution Requirements—

(1) SPECIFIC STATUTORY AUTHORIZATION—Consistent with section 8(a)(1) of the War Powers Resolution, the Congress declares that this section is intended to constitute specific statutory authorization within the meaning of section 5(b) of the War Powers Resolution.

(2) APPLICABILITY OF OTHER REQUIREMENTS—Nothing in this resolution supercedes any requirement of the War Powers Resolution.

The Bush administration subsequently cited the law as providing authority to the president to combat terrorism everywhere, including within the United States.

The result: Congressional leaders came away claiming that they had retained an important role in limiting the president's expansive war powers claims, and the president came away claiming that he had the exclusive power over that decision, even on a preemptive basis. There was little serious or sustained debate within Congress on the matter. The president got much of what he wanted; what he did not get, he claimed.

The President Acts

On September 24, 2001, President Bush reported to Congress—"consistent with the War Powers Resolution" and PL 107-40 (the Use of Force Resolution)—that in response to the terrorist attacks on September 11 he had ordered the deployment of forces "to a number of foreign nations in the Central and Pacific Command areas of operations." He stated that he might find it necessary to commit "additional forces into these and other areas of the world" and that he could not predict "the scope and duration of these deployments" or the "actions necessary to counter the terrorist threat to the United States."[31]

Two weeks later, on October 9, President Bush again reported to Congress, "consistent with the War Powers Resolution" and PL 107-40, that on October 7, 2001, U.S. armed forces had begun combat operations in Afghanistan against Al Qaeda and the Taliban. The president carefully framed his decision to commence military action so as not to invoke the specific clause in the War Powers Act that would potentially trigger the sixty-day withdrawal clock, but rather stated more generally that he was reporting to Congress "consistent with the War Powers Resolution." What this means is that he was abiding by the legal requirement in the resolution that he inform Congress of his actions, but not the specific part of the resolution—the part leading to the requirement that he remove troops from hostilities after a sixty-day period—that presidents have always maintained is an unconstitutional infringement on their commander-in-chief power.

More interestingly, he deliberately avoided citing the specific statutory authority to use military action against those responsible for 9/11 granted to him in PL 107-40, stating only that he was reporting to Congress "consistent with PL 107-40." Instead, Bush stated that he took actions "pursuant to my constitutional authority to conduct U.S. foreign relations as Commander in Chief and Chief Executive." This amounted to a carefully parsed argument that *the president does not need explicit congressional authorization in the first place to commit the country to war.*

In that case, why might the president have sought the Use of Force Resolution in the first place, seeing that he claimed to have the constitutional authority to do what was necessary in his view to deal with the perpetrators and even prospective perpetrators? The answer boils down to politics, on both sides of the constitutional divide.

The members of Congress certainly planned to do something post-9/11—at the very least to express their outrage and the need for swift action. For the president, action by the board of directors would afford additional political cover. If Congress agreed to give him wide-ranging discretion, then the matter would be settled for all intents and purposes. President Bush could proceed without any expectation that he would have to return to Capitol Hill for authorization to conduct any further action.

Authorizing War on Iraq

In the summer of 2002, the Bush administration began to lay the public groundwork for addressing what it stated was a threat posed by Iraq: Saddam Hussein's regime had acquired, or was in the process of acquiring or developing, weapons of mass destruction. At that time it was clear that there were sharp divisions in Congress over the wisdom of taking direct military action against Iraq.

In addition to opposition from Democrats, who had a slim 51–49 majority in the Senate but were in the minority in the House at the time, a number of prominent Republicans had joined Democratic opponents of authorizing the use of force against Saddam Hussein and the Iraqi government. Among those members of the president's party who had expressed deep reservations over the wisdom of invading Iraq were House majority leader Dick Armey and influential Republican senators Chuck Hagel of Nebraska and Richard Lugar of Indiana, both senior members of the Foreign Relations Committee. The White House was keenly aware of these divisions in the Congress and was especially concerned about the dissenting views among Republicans.

To counter opposition, the administration enlisted the active support of House majority whip Tom DeLay, who pulled no punches in criticizing fellow Republicans who had questioned congressional action in support of authorizing the invasion. Vice President Dick Cheney was also a public and, more importantly, private advocate in the halls of Congress for the president's position, bringing to bear his considerable powers of persuasion on any potentially recalcitrant Republicans.

Some congressional proponents of bringing down Saddam Hussein argued that the president required no additional authority from Congress. Many in that group, however, believed that it was nonetheless important politically to receive congressional approval. The chairman of the House International Relations Committee,

Henry Hyde of Illinois, a well-respected, longtime member of the body, advised the White House to seek congressional approval even though he believed it was not required:

> The White House should be mindful of the important distinction between what the president can do and what he ought to do. . . . Any policy undertaken by the president without a popular mandate from Congress risks long-term success.[32]

The White House, in response, stated its intention to "consult" with Congress, but maintained the position that the president was not required to seek or to receive congressional approval. White House spokesman Ari Fleischer stated: "In all cases, the president will consult with Congress because Congress has an important role to play."[33] Exactly what role he was talking about was unclear. Was it the advisability of consulting with Congress? Or was Fleischer mindful of Congress's appropriations power? Perhaps both—the ambiguity may have been deliberate.

Make no mistake about it: The White House was fully prepared to combat any assertions of congressional prerogatives it might have considered too bold. White House lawyers prepared a legal brief stating their position that the president did not require congressional approval to take military action. In the brief, they cited three separate legal authorities already in place: PL 101-1, the joint resolution passed in 1991 that authorized President Bush's father to conduct the Persian Gulf War, which they maintained was still in effect; PL 107-40, the Use of Force Resolution, which a year earlier had authorized the president to take action against those involved in the 9/11 attacks (including the aforementioned nonbinding "whereas" clause in the preamble to the act); and the authority to use military forces to enforce the 1991 UN resolution regarding Iraq's promise to disclose and disband its biological, chemical, and nuclear weapons programs.[34]

On September 4, President Bush convened the congressional leadership from both parties at the White House to inform them of his intention to seek formal congressional support for taking military action against Iraq and to tell them that he would be making his case to the United Nations as well. On September 12, the president addressed the United Nations General Assembly, setting out his concerns over Iraq. He stated that if Iraq continued to fail to comply with UN Security Council resolutions requiring it to undergo regular inspections for weapons of mass destruction, the United States would take action to see that those resolutions were enforced.[35]

On September 19, 2002, the White House sent a draft joint resolution to the congressional leadership that would authorize the use of military force against Iraq, "to restore international peace and security in the region."[36] Hyde's argument apparently won out: The president believed that he did not need to have Congress go along, but that its support could prove useful in the long run. In addition, in political Washington, conducting the vote could only redound to his party's benefit. It looked likely to pass both chambers, and it would put wavering Democrats on the spot with the elections coming up. In mid-October, after lengthy debate, the House voted 296–133, and the Senate 77–23, in favor of authorizing the use of force. Although the president did not get everything he wanted, he did receive wide latitude in the conduct of the war in the event that he chose to invade Iraq.

Again, the politics of the matter were difficult for advocates of congressional prerogatives. The president was adamant that he had information that showed evidence of a secret weapons of mass destruction program in Iraq, and he even hinted at possible connections between Osama bin Laden's Al Qaeda and Saddam Hussein. The president had the upper hand, and Congress acquiesced, giving him full authority to use force against Iraq.

As noted earlier, this ability of the White House to manage information and control the terms of the debate in national security policy has no real parallel in domestic policy. In foreign affairs, the president is the only one in a position to see the whole picture, and presidents never hesitate to press that point. In an era of highly sensitive intelligence gathering on threats to American interests, Congress is at a decided disadvantage in any effort to check the president when he is initially deciding whether to commit troops.

In signing the authorization for force, President Bush explained that he had consulted extensively with Congress in the preceding months, that his views and those of Congress were the same on "the important question of the threat posed by Iraq," and that he planned to continue "close consultation in the months ahead." Nevertheless, he again stated his position, as he had in signing PL 107-40 immediately after the 9/11 attacks, that he did not need the board of directors' permission to use military force:

> My request for [congressional authorization] did not, and my signing this resolution does not, constitute any change in the long-standing positions of the executive branch on either the President's constitutional authority to use force to deter, prevent, or respond to aggression or other threats to U.S. interests.[37]

It is particularly important to note that the president reaffirmed his belief that he had the authority not just to use force in the face of aggression, but also that he had the authority to act preemptively to "deter . . . threats to U.S. interests."

The law did require that certain conditions be met before military operations were initiated (in particular, that efforts be made through diplomatic channels to encourage Iraqi compliance with the UN inspectors looking for evidence of weapons of mass destruction), and it also required the president to submit written reports to Congress every sixty days on matters related to the statute. In addition, and counter to the president's wishes (his initial proposal would have authorized the use of force throughout the Middle East), the authorization limited military activity to Iraq. But the authorization set no time limit on military operations, nor did it specify the conditions under which the United States might terminate its deployment of armed forces in Iraq. In addition, it specified no limits on the level of military force that might be required to accomplish the objectives it set forth. Rather, it seemed to suggest that the president could make that determination. According to the bill, the president was authorized to use the armed forces

> as he determines to be *necessary and appropriate* in order to (1) defend the national security of the United States against the continuing threat posed by Iraq; and (2) enforce all relevant United Nations Security Council resolutions regarding Iraq. (PL 107-243, emphasis added)

This "necessary and appropriate" clause seemed, in effect, to mean that Congress legislated away, at least for the time being, any authority it might have over the conduct of the war. As such, the Use of Force Resolution for the Iraq War typified Congress's ongoing acquiescence to presidential prerogatives in war powers.

Antiwar Democrats Take the Congress

The November 2006 elections ushered in a new era in Congress. After twelve years of Republican rule, broken up only by a year and a half of Democratic control of the Senate from mid-2001 to 2002, Democrats swept to victory.

Although analysts differed on the relative weight of various factors that influenced voters, most focused on two big ones: Republican scandals and the unpopular war continuing in Iraq. The Democratic majorities felt that they had a mandate from the American people to take the reins away from the president and draw down the American presence in an Iraqi conflict that Democrats asserted had degenerated into a civil war among various religious and regional factions that had spun out of control. The stage was set for a showdown.

First, in January 2007, just as the Democrats took over, the president snubbed his nose at them by announcing the start of a 30,000-troop *surge* in Iraq, a policy meant to secure more regions of the country that had been rife with violence. Instead of following the polls and scaling back American troop levels, he invoked his commander-in-chief power to increase American involvement.

In the immediate wake of the new policy, in early February 2007, President Bush submitted to Congress a request for supplemental appropriations for the current fiscal year to fund the ongoing wars in Iraq and Afghanistan. The Democratic majority in Congress believed that it had been presented with a clear opportunity: to use language in the supplemental appropriations bill to force the reduction of the number of combat forces deployed in Iraq over the next several months.

Agreeing on a provision for troop withdrawal proved far more difficult for the newly elected Democrats than they had anticipated. Despite the fact that they owed their majority in part to the public's desire to end the war, there were deep divisions within the party, especially in the House. A number of the newly elected Democrats were from traditionally Republican or marginal districts, and the party leadership was aware that, for them, voting against the war might translate into a short career in Congress. The majority of members of the Blue Dog Coalition (a group of forty-five moderate Democrats who usually coalesced around budget and national defense issues) was opposed to attempts to require the administration to withdraw troops. On the other end of the spectrum was the more numerous Out of Iraq Caucus, members of which, as their name suggested, advocated a quick end to the war.

Newly elected speaker Nancy Pelosi, who herself represented a liberal, antiwar constituency in San Francisco, was keenly aware of the challenges confronting her in balancing these interests in trying to craft a troop withdrawal provision. Despite the public's dissatisfaction with the war, opponents of troop reductions quickly portrayed any attempt to reduce the military forces as being a vote to abandon U.S. troops in the midst of a war.

In crafting a bill, the speaker had to hold on to moderates in the party with a less restrictive troop withdrawal provision, and at the same time keep antiwar members in the fold with something meaningful enough to gain their support. The challenge in passing a troop withdrawal provision was made more daunting by the slim margins by which the Democrats controlled the chambers—233–202 in the House and only 51–49 in the Senate. And even that 51–49 margin was misleading when it came to the war. Connecticut's Joe Lieberman had been reelected on an independent slate after losing the Democratic primary, and although he was a Democrat for most purposes (he voted with the party on organizational matters and attended the party caucus), the major point of contention in the election had been over his enthusiastic support of the president's war policies.

The initial version of the president's supplemental appropriations request, passed by the Appropriations Committee in the House in mid-March, set a binding deadline for troop withdrawals to begin by August 31, 2008. It also contained nearly $30 billion in additional spending over and above the president's request, about half of which was for Democratically sponsored domestic programs, which the leadership had included in order to secure the votes of wavering members. The White House indicated early on that the president would veto any bill that included any troop withdrawal language at all *or* additional unrelated spending above his request.

The bill passed the House in late March along a mostly party line vote, with fourteen Democrats voting opposed and only two Republicans in favor. The Senate version of the bill passed a few days later; that bill would have required the president to begin redeploying troops in the summer of 2007 and to withdraw them by March 31, 2008. The troop withdrawal provision, however, was only advisory and explicitly not binding. Senate majority leader Harry Reid was unable to muster the necessary Senate supermajority for any language stronger than that.

In the conference committee for the supplemental appropriation, House and Senate Democrats modified the troop withdrawal provisions. The new version would require the president to certify that, by July 21, 2007, Iraq was making sufficient progress toward satisfying a set of benchmarks (to move toward self-sufficiency and self-government) that the president had set forth earlier in the year as part of his troop surge strategy. If he determined that the benchmarks had been met, gradual troop withdrawal would begin in October, with a nonbinding goal of complete withdrawal by April 1, 2008. The bill also contained some $20 billion in spending above the president's request, about half of it for domestic programs, including money for recovery from Hurricane Katrina and for veterans' health care.

On May 1, 2007, President Bush vetoed HR 1591, the U.S. Troop Readiness, Veterans' Care, Katrina Recovery, and Iraq Accountability Appropriations Act, as he had promised. He stated that the bill was

> unconstitutional because it purports to direct the conduct of operations of war in a way that infringes upon the powers vested in the presidency by the Constitution, including as commander in chief of the Armed Forces.[38]

The president invited the congressional leadership to the White House the following day, but he made it clear that there would be no compromise on any troop withdrawal provisions. The following day the House voted in an effort to override the president's veto, but failed by a vote of 222–203—far short of the two-thirds needed.

After considerable further debate, the Democrats later that month offered up a bill that contained a watered-down version of the troop withdrawal provision, one that had in fact been drafted by a Republican, Virginia senator John Warner, a leading voice and authority on military affairs. The new bill dropped any timeline for troop withdrawals and instead included language that merely would tie the Iraqi reconstruction aid requested by the president to the issuance of administration reports on the government's progress toward certain benchmarks. Even with the absence of troop withdrawal language and pared-down domestic spending, the speaker was only able to secure passage of the bill in the House with a deft procedural move (described in Chapter 4) that split the bill, thereby allowing a majority of Democrats to oppose the war supplemental component and a majority of Republicans to oppose the domestic spending component.

The president signed the bill into law on May 25, 2007, nearly four months after he submitted his initial request.

The Democratic leadership pledged to continue to press the administration for a timeline for troop withdrawals. They believed strongly that, as casualties mounted and the public turned increasingly against the war and the surge policy, gradually more and more Republicans, fearing catastrophe in the 2008 electoral cycle, would see the writing on the wall and agree to a legislative timetable for troop reductions and withdrawal. Eventually, whether or not the president himself came around to this view, the Congress would act with a veto-proof majority to impose its policies.

Although a few more Republicans did begin to see things the Democrats' way, the Democratic leadership was never able to muster anything close to a veto-proof majority. The Senate spent a good bit of its summer of 2007 debating withdrawal provisions, but none were successful. The Congress, despite its seeming mandate from the 2006 elections, was unable to assert its war powers prerogatives through language in an appropriations bill or any other legislative vehicle.

Keep in mind, however, that even had Congress succeeded in getting something into law overriding a presidential veto, the president probably would have resisted, maintaining that the board's efforts to manage the conduct of the war violated his commander-in-chief power. This would have precipitated a historic constitutional confrontation.

Ultimately, though the Democrats' majorities in the chambers created the expectation that they could do something to affect the course of the war, the reality was
that they were unable to accomplish anything while President Bush remained in the
White House. And needless to say, the idea to simply cut off funding for the war by
refusing to pass an appropriation was not entertained. When thousands of Americans are in harm's way, it is almost unimaginable that any Congress would risk being
charged with deserting the troops.

In the realm of oversight, the Democrats were not much more effective. In several high-profile hearings, major Bush administration figures were put under the klieg
lights to explain and defend what Democrats regarded as failed policies. And numerous members of Congress made high-profile trips to the war zone to see for themselves whether progress was being made. In particular, there were three eagerly
awaited hearings with the top commander in Iraq, General David Petraeus. His reputation for straight shooting encouraged Democrats, who were looking to get a respected figure on the record expressing a pessimistic view of the prospects for the
troop surge and other Bush policies. Presumably this would give Republicans in Congress an opening to rethink their support of the surge. But Petraeus did not provide
Democrats with the fodder they needed, and eventually congressional committees
moved on to smaller-bore issues regarding contracting practices related to the war.

CONCLUSION: CONGRESS AND WAR
IN THE TWENTY-FIRST CENTURY

The relationship between the president and Congress was constitutionally established to invite struggle.[39] It was meant to give each political branch the leverage to
challenge the other's prerogatives in order to prevent either one from abusing its
power. For the most part, the relationship between the branches involves a shared
and relatively balanced exercise of power. Of course, the relationship has tensions
built into it. This normal relationship involves wrangling over the interpretation
and implementation of authorizing and appropriations laws, and it is not at all uncommon for disagreements to crop up about the level of meddling in agency affairs
that is appropriate for the legislative branch.

In the day-to-day relations between the board of directors and the government
agencies and the president, these tensions are almost always worked out in the political arena. Accommodations are reached that usually respect the prerogatives of
both the Congress and the executive. Because each side has a great deal of leverage,
each side has the means to protect those prerogatives. Only rarely do disagreements

rise to the level of court cases, and when they do, more often than not the federal judges refuse to get involved, forcing the branches to work things out. The sharing of power pertains in almost all areas of policy, whether in the domestic sphere or in the shaping of policy at the State Department and in the defense and intelligence areas. (We saw in Chapter 4 that Congress went so far as to reorganize the entire intelligence function of the government in 2004 through comprehensive legislation.)

In the limited but tremendously important cases of war powers and covert operations, however, the situation is entirely different. The Congress has been overtaken by the executive in recent decades. The idea that only Congress has the power to commit the nation to war seems to be a relic of the past. No war has been officially declared since 1942, and presidents feel that they do not need congressional approval to commit troops in potentially hostile regions or even to initiate the overthrow of a regime through covert operations. In fact, in 1973 Congress went so far as to give presidents blanket authorization to commit troops abroad for sixty days without its approval. A lot can be done with modern military technology in that period of time.

Most crucially, no president has accepted the constitutionality of that sixty-day time frame. The commander-in-chief power, together with other Article II provisions concerning foreign relations and the broader "executive power," gives the president (at least from his perspective) the permanent authority to use military force to protect or advance American interests. That power was always meant to include the presidential prerogative to repel imminent threats, especially when Congress is not in session. It may not originally have been meant to include the authority to commit the armed forces when there was opportunity for full-fledged congressional debate.

The presidential prerogative to use force without congressional approval evolved rapidly following World War II as a response to the Soviet threat. Now presidents claim the need to act swiftly. They are the only ones with full information and the ability to see the whole picture; the argument is that the nation's security in a dangerous world depends on nearly total deference to the president in determining threats to American interests.

Let us suppose that presidents are correct in claiming full authority to commit the nation to war stemming from the commander-in-chief power and other constitutional provisions. Their constitutional duty, then, is to use their best judgment in defining the vital interests of the nation and then using American military might if necessary to protect those interests. It is in the area of appropriations that the relationship between the branches has the potential for more contention, and even constitutional confrontation, as was noted in the section on the Iran-Contra Affair. Congress, for its part, has unchallenged control over the purse strings of the government. If the members of Congress, using their good judgment, refuse to pro-vide the funding for an operation or forbid the use of funds in a particular sphere, as was the case with the Boland Amendment, the president may be unable to do what he deems necessary.

No one said the Constitution was perfect. In the case of war powers, two consti-tutional prerogatives meet head on, and it is not clear what should happen. In a rel-atively minor venture, the president could probably move funds around to achieve his objectives (although lying about it to Congress could get him in trouble, as sev-eral members of the Reagan administration found out in the 1980s). If push came to shove in a more major military action, it might be that the power of the purse would win out. Of course, it is hard to imagine the Congress denying funds to sup-port an ongoing operation when troops are in harm's way. Politics invariably mili-tate in favor of supporting the troops.

———————

Congress has become almost a bit player in the decision to go to war. The members usually weigh in, but it is not clear that their advice is heeded or wanted by the com-mander in chief. The scale has tipped way over in the executive's direction. Having said that, going to war is still fundamentally a political decision. Although presi-dents claim the right to identify the national interest and to act to protect it, the les-son from history is that it is always better to have as many powerful people on your side as possible.

Presidents Johnson and Nixon failed to make an argument for the Vietnam War persuasive enough to keep the nation on their side, and they paid the price. As the war dragged on and opposition mounted, both were stymied in their efforts to pur-sue other policy goals. The Johnson administration was brought down as a result of his unpopular war policies (Johnson shocked the nation by choosing not to run for reelection in 1968); his proposals for ending poverty once and for all and creating the "Great Society" went down with it. Similarly, vehement opposition to Vietnam made it impossible for Nixon to achieve his ambitious goals on the domestic front, and his various efforts to quash that opposition indirectly led to the Watergate scan-dal and his forced resignation in 1974.

Even President Reagan paid a heavy price for unpopular, unilaterally pursued for-eign policy actions. In 1986 and into 1987, his popularity cratered as more infor-mation came out on the Iran-Contra Affair. He was faced with a crisis that led to the replacement of his chief of staff and much of his foreign policy team. His adminis-tration foundered for months before regaining its footing.

More recently, President George W. Bush's political standing took a hit from the deteriorating situation in Iraq, beginning in 2004. Although he maintained his policies with regard to the war, his political leverage in other areas of great interest to him, including entitlement and immigration reform, virtually disappeared. His party suffered badly at the polls both in 2006 and in 2008 because of it.

For political and practical reasons, presidents need support for their actions from Congress. Congress can make life very difficult for the chief executive. After all, members of Congress have a big megaphone. Hearings, press conferences, and other public displays affect public opinion and a president's standing. Congressional efforts to tie the president's hands in the conduct of war through appropriations limitations may rarely be successful, but they may also force the president off his game plan. At the very least, it may be impossible for the president to get more of what is needed to pursue his desired ends.

Also keep in mind that any major commitment of troops is likely to have wide-ranging economic, diplomatic, and other policy effects that will have to be addressed in legislation. Congressional prerogatives in most of these other areas are unquestioned. Again, the legislative branch's cooperation will be needed to further the president's objectives.

The alternative is to bring Congress—ideally both parties in Congress—into the consultative process from the beginning. Giving Congress a stake in the outcome of a foreign entanglement makes it a partner. In almost all areas of government policy, there is no choice: The president must share power with the Congress. With the war power, however, the question of whether or not to collaborate with Congress has become, in an important sense, a matter of choice for the president. As a practical consideration, fostering a trusting working relationship with Congress is the wiser course—in fact, it is just as important in the matter of war as in any other realm of policy. Four administrations in the last forty-five years have suffered grievous political wounds for their failure to do so.

QUESTIONS FOR DISCUSSION

1. No one doubts that the president can act unilaterally to commit troops to combat if the nation is under imminent threat. But when there is time for full debate, should Congress or the president have the right to decide whether to commit troops to battle? More generally, should Congress assert itself in the area of foreign policy and war powers? Why or why not?

2. Why do presidents seem regularly not to consult with Congress on matters pertaining to war, even though the failure to do so has led to severe political problems for several recent administrations?

3. What do you think would have happened if the Congress had successfully
   overridden President Bush's 2007 veto of the supplemental spending legislation
   that would have put in place a timetable for the withdrawal of troops from Iraq?
   Would the president have followed the law? What might have happened had he
   not done so?

SUGGESTIONS FOR FURTHER READING

Calabresi, Stephen G., and Christopher S. Yoo. 2008. *The Unitary Executive*. New
    Haven, CT: Yale University Press.
Fisher, Louis. 2004. *Presidential War Power*, 2nd ed. Lawrence: University Press of
    Kansas.
Goldsmith, Jack L. 2007. *The Terror Presidency*. New York: Norton.
Howell, William G., and Douglas L. Kriner. 2009. "Congress, the President, and the Iraq
    War's Domestic Political Front." In *Congress Reconsidered*, 9th ed., edited by Lawrence
    C. Dodd and Bruce I. Oppenheimer, pp. 311–336. Washington, DC: CQ Press.

NOTES

1. Quoted in Jeffrey F. Addicott, *Terrorism Law* (Tucson: Lawyers and Judges, 2004), pp. 347–348.

2. Ronald J. Ostrow, "Legal Experts Split over Bush's Power Policy: Talk of Launching an Offensive Against Iraq Sparks Questions About the Need for Congressional Approval," *Los Angeles Times*, November 13, 1990, p. A13.

3. See Robert Mann, *A Grand Delusion* (New York: Basic Books, 2002), ch. 34.

4. Robert C. Byrd, "Preserving Constitutional War Powers," *Mediterranean Quarterly* 14, no. 3 (2003): 2.

5. Louis Fisher, *Presidential War Power* (Lawrence: University Press of Kansas, 1995), p. 1, quoting Edwin B. Firmage, "War, Declaration of," in *Encyclopedia of the American Presidency*, edited by Leonard Levy and Louis Fisher (New York: Simon & Schuster, 1994), p. 1573.

6. Louis Fisher, *Presidential War Power*, 2nd ed., rev. (Lawrence: University Press of Kansas, 2004), pp. 2–3 (emphasis added).

7. Jennifer K. Elsea and Richard F. Grimmett, "CRS Report for Congress: Declarations of War and Authorizations for the Use of Military Force," Congressional Research Service, March 8, 2007, p. 1.

8. Kathryn L. Einspanier, "Burlamaqui, the Constitution, and the Imperfect War on Terror," *Georgetown Law Journal* 96, no. 3 (2008): 990.

9. For a range of sympathetic views, see David Gray Adler, Larry N. George, and Arthur Schlesinger Jr., *The Constitution and the Conduct of American Foreign Policy* (Lawrence: University Press of Kansas, 1996).

10. Arthur Schlesinger Jr., "Bush's Thousand Days," *Washington Post*, April 24, 2006, p. A17.

11. James Madison, *The Federalist Papers*, No. 58.

12. A useful discussion of this issue can be found in Noah Feldman and Samuel Issacharoff, "Declarative Sentences: Congress Has the Power to Make and End War—Not Manage It," slate.com, March 5, 2007, available at: http://www.slate.com/id/2161172/; and Robert McMahon, "Balance of War Powers: The U.S. President and Congress," Council on Foreign Relations, April 17, 2007, available at: http://www.cfr.org/publication/13092/balance_of_war_powers.html.

13. In the last couple of decades, an argument has been made in some quarters that Congress's power to declare war means that Congress has the power to recognize the existence of a war already in progress. The argument is that the commander-in-chief power and other Article II provisions were always meant to give the president the power to assess the international situation and commit the nation to war and to have Congress follow up with an official "declaration." Taking this position is Albert Jenner, "Fixing the War Powers Act," *Heritage Lectures*, no. 529 (May 22, 1995), available at: http://www.heritage.org/research/nationalsecurity/hl529.cfm.

14. David Gray Adler, "The Constitution and Presidential Warmaking: The Enduring Debate," *Political Science Quarterly* 103, no. 1 (1988): 1–36.

15. Quoted in Edward Keynes, *Undeclared War* (State College: Pennsylvania State University Press, 2004), p. 2.

16. Quoted in ibid.

17. John Yoo, *The Powers of War and Peace* (Chicago: University of Chicago Press, 2006).

18. See *United States v. Curtiss-Wright Export Corporation* (1936).

19. Quoted in Richard Benedetto, "Remember When Partisan Politics Stopped at the Water's Edge?" *USA Today*, November 18, 2005, available at: http://www.usatoday.com/news/opinion/columnist/benedetto/2005-11-18-benedetto_x.htm.

20. "Labor Decides to Mugwump It," *Time*, July 31, 1972.

21. Quoted in *The American Experience: The Presidents*, PBS special, available at: http://www.pbs.org/wgbh/amex/presidents/36_l_johnson/l_johnson_foreign.html.

22. Alfred Cumming, "Statutory Procedures Under Which Congress Is to Be Informed of U.S. Intelligence Activities, Including Covert Actions," Congressional Research Service, January 18, 2006.

23. Cumming, "Statutory Procedures Under Which Congress . . . ," pp. 7–8.

24. Fox Butterfield, "Casey Said to Have Failed to Follow Arms Rule," *New York Times*, April 3, 1987, available at: http://query.nytimes.com/gst/fullpage.html?res=9B0DE1D 6103DF930A35757C0A961948260.

25. The War Powers Act states that the sixty-day period begins when troops are introduced into "hostilities or into situations where imminent involvement in hostilities is clearly indicated by the circumstances." Bizarrely, the bill provides that the parliamentarian of the Senate, normally a lawyer with no necessary expertise in international or military law, must determine what constitutes "hostilities" or "imminent involvement in hostilities."

26. Presidents have also maintained that key provisions of the act constitute a legislative veto, which was declared unconstitutional in the 1983 *Chadha* ruling.

27. David Johnston, "Poindexter, Plain yet Puzzling Figure in Iran-Contra Affair, Goes on Trial Today," *New York Times*, March 5, 1990, available at: http://query.nytimes .com/gst/fullpage.html?res=9C0CEED91639F936A35750C0A966958260&sec=&spon=& pagewanted=all. For more detail, see Special Committee to Investigate the Iran-Contra Affair, "The Iran-Contra Report," November 18, 1987, available at: http://www.presidency .ucsb.edu/PS157/assignment%20files%20public/congressional%20report%20key%20 sections.htm.

28. George W. Bush, remarks of September 12, 2001, *Public Papers of the Presidents of the United States, 2001*, vol. 2 (Washington, DC: U.S. Government Printing Office, 2003), p. 1100.

29. Donald Wolfensberger, "Congress and Policymaking in an Age of Terrorism," in *Congress Reconsidered*, 8th ed., edited by Lawrence C. Dodd and Bruce I. Oppenheimer (Washington, DC: CQ Press, 2005), pp. 346–347.

30. George W. Bush, *Public Papers of the Presidents of the United States, 2001*, vol. 2 (Washington, DC: U.S. Government Printing Office, 2003), pp. 1124–1125.

31. Cited in Richard F. Grimmett, "CRS Report to Congress: The War Powers Resolution: After Thirty-Three Years," Congressional Research Service, updated May 1, 2007, p. 47.

32. Miles A. Pomper, "Bush Hopes to Avoid Battle with Congress over Iraq," *CQ Weekly*, August 31, 2002, p. 2252.

33. Quoted in David Rennie, "Cheney Call to Arms Against Saddam," *Telegraph*, August 27, 2002, available at: http://www.telegraph.co.uk/news/worldnews/middleeast/iraq/ 1405532/Cheney-call-to-arms-against-Saddam.html.

34. Pomper, "Bush Hopes to Avoid Battle with Congress over Iraq," pp. 2252–2254.

35. Jennifer Elsea and Richard Grimmett, "CRS Report to Congress: Declarations of War and Authorizations for the Use of Military Force: Historical Background and Legal Implication," Congressional Research Service, updated March 8, 2007, p. 19.

36. Cited in Grimmett, "CRS Report to Congress: The War Powers Resolution: After Thirty-Three Years," p. 48.

37. Elsea and Grimmett, "CRS Report to Congress: Declarations of War and Authorizations for the Use of Military Force," p. 20.

38. Quoted in Jennifer K. Elsea, Michael John Garcia, and Thomas J. Nicola, "CRS Report to Congress: Congressional Authority to Limit U.S. Military Operations in Iraq," Congressional Research Service, July 11, 2007, p. 1.

39. On the relationship between the branches in foreign policy, see Cecil Van Meter, *Invitation to Struggle: Congress, the President, and Foreign Policy*, 4th ed. (Washington, DC: CQ Press, 1992).

CHAPTER EIGHT

THE BOARD OF DIRECTORS
IN THE TWENTY-FIRST
CENTURY

The political institutions in a nation as dynamic and diverse as the United States reflect that dynamism and diversity and are ever-changing. This has been true throughout the sweep of American history.

Having said that, in many ways the board of directors of the U.S. government looks a lot like it did in the twentieth century and even, in many ways, like it did before that. As we learned in Chapter 2, the fundamental nature of Congress was established more than two hundred years ago in the Constitution, and very little in that document relevant to the Congress has been changed. As a result, the institution has in many ways stayed the same.

A lot of critics of the contemporary Congress wistfully recall the day when Congress was a problem-solving, productive, bipartisan, and downright chummy place. Usually they are thinking of a post–World War II "era of consensus" that existed some time from about the late 1940s to the mid-1960s. Most of the gauzy reminiscences of this era conspicuously leave out such events as Senator Joseph McCarthy's controversial efforts to root out Communists from the Army and the State Department (and his subsequent censure by the U.S. Senate); the intensely contentious debates over civil rights and the federal role in education and other areas; the hardball tactics used by President John Kennedy and Speaker of the House Sam Rayburn in 1961 to give the newly elected president even a slim chance to pass his top agenda items; the multiple filibusters in the Senate opposing basic equality for African Americans; and so on.

Congress is what it is: a rough-and-tumble, partisan place whose members search for advantage in order to serve their constituents and help their party gain or retain majority status. It's no use pretending it can be anything else. Understanding the Congress involves, first and perhaps most importantly, understanding its limitations.

The first section of this chapter covers those limitations, which can be summed up succinctly: The institution is inherently slow, parochial, and unable to plan. We have seen throughout the book (and review here) the impact of these characteristics on the lawmaking process.

But political institutions, as suggested, need to change as society changes in order to stay relevant. It is true that Congress's traits are not entirely determined by its fundamental nature; the environment has shaped the institution in important ways as well. The next section, "It's Not All 'Nature': The Environment Shapes the Contemporary Congress," summarizes the recent changes in the larger political environment that have had the greatest impact on the institution. Three that we have seen time and again throughout this book are particularly notable. First, the American party system (not part of the original "genome") underwent substantial changes in the latter decades of the twentieth century; because of this, Congress has become a much more leadership-controlled institution than it was even just twenty years ago. Second, members are pulled away from their role as the board of directors to attend to constituent and electoral matters more than they ever have been. And third, the tremendous increase in interest group activity has significantly changed the legislative environment for the board of directors.

The goal of this chapter, and the subject of the last section, is to answer the question: Can an institution set up like Congress work in the twenty-first century? At this writing, the United States is involved in two major wars, has an economy struggling to come out of a deep recession, and faces domestic budget challenges of unprecedented magnitude. It is an open question whether the board of directors is up to the task of addressing these challenges.

First, we need to look at how Congress has historically coped with, or tried to compensate for, its inherent limitations in order to maintain its relevance in a changing world. As we shall see, it has done so both by making internal efforts at reform and by looking outside the institution itself. The members' implicit and sometimes explicit recognition of the institution's limitations has often led it to employ flexible approaches to pressing issues.

The chapter wraps up by taking a therapeutic approach: identifying the ways in which the institution is failing to meet its responsibilities as a board of directors of the federal government and diagnosing the root causes of those failings. The road to better health for the institution can only come after this sort of analysis.

It turns out that, in the twenty-first century, the board in fact fails to meet its responsibilities in all three areas that are the focus of this book. Authorizing bills are not updated on schedule, the budget process has broken down some years and is almost never completed on time, and oversight is done with less rigor than in the past. What are the causes of these deficiencies?

One cause is the heightened partisanship in the Congress. Sharp partisan differences are not by any means an entirely bad thing. When political parties offer clear, principled choices to the voters on the major issues of the day, the effects can be salutary. The middle-of-the-road approach is not always the right one for every problem that policymakers and the nation face. But having said that, and considering the particulars of the legislative process as described in this book, the level of partisan polarization in the system today does have potentially disabling consequences. What does Congress need to do to avoid partisanship that paralyzes? Are there any models out there that offer hope?

The second and even more serious and thoroughgoing problem facing the Congress is the imbalance that has developed between members' legislative and representative roles. Being an effective board of directors takes time—time to hold hearings and otherwise evaluate how agencies are carrying out programs, time to develop authorizing and appropriations bills that enable executive branch officials to do their jobs in the interest of the American people, and time to take a thoughtful look at the more intractable long-term problems facing the nation. Unfortunately, members are compelled by larger forces to spend more of their scarce time on constituent meetings and, especially, fund-raising and other activities associated with campaigning. The result: Much less time has been spent in recent years on legislative and oversight business just as the problems facing the government have necessitated more of the sustained attention of the members. Politicians' ability to take steps in the direction of righting that imbalance will go a long way toward determining how effective an institution Congress will be in the twenty-first century.

CONGRESS'S INHERENT LIMITATIONS

Understanding the Congress is to a significant degree a matter of understanding the consequences of what is imprinted on the institution's genome. The Framers of the Constitution did not work from an efficiency model in developing the branches of government. They wanted a government that would put into law (Congress's job) and carry out (the job of the executive branch agencies) good public policy. But their primary concern was establishing a republic that would have built-in safeguards against the abuse of power. Protecting the liberties of the people was job one in their eyes.

The political scientist James Sundquist says that Congress is by its very nature slow, parochial, and unable to plan.[1] Left to its own devices, the institution tends toward inaction, is more likely to legislate in the service of state and local concerns than national ones, and has a great deal of difficulty pursuing an agenda in a concerted and systematic way.

Speaking to the first point, the legislative process is by its nature plodding. A good lawmaking process is a thorough one; the work of the experts on the committees and the subcommittees necessarily takes time. Speed and efficiency usually come at the cost of thoroughness. A hastily considered bill is usually one that needs to be revisited before long.

On complex legislation, often more than one committee in each chamber weighs in with hearings and markups. The requirement that a bill, in order to be passed, must be approved, in identical form, by two chambers with profoundly different perspectives—stemming from different term lengths and different types of constituencies—throws another wrench in the works. Time-consuming effort is required to forge the compromises necessary to win enough votes in both chambers to pass the final version of a bill.

In addition, government programs ordinarily necessitate both an authorization in law and a subsequent appropriation to be put into operation. Congress has, in effect, divided the process of thinking through what should be done (the authorization process) from the funding (the appropriations process) of the actual activity. Because that funding decision—made annually for most programs—is often affected by each year's new budgetary circumstances, it can be harder to fund certain activities up to the authorized level.

No discussion of the deliberate nature of the legislative process can proceed without focusing on the Senate. The Senate was created by "the Great Compromise" to give every state equal representation. Senators have always taken that equality principle very seriously. Each and every one values the numerous prerogatives they have in Senate procedure to defend and advance the interests of their state. The chamber has always tended to move very deliberately, providing the brake to the House of Representatives' accelerator.

As a practical matter, Senate rules afford every senator the ability to bring the chamber to a halt for at least a few days, and supermajorities are usually needed to pass significant legislation. (The House runs on an almost purely majority-rule principle, which enables its leadership, assuming they have the votes, to move legislation on a very swift timetable. The concerns of the minority simply do not always have to be taken into account.) Savvy senators know how to use every prerogative to their advantage. One Capitol Hill reporter says that Senator Mary Landrieu of Louisiana is particularly adroit at stalling Senate action to her advantage. Her strategy is to wait until a holiday is coming up, when senators head back to their home state for an extended period of time—maybe one or two weeks or even more. As the holiday approaches and senators are getting anxious about making their flights, she objects to consideration of a crucial bill—in effect placing a hold on the business of the Senate. The process to break that hold may take days if she utilizes every avenue available to her. Senate leadership is forced to consider her immediate needs if they want to move the important bill.[2] These needs usually involve funding for infrastructure in her state.

There is another reason Congress fails to act swiftly (and sometimes fails to act at all): It is often more advantageous to keep an issue alive than to resolve it with decisive legislative action. In short, winning a legislative battle is not always good politics. Congress's *failure* to pass a constitutional amendment banning gay marriage keeps a useful issue alive for Republicans in the next election cycle. Similarly, Congress's *failure* to forge a compromise on raising the minimum wage enables Democrats to keep an issue they can exploit on the agenda for the next campaign.

A good example of legislative success coming at a political cost occurred in the summer of 1996. As described in Chapter 4, that year congressional Republicans spearheaded the passage of welfare reform legislation, which ended no-strings-attached government payments to poor single mothers. Republicans had for years been able to capitalize on Democrats' support of the program, charging them with providing a steady stream of taxpayer money to people who were doing nothing to get out of poverty.[3] In some areas of the country, the issue was a linchpin of successful GOP campaigns. Fixing the program (forcing recipients to take steps toward finding jobs or eventually be cut off) had the political effect of taking a very useful issue off the table.

Having said all this, it is certainly not impossible for Congress to move with alacrity, even on major items. It *can*, at times, move expeditiously.

Crisis conditions sometimes drive the board of directors to move bills rapidly, short-circuiting much of the process, especially the committee deliberations that are so crucial to bringing expertise to bear on the issues. In March and April 1933, Congress passed in short order several major bills that created new agencies and dozens of new programs, at the behest of President Franklin Roosevelt, in an attempt to deal with the worsening Great Depression. In many cases no hearings were held, and the bills themselves were mere outlines.

After the September 11, 2001, attacks on the homeland, Congress moved very quickly to authorize military action and give the president enhanced law enforcement tools with the so-called PATRIOT Act. Essentially the president got all the tools he wanted to counter terrorism in the United States. Congress had second thoughts and rescinded some of the more controversial provisions in 2006.

In 2009, President Obama, citing the deepening recession and the urgent need to get more money into the economy to generate jobs and spending, persuaded the Congress to pass the $787 billion American Recovery and Reinvestment Act (ARRA). Just four weeks into his administration, the bill was ready for his signature. It represented more overall stimulus, in the form of mostly domestic spending and tax cuts, than any other legislation since at least World War II.[4]

Quick action comes at a cost. Invariably the normal deliberative process is short-circuited—there are few or no hearings, little careful consideration is given at the subcommittee or even committee level, and sometimes even floor debate is sharply limited. (Members had virtually no opportunity to amend the 2009 ARRA.) Decisions made in haste do not always stand up well to the test of time. The creation of the Department of Homeland Security in 2002 involved relatively little deliberation considering the scope of the task of bringing twenty-two disparate agencies together into a coherent whole. The new department has had to be reorganized many times in the years since its establishment. Box 8.1 provides another example of hasty decision-making that led to potentially unintended consequences: the establishment of the Troubled Asset Relief Program (TARP) in the Emergency Economic Stabilization Act, passed after the near-collapse of the financial system in September 2008.

The second of Congress's immutable traits, related to its representative role, is its parochialism. This is another way of saying that members of Congress look after their own. The members are elected by the people in discrete districts and states—Congress was created to represent us where we live, not just as a nation. Voters have always held representatives and senators accountable for how well they are able to address constituent needs. As we have seen, it is this principle of accountability that is the bedrock of a republican system of government. The idea is that people in power are less likely to abuse their authority if they have to stand for election on a regular and frequent basis.

One cannot overstate the importance of the constituency connection for members of Congress. Nearly everything the board of directors does in carrying out its lawmaking and oversight powers is influenced by the local and state perspective. The political scientist Garry Young puts it this way: There is a certain grain to the policymaking tendencies of Congress, and as with cutting a piece of wood, going with that grain is a lot easier than going against it.[5] What he means is that legislation that addresses particular local and state concerns stands a better chance of passing than legislation that does not.

A federal education program that guarantees funding for every congressional district is much more likely to pass than one that sends taxpayer money only to needy areas. The second program may be more defensible from a policy standpoint on the grounds that it saves taxpayers money by focusing resources where they are needed the most, but the first is the more likely legislative success story because every member would see a benefit for his or her district or state.

When Congress was contemplating the distribution of homeland security funding for states in the aftermath of the September 11, 2001, attacks, proposals that "shortchanged" sparsely populated states based on threat assessments (some government assessments recommended pouring funds into the big cities and other likely targets) were attacked by small-state senators who wanted their first responders to receive a good share of federal funds.[6] It goes without saying that senators from Alaska, Wyoming, and other states not high on the threat assessment list made sure their states got what they viewed as a fair shake.

The committee system in Congress, set up to provide for specialization and policy analysis, in many ways tends to reinforce the parochial perspective of the membership. Although members get on committees for all kinds of reasons—power within the chamber, policy interests, ideology—early in their careers they do everything they can to secure an assignment on a committee that addresses the economic needs of their constituents. Farm state senator John Thune (R-SD) pulled out all the stops to make sure he got on the Agriculture Committee; Susan Davis's (D-CA) first job after getting elected in 2000 was to persuade her party's Steering Committee that she needed a slot on the Armed Services Committee to address the needs of the thousands of Navy families in her San Diego–based district.

It should be noted that the often-reviled but undeniably influential "special interest groups" are most effective when they can demonstrate to members of Congress the local impact of their agenda. If jobs are at stake or numerous constituents are mobilized, the group, whether it is an advocacy organization, a local government, or a corporate concern, is much more likely to get what it wants.

The Obama administration's efforts in 2009 to scale back some of the big-ticket weapons systems that were developed decades ago to counter the Soviet threat ran into vigorous opposition for just this reason. A single weapon system or fighter jet is likely to be manufactured in numerous states (the F-22 fighter jet has component parts made in forty-four states) and sometimes hundreds of congressional districts;

scaling back production can cost thousands of jobs. Former Office of Management and Budget official Gordon Adams says, "The thing about weapons and bases is they are backyard issues for members of Congress. It's not like foreign aid. It's about contracts in my district, contributors to my campaign, things that directly affect my prospects of staying in office and my ability to say to my constituents, 'I got one for you!'"[7]

Third, Congress is unable to plan. The very cumbersomeness of the legislative process makes planning by the Congress problematic. It is very difficult to follow through on a concerted agenda when there are so many veto points in the path of a bill. Legislation can be stalled in committees and subcommittees by clever members

---

BOX 8.1
CONGRESS ACTS FAST: THE BAILOUT
OF THE U.S. FINANCIAL SYSTEM

Financial markets in the United States and around the world face a dire emergency requiring urgent and decisive action. Some key parts of the credit market are on the verge of gridlock, resulting not just in the collapse of major financial institutions but also in credit disruption that is severely weakening the long-term prospects of non-financial companies. And while this is currently most visible in Wall Street and in the financial sector, it is only a matter of time before the fallout hits Main Street, with potentially devastating economic effects for typical American households.*

This was the diagnosis of the Heritage Foundation. The memo, written by Stuart Butler and Edwin Meese III, went on to support the aggressive intervention in the crisis proposed by the Bush administration's Treasury Department. Normally a conservative, market-oriented think tank, the Heritage Foundation lined up with many liberals in support of immediate and comprehensive legislation. The proposal would give unprecedented powers to the Treasury Department to spend up to $700 billion buying up "toxic" debt owned by the major financial institutions.

Although the so-called Emergency Economic Stabilization Act of 2008 was passed into law on October 3, 2008, only about two weeks after the administration proposal was put forth, the road to final passage was not an easy one.

On September 28, the House rejected the Treasury plan by a vote of 228–205, even though members were warned by the president, presidential candidates Barack Obama and John McCain, and most of the congressional leadership that

in opposition. Interest groups watch Congress's mostly open deliberations very carefully and have often successfully waylaid seemingly popular measures by waging extensive campaigns to drum up a public outcry. Senators can put holds on legislation to gum up the process.

Ultimately, Congress, when viewed as a single entity, cannot plan *because it is not actually a single entity.* Time and again we return to the institution's bicameral nature. Even if leadership can make one or the other chamber work efficiently (usually the House), there is no guarantee that the other chamber will go along. The chambers were formed, by design, with different interests and needs. It is rare that the two will see eye to eye on major legislation and move in a swift and timely manner. The

---

immediate action was imperative to avoid an economic meltdown. Speaker Nancy Pelosi's strongly worded speech on the House floor blaming Republicans for the economic mess did not help matters, but opposition was strong even among some in her party. Many Democrats objected to bailing out major financial institutions when people in Middle America were hurting. Some Republicans objected to such a blatant betrayal of free market principles. Ultimately the issue turned into a political football, with major divisions within the Republican membership of the House sinking the effort.

The Senate saved the legislation. A bipartisan group of senators worked long hours in consultation with Treasury secretary Henry Paulson and House leadership, crafting a bill with enough sweeteners—tax breaks for small businesses and for some in the middle class, as well as a change in the cap on federal insurance for bank deposits—to find sufficient support in both chambers.

But hastily formed legislation of this magnitude is bound to have its flaws. In little more than one month, institutions that had received financial support were criticized sharply for using their new funds in ways that contravened the purpose of the bailout legislation. And the Treasury Department had exploited a gray area in the legislation by putting in place a change in tax law that many experts believed was actually illegal and that resulted in a huge windfall for banks.[†]

* Stuart M. Butler and Edwin Meese III, "The Bailout Package: Vital and Acceptable," Heritage Foundation, WebMemo 2091, September 29, 2008, available at: www.heritage.org/Research/Economy/wm2091.cfm.
† Amit R. Paley, "A Quiet Windfall for U.S. Banks," *Washington Post*, November 10, 2008, p. A1.

fact is that the Congress does not have the equivalent of a central nervous system. Our bodies have the capacity to coordinate the left and right sides, making it possible for us to hit a softball or juggle, but Congress's two sides have only ad hoc means to forge compromises. These days conference committees have fallen out of favor, and instead the leadership of the two chambers, usually in conjunction with White House negotiators, work informally to cobble together agreements on many major pieces of legislation. These efforts require a great deal of heavy lifting and as a result do not always bear fruit.

Newt Gingrich learned this the hard way. When he became speaker of the House after the stunning landslide Republican takeover of Congress in the 1994 elections, he assumed that, by a massive show of political, oratorical, and legislative force, he could dominate the whole Congress, building so much popular support for his programs that the Republican-controlled Senate and even the Democratic president would be forced to sign on to it. He moved swiftly on the ten-point "Contract with America" agenda, passing nine of the ten agenda items in fewer than one hundred days. (The only item that did not muster sufficient support was the effort to impose term limits on Congress by constitutional amendment, which requires a two-thirds vote.) Many of the bills garnered large majorities that included dozens of Democrats. But then there was the Senate. Most of the "Contract" items either were delayed or altered substantially there; the majority did not make it into law at all. In addition, the president was able to sustain a veto on one item. The lesson was clear: A bicameral legislature arranged like ours puts nearly insuperable obstacles in the way of the implementation of a concerted congressional agenda even under extraordinary circumstances.

The upshot is that the branch of the federal government that the Framers saw as the most important is constitutionally slow, narrowly focused, and unable to plan. But what if a crisis requires decisive action? Sometimes complex, major issues must be resolved in the interest of the whole nation. What then? What if there *must be* a plan? How does the board of directors respond? We get to these questions later, but first we look at some of the ways in which the environment has changed the Congress and how it conducts its business directing the work of government.

IT'S NOT ALL "NATURE": THE ENVIRONMENT SHAPES THE CONTEMPORARY CONGRESS

As suggested at the beginning of the chapter, political institutions in a dynamic society change, sometimes in significant ways, over time. Congress's essential characteristics are set in certain respects—as discussed in the previous section—but the full story is not all about "nature." "Nurture" also plays an important role in forming the traits of the institution. Assessing the board of directors in the twenty-first century requires looking at recent changes in the political landscape that have shaped the contemporary Congress. We begin with the changes in the party system, and then we look at the changing electoral and constituent pressures that members of Congress face in their representative role. We finish with a discussion of the effect of the explosion of interest group activity in Washington on the work of the board of directors.

A More Partisan Place

The political party system was not envisioned by the Framers of the Constitution, although something resembling a party system developed not too long after the founding period. In the nineteenth century, Congress began to organize much of its business along party lines, to the point where the parties eventually were officially recognized in the rules of the House and Senate. And as developed in Chapter 2, today parties are in charge of committee assignments and the development of the legislative agenda in the two chambers. As such, the party system is the most important non-inherent characteristic of the institution.

The journalistic and "inside-the-beltway" conventional wisdom is that over the last thirty years Congress and American politics in general have become much more divided along party lines than they had been. In fact, there is little doubt that the two parties in Congress have become more polarized. Political scientists point to various ways to measure this phenomenon. Data show that members of Congress are more likely to vote with the majority of their party on the floor of the House or Senate today than they were twenty, thirty, or forty years ago.[8] Also, the voting behavior of members of the two parties in Congress has become more liberal on the Democratic side and more conservative on the Republican side. There is less ideological variation within the parties than there was several decades ago.[9]

A Short History of the Parties

The key factors leading to the increased ideological homogeneity within the congressional delegations of the Democratic and Republican Parties were the rise of polarizing social issues in the middle decades of the twentieth century and the consequent change in the makeup of the party coalitions. The evolution of the two parties' coalitions, particularly in the last forty years or so, has gone unmistakably in the direction of what is called *ideological sorting*. A short history lesson is required to understand exactly what has happened.

The Democratic Party's history goes further back than the Republicans' (even though the Republican Party is often called the Grand Old Party, or GOP). Democrats trace their lineage to Thomas Jefferson and Andrew Jackson. In fact, most state parties still have Jefferson-Jackson dinners to bring supporters together for fund-raising and other purposes. The party was rooted in two principles: promoting the cause of the working man (originally thought of as a small farmer or tradesman) and permitting states to have control over their domestic affairs free of federal interference, sometimes called *states' rights*.

In the South (the eleven states that were part of the Confederacy, sometimes expanded to include border states such as Kentucky, Oklahoma, and Missouri), the Democratic Party became the political force behind slavery, and after slavery was abolished, it became the force behind the segregated system of legal apartheid dividing the races that lasted from its start in the 1880s and 1890s until the civil rights movement overturned it in the mid-1960s. Southern Democrats tended to hold very conservative positions across the board, and not just on racial issues: They were pro-defense, anti-union, and generally opposed to federal intervention in local affairs.

In other parts of the country, the Democrats evolved very differently as the twentieth century progressed. State and local party units in the industrial North and Midwest were very likely to be pro-union and very strongly in favor of a range of government services. In some major cities—Chicago, for example—the party was instrumental in assimilating masses of immigrants from Poland, Ireland, and other European countries. In some places, American blacks played a role in the party machines. With Catholics and Jews often serving in important leadership roles, Democrats in some parts of the country were diverse, especially as compared to the overwhelmingly white and Protestant southern members of the party.

The party held together despite its profound differences at the state level because of the shared belief that, in the end, states should run their own affairs. The party had some tumultuous conventions in the late 1890s and into the 1920s because of the widely varying views of the different state parties, but as long as the more liberal members of the party did not meddle with the South's settled segregationist system, accommodations could usually be reached.

Things began to get trickier in the 1930s when a Democrat—in fact, a big-government, pro-union liberal, Franklin Roosevelt—dramatically expanded the reach of the federal government into states' affairs. This was a change that many leading southern Democrats had feared, as they believed it would be the first step toward the federal government trying again to desegregate the region—an effort that had failed, as undertaken by Republicans, after the Civil War. But Roosevelt was very careful not to get into the internal affairs of southern states when it came to race relations. He had won all those states easily, but he knew that meddling in racial matters might well cost him and his party at the ballot box in future elections.

What had developed in the first several decades of the twentieth century was a Democratic Party at the congressional level that had some of the most liberal people in the Congress—followers of Roosevelt who supported an expanded federal role— and some of the most conservative—most of the 125 or so southern Democrats in the House and Senate who were strict segregationists and suspicious of the federal government.

Republicans, for their part, also have a mixed ideological heritage. The party was formed in the 1850s from the remnants of the disintegrating Whig Party and various social movements and smaller parties. The driving force was opposition to slavery— or at least opposition to its spread to the territories and new states. The various fragments of smaller parties and movements that formed the Republican Party were favorably disposed toward a stronger central government to achieve their ends. More broadly, many Republicans also supported federal action in the service of promoting a better business environment for American industry.

With the successful prosecution of the Civil War by Republican president Abraham Lincoln, the party was dominant and intent on enforcing its views on the formerly Confederate states. This initially took the form of a military occupation of the South; eventually, after the occupation was ended in 1877, the party acted on its interest in securing the rights of the freedmen in the region. The party in Congress wished to use the federal government as an instrument for social change in the recently occupied areas. But the white South—represented by the Democrats— resisted. And it won out. The generation of so-called Radical Republicans who were willing to fight for civil rights for newly freed slaves and other black Americans either became weary from the struggle or passed on. They were gradually replaced by other Republicans who, while sometimes liberal on questions of social equality, were more interested in using government in less controversial ways, mainly to promote business.

By the middle of the twentieth century, the party was characterized by a similar if somewhat scaled-down version of the schism within the Democratic Party. The Republican Party included some very liberal members in the Northeast and parts of the Midwest (so-called Progressives) who wanted to see the federal government do much more than just protect and encourage industry, as well as some members in the Midwest and the growing West who advocated a laissez-faire approach to the economy— lower taxes and a smaller government. Although Republicans in midcentury had no pro-segregation wing to speak of, they did have large internal differences on the role of government in addressing social problems, including racial injustice, and regulating the economy; consequently, by this time, Republican members in Congress spanned the political spectrum.

In the 1950s and into the 1960s, Congress had many contentious debates on the major issues of the day, including the role of the federal government in education and in regulating the economy and the status of civil rights for African Americans. But these debates typically did not break neatly along party lines. Both parties had lots of people on both sides of these and other major issues. Each party had both strong conservatives and strong liberals. The coalitions in support of this or that specific policy shifted constantly as a result. The Congress and the country were polarized on many important questions, but that polarization was not principally along party lines.

The Sorting Begins

There are disagreements on exactly when the change that resulted in the more ideologically consistent, polarized parties of today began in earnest, but most people point to some time in the 1960s. The decisive year was probably 1964, during which:

1. Lyndon Johnson, a Democratic president—and a southern one at that (he was from Texas)—put his considerable political capital and skills behind the Civil Rights Act, legislation that would end once and for all legal segregation in the South. He told aides privately that, by supporting this bill, he had lost the South for the Democratic Party for a generation. (As it turned out, he underestimated the length of time.)

2. The Democratic Party, traditionally the party of states' rights, moved for the first time as a national party at its national convention to penalize a state party for refusing to seat an African American in its delegation. (The all-white Mississippi delegation was challenged by a rump group, the Mississippi Freedom Democratic Party, which protested the segregation policies of the state party.) This was a crucial break from past practice. Up until that time, the party had heeded each state's right to choose freely its own delegation without national interference.

3. The Republicans nominated a resolutely small-government, anti–New Deal, pro–states' rights conservative for president, Senator Barry Goldwater of Arizona.

The result of these events was that the national Democratic Party moved unmistakably in the liberal direction, upstaging the conservative wing of the party at the convention and in the Congress. Conversely, the Republican Party went full force

TABLE 8.1   *Ideological Sorting of the Parties on Major Issues*

	PRE-1964	POST-1964
Democrats	Party split, with southern Democrats opposed to desegregation and often resistant to government regulation of the economy; the rest of the party tended to be pro–civil rights, pro-union, and in favor of government regulation.	Party becomes increasingly uniform in support of affirmative action, liberal on other social issues, and in favor of government regulation and social programs.
Republicans	Party split, with largely northeastern faction for desegregation and favorably disposed to government regulation of the economy; the rest of the party was more likely to oppose government regulation and was mixed on the question of desegregation.	Party becomes increasingly uniform, with conservative positions on social issues and in opposition to more taxes, government regulations, and social programs.

against its liberal elements by nominating a rock-ribbed anti–federal intervention conservative for president. These changes proved lasting. Ever since, at the national level in presidential campaigns, Democrats have been pro–civil rights, liberal on social issues (abortion, the rights of the accused, gay rights, and so on), and strongly in favor of government intervention in the economy. Successful Republicans at the national level have opposed affirmative action and forced integration, attempts to liberalize on social issues, and any increased federal role in the economy. Table 8.1 depicts these changes in the two parties.

It took some time, however, for these developments to filter down below the presidential level. At the congressional level, it is hard to defeat an incumbent, and voters are not necessarily tied to party labels as long as their representative is attuned to and delivers for the district. In some of the most conservative parts of the South, amazingly enough, there were hardly any qualified Republicans available to run for House seats or even Senate seats in the 1960s and even into the 1980s. In fact, in the 1980s, while the South was stronger than any region for the Republican presidential candidates (Ronald Reagan in 1984 and George H. W. Bush in 1988), it remained the strongest for the Democrats in the House of Representatives.

Similarly, many liberal Republicans remained in Congress, especially from the Northeast. Many southern Democrats were far more conservative than their presidential candidates (and would not campaign with them), and most northeastern congressional Republicans were far more liberal than their presidential candidates.

Having said that, these gradual changes were leading to what would soon be change on a grander scale. The 1994 elections were the tipping point in the South. Moderate or conservative southern Democrats were replaced in large numbers by conservative southern Republicans in the House and Senate. (Some conservative Democrats who survived that year switched parties to become Republicans.) As a result, the Democrats became a much more uniformly liberal party in Congress in short order. In 2006 and 2008, Republicans lost the bulk of what remained of their northeastern liberals and moderates, leaving the party more uniformly conservative in Congress than it had ever been. The *New York Times* described moderate Republicans at that time as "an endangered species."[10] (The 2008 election left the GOP with no representation in the House in all of New England.) Now the vast majority of members line up with their party on most issues of the day.

As noted earlier, Congress has always had contentious issue debates. The difference in the modern era is that these debates split the Congress along party lines. The Congress has long been *organized* along party lines; now the party in control is in a much better position to use its power in an attempt to pursue an ideological agenda. When the parties were more ideologically diverse, the party leaders could not do that. The imperative on most issues in those days was to build cross-party coalitions.

The other factor that has contributed to bitter partisanship in this era is the narrowness of the margins between the parties in the two chambers for most of the time since 1994. Every election cycle, both parties have believed that they have a fighting chance to take over one or both of the chambers, or at least close the gap considerably.[11]

It was not always so. For most of the period from 1958 to 1994, Democrats had commanding majorities in the House. By the mid-1960s, Republicans had become resigned to the fact that they were unlikely to take back the chamber anytime soon. This was often the case in the Senate as well, although the 1980 surprise takeover of the Senate by the Republicans changed that thinking.

Republican resignation to minority status in those days led them to a more accommodating stance. They felt their interests were best served by attempting to work with Democrats and helping to smooth Democrats' interactions with Republican administrations in exchange for help with projects for their districts and certain concessions on major legislation. Democrats were open to this, as it is always easier to pass legislation, especially in the Senate, when it is presented in a bipartisan way. Relations between the leadership of the two parties at the time were characterized by a spirit of relative comity.

Close margins change the calculus in the Congress. When your party's hold on power is precarious, you are much less likely to help members of the minority; you do not want them to be able to return to their districts or states touting legislative accomplishments. The minority, for its part, tends not to cooperate to help the majority with its agenda items. Minority members do not want majority members to have legislative accomplishments to run on. A "do-nothing" Congress puts the minority in a stronger relative political position for the next electoral cycle.

The 2008 elections changed the calculus a little bit. Democrats came away with large majorities in both the House and Senate—securing a 257–178 margin in the House and a 58–41 margin in the Senate. Republicans seemed less likely to be able to retake the majority in a single election cycle. Still, the parties remain ideologically homogeneous for the most part, and the partisan atmosphere remains highly charged.

The ideological sorting of the parties means that clear partisan divisions are here to stay for the foreseeable future. The effect of this change in the party system on the Congress almost cannot be exaggerated. When the two sides have very different views on the major issues of the day, the odds for cooperation and comity go down. And sometimes, even when there can be a meeting of the minds across party lines, members of the minority party choose not to cooperate for fear of assisting the majority party's electoral prospects.

Party Leadership Ascendant

As the parties sorted themselves out ideologically in the 1960s and 1970s, Congress—particularly Democrats in the House—implemented rules changes that had the potential to enhance the power of party leaders. By the mid-1990s, a sea change had occurred in the way Congress went about its business directing the work of government.

In some ways this new system resembled the one that existed in the late nineteenth and early twentieth centuries, when party leaders often were able to exert their will, controlling the agenda of the House and sometimes even the Senate. The leadership in those days ran roughshod over the prerogatives of the committees and the whims of rank-and-file members.

Eventually this heavy-handed control proved too much for many members. Such a system restricted their freedom and control over the issues that mattered to them. Many found themselves in regular disagreement with their leadership and chafed at having to kowtow to those leaders in order to secure good committee assignments and chairmanships. By about 1920, a system that rewarded seniority and insulated committees from outside pressures from the caucus or the leadership had developed, and this system would flourish throughout the middle decades of the twentieth century.

Democratic reformers in the late 1960s and early 1970s wanted to change all that. They felt that the party in power should be able to pursue an ideologically coherent, party-based agenda and not be hamstrung by the whims of a few senior members who chaired committees and who were out of step with the caucus. At the time the reformers were targeting the conservative southerners in their midst, whom the majority of the party saw as thwarting the will of the people. Leadership was given the tools to make the House work the majority's will, especially by giving the speaker control of the Rules Committee and the caucus the power to ignore seniority in picking committee chairs. But change happened slowly. Democratic leaders in the 1970s until the early 1990s were not always assertive in the use of their newfound powers.

As we saw in Chapter 4, it was the Republican leadership in the House that took full advantage of the 1970s-era rules changes after the Republican Revolution of 1994.[12] For most of its twelve-year reign, the leadership had its way on the floor, where it controlled the agenda, and in naming committee chairs. Democratic speaker Pelosi followed up in the 110th Congress by taking full control of the agenda; she was unable, however, to dictate committee chair positions.

Even in the Senate, the party leaders on both sides have been more active. They have often asserted themselves in negotiations over legislation in ways that would have been unthinkable a generation ago, and they have been active in managing message and public relations. For the most part, however, the Senate is still tradition-bound. Leadership cannot move an agenda the way it is done in the House, and the seniority system still determines the selection of committee chairs. Change moves at a glacial pace in the U.S. Senate.

In many respects, the rank and file have acquiesced in the accretion of power by party leaders. Members are well aware of the stakes in each upcoming electoral cycle. Losing the majority means losing control of the distribution of federal funds and the agenda more broadly; conversely, for the minority, gaining control comes with those valuable perks. The rank and file have been willing, in both parties, to give up some prerogatives at the committee and subcommittee levels in order to further the broader aims of their party. The mantra is to stay on message, do not help the other side, and stick with the party on legislation if at all possible. Someone has to manage this process, and it makes sense to give elected leadership that authority.

What has developed is a much more tightly managed legislative process—tightly managed by the leadership. As Barbara Sinclair says, and as we saw in Chapter 4, "unorthodox lawmaking" has become the norm.[13] If the regular process—major legislation being examined in one or more committees and subcommittees by dozens of members—is too slow or yields an unacceptable result, the leadership steps in to engineer a solution more friendly to the majority party. This may involve skipping stages on the "how a bill becomes a law" chart and including only a relatively few members in the discussions (and often few if any minority party members). The regular process can be too messy and fraught with too much uncertainty.

Many members, and certainly the leadership, believe that the old ways are not suited to the modern media environment. Congress is a complex and confusing place that too often moves slowly. Someone needs to try to streamline it and translate it to the new media. The leadership takes on this task.

The resurgence of leadership and the resultant use of unorthodox lawmaking are in large part products of the increase in partisanship in congressional politics and in American politics more broadly. Leaders are granted the power to assert themselves when members understand that the fate of their party is at stake.

Electoral Pressures

A politician running for office one hundred or more years ago took a very different approach from the way politicians run today—and the process was nowhere near as taxing or as time-consuming. Nominations for office were controlled by local and state party leaders. Any potential candidate for Congress had to have had inside connections, usually gained by having been active in party politics. The party organizations would also normally take care of most of the business of running the general election for their candidates.

But this began to change in the first few decades of the twentieth century with the advent of primary elections as a means to choose nominees for the parties. Increasingly candidates for office might have to win two elections—the primary and the general—in order to gain a seat.

The primary presented a new challenge for aspiring politicians. In the general election candidates could easily differentiate themselves from their opponent just by virtue of their party label, but in a primary some other tack had to be taken. A Democrat running against other Democrats had to convince voters that he or she was the better individual to represent the party. This was the beginning of what political scientists now call "candidate-centered" politics.

What was rapidly developing was a campaign politics based on personality, which was aided and abetted by the advent of television and sophisticated advertising techniques. By the midtwentieth century, candidates often ran away from their party label and appealed directly to the broader electorate, many of whom did not neatly fit into the Democratic or Republican box. With candidate-centered politics, it also took more time and effort for a person to get elected to a high-profile position such as one in Congress. Candidates had to establish their name to get the nomination, then start over again in the general election campaign.

In Chapter 3, we saw in detail what it takes to run for Congress in the twenty-first century. Candidates have to set up what amounts to a small or medium-sized business. In many respects, House and Senate candidates, Democrat or Republican, are on their own in setting up the campaign enterprise. They may get vital help from their party, but it is *their* campaign, and they have to put in tremendous time and effort in order to be competitive and even to get their name on the ballot.

Perhaps most importantly, it is the fund-raising that presents the biggest challenge. The cost of running for office has skyrocketed. A competitive House race is about three or four times as expensive as it was just fifteen years ago, with competitive races requiring between $2 million and $3 million and sometimes more. Fund-raising for Senate races is even more burdensome, with costs hitting $10 million or more in some states.

The reform impulses that resulted in changes in the campaign finance laws in 1974 made fund-raising a more burdensome and labor-intensive task than it used to be. With the contribution limits that were part of that legislation, more people now have to be contacted in order to raise enough money.

The demands on members' time to raise the requisite cash are incredible. One member of the House who was running for a Senate seat in 2008 spent nearly every working day in Washington in the spring and summer of that year, from 9:00 AM to 6:00 PM, in a cubicle in his party's senatorial campaign committee offices making fund-raising phone calls, leaving the room only for floor votes. Members attend breakfast fund-raisers before work and go to evening fund-raisers after work. Most sitting members of the Senate retain permanent campaign fund-raising offices near Capitol Hill, as do many House members.

The pressure to spend time back in the district, whether for fund-raising or more generally for meetings and politicking, is intense. There are constant demands from constituent groups and donors for face time. So not only do members have to spend more time than ever before raising money, but they are faced with a much more organized electorate as well. Technological advances, especially the Internet, have made citizen organizing around shared interests easier than ever. Contact time with the senators and representatives is very important to attentive constituencies and, needless to say, very time-consuming for the members.

Representatives' and senators' scarce staff resources are stretched more thinly than ever. First the fax machine and now e-mail have made contacting members of Congress a snap. The staff in the district or state and in Washington are inundated with messages and letters and faxes. Most offices have a policy of responding to every communication in at least a perfunctory manner. The more thoughtful inquiries require more detailed responses. It is highly embarrassing to be confronted at a town hall meeting or another venue by constituents who have not received a satisfactory response from the office or, worse yet, have received no response at all. Members from competitive districts sometimes find that they have few resources to do much more than address constituent questions and needs.

Members rarely lose reelection campaigns, but this happy situation for them does not happen by accident. They must tend to constituent needs, bring home the bacon in appropriations legislation, raise money in the hopes of discouraging potential opposition, and help the party fund operations for more vulnerable colleagues. Pitching in by raising money for the party serves the purpose of enhancing one's own chances for a better committee assignment, committee or subcommittee chair, or leadership position, which in turn enables one to deliver more for constituents.

As a result of this changed environment, members are not in Washington as much as they used to be. There was a tipping point sometime in the 1970s or early 1980s when members began to demand more time at home. Larger social and economic forces were also at work.

First, by that time commercial jets had made it possible to travel regularly to almost anywhere in the country. Members could now get home every weekend (which most do, especially in the House).

As members felt compelled to go home more often, it became the norm for them not to have their family with them in Washington. Why bring the family to the capital city when it would be less unsettling for the children and less expensive to raise them back home in the district—where members were spending a good bit of their time anyway? It was also good politics for members to have their district home truly be their primary residence.

The social changes of the time reinforced this trend. More and more members had a spouse (usually a wife) with a career. Women's liberation had opened up more opportunities for talented women, and many were unwilling to leave their career to follow their husband to Washington.

In the twenty-first century, members' representative role puts a great deal more pressure on them than in the past. The lawmaking environment in Washington has changed as a result. There is a substantial potential cost when members have to focus so much effort on their constituent service, fund-raising, and other reelection efforts, and one is that the board-of-director duties may get short shrift. The fact is that members are not in Washington to work on legislation and oversight as much as they used to be. We return to this topic at the end of the chapter.

The Growth of the Lobbying Industry

Chapter 2 covered the tremendous expansion of interest groups—"hyperpluralism" is the term coined by the journalist Jonathan Rauch—that began after the explosion of government activism in the period from about 1965 to 1971. At that point, the federal government became involved, through programs and regulatory measures, in literally every aspect of American life. No area of business, no occupation, no state or local government unit, no educational establishment, not even any area of citizens' personal lives, was untouched by federal law or agency regulations.

As a result, businesses that did not want to be at a competitive disadvantage had to try to influence the board of directors. County, city, and state governments that did not want to miss out on their fair share of federal program dollars had to make their presence felt. Blind people, old people, dentists, electricians, artists, social workers, real estate agents, auto dealers, and many other categories of people had to organize in order to protect what they got from the government or, better yet, to promote and advance their interests. Universities had to come to DC and meet with members of Congress or miss out on research grants. People who believed strongly in women's rights, gay rights, affirmative action, the rights of the unborn, school prayer, or the need to protect the environment had to press their case in the halls of Congress. What they all did was band together and hire Washington representatives—also known as lobbyists.

This changed dynamic has affected the board of directors in profound ways. As government has gotten larger, more complex, and more involved in many more aspects of American society, the demand for information on Capitol Hill to inform the authorizing and appropriations processes has also increased. And at the ready are the lobbyists—a steady stream of professionals adept at getting information on complex issues to the members and their staffs in a usable format on a moment's notice. Many of them are well equipped to develop specific legislative solutions to, for example, change the tax code to encourage a certain type of economic activity, or perhaps more effectively to address specific environmental hazards.

Congress is a very busy place, with a great deal going on at any given time. It almost cannot be exaggerated how hectic the policymaking process is. We have seen the kind of pressure that members are under in the performance of their representative role. Most staffers and members are generalists, and most staffers and members have a limited amount of time to look at any particular issue. Communicating complex matters takes a great deal of finesse, and the professionals in the lobby firms are good at it. They know the legislative process—many were staffers or even members before going into the private sector—and they know what works and when to press their case. The lobbyists are a constant presence, and their knowledge of the issues and the process makes them invaluable. The board of directors literally cannot function without them.

Interest groups further insinuate themselves into the process by becoming integral to many members' reelection efforts. Many groups contribute to campaigns through their political action committees (PACs). Some groups specialize in bundling together donations from various groups or individuals, effectively amplifying their influence. Others are adept, even without a PAC, at helping candidates or one of the parties with getting out the vote and other essential campaign activities. As noted in Chapter 2, *effective interest groups understand the connection between members' two roles and are expert at highlighting the state and district effects of the government programs and public policy issues the board of directors is handling.*

There is a downside to all of this—namely, that these groups have an *interest*, literally, in what gets in law. That is to say that lobbyists, by definition, are advocating on behalf of a private interest or a particular viewpoint. To the extent that the policymakers are getting their information exclusively from sources that have an ax to grind, the larger public interest may not always be as big a part of the equation as it should be.

We return to this problem at the end of the chapter. Suffice it to say at this point that the board of directors, in overseeing the vast $3.5 trillion federal government—an entity approximately one-fourth the size of the entire U.S. economy—needs information. And reliable information, persuasively presented, is the coin of the realm. When billions of dollars are at stake in the legislative process, a lot of people want to have a say in how it is distributed. When Congress is contemplating government action that will affect the health care system (a full 16 percent of the entire economy) or the energy sector or the financial sector, the members and their staff are deluged with proposals and arguments.

A tremendously competitive policymaking arena has developed on Capitol Hill. The key players include interest group representatives and the government agencies that report to Congress (most are required to do so by law) on the conduct of the programs they are running and that sometimes recommend legislative changes so that they can serve their missions more effectively. The difference today is the ubiquity of those interest groups. In the policymaking arena, the professional persuaders often have the upper hand.

CAN CONGRESS WORK IN THE TWENTY-FIRST CENTURY?

This chapter started by cataloging Congress's inherent limitations. The institution was built to be deliberate, district- and state-focused, and unable to pursue a concerted agenda. It has always had these attributes, and always will. But there are times when there absolutely must be a governing plan, or when a compelling argument is made that the national perspective should take precedence.

Certainly this will be the case in the coming years as the board of directors is forced to face the budget challenges described in Chapter 5. The costs of Medicare and Social Security in particular will get much greater in the next decade with the aging of the baby boom generation—the demographic "lump in the snake." The effects of these costs may be catastrophic, according to GAO.[14] If major changes are not made, the costs will eat into the ability of the government to support infrastructure improvements, research and development in the energy area, homeland security funding, the modernization of the armed forces, and other pressing matters. GAO projects a dramatic increase in the national debt, with resultant inflationary pressures and economic distress.

But frankly, Congress often resists looking at the big picture and refuses to act on an agenda put forth by one of the parties, or more often by the president. Congress typically insists on its prerogative to take its time through the legislative process, considering every angle and protecting the interests of the members' constituencies. It is far more common that a comprehensive program is stymied than that one is passed in any recognizable form. Most of the Republicans' 1995 "Contract with America" wallowed in the Senate. President Clinton's plans to reform the entire health care system the previous year never even came to a vote, despite his best efforts. President Carter proposed comprehensive energy reform in 1978 in response to the debilitating energy crisis—it went nowhere. Earlier in the 1970s, President Nixon wanted to remake the federal-state relationship with what he called "New Federalism." He had no success. In 2005 President Bush put forward a plan for reforming the major Social Security programs. He never got a vote either. The list goes on.

But Congress has at times openly acknowledged its shortcomings, sometimes by showing a willingness to find a way to compensate for its natural weaknesses. There are three common approaches: (1) delegating responsibility to the executive branch, (2) setting up a commission to find a solution, and (3) legislating reform. Essentially what Congress is trying to do when addressing its own weaknesses is to find a way to remain relevant in the important policy debates of the day. We are likely to see Congress continue to rely on these approaches in the future as it attempts to grapple with the challenges of the twenty-first century.

Delegating Responsibility to the Executive Branch

The congressional history of the middle decades of the twentieth century—from roughly 1920 to 1970—was one of voluntary abdication of decision-making responsibility to the executive branch in a whole host of areas.[15]

There were various reasons the board of directors abdicated when it did. First, in the early part of the twentieth century scientific public management theories came into vogue. The idea was that, with the increased complexity of modern life and the growing role of government, many things were too important to leave to the hurly-burly of partisan politics and the parochial deal-making of legislative bodies. Legislatures were seen as corrupt and prone to pork barrel spending and favoritism. Instead, the idea was to have professional civil servants who would not be beholden to one party or the other and who, as specialists in their fields, would make rational, data-driven decisions on allocating resources for addressing problems and improving infrastructure.

At the county and municipal levels, these ideas took hold in much of the nation. But Congress never gave up its most important power—the power of the purse. Nor did it give up its authority to authorize in law what the government does. It did, however, increasingly delegate regulatory and other key decisions to the bureaucrats in executive branch agencies, particularly when highly technical, sensitive, or scientific matters were involved. The Securities and Exchange Commission (SEC) was given the authority to regulate the stock market, the Environmental Protection Agency (EPA) was made responsible for regulations on pollutants, the Nuclear Regulatory Commission (NRC) was established to ensure the safety of nuclear power plants, and so on.

The board, at times, has even allowed agency officials a great deal of leeway in allocating resources for government programs and even in deciding where to locate agency offices that hire numerous people for secure government jobs. In addition, the members increasingly ceded management responsibilities to the president, who was given the Executive Office of the President in 1939 so that he could better coordinate all of the far-flung activities of the fast-growing federal government. At the time, the president was given considerable authority by Congress to reorganize executive agencies and define missions.

Of particular note, in 1921 Congress required the president, with the passage of the Budget and Accounting Act, to submit to it a budget—basically an agenda—for the upcoming fiscal year. This gave him the opportunity to suggest legislative proposals to fix big problems. He always had had the right to offer up legislation—the Constitution authorizes the president to report to Congress on the state of the Union and suggest any legislative measures he deems necessary. (President Woodrow Wilson was the first regularly to do so, beginning in 1913.[16]) The 1921 law also gave the president an institutionalized process by which to propose legislation in a more comprehensive way, and the resources to follow through with such proposals. Essentially this law was an admission of weakness by members of Congress—they desperately needed *someone* to look at the big picture for them.

In fact, as we saw in Chapter 5, Congress's budget process—and in many ways its authorizing process—begins with an assessment of the president's request in his budget plan. Thus, in a formal way via this act, the board of directors gave the president the ability to look at the big picture and, in effect, set the agenda. And every president since Franklin Roosevelt has tried to do so. If a plan for action on big-picture issues is going to be on the table, it is more likely than not going to come from the president. The expression "the president proposes, and the Congress disposes" derives from this tradition of deference on agenda-setting that came about in the middle decades of the twentieth century.

None of this is to say that the Congress is acquiescent. Usually it is not. To the extent that there is action on major issues, it usually happens at a deliberate pace, and Congress leaves an indelible mark on the final product. Sometimes, when a president is in a weakened political position, it is Congress that gets the bulk of what it wants on the major issues. It is rare, however, for even strong presidents to have their way with the Congress.

Earlier chapters have touched on a few of those rare times when presidents have moved an agenda with little resistance. One of those times was in the 1930s. For an unprecedented period stretching over about three or four years, Franklin Roosevelt got what he wanted passed, and mostly in the form he wanted. He was a highly skilled politician and persuader, he had an electoral mandate that included huge congressional majorities for his party, and the Great Depression was a crisis of unmatched severity.

Similarly, Lyndon Johnson capitalized on a time of great unease after the assassination of John Kennedy to pass rafts of important legislation in 1964 and 1965. He was aided by a landslide triumph for his party in the 1964 elections and his own tremendous political skills. No one was better than Johnson at knowing what motivates members of Congress and doing what it took to get their votes.

To a somewhat lesser degree, another talented politician, Ronald Reagan, capitalized on a great political victory in 1980 (his party took over the Senate and replaced thirty-three Democrats in the House to give a conservative cross-party coalition, if not Republicans alone, a working majority on key issues) and an economic crisis to move his agenda through the Congress in speedy fashion in 1981.

What is notable is that these three cases are the exceptions. No other president in the last one hundred years has had the same kind of success. Most have had ambitious agendas, but they usually ran into serious obstacles on Capitol Hill that either forced them to seriously alter their original plans or even to abandon them.

The bottom line is that Congress looks to the executive branch for guidance and frequently gives top-ranking officials a great deal of delegated authority to address new issues and problems. This is wise; after all, Congress has put in place a great body of expertise in the executive branch in all the agencies established through its authorizations and appropriations laws. It would be silly to ignore this enormous resource—and in fact there are times when Congress *must* rely on the executive branch to compensate for its own shortcomings. But the board retains its power to come back at the executive if it does not like what it sees. It relies on hearings and other forms of oversight to persuade agency officials to do things its way. It may pass new legislation providing clearer guidance on policy matters or more restrictions on how money is spent. In particular, it is through the annual appropriations process, in which the most regular and rigorous assessment of government programs takes place, that Congress exerts itself as the board of directors of the federal government.

The Commission Solution

A lot of major issues are very difficult for the locally focused Congress to handle, particularly those that are highly intricate and apt to bring pain to the people back home. The time-tested solution: form a bipartisan commission, made up largely of former public officials, to come up with a solution that is relatively free from politics and focused on the national interest.

At the end of Chapter 5, we saw that a bipartisan commission was formed in the early 1980s, headed by Alan Greenspan, to address the approaching insolvency of Social Security. (In fact, Social Security had run out of dedicated funds one year, and Congress had to authorize it to poach from general revenue to meet its commitments.) A small and select group, comprising leading Democrats and Republicans, met out of the public eye and formed a plan. With President Reagan and Democratic speaker Thomas P. "Tip" O'Neill signing off, it passed the Congress despite having decreased old-age benefits and raised taxes on many elderly. Congress seemed to know that it could not have had productive, open deliberations on such a sensitive and important program in the normal legislative process and still have managed to produce a workable solution.

Similarly, Congress has recognized that closing and realigning military bases (the economic engines of many communities across the country) is both necessary in the aftermath of the Cold War and too difficult to handle in the regular legislative process. Instead, Congress set up the Base Closure and Realignment Commission (BRAC) in the late 1980s. Five rounds of closures and realignments have been passed into law since then. The latest round was initiated in 2005. Here is how BRAC described its activities that year:

> Welcome to the 2005 Defense Base Closure and Realignment (BRAC) Commission's official website. Our goal is to assist the American public, including

interested stakeholders, to fully understand the open and transparent process through which our work is conducted. The website will also serve as a means by which you may share your thoughts, concerns, or suggestions with the Commissioners. Your input is appreciated.

The Congress established the 2005 BRAC Commission to ensure the integrity of the base closure and realignment process. As directed by law, the Commission will provide an objective, non-partisan, and independent review and analysis of the list of military installation recommendations issued by the Department of Defense (DoD) on May 13, 2005. The recommendations provided by DoD are extremely complex and interrelated and will require in-depth analysis and careful attention to detail. The Commission will follow a fair, open, and equitable process, as set forth by statute. The Commission's mission is to assess whether the DoD recommendations substantially deviated from the Congressional criteria used to evaluate each military base. While giving priority to the criteria of military value, the Commission will also take into account the human impact of the base closures and will consider the possible economic, environmental, and other effects on the surrounding communities.[17]

After BRAC made its final decisions as to what closures and realignments to recommend, it was up to Congress to vote on whether to accept the report. *Congress did not permit itself, by statute, to amend the report in any way.* The recommendation would come to an up-or-down vote, with no opportunity for individual members to pick it apart on either chamber floor, as would surely have happened if they had been free to do so in the normal amending process or if the report had been subject to subcommittee and committee markups. A great deal is at stake in these decisions, from jobs to whole local economies. Congress, knowing that its innate inability to plan and its tendency to protect narrow constituent concerns would prevent it from agreeing to a comprehensive realignment of military facilities without dispensing with the regular process, in effect tied its own hands by forcing a vote on the whole lot of commission recommendations.

The procedures followed by the 9/11 Commission, as described in Chapter 4, were different. While that commission was also bipartisan and was to present the board of directors with a comprehensive proposal (dealing with the intelligence lapses that came to light after the 9/11 attacks), the board did not require itself to take or leave the commission's plan as a whole. Instead, members implemented some suggestions but not others. In fact, they passed thirty-nine of the forty-one official recommendations.

More commonly, commissions are established to avoid directly addressing major issues that are too politically difficult to tackle. Several commissions have been established to tackle the entitlement crisis—going back to the Grace Commission in the 1980s and the Kerrey-Danforth Commission in the 1990s—but their recommendations were never adopted. Some commissions can be very helpful in breaking the gridlock on Capitol Hill, but others serve just to further it.

Legislating Reform

From time to time, Congress comes clean. It publicly recognizes its inherent tendency to serve narrow special interests and to avoid addressing bigger issues in a decisive way. A common solution: corrective surgery by means of "reform." The approach of choice is usually campaign finance reform.

The theory is that big corporations and other powerful entities have outsized influence over the legislative process and that this influence is largely traceable to their campaign donations. By reforming the campaign finance system and limiting the amount of special interest money in politics, members of Congress will be free to focus, undistracted by pesky campaign donors, on the big issues—such as streamlining the tax code, cutting off subsidies for wealthy farmers and oil companies, and other controversial matters that affect the wealthy and big business.[18]

The two most significant efforts to do just that were the Federal Elections Campaign Act (FECA, 1972, substantially amended in 1974) and the Bipartisan Campaign Reform Act (BCRA, or McCain-Feingold, 2002). The 1970s acts required full disclosure of candidates' funding sources and put strict limits on interest group donations to campaigns. PAC contributions were limited to $5,000 per election (primary and general) to a candidate. Individual donations were capped at $1,000.

BCRA adjusted some of those amounts to keep up with inflation and put an end to a major loophole that special interests had used to funnel unlimited amounts of money to the political parties—the "soft money" loophole. It restricted campaign activities by special interests in other ways as well, many of which are still, at this writing, being contested in the federal courts.

Although these efforts may be defensible on their merits, they have been nowhere near the panacea that their advocates believed them to be. Interest groups have always influenced members of Congress *whether or not they form PACs and contribute to campaigns.* As we have seen, they do this by bringing the local effects of policy to members' attention. Members have always been locally focused. The fact is that corporate interests will have the opportunity to make their views known to members and exert influence as long as the companies in question continue to employ people and contribute to the larger community. Campaign contributions help interest groups gain access to make their case, but they are not a necessary component of effective lobbying. Groups such as the National Association of Counties (see Chapter 2) do not feel handicapped by the fact that they do not have a PAC.

There are also periodic reform efforts aimed at special interest influence that focus on the dispensing of favors to members. These happen after a spate of ethics scandals in which members are found taking bribes or otherwise abusing the public trust.

In the last fifteen years or so, Congress has gradually put more and more restrictions on the kinds of gifts, meals, sports tickets, and other services members may accept from individual lobbyists or groups. Significant restrictions were put in place by the new Republican majority in 1995 on the heels of a series of embarrassing revelations and a few indictments largely involving Democrats in the years leading up to the Republican takeover. Similarly, Democrats imposed yet stricter rules when they took control of Congress in 2007 after several Republicans came under investigation or were indicted for accepting bribes or other bad behavior. In particular, members of Congress have focused on earmark reform in the aftermath of the scandal involving Representative Randy "Duke" Cunningham (R-CA), who received sizable kickbacks from corporate interests in exchange for inserting earmarks in appropriations bills to funnel federal money to those companies for various projects. The idea of the reforms is to shine a light on the earmarking process by listing all of them, with the requesting members' names, in report language attached to bills and requiring that all requests for earmarked funds be posted on members' websites.

Unfortunately, however right-thinking these reforms are, they, like campaign finance reform efforts, are oversold. Shining a light on shady behavior is certainly a good thing, but such efforts do not end the influence of interest groups or enable members to focus in a disinterested fashion on controversial issues. The influence of outside groups is largely based on their ability to bring useful information to the attention of members, especially information about the effects of legislative proposals on local economies or the larger American economy; for the most part, access is not based on the ability of these groups to wine and dine, bribe, or otherwise line members' pockets. Members want to serve their districts and states, and interest groups that are worth their salt help them do it.

What should be clear is that regardless of the value of reforming the campaign finance system, or putting more restrictions on the favors that outside groups can do for members, or shining a light on the earmarking process, Congress cannot legislate away its inherent tendencies. The rhetoric of campaign finance reform and ethics reform is intoxicating, but it cannot alleviate Congress's parochial focus or its difficulty in dealing speedily with big, intractable problems. Having said that, it is a safe bet that members of both parties will continue to push for more reforms, arguing that reforms hold the potential to "solve" the problem of special interest influence on the legislative process—because it is good politics to do so.

———

The lesson from this discussion is that Congress does attempt to manage its inherent limitations, even if they cannot be removed. Campaign finance and ethics reform cannot remove those limitations (despite the claims of some proponents), and neither can commissions—but they can help, and, indeed, the "commission solution" has at times been essential in addressing some otherwise intractable problems.

In addition, the board of directors will continue to delegate responsibility to the executive branch. It is wise to do so; furthermore, it is simply impossible for the board not to, given the size and scope of the federal government. Congress regularly cedes quasi-legislative authority to the agencies in areas where technical or controversial regulations must be promulgated to implement the law. But the board will never give up its essential authorizing and funding powers. It is these that give it the leverage to change agency behavior through oversight or, of course, by changing the law and taking back the delegated powers.

LOOKING AHEAD: A THERAPEUTIC APPROACH

Congress's fundamental nature makes it impossible for it to achieve some idealized level of performance. Anyone looking for Congress to move expeditiously and harmoniously on the major issues of the day, while at the same time giving careful consideration to expert opinion and a wide variety of views, is living in a fantasyland. The institution simply cannot meet that sort of standard.

It is better to grade Congress on a curve. Given its inherent limitations, how does Congress do? Is it obviously better or worse than other democratically elected legislatures around the world at tackling complex issues?

There is no consensus answer. Most political scientists would say that the U.S. Congress does not fare too badly by comparison, although in one sense there are not too many comparable counterparts. Very few legislatures around the world have the kind of responsibilities that Congress has. Our legislative body is the board of directors, with funding and authorizing authority over a vast government; most legislatures do not have that level of power. The branches are usually not coequal in other democracies—typically the executive has more unchecked authority than is the case in the United States.

As we have just seen, Congress's enhanced responsibilities compared to other legislatures compel it to be creative in dealing with difficult issues. The board of directors has chosen to delegate power and responsibility to the executive branch, and it often uses commissions in an attempt to get past its parochial nature. With the exception of the fraught relationship between the branches in warmaking and intelligence (covered in the last chapter), Congress has always retained full authority to reclaim delegated authority or reject commission proposals in other spheres of policy, even if it sometimes chooses to delegate. It is exactly this flexibility that has allowed Congress to retain its place at the center of our political system.

But as we have seen in this book, *the board of directors often fails adequately to perform its essential functions—authorizing, funding, and supervising the federal government.*

Today many government agencies function under lapsed or outdated authorizations. Congress, in effect, does not keep up with its responsibility to think through what the government should do. Instead, too often it updates agency policy in a haphazard manner, if at all. Sometimes it does so by way of provisions attached to appropriations bills, without proper consideration or much in the way of hearings. The failure of the board systematically to address authorizations leaves many agencies in a kind of limbo that makes the planning that is crucial for government agencies to function efficiently and effectively much more difficult.

Second, the board has failed miserably in funding the operations of the federal government on a timely basis. Its average number of appropriations bills completed on time from 1997 to 2008 was only one and a half out of twelve. (It has been almost twenty years since the appropriations bills have each received full attention and scrutiny in both chambers.) As a result, Congress normally leaves large swaths of the government on continuing resolution, sometimes for a large part of the fiscal year and even, in 2007, for the whole fiscal year. Programs are put on hold, contracts have to be suspended, and budgets are usually insufficient to maintain the same level of services. This is not good government, to put it mildly.

Third, Congress conducts less rigorous oversight of agency business than it did in years past. As the elected representatives of the people, the members of the board have the responsibility to keep tabs on how programs are run and taxpayers' money is spent. When congressional oversight falls through the cracks, agency officials are less accountable for their actions, an important fact in view of the sort of discretion so many of them are granted by the board.

When a person exhibits destructive or antisocial behavior, psychoanalysts say that the first task is to recognize the problem. For Congress, we can see the manifestations of bad behavior in the authorizing and appropriations processes as well as in the conduct of oversight. A successful therapy must then involve diagnosing the root causes of the problematic behaviors.

There are two in particular. First is the level of partisanship in Washington. Keep in mind that partisanship, in and of itself, is not a bad thing. After all, the two parties differ on fundamental questions—such as the role of government, the appropriate level of taxation, and moral issues—in ways that sometimes make it impossible or next to impossible to come to a meeting of the minds. But given the way Congress is structured, a supercharged partisan atmosphere that creates a deep-seated lack of trust and an inability to work together *is* a problem, and one that threatens to undermine the institution's ability to conduct its basic responsibilities as the board of directors of the federal government.

Second is the imbalance that has developed between the two roles of members of Congress. Consider an analogy: A type-A workaholic is often encouraged to strive toward work-life balance. The idea is not to get so wrapped up in one's job as to neglect one's health and one's family. For members of Congress, the problem is only slightly different—they need to strive to maintain "work-work balance" between their two jobs, that is, between the representative and legislative roles. But in the twenty-first century all sense of balance and proportion has been lost. The representative role has become prominent at the expense of members' important duties in directing the work of government.

Problem Number One: Partisanship

Most observers believe that both the institution and the political system more broadly are infected by a plague of venomous partisanship. And there is some truth to that. But it should be remembered that partisanship and invective have been with us from the beginning in this country—really in a sense even before there officially were parties! The period of relative comity between the parties from the late 1950s up into the 1980s, to the extent that it existed at all, was due in significant measure to the large margins that Democrats usually held in Congress. Republicans were resigned to their lot in life as a permanent minority, and a "get along–go along" mentality held sway at least some of the time.[19]

The question of whether partisanship is good or bad for the country is not as easy to answer as some make it out to be. The prevailing wisdom is critical of strong and assertive partisanship. Ronald Brownstein of the *National Journal* says that our political party system is more partisan and polarized than the public is.[20] Former members of Congress regularly lament that the two sides do not work together as much as they once did. There used to be more opportunities to work toward consensus, they say.

We have already addressed this issue in one respect: There really was no time when things were perfectly harmonious in Congress. There have always been divisions in our society and in the Congress on the major issues; in the past, those divisions were often every bit as sharp as the ones we see today, and sometimes more so. *The divisions did not, however, always divide along party lines, as they tend to now.*

Former congressman Van Hilleary of Tennessee makes the point that factional divisions have characterized U.S. politics going back to the intense feuds between Alexander Hamilton's Federalists and Thomas Jefferson's Democratic-Republicans, the conflicts that fueled the Civil War, and so on. He says that, in one sense, sharp partisanship with clearly drawn lines plays an important role in the policymaking process.[21]

Hilleary notes that we have accepted for centuries the value of the adversarial process in the courtroom, where the prosecutor makes the best case for the state and the defense attorney makes the best case for the defendant. Neither side is trying to put forth some sensible middle ground, and that is the way it is meant to be. That system is set up to highlight polarized views, the theory being that a more just result will be arrived at only after the airing of those views. Hilleary suggests that perhaps the policymaking process works best only after a public airing of the clearly distinct views and arguments of the two sides.

The journalist Matthew Yglesias makes a companion case that the parties in American politics finally make sense in the contemporary, post-1964 era. Surely, he suggests, it is a good thing that voters now know more surely what they will get when they vote for one party or the other.[22]

Today there is no doubt that the relations between Democrats and Republicans on Capitol Hill are testy at best. In the House in recent years, key leaders of the two parties have at times barely been on speaking terms. At some level this is to be expected, and it will never fully go away. But it is a problem for one central reason: Bipartisanship is *required* to get anything done on Capitol Hill, except in very rare cases. The de facto rule for passage in the Senate is sixty votes. This almost always requires accommodation and bipartisanship. Unfortunately, not everyone recognizes this.

To the extent that partisanship entails efforts simply to score points at the expense of one's adversary's (as opposed to genuine expressions of a particular viewpoint, as Hilleary's model suggests), poisoning the atmosphere for compromise, the Senate cannot work. What happens if the minority party simply refuses to negotiate? The same result. In the twenty-first century, senators take full advantage of their prerogatives—especially the hold or the threat of a filibuster—to derail important legislation. It is most important to note that the use of these tactics has increased dramatically in recent years.[23]

The House also presents an interesting dilemma for its leadership. The chamber's rules are set up to facilitate the passage of the majority's agenda. The parties in the House are dominated by strong liberals (the Democrats) and strong conservatives (the Republicans). But the problem is that *neither party can get the majority in the chamber without electing a sizable number of moderates.* It is next to impossible to elect an ideologically pure majority. The leaders are pressured by the majority of their caucus to pursue a true "blue" or true "red" agenda. But putting in place an ideological agenda may well lead to the loss of the districts represented by more moderate party members in future election cycles, and potentially even to the loss of control of the chamber.

Republican speaker Dennis Hastert (1999–2007) ultimately was undone by this dilemma. He and his leadership team pushed very hard, in tandem with President Bush, for a conservative agenda in the first decade of the twenty-first century. This made the political life of Republican House members from districts with a lot of Democrats and independents increasingly more difficult to navigate. Many of them lost their seats in 2006, giving the Democrats the majority. Still more fell in 2008, and others quit in frustration.

Speaker Nancy Pelosi is now walking the tightrope with her liberal caucus majority and what she calls her "majority maker" moderates—many of whom come from Republican-leaning districts. (In the 111th Congress, forty-nine House Democrats represent districts won by John McCain against Barack Obama, and more than eighty represent districts that voted for George Bush over John Kerry in 2004.[24]) How well she can keep up that act, balancing the needs of the moderates and the liberals, will go a long way toward determining how long the Democrats are able to maintain the majority.

Recent history indicates that the approach to the legislative process is the same in the House regardless of the party in control. Each party (the GOP from 1995 to 2007 and now the Democrats since 2007) has felt a great deal of pressure to move an ambitious agenda in order to satisfy its base and prove its worth to the American people. Often the members have had to streamline the legislative process in order to achieve their ends, and in fact jettisoning the regular process—"unorthodox lawmaking"—is now often the norm. Leaders are willing to ignore committee prerogatives, bills receive less scrutiny by the expert members and staff on those committees and subcommittees, hearings are shorter or sometimes are not even held, amendments are often prohibited on the floor—in short, the deliberative process is short-circuited, and the legislative product too often suffers as a result.[25]

In recent years, intense partisanship has led to efforts by the House, in tandem with the president, to steamroll the Senate. The idea has been to take advantage of the Senate's slow pace by moving something the president supports through the House quickly and gearing up the president's extensive press office for a public relations campaign to create a sense of urgency for the legislation. The aim is to force the Senate to accept the House version with little or no adjustment. This process was tried by the George W. Bush administration in conjunction with Speaker Hastert, and it occasionally worked when the president's political position was strong. But attempts such as these to marginalize the Senate in the service of a political or ideological agenda take a great deal of heavy lifting and are far from reliable. They simply cannot be achieved with any consistency.

Is There a Workable Model Out There?

It is instructive to consider the legislation that does regularly make it through the Congress in a timely fashion: the yearly reauthorization of the activities of the Defense Department. This massive bill sets the policies for a more than $600 billion entity entrusted with defending the security of the nation, and it is about as important as any other single thing Congress does. Each year it gets done, even while immigration reform and other ambitious plans stall and appropriations bills get shoveled together into omnibus packages months into the new fiscal year.

How does Congress do this? Some people point to the strong imperative that members feel when working on legislation that affects the men and women who put their lives at risk in defense of the country. And that is certainly a factor. From a procedural standpoint, however, the key is the tradition of bipartisanship practiced by the Armed Services Committees in the two chambers. Bipartisanship happens on the Hill, but it is episodic and not deeply ingrained almost anywhere else. Sometimes a bipartisan process is claimed when the majority is able to persuade a few members of the minority to join them. President Bush claimed bipartisanship when a handful of Democrats signed on to his tax cut bill in 2001. President Obama did the same when three Republicans came on board to vote for the American Recovery and Reinvestment Act in 2009. But this is not the real thing.

Consider that the whole of the Armed Services Committees' membership and staff share information and work together on the defense authorization bill. Everyone understands that the majority has the upper hand at the end of the day, but the internal processes are cooperative. That is true bipartisanship, and it explains why the final product that these committees come up with passes by overwhelming margins most years. The Senate *can work* if and only if real efforts are made at developing consensus.

Not only is national defense policy made on a bipartisan basis, but so is legislation in other areas, such as farming and public works. The Farm Bill and transportation reauthorizations usually move through Congress on a bipartisan basis, with divisions more likely to be drawn on regional than partisan lines. Even education policy, once a source of great ideological division, does not divide the parties in the way it used to. In recent years Congress has had success in coming together to change federal policy, sometimes in major ways, at the elementary, secondary, and college and university levels.

An issue is not always resolvable, however, just because the policy debate does not divide the parties. Immigration policy and trade policy have become particularly contentious in recent years. The differences in these two areas do not break down along partisan lines, but legislative agreements have proven elusive.

These exceptions do not change the rule: Bipartisanship is the sine qua non of the legislative process. Recognizing that reality is the first step toward addressing Congress's failings. Cooperative processes are required if the board is to get its legislative work done on a timely and consistent basis.

Partisanship and Oversight

A highly partisan atmosphere creates a more intractable problem for Congress as it approaches its duty to supervise the work of the federal agencies. In recent decades oversight has gotten short shrift when Congress and the White House are controlled by the same party.

This was not always the case. As noted in Chapter 6, Senator Harry Truman conducted vigorous and often embarrassing investigations of President Roosevelt's administration in the early years of World War II. The Republican Congress did not lay off President Eisenhower in the early 1950s. As we saw in Chapter 7, Lyndon Johnson's conduct of the Vietnam War received intense scrutiny from the Democratically controlled Congress of the day. And Jimmy Carter was not let off easily either by the Democratic Congresses with which he served.

In more recent years, the trend has been for Congress to conduct only perfunctory oversight during times of unified government. On the other hand, in times of divided government in the last two decades, both parties have hired dozens of investigators to go after alleged wrongdoing in the executive branch, and they have inundated the White House and agency personnel with subpoenas demanding documents and testimony.[26] Sometimes it seemed as though key officials were spending more time trying to cope with congressional demands than actually doing the work of the agencies.

Oversight has too often become more about scoring political points than about ensuring the efficient implementation of government programs and the wise stewardship of taxpayer money. Of course, oversight cannot help but have a political element to it—lawmakers are always trying to look good by exposing waste, fraud, and abuse in the government. But to serve the public they need to reassess their institutional responsibility to oversee the executive vis-à-vis their desire to score political points in the larger battle between the parties. Most observers do not think the prospects for a turnaround are good.

Problem Number Two: Congress's "Work-Work Imbalance"

In recent years members of Congress simply have not been in Washington as much as they used to be. The American Enterprise Institute's Congress-watcher, Norman Ornstein, made these comments regarding the congressional workload in a 2006 *Washington Post* article:

> The total of 97 calendar days [in session in 2006], counted generously, is the smallest number in 60 years and the days of what Harry Truman derided as that "do-nothing 80th Congress."
>
> During the 1960s and '70s, the average Congress was in session 323 days. In the 1980s and '90s, the average declined to 278. The days in session have plummeted since; it's likely that the average per two-year Congress for the first six years of the Bush presidency will be below 250.
>
> Of course, days in session and days voting don't give a full picture of Congress and its work. Committees and subcommittees hold hearings, do oversight and mark up bills. Still, the average Congress in the 1960s and '70s had 5,372 committee and subcommittee meetings; in the 1980s and 1990s, the average was 4,793. In the last Congress, the 108th, the number was 2,135. We do not have final figures yet for 2005, but they are likely to be lower yet, and with oversight practically nonexistent.[27]

Table 8.2 shows the days in session in the House from the 95th Congress in the 1970s through the 110th Congress. The bottom line is that the House of Representatives in the twenty-first century is in session about 20 percent fewer days than it was through the 1960s and 1970s. The numbers are only slightly better in the

TABLE 8.2   *Days in Session, U.S. House, 95th through 110th Congress*

CONGRESS	DAYS IN SESSION
95th (1977–1978)	324
96th (1979–1980)	326
97th (1981–1982)	298
98th (1983–1984)	317
99th (1985–1986)	282
100th (1987–1988)	309
101st (1989–1990)	288
102nd (1991–1992)	280
103rd (1993–1994)	267
104th (1995–1996)	311
105th (1997–1998)	253
106th (1999–2000)	278
107th (2001–2002)	272
108th (2003–2004)	248
109th (2005–2006)	226
110th (2007–2008)	281

Source: *Library of Congress.*

Senate—the upper chamber in the twenty-first century is in session about 15 percent fewer days than it was in the midtwentieth century.[28]

Why do these statistics matter? It takes a lot of work to direct something as large, complex, and multifaceted as the $3.5 trillion federal government. Certainly it is a full-time job for the 535 elected representatives of the people. But of course, this is only one of their jobs. As a practical matter, getting reelected has to be priority number one for the members—after all, what good can they do for the people if they lose their seat? The problem is that what is required to run for reelection has cut into the time needed to serve the legislative role and establish policy for the agencies of government.

The Serious Business of Directing the Work of Government

At this point we come full circle to the premise of this book: Congress can only be understood in a meaningful way in the context of its relationship with the executive branch. The Framers of the Constitution put in place a system in which interaction between the branches is *required* for the system to work well. The quality of Congress's work as the board of directors is, in many respects, conditioned by the quality of its interactions with the agencies and departments of government.

The agencies and departments are given legally established missions to fulfill. The Defense Department is in place to be prepared to fight wars and take other actions to further the security of the nation. The National Institutes of Health were created to conduct basic scientific research to improve treatment and find cures for cancer, AIDS, mental health problems, and so forth. The Transportation Safety Administration focuses on threats to air travel. These are inherently complex challenges requiring specialized expertise and training and often wide-ranging legal authority. The government agencies hire people to do the work, many of whom dedicate their entire careers to an agency's mission.

In order for the agencies to serve their missions effectively, they need an up-to-date legal framework and authorities that only Congress can provide. Agencies also need funding to achieve their objectives, and of course, only Congress can provide that. Often agencies need to be given a great deal of flexibility to do their work in a rapidly changing world.

It is critical that the agencies tell Congress what they need in law—in both authorizations and appropriations statutes—to be able to carry out their missions. This is not as easy as it sounds. Congress is absolutely inundated with information on government programs, much of it most effectively conveyed by lobbyists in the service of a particular private interest. In the current environment, and with the board's truncated schedule in Washington, the disinterested information coming from the scientists and policy specialists in the agencies sometimes gets lost in the shuffle—especially since agency officials often do not understand Congress or how to approach and provide information to the key people. By comparison, the skilled lobbyist's case on behalf of a private concern can be very persuasive.

The problem goes both ways. Not only do the agencies have trouble establishing and nurturing the kinds of relationships they need to have on Capitol Hill to influence the legislative process, but the members of the board are not taking the time to do the necessary painstaking work. The institution conducts much less oversight than it used to. Thorough oversight is an essential ingredient for good legislation. As noted already, Congress is also not keeping up with its funding and authorizing responsibilities.

The Effect of Earmarking

Congress's "work-work imbalance" has changed congressional behavior in other ways as well. The focus on the representative role has affected how Congress approaches the authorizing and funding legislation it does complete. The practice of earmarking program money to address particular constituent needs, as noted in Chapter 5, has increased manifold in just the last fifteen years. The major infrastructure legislation Congress regularly addresses—such as water projects (approximately every two years) and transportation funding (approximately every five years)—has in the last three decades become almost exclusively pork barrel bills. Broader purposes—enhancing economic efficiency, sustainability, and other national priorities—have gotten short shrift.

Agency budgets across the government have come under increasing pressure as a result. Programs meant to address problems based on formulas or competitive processes have been picked apart with earmarks. Agency officials coming to the board of directors for more flexibility in their budgets often find themselves running into a brick wall. Members believe that they know best what is in the interest of the people and jealously guard their constitutional right to direct government spending where they see fit.

Often, in this era of scarce resources, the final funding decisions are almost literally made with a meat cleaver. The appropriators roll several bills together into an omnibus package and, to meet the 302(a) allocation limits (or to find the funding for earmarks), simply cut spending equally across all agencies without regard to needs or good government requirements. The information provided by the agencies is a negligible part of that equation.

Earmarking on defense funding bills has put a considerable burden on the armed services. Invariably, money for special district-based defense-related projects comes out of operation and maintenance accounts—that is, spare parts, equipment and weapons maintenance, troop training, and combat operations. These accounts, of course, are particularly hard hit in time of war. Defense policy experts suggest that the detrimental effects on force readiness have been considerable this decade.[29]

Congress's "work-work imbalance" has probably also affected its willingness to assert its constitutional prerogatives in the area of war powers. As described in Chapter 7, in general members prefer to defer full responsibility for decisions to commit troops to war, as well as the conduct of war, to the president. It is more convenient not to take responsibility for these decisions, while still reserving the right to criticize executive decisions when things go wrong or casualties mount. In this area, as well as in all the others discussed here, Congress badly needs to take its legislative and oversight responsibilities more seriously and recalibrate the balance between the two roles it serves.

Can the "Work-Work Imbalance" Be Corrected?
This chapter has been an exercise in identifying Congress's failings and the root causes of those failings—the first steps in the direction of a solution. In tandem with

that effort, this chapter has also tried to tamp down expectations. The Congress has its limits; solutions have to be realistic.

What is it reasonable to expect from Congress? Congress is naturally slow, parochial, and unable to plan, but it must continue to find ways to improvise and adjust when circumstances demand concerted action. In addition, partisanship at some level will always be with us, but leaders in Congress cannot allow it to destroy the working relationships between the parties that are needed to move bills through the process. The Wall Street bailout bill of 2008 mentioned earlier was nearly torpedoed by acrimonious partisanship in the House. It was saved when the Democratic and Republican leaders of the Senate caucused behind the scenes and brought forward a workable package to address the impending crisis. The bill had its flaws, but the crisis was dire, and there was a consensus that something decisive or even drastic had to be done. These relationships across party lines are necessary for Congress to do its job responsibly within the separated system.

Some action also needs to be taken to readjust the balance between the members' legislative and representative roles. Much too much is at stake for the problem to be ignored. It is not an exaggeration to say that Congress's ability to do a responsible job directing the government and remaining a relevant player in the major issues of the day depends on it. It is only Congress that can provide the legal framework and the funding for government programs. It is essential that the board of directors do so carefully and well.

Obviously this will require more time in Washington and marginally less time focused on reelection and constituent service. Norman Ornstein and Tom Mann from the Brookings Institution suggest that "the best reform would be to require Congress to hold sessions five days a week for a minimum of 26 weeks a year, with members spending two weeks on, in Washington, and two weeks off, in their home districts. Members of Congress should not be distracted by permanent campaigning; accordingly, fundraising in the capital should be banned when the legislature is in session."[30]

Whether these proposals are at all feasible is debatable. But the direction we need to go is not. Members need to spend more time in Washington and less time at home. Happily, there are some good signs in the 111th Congress. At this writing, Congress is on track to be in session much more than recent Congresses, and the current pace of hearings on legislative proposals is encouraging as well. Whether this change has been spurred by the economic crisis and the excitement of a new administration and will prove only to be a blip in the larger trend remains to be seen.

CONCLUSION

The aim of this book has been to give readers an understanding of Congress as it directs the work of the federal government. Essentially, this is Congress in its *legislative* role, developing laws to establish what agencies do in the interest of the American people and then deciding what funds can be allocated for those purposes. The institution cannot be understood in any sophisticated way without seeing it in the context of this relationship with the executive branch agencies that actually do the work of government.

It is also true that Congress's actions as the board of directors of the federal government cannot be understood in isolation from its other responsibility—the representative role. Members of Congress are constantly attuned to the needs and concerns of their constituents. Those needs and concerns inform everything they do in their lawmaking role. The pressures of that representative role are intense and, as we have seen, tend to overshadow their authorizing, appropriations, and oversight duties.

The vast majority of members of Congress are hardworking and talented people trying to do the right thing as they see it. But they have, in essence, two very difficult jobs. Directing the federal government while being available to constituents and doing what needs to be done to get reelected is a tremendous challenge—maybe an impossible one, the way the system is structured now. As a result, it is no surprise that authorizations of major agencies lapse and fall out of date. It is also no surprise that the board has trouble finding the time each year to consider carefully the funding requirements of every agency of the government when they have so much on their plate. Both of those responsibilities carry with them the need to conduct oversight to determine which programs are working, which ones need more funding, and what changes need to be made so that agencies can better serve their missions and the American people. Oversight is done unsystematically and is too often undertaken to score political points in anticipation of the next election rather than to ensure good government.

The Constitution sets up Congress as a powerful player in our separated system of government. As we look ahead, there is a lot for it to consider.

The twenty-first century presents major policy challenges that we can anticipate and surely some equally as daunting that we cannot. A growing consensus is developing that global climate change presents a host of profound domestic policy dilemmas. The Defense Department and the intelligence agencies also list it as one of the top national security challenges in the new century. In addition, the baby boom generation is set to retire in earnest beginning in 2011 and will be ready to claim full Medicare and Social Security benefits at that time. Everyone recognizes that this eventuality could bankrupt the government in the not-too-distant future. The key component of the problem is the health care system, which, while delivering miracles on a daily basis, is inefficient and tremendously costly.

In these areas and many, many more, the government *has* to act. With the need to pass laws to address the challenges of the twenty-first century, Congress will remain a central player. The quality of its work will determine the kind of future we have.

QUESTIONS FOR DISCUSSION

1. In dealing with the many problems facing the nation in the coming years, would it be wise for the board of directors to delegate more to the president on the big issues? Should it rely on commission recommendations more? Or is there some way Congress can restructure how it does its legislative work in order to help it cope with complex, large-scale problems?

2. Can you think of any practical solutions for Congress to deal with its "work-work imbalance"?

3. There are good reasons why people are partisan—after all, political parties are the main vehicles in a democratic political system for pursuing strongly held beliefs and viewpoints. Is there a point where partisanship goes too far? If so, can you identify that point?

SUGGESTIONS FOR FURTHER READING

Brownstein, Ronald. 2007. *The Second Civil War*. New York: Penguin Press.

Mann, Thomas E., and Norman J. Ornstein. 2009. "Is Congress Still the Broken Branch?" In *Congress Reconsidered*, 9th ed., edited by Lawrence C. Dodd and Bruce I. Oppenheimer. Washington, DC: CQ Press.

Ornstein, Norman J., and Thomas E. Mann. 2006. "When Congress Checks Out." *Foreign Affairs*, November 30.

Smith, Steven S., and Gerald Gamm. 2009. "The Dynamics of Party Government in Congress." In *Congress Reconsidered*, 9th ed., edited by Lawrence C. Dodd and Bruce I. Oppenheimer, pp. 141–164. Washington, DC: CQ Press.

Sundquist, James L. 1981. *The Decline and Resurgence of Congress*. Washington, DC: Brookings Institution Press.

Wheeler, Winslow. 2004. *The Wastrels of Defense*. Washington, DC: U.S. Naval Institute Press.

NOTES

1. James L. Sundquist, *The Decline and Resurgence of Congress* (Washington, DC: Brookings Institution Press, 1981), ch. 7.

2. Joe Schatz of *Congressional Quarterly*, interview with the author, April 23, 2009.

3. For a good description of how welfare and other racially tinged issues played politically in the 1980s, see E. J. Dionne, *Why Americans Hate Politics* (New York: Simon & Schuster, 1991), ch. 3.

4. David M. Herszenhorn and Carl Hulse, "Deal Reached in Congress on $789 Billion Stimulus Plan," *New York Times*, February 11, 2009, p. A1.

5. Garry Young, interview with the author, October 24, 2007.

6. See Veronique de Rugby, "What Does Homeland Security Spending Buy?" American Enterprise Institute Papers and Studies, June 5, 2009, available at: http://www.aei .org/paper/21483.

7. Quoted in R. Jeffrey Smith and Ellen Nakashima, "Pentagon's Unwanted Projects in Earmarks," *Washington Post*, March 8, 2009, p. A1.

8. Mark Brewer, *Parties and Elections in America*, 5th ed. (Lanham, MD: Rowman and Littlefield, 2007), pp. 403, 405.

9. Probably the definitive work on this topic is Keith T. Poole and Howard Rosenthal, *Ideology and Congress* (Piscataway, NJ: Transaction, 2007). See also Gary C. Jacobson, *The Politics of Congressional Elections*, 7th ed. (New York: Longman, 2009), p. 246.

10. Claudia Dreifus, "A Science Advocate and an 'Endangered Species,' He Bids Farewell," *New York Times*, May 9, 2006, available at: http://www.nytimes.com/2006/05/09/ science/09conv.html.

11. The 2008 congressional election romp for the Democrats may, however, put control of the House and Senate out of the reach of Republicans in 2010. However, Republicans know they *can* gain control; the leadership will have that as its primary goal, at least by 2012.

12. Ronald Brownstein, *The Second Civil War* (New York: Penguin Press, 2007).

13. Barbara Sinclair, *Unorthodox Lawmaking*, 3rd ed. (Washington, DC: CQ Press, 2007).

14. See U.S. GAO, "The Nation's Fiscal Outlook: The Federal Government's Long-Term Budget Imbalance," available at: http://gao.gov/special.pubs/longterm/.

15. Sundquist, *The Decline and Resurgence of Congress*, chs. 3–6.

16. Sidney Milkis and Michael Nelson, *The American Presidency: Origins and Development, 1776–2007* (Washington, DC: CQ Press, 2007).

17. See "2005 Defense Base Closure and Realignment Commission Report," available at: http://www.brac.gov/.

18. David Mayhew, *Congress: The Electoral Connection* (New Haven, CT: Yale University Press, 1974), pp. 178–179.

19. William F. Connelly and John J. Pitney, *Congress's Permanent Minority: Republicans in the U.S. House* (Lanham, MD: Rowman and Littlefield, 1994).

20. Ibid.

21. Van Hilleary, speech delivered July 24, 2008.

22. Matthew Yglesias, "The Case for Partisanship," *The Atlantic*, April 2008, available at: http://www.theatlantic.com/doc/200804/comment.

23. For historical perspective and analysis on filibusters, see Gregory John Wawro and Eric Schickler, *Filibuster, Obstruction, and Lawmaking in the U.S. Senate* (Princeton, NJ: Princeton University Press, 2006); and George Will, "The Democrats' Disharmony," *Washington Post*, April 30, 2009, available at: http://www.washingtonpost.com/wp-dyn/content/article/2009/04/29/AR2009042904018.html.

24. Republicans hold only five seats in Obama districts.

25. See Norman Ornstein and Thomas Mann, *The Broken Branch* (Washington, DC: CQ Press, 2006).

26. Alexis Simendinger of *National Journal*, speech delivered September 12, 2007.

27. Norman Ornstein, "Part-Time Congress," *Washington Post*, March 7, 2006, p. A17.

28. Norman J. Ornstein, Thomas E. Mann, and Michael J. Malbin, *Vital Statistics on Congress 2008* (Washington, DC: Brookings Institution Press, 2009), p. 125.

29. See, for example, Winslow Wheeler, *The Wastrels of Defense* (Washington, DC: U.S. Naval Institute Press, 2004), p. 11.

30. Norman J. Ornstein and Thomas E. Mann, "When Congress Checks Out," *Foreign Affairs*, November 30, 2006.

APPENDIX:
100 YEARS OF CONGRESS: 1910–2010

100 Years of Congress: 1910–2010

For Party Control and Presidents:
■ denotes Democratic Party   □ denotes Republican Party

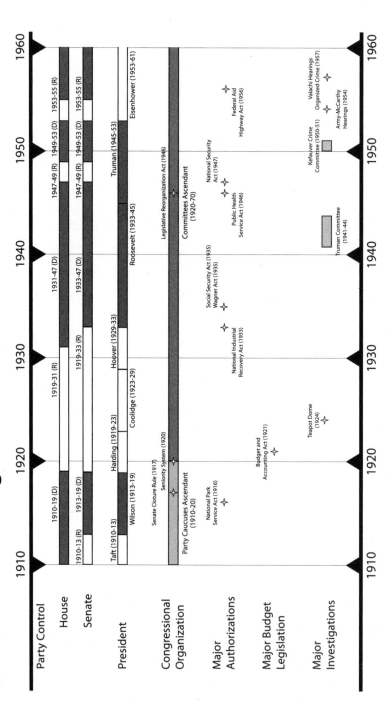

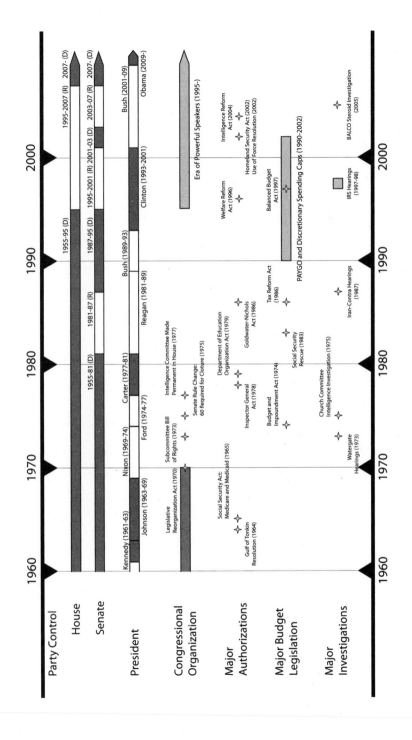

Party Control

| | 1960 | 1970 | 1980 | 1990 | 2000 |

House
1955-95 (D) | 1995-2007 (R) | 2007- (D)

Senate
1955-81 (D) | 1981-87 (R) | 1987-95 (D) | 1995-2001 (R) | 2001-03 (D) | 2003-07 (R) | 2007- (D)

President
Kennedy (1961-63) | Johnson (1963-69) | Nixon (1969-74) | Ford (1974-77) | Carter (1977-81) | Reagan (1981-89) | Bush (1989-93) | Clinton (1993-2001) | Bush (2001-09) | Obama (2009-)

Congressional Organization
Legislative Reorganization Act (1970)
Subcommittee Bill of Rights (1973)
Senate Rule Change: 60 Required for Cloture (1975)
Intelligence Committee Made Permanent in House (1977)
Era of Powerful Speakers (1995-)

Major Authorizations
Social Security Act: Medicare and Medicaid (1965)
Inspector General Act (1978)
Department of Education Organization Act (1979)
Goldwater-Nichols Act (1986)
Tax Reform Act (1986)
Welfare Reform Act (1996)
Intelligence Reform Act (2004)

Major Budget Legislation
Gulf of Tonkin Resolution (1964)
Budget and Impoundment Act (1974)
Social Security Rescue (1983)
Balanced Budget Act (1997)
Homeland Security Act (2002)
Use of Force Resolution (2002)
PAYGO and Discretionary Spending Caps (1990-2002)

Major Investigations
Watergate Hearings (1973)
Church Committee Intelligence Investigation (1975)
Iran-Contra Hearings (1987)
IRS Hearings (1997-98)
BALCO Steroid Investigation (2005)

| | 1960 | 1970 | 1980 | 1990 | 2000 |

GLOSSARY OF KEY TERMS

302(a) allocation   The section of the budget resolution that determines each committee's spending allocation for legislation pertaining to the next fiscal year. Most attention is paid to the allocation for the Appropriations Committees covering discretionary spending.

302(b) allocation   The subdivision of the 302(a) allocation made by the Appropriations Committees. In each chamber, the Appropriations Committee allots a portion of the 302(a) to each of its twelve subcommittees (constituting the 302[b] allocations) to fund the agencies in each subcommittee's jurisdiction for the next fiscal year.

"A" committees   A subset of Senate committees including most authorizing committees. Senators are guaranteed one A committee assignment and may have as many as two.

Accounts   The unnumbered paragraphs in appropriations bills that provide budget authority to the agencies. Each account usually covers a broad range of programs and expenses in a given agency.

amendment in the nature of a substitute   An amendment offered as a replacement to the bill being considered on the floor.

amendments between the chambers   The process of passing a bill back and forth until one chamber agrees to the version passed in the other chamber. One of the principal methods of resolving the differences between the two chambers on pending legislation.

Apportionment   The process of distributing the 435 House seats among the states after the decennial census. The "method of equal proportions" is currently used by the Census Bureau to determine how many representatives each state gets.

Appropriations Committees   The committees in the House and Senate that write the bills that control the funding for the discretionary portion of the federal government.

assistant leader   The second-ranking party leader in the Democratic and Republican Parties in the Senate. Sometimes called the "majority whip" or the "minority whip."

authorization of appropriations   The section of authorizing legislation that sets a funding ceiling for discretionary programs.

authorizing committees   The committees in the House and Senate that write legislation that sets agency policies. These committees also have oversight responsibilities for the agencies in their jurisdiction.

authorizing power   One of Congress's three powers as the board of directors of the federal government, this power, granted in Article I of the Constitution, gives Congress the authority to determine the policies of executive branch agencies.

Bipartisan Campaign Reform Act (BCRA)   Legislation signed into law in 2002 that updated and revised existing campaign finance law and, among other things, put an end to unlimited so-called soft money contributions and adjusted the contribution limits for individual donors to campaigns for federal office. Often called "McCain-Feingold" in honor of the two senators—Russ Feingold (D-WI) and John McCain (R-AZ)—who were its principal sponsors.

budget authority   The authority provided in law that enables agencies to obligate money in order to carry out government programs.

budget request   See "president's budget"

budget resolution   See "Concurrent Budget Resolution"

candidate-centered politics   Campaign politics focused on individual candidates rather than parties. Candidate-centered politics developed in the twentieth century as parties began using primaries to select nominees, forcing candidates to distinguish themselves based on personal characteristics.

caucus   The official meeting of the members of one party in either the House or the Senate for the purposes of conducting official business, such as selecting members for leadership positions or discussing legislative strategy. House Republicans call their meeting of party members a "conference."

caucus chair   Member chosen by the Democrats or Republicans in the House or Senate to lead meetings of the party members and to take on other duties. House Republicans call this member the "conference chair."

chairman's mark   The version of a bill developed by the chair of a subcommittee or committee that is brought up for discussion, amendment, and vote in that subcommittee or committee.

chief of staff   The staff member who is in charge of a senator or representative's personal office. Sometimes referred to as "administrative assistant (AA)."

closed rule   A type of special rule governing debate on the House floor that permits no amendments to the legislation under consideration. See "structured rule."

cloture   A Senate procedure that puts a limit on floor debate and nongermane amendments. Cloture requires sixty votes to be "invoked," after which a vote takes place after thirty hours on the motion or bill under consideration.

commander-in-chief power   The power granted to the president, in Article II of the Constitution, over the armed forces and over the state "militias" "when called into the actual service of the United States."

"commission solution"   The term coined here for Congress's practice of establishing commissions—panels of experts who study pressing or long-term problems facing the nation. A commission is usually required to report its findings or provide a legislative solution, which Congress may or may not be required to act upon.

committee jurisdiction   The policy domain (including the operations of the relevant federal agencies) given each congressional committee by the parent chamber.

Committee of the Whole   A committee whose membership includes the whole House of Representatives. Most important legislation in the House is handled by the Committee of the Whole before it is voted on by the House of Representatives. The Committee of the Whole offers a streamlined method to handle most debate and amendments on the floor of the chamber.

committee referral   The process, managed by the parliamentarian of the House or Senate, that determines which committee should receive the bills introduced by members of Congress. Parliamentarians make this decision based on the established committee jurisdictions.

committee staff   The people who are hired by and work for the chair or ranking member of a committee to do research on legislation, set up hearings, and attend to other business of the committee.

Concurrent Budget Resolution   A resolution agreed to by the full House and Senate that sets the parameters for all budget-related legislation to be handled that year. Also called the "budget resolution," it includes spending and revenue targets, sets the limits on discretionary spending, and may include instructions for tax bills or mandatory spending legislation.

conference chair   The term used by House Republicans for their party equivalent of a "caucus chair."

conference committee   An ad hoc panel comprising members from both chambers and selected to iron out the differences between similar legislation passed by the House and Senate. Often simply called "conference."

conference report   The final version of conference committee deliberations to iron out the differences between similar legislation passed by the House and Senate. The conference report must be agreed to by the majority of each chamber's delegation to the conference and is subsequently sent to both chambers for final approval.

continuing resolution (CR)   The legislation that keeps government agencies running when Congress has failed to pass appropriations bills by the beginning of the fiscal year.

cracking   A process sometimes used by majority partisans in a state legislature when they redraw congressional district lines. Its purpose is to distribute the minority party's supporters more thinly across congressional districts so that the majority party can maximize its representation from the state in the House of Representatives. Historically has referred to the process, now unconstitutional, by which voters of a racial or ethnic minority are distributed in such a way as to minimize their chances of electing one of their own to office.

deficit   The difference between government revenues and government expenditures when expenditures outpace those revenues.

direct spending   The program funding provided, usually by formula, in authorizing law. Also called "mandatory spending."

discretionary program   A government program that receives its funding in an annual appropriations bill.

discretionary spending   Spending that is controlled annually in appropriations legislation, including program funds and, more generally, agency operating funds.

district office Member offices set up in districts and states to address directly constituent needs and concerns, usually those related to federal government programs and services.

earmark A specification by Congress, usually in an appropriations bill or report language attached to an appropriations bill, of the location or recipient of federal funding, thus circumventing the established merit-based formulas or competitive allocation processes handled by the executive branch.

entitlements See "mandatory programs"

executive power The broad grant of power given the president at the beginning of Article II of the Constitution.

executive privilege The doctrine that asserts that the president and other high officials of the executive branch should be able to keep certain communications private if disclosing those communications would disrupt the functions or decision-making processes of the executive branch.

exclusive committees The five House committees—Appropriations, Energy and Commerce, Financial Services, Rules, and Ways and Means—that are given special status by the rules of both parties. Members who secure membership on one of these committees may not serve on any other committees unless granted a waiver by the party leadership.

favorable report Action taken by a committee giving approval to legislation under its jurisdiction with the hope that such legislation will be taken up for floor consideration.

Federal Elections Campaign Act (FECA) A law passed in 1974 that put strict limits on campaign donations and instituted rigorous reporting requirements for congressional campaigns.

fencing off (funds) Action by Congress (through a provision in appropriations law) to prohibit an agency from using some portion of appropriated funds until certain administrative plans to implement a program are approved by the Appropriations Committees. Such a provision constitutes an unconstitutional "legislative veto" but is nonetheless commonly used by Congress and not contested by agencies.

filibuster A delaying tactic that may be used by members of the Senate to stop legislation from coming to a vote. A supermajority of sixty senators is required (see "cloture") to limit debate and move toward a vote.

fiscal year For accounting purposes, the federal government year begins on October 1 and goes twelve months through September 30 of the following calendar year.

franking The allowance given to each member of Congress, through his or her chamber, to send mail to constituents free of charge; often called the "franking privilege." Congress reimburses the Postal Service through its legislative branch appropriation.

functional categories Broad categories of federal spending included in the Concurrent Budget Resolution. The functional categories do not align perfectly either with the government departments and agencies or with congressional committee jurisdictions. They are meant to facilitate discussion in Congress on the goals and purposes of federal spending.

funding power One of Congress's three powers as the board of directors of the federal government; often called "the power of the purse." Congress is given this power to determine the budgets for the federal agencies in Article I, Section 9, of the Constitution.

general election The final election in a campaign, usually between a Democrat and a Republican, that determines the winner of a House or Senate seat.

general provisions A component of appropriations law, identifiable by section numbers, that gives specific instructions to agencies on a wide range of matters.

germaneness The House has a general rule that amendments must be directly related ("germane") to the legislation under consideration. In the Senate, germaneness applies to appropriations bills (although it is not uncommon for the rule to go unenforced) and to bills under consideration after cloture has been invoked or by unanimous consent agreement.

gerrymandering The process of drawing House district lines to benefit an incumbent or a particular party or to improve the chances that a candidate from a racial or ethnic minority will win the seat.

Great Compromise The deal struck between big and small states at the Constitutional Convention that led to the establishment of a bicameral Congress.

hearings Public committee or subcommittee meetings (initiated by the chair) that are intended to gather information from witnesses on pending legislation, to look into the operations of agencies and programs, or to investigate potential wrongdoing at agencies or in the private sector. Senate committees hold hearings on nominations to the federal courts and the top-level executive branch positions. Hearings involving classified information are not held in public.

hold Action by a senator to deny the majority leader unanimous consent to proceed with legislative business. The hold delays that business until it is withdrawn (often after a deal is negotiated with the senator or senators placing the hold) or until the leader successfully forces action by invoking cloture.

hotlining A tool of the Senate majority leader to apprise the entire chamber (by e-mail and phone) of legislative business he would like to bring up on the floor, usually the next day, by unanimous consent. Hotlining enables the leader to expedite that business. Members may notify the leader of their objections, thus denying unanimous consent.

hyperpluralism A term coined by Jonathan Rauch referring to the dramatic proliferation of interest group activity beginning in the 1970s.

ideological sorting The process by which the adherents of the two parties began to divide increasingly along ideological lines, to the point where the Democratic Party is now more uniformly liberal and the Republican Party more uniformly conservative than they have been in the past. Sorting by ideology became especially noticeable beginning in the 1960s.

incumbent The current occupant of a political office.

independent expenditure Money that may be spent on an unlimited basis by the political parties on behalf of congressional candidates. Independent expenditure campaigns must not be coordinated in any way with the candidate campaigns.

interest on the debt The money spent by the Treasury to service the accumulated debt owed by the federal government.

joint explanatory statement (JES) Nonstatutory language added to the final version of legislation to explain how the two chambers came to agree on the final version. Part of the "conference report," the JES often includes instructions from Congress on how to implement the law, requests for reports on the ongoing conduct of government programs, and earmarks. The generic term "report language" encompasses the joint explanatory statement.

leadership staff   Congressional staff hired by party leadership to assist in their duties.

leadership PACs   Political action committees set up by federal politicians as a means to contribute to their fellow party members' campaigns and their party committees and to support their own campaign-related expenses.

legislative assistant (LA)   The staff position in a representative's or senator's Washington office that is responsible for researching and tracking a certain set of policy issues.

legislative correspondent (LC)   The staff position in a representative's or senator's office that is responsible for drafting responses to constituent correspondence.

legislative director (LD)   The staff position in a representative's or senator's Washington office that is responsible for overseeing the legislative interests of the member.

legislative role   One of two central roles that the Constitution gives to members of Congress. The legislative role is the congressional responsibility to direct the work of government through authorizing and appropriations legislation and by conducting oversight of agencies and programs.

legislative veto   The provision in legislation that enables a committee or chamber of Congress to reject an executive branch plan of action. Legislative vetoes were ruled unconstitutional in 1983; nonetheless, Congress continues to put them in legislation. See "fencing off (funds)" for the most common type.

limitation language   The provision in appropriations law that prohibits an agency from spending money for a particular purpose.

lobbyist   A person who is hired to persuade members of Congress to support the legislative concerns of a particular interest group.

majority leader   In the Senate, the senator selected by the majority party to schedule legislation and otherwise pursue the majority party's agenda in the chamber. In the House, the member selected by the majority party to develop and plan legislative strategy. The majority leader in the House is second in command to the speaker.

majority whip   The House member selected by the majority party to count votes and marshal support for the legislative agenda. The equivalent position in the Senate is usually referred to as the "assistant leader."

mandatory program   A government program that is established and funded based on criteria set forth in authorizing legislation. Mandatory programs are not subject to the annual appropriations process.

mandatory spending   Spending on programs for which formulas or criteria are set forth in authorizing legislation. Mandatory spending is not under the control of the appropriations committees.

markup   The process of considering legislation (see "chairman's mark") in subcommittee or committee meetings. Most markups are held in public, and members on the panel are given the opportunity to offer and vote on amendments and the entire bill.

members' representational allowance (MRA)   The allotment given to House members to pay for all office-related expenses. The MRA for the 111th Congress was about $1.4 million per year, with some variation depending on travel costs for individual members. Senators also get an allowance (not called MRA) that is based on population but not strictly proportional.

minority leader   In the Senate, the senator selected by the minority party to lead negotiations with the majority leader on legislative agenda items. The minority leader is also usually the chief spokesperson for the party. In the House, the member selected by the minority party to speak for the party and sometimes devise strategies to thwart the majority party's agenda.

minority whip   The House member selected by the minority party to keep tabs on the views of the minority members on pending legislation. The minority whip is also often the member who tries to keep the party together in opposition to the majority's agenda. The equivalent position in the Senate is usually referred to as the "assistant leader."

modified open rule   See "open rule."

motion to recommit   A motion put forward on the floor by the minority party, after debate has been completed on a bill, to send the bill back to committee for reconsideration. A successful motion normally does not result in reconsideration but rather in the bill's failure. Motions to recommit may include instructions to the relevant committee to make particular changes.

necessary and proper clause   The provision in Article I of the Constitution that has the effect of giving Congress wide latitude to do legislatively what is "necessary and proper" to carry out the powers given to it in the article.

obligations   Contractual arrangements made by government agencies for services rendered by nonfederal entities (often in the private sector) or other agencies of the federal government.

Office of Management and Budget (OMB)   The agency within the Executive Office of the President that has the principal duty of putting together the president's budget, based on the input of all federal agencies. OMB also monitors the progress of the president's priorities on Capitol Hill.

ombudsman   The person who serves the public by looking into their problems with government agencies. Members of Congress serve this function for their constituents.

open rule   A type of special rule governing debate on the House floor, an open rule permits any germane amendments to the legislation under consideration. A "modified open rule" normally permits any amendments as long as they have been submitted to the Rules Committee in advance.

outlays   Payments made by the government for services rendered (see "obligations").

oversight   One of the three key powers held by Congress in its role as the board of directors of the federal government, this implied power gives Congress the right to look into the performance and conduct of government programs and agencies. Congress cannot effectively do its legislative work of authorizing and funding the government without the ability to get information from the executive branch agencies as to how programs are working.

packing   Sometimes used by majority partisans in a state legislature as they are redrawing congressional district lines, packing is a way of putting as many minority party supporters in as few districts as possible, thereby giving the majority party a near-lock on the state's other congressional districts.

passback   Action by the Office of Management and Budget, usually in late November or early December, in which it "passes back" to the federal departments and agencies a draft presidential budget for the next fiscal year (the one starting approximately ten months later). The agencies can appeal the OMB draft budget.

personal office   The offices of representatives and senators in Washington and in their districts and states. The personal offices deal with legislative matters (in the Washington office) and address the concerns of constituents (see "ombudsman").

personal staff   Aides hired by members of Congress to deal with legislative matters and more generally address the concerns of constituents.

pluralism   The idea that political power in society is not held by a defined narrow elite but rather is distributed among a wide range of overlapping groups, any one of which is not in ascendance permanently or even for a long period of time.

pocket veto   If a bill passes Congress within the last ten days of a congressional session and the president chooses not to sign it or veto it, the bill dies when Congress adjourns, and the president can thus, in effect, veto legislation without taking any action.

political action committee (PAC)   The fund-raising and campaign-contributing arm of an interest group (a business, labor union, or other sort of association or advocacy organization). A PAC raises money from its members or employees and contributes those funds to the election campaigns of candidates it wishes to support.

post-committee adjustments   Action by party leadership in Congress to alter legislation after it is reported out of committee.

prerogative view   The theory that the president has an "undefined residuum" of power, implied by the "executive power" provision at the beginning of Article II of the Constitution, and that this enables him to take actions in a time of crisis that, although not always strictly legal, are in the nation's best interest.

presentment clause   The Article I constitutional provision that requires legislation to pass the House and Senate in identical form before it is sent to the president for his consideration.

president's budget   The comprehensive document developed at the president's direction every year stating his budgetary and legislative priorities for the coming fiscal year and beyond. Delivered to Congress in early February, it kicks off the congressional budget process.

primary election   An election held to determine a party's candidate for the general election.

professional staff member (PSM)   Aide hired by either the chair or ranking member of a committee to handle legislative matters in the committee's jurisdiction.

ranking member   The top-ranking minority party member on a committee given the power to hire professional staff to support his or her legislative priorities. Normally the ranking member becomes chair when his or her party wins the majority in the chamber.

reconciliation instructions   An optional provision in the Concurrent Budget Resolution that directs authorizing committees to report out legislation related to taxes and/or mandatory programs. That legislation is subsequently protected from filibuster on the Senate floor.

redistricting   Action taken at the state level to draw House district lines based on the results of the decennial census.

report language Nonstatutory provisions attached to a bill as it goes through the legislative process. Report language is intended to make clearer to agency officials and other interested parties Congress's intentions in the law and may include earmarks, requirements for reports, and suggestions regarding the implementation of government programs.

representative role One of two central roles that the Constitution gives to members of Congress. The representative role is derived from a member's connection to the voters of the district or state that put him or her in office. The American republic was based on the notion that the elected representatives would be *accountable* to the people who put them in office.

republic A government in which sovereignty is vested in a voting citizenry that elects representatives to exercise power on its behalf.

"right-eye-dominant" A term coined here to describe the tendency of members to vote on legislation consistent with their constituents' views even if their own analysis or ideology might lead them to vote differently.

Rules Committee The House committee that determines the guidelines for consideration—including the amending process and the time allotted for debate—of most important legislation on the floor.

select committees Committees of Congress whose membership is determined by the leadership of the parties in a particular chamber rather than by the parties' Steering Committees.

self-executing provision The provision in a special rule that, if that special rule is approved by the full House, has the effect of amending the pending legislation before it comes to the floor; often used to implement post-committee adjustments.

speaker of the House The position established in the Constitution that serves as the presiding officer of the House of Representatives. The speaker also serves as the leader of the majority party overseeing the legislative agenda of the chamber.

special interests See "interest groups."

special rule A resolution developed by the Rules Committee that determines the guidelines for consideration—including the amending process and the time allotted for debate—of most important legislation on the floor. A special rule guiding debate is subject to a vote before the pending legislation is brought up for consideration.

split referral One method of referring legislation to committees in the House, the split referral may be employed by the majority party leadership to send a bill to more than one committee when the bill does not fit neatly into one committee's jurisdiction. Usually leadership sets a deadline for each committee to complete consideration of the relevant portion of the legislation.

stacking votes A common method of handling voting on amendments in the Committee of the Whole in the House of Representatives. Debate is conducted on several amendments with no votes taken. When debate is complete, members are summoned to the floor to vote serially on the amendments.

staff director A common term for the top aide to the chair or ranking member of a committee.

Steering Committee The party committees in the House and Senate that handle committee assignments and other important business.

structured rule   A type of special rule governing debate on the House floor that permits only certain types of amendments; sometimes called a "modified closed rule." See "closed rule."

"super A" committees   The Armed Services, Appropriations, Finance, and Foreign Relations Committees, which are considered the most important committees in the Senate. Members are guaranteed by their party an assignment on one super A committee. Democrats have an additional committee in the super A category—the Commerce, Science, and Transportation Committee.

supplemental appropriations   Additional appropriations provided during the fiscal year for agencies that were not given the funds in the regular appropriations process the previous year to handle some unforeseen circumstance.

suspension of the rules   A method in the House to expedite consideration of (usually) noncontroversial legislation. Passing a bill under "suspension" requires a two-thirds vote. Debate and amendments are strictly limited.

unanimous consent   In this procedure meant to expedite consideration of legislation, usually in the Senate, every member agrees to proceed regardless of whether rules of the chamber are being violated.

unanimous consent agreement (UC agreement)   Carefully crafted agreement in the Senate, usually negotiated by the majority and minority leaders, that limits debate and structures the amendment process. As the term implies, all members are party to the arrangement.

unitary executive   The theory that the Constitution strictly limits Congress's power to be involved in executive branch decision-making, including setting criteria for hiring agency officials and developing administrative plans.

"unorthodox lawmaking"   A term coined by the political scientist Barbara Sinclair to describe the increasingly common practice in Congress of using creative approaches to the legislative process.

whistleblowers   Agency officials who report wrongdoing at the workplace, usually to Congress or to agency inspectors general. Whistleblowers usually have some statutory protections from retribution.

"work-work imbalance"   A term coined here to describe the increasing pressures on members of Congress to focus on their representative role at the expense of their legislative role.

INDEX